The Bible and American Culture

"No book in American history has had a greater historical or cultural impact than the Bible. Yet not until Setzer and Shefferman's splendid anthology has the Bible's wide influence been sampled in a handy, one-volume collection. This reader is a treasure for all who seek a deeper understanding of the American religious experience."

Peter J. Thuesen,
Indiana University-Purdue University Indianapolis, USA

"The interplay between biblical text and American religiosity is on full display in this valuable collection of primary sources. Setzer and Shefferman have put together a diverse and thoughtful range of sources that demonstrate the unique place of the Bible in American culture from the days of the Puritans to the modern and post-modern worlds of biblical interpretation. This is precisely the kind of sourcebook that will well serve both students of the Bible and students of American religion and culture. Highly recommended."

Jeffrey S. Siker, *Loyola Marymount University, USA*

From political speeches to pop songs, the biblical presence in American culture is hard to ignore. This sourcebook gathers and contextualizes a remarkable series of primary texts to illuminate the varied uses of the Bible in American life. Topics covered include the publication and distribution of the Bible; the use of the Bible in debates over slavery, homosexuality, feminism, and civil rights; and biblical sources in works of art, music, poetry, and fiction. The book provides a clear understanding of the centrality and influence of the Bible from the period of the first European settlers to the present day. It is invaluable for students taking courses on religion and American culture, and on the history of religion in the United States.

Claudia Setzer is Professor of Religious Studies at Manhattan College, USA.

David A. Shefferman is Assistant Professor of Religious Studies at Manhattan College, USA.

The Bible and American Culture

A Sourcebook

**Edited by Claudia Setzer
and David A. Shefferman**

Routledge
Taylor & Francis Group

LONDON AND NEW YORK

First published in 2011
by Routledge
2 Park Square, Milton Park, Abingdon, OX14 4RN

Simultaneously published in the USA and Canada
by Routledge
711 Third Avenue, New York, NY 10017

Routledge is an imprint of the Taylor & Francis Group, an informa business

British Library Cataloguing in Publication Data
A catalogue record for this book is available from the British Library

Library of Congress Cataloging in Publication Data
The Bible and American culture : a sourcebook / edited by Claudia Setzer and David A. Shefferman.
  p. cm.
  1. Bible–History–Sources. 2. United States–Religious life and customs–Sources. 3. Religion and culture–United States–History–Sources.
  I. Setzer, Claudia. II. Shefferman, David A.
  BS447.5.U6B52 2011   220.0973–dc22
  2010050163

ISBN: 978-0-415-45196-3 (hbk)
ISBN: 978-0-415-57811-0 (pbk)

Typeset in Baskerville
by Bookcraft Ltd, Stroud, Gloucestershire

Contents

List of figures

Acknowledgments

Our student assistant remarked that this book was "more than the sum of its parts." This is true for any book, but especially this one. Our students provided the first inspiration to provide a collection of ready texts for their exploration.

This book would not have happened without the enthusiasm of editor Lesley Riddle, who recognized the need for a book like ours. Amy Grant ably shepherded us through the first stages of the project. We are especially grateful to Katherine Ong, for diligence in handling many of the details of production, and for her unwavering courtesy and patience in the face of a steady stream of our email queries.

We have benefited from numerous digital collections that make available precious documents from America's past. We relied particularly on Google Books, Documenting the American South at the University North Carolina at Chapel Hill, Making of America at the University of Michigan, the Avalon Project at Yale University Law School, Sabin Americana administered by Gale-Cengage Learning, and the digital collections at the New York Public Library. We appreciate the website "Famous Trials," created by Professor Douglas Linder at the University of Missouri-Kansas City School of Law.

The Smithsonian Institution has proved helpful and generous in providing a recording and images from their collections. The National Gallery of Art and the American Folk Museum also graciously permitted use of images.

Manhattan College has supported this project with a summer grant and a sabbatical grant. Dean Richard Emmerson kindly provided funding for a summer assistant. Joseph Smith, our assistant, gave us invaluable help in organizing and tracking down permissions.

Our colleagues at Manhattan College enable a nurturing atmosphere of intellectual exchange. For specific bibliographic recommendations and advice, we thank Judith Plaskow, David Witzling, and Jeff Myers. We appreciate Joseph Lennon for introducing us to the poet Samuel Menashe and his work.

Other colleagues in the field have helped us to sharpen and clarify our work, including Lynn Neal, Patrick Alexander, and Stephanie Cobb. We especially value the comments of Peter Thuesen and our anonymous readers at Routledge Press. Our book is much richer because of them.

On artistic matters we profited from the counsel of Tobi Kahn and Leora Visotzky. Tobi was especially gracious in allowing us to use an image of his work, in making available his essay "On Beauty," and in taking time to talk with us.

Our extended families have helped by shouldering childcare, encouraging our progress, and showing pride in our work. We are both fortunate to have spouses who are intellectual companions as well as loving partners. Nereida Segura-Rico and Michael R. Greenwald provided time and space to work, critical editing, as well as firm, but gentle advice. They champion us to others, while encouraging us at home.

Last, we are grateful to each other. After three years of working together on the project, we are better friends and scholars. We both know that we could not have done such a book alone. It is truly more than the sum of its parts.

We dedicate this book to our children, Leora, Alex, Nora, and Leah, who give us unending delight. This book is about America's past and present, but they are its future.

Introduction

THE PLACE OF THE BIBLE IN THE PARADOX OF AMERICA

President Barack Obama, in a visit to Turkey in April 2009, assured his hearers that although the United States contained a large number of Christians, "we are not a Christian nation, or a Jewish nation, or a Muslim nation. We are a nation of citizens who are bound by ideals and a set of values" (Pasha 2009). Yet less than three months earlier, in his inauguration speech he stirred his hearers by referring to the apostle Paul's First Letter to the Corinthians 13:11, "the time has come to set aside childish things," advising them to carry forward "the God-given promise that all are equal, all are free, and all deserve a chance to pursue their full measure of happiness" (20 January 2009).

These few words show the peculiar paradox of America, a republic whose government guarantees free expression and does not promote religion, but whose public discourse regularly uses biblical ideas and language as the lingua franca. In lacing his speech with a biblical quotation and references to God, Obama was not unusual. He followed the pattern of virtually every other president since Washington.

In this book, we gather materials that illustrate the continuing relationship between these two parts of the American temperament. *The Bible and American Culture* seeks to illuminate the Bible's curious but essential role in American history and culture. Readers have never had the benefit of an anthology of primary documents on this topic. We hope that this edition, by giving more immediate access to texts, will allow everyone a chance to engage with the material. As a biblical specialist and an American religion specialist, we write as teachers who wish to account for the Bible's persistent but varied presence across American history both for ourselves and our students, leading to critical reading and self-reflection.

Our volume necessarily builds upon a substantial body of secondary literature. In 1982 Oxford University Press published an indispensable collection, *The Bible in America: Essays in Cultural History* (Hatch and Noll 1982), while at the same time the Society of Biblical Literature (SBL) released the first volumes in a six-part "Centennial" series, *The Bible in American Culture*, examining the Bible's past and present roles in education, popular culture, arts and letters, law, and other specific arenas of American life (Frerichs 1988; Phy-Olsen

1985; Gunn 1983; Johnson 1985; Barr and Piediscalzi 1982; Sandeen 1982). The debt we owe to these works and others will be clear throughout this book.

Our own interpretive proclivities and analytical perspectives shape this collection, however. The selection, trimming, and organizing of materials, our second-order, interpretive "framings," and our introductory essays to each chapter develop from certain assumptions. First, we maintain the ubiquity of the Bible in American culture and history. As Nathan O. Hatch and Mark A. Noll say in the introduction to their 1982 book, it is true not only "that Scripture has been nearly omnipresent in the nation's past" but also "that the actual use of the Bible in American life has been attended with considerable complexity and decided ambiguity" (4).

Our second assumption recognizes that the "considerable complexity and decided ambiguity" that accompanies the actual use of the Bible stems from the reality that "the Bible" always has been, and remains, a highly charged and open signifier in American life. Signifiers – as the word suggests – convey meaning and significance, so the characterization of the Bible as highly charged and open indicates not only that Americans have understood and valued the Bible in a variety of ways but also that the different meanings have cut against each other in real, sometimes conflicting terms. The results are a mixed legacy of biblical interpretation. The biblical text has been a hopeful alternative narrative of reality for oppressed groups, a spur to care for the poor and to eradicate injustice, and a source of inspiration for artists and writers. Yet, the Bible has been used to justify slavery, or the seizing of land. Today some T-shirts and bumper stickers sport the seemingly innocent "Pray for Obama: Psalm 109:8." The hostile sentiment is revealed when one knows that the verse says "May his days be few; may another seize his position." The following verse, "May his children be orphans, and his wife a widow" suggests some may be using the Bible to hope for the assassination of a president.. We have attempted to present prominent and influential uses of the text in American history, whether for good or ill.

Our third assumption is that certain understandings and uses of the Bible derived from Protestant Christianity have continued to predominate in American culture for hundreds of years. Sacvan Bercovitch, Catherine Albanese, and others argue that the legacy of biblical interpretation of the Puritans, those intrepid European religious seekers of the seventeenth and eighteenth centuries, has been especially profound and lasting in American life. As Bercovitch argues in an important 1983 essay included in one of the SBL volumes,

> the major legacy of Puritan New England is not religious, or moral, or institutional ... The distinctive contribution lies in the realm of rhetoric. The Puritans provided the scriptural basis for what we have come to call the myth of America. In this sense their influence appears most clearly in the extraordinary persistence of a rhetoric grounded in the Bible, and in the way that Americans keep returning to that rhetoric, especially in times of crisis, as a source of cohesion and continuity.

(Bercovitch 1983: 219)

In *America: Religions and Religion*, her popular textbook on American religious history, Albanese (1999) takes Bercovitch's argument even further. She insists that the Puritan's unique, biblically grounded "rhetoric" laid the foundations for an evolving yet enduring, collectively (though unconsciously) observed "American religion" that she labels "public Protestantism." Similarly, a recent article by John Lardas Modern (2008) illustrates the evangelical media practices of the nineteenth century, which successfully created out of that Puritan heritage a comprehensive public piety, which he calls "evangelical secularism."

BIBLICAL ARCHETYPES AND THE IDEA OF "AMERICA"

In underscoring its lasting legacy, we figure the Puritan perspective as both exceptional and exceptionalist. The Puritans saw themselves as uniquely commissioned. They found in the Bible justification for their endeavors not only as part of but rather as the end of biblical prophecy. As Bercovitch puts it, "the New England emigrants ... discovered America in the Bible; and they found the texts they sought in biblical passages" that ultimately pointed to them as the "holy remnant" who would usher in the final Kingdom of God in a "New World" (1983: 223). It was the Puritans, Bercovitch notes, who first used the word "Americans" in reference to European immigrants. The identity was the pillar of a new and peculiar myth of Americans as exceptional "chosen" people divinely ordained to bring a grand biblical narrative to God's predetermined conclusion.

Mark Noll, in *America's God*, delineates the biblical roots as well as the singular development of American exceptionalism. Noll identifies the particular synthesis in American culture of Evangelical Protestant religion, republicanism, and Common Sense philosophy. Evangelical Protestantism, characterized by a reliance on biblical authority, and translation of faith into activism, dominated American public life, even among non-evangelicals. Republicanism, a term that has engendered much discussion, is a secular political ideology that rests on power proceeding from consent of the governed, the virtue of civic participation, and the value of a constitution and rule of law. Common Sense was a moral philosophy that originated in Scotland, flourishing in the eighteenth century, which stressed that the senses and inherent common sense were the basis of moral reasoning. The common person could access ethics outside of church authorities or intellectual elites. By extension, Common Sense approached the Bible as a book of facts accessible to anyone via ordinary perception. Noll says, while Americans believe in an exceptional destiny for themselves on which the rest of the world depends, this "Christian republicanism" makes them quite unique in a different way. Discussing the period of the late eighteenth century, just after the Revolution, he notes, "American Christians, despite substantial conflicts among themselves, took for granted a fundamental compatibility between orthodox Protestant religion and republican principles of government. Most English-speaking Protestants outside the United States did not" (2002: 54).

In Noll's estimation, that uniquely American fusion of perspectives meant that in public discourse from the Revolution through the Civil War "the Bible was not so much the truth above all truth as it was the story above all stories" (1982: 43). Its story remains intertwined in the events, movements, and debates of the country, for good and ill, often in ways that are not obvious. When audiences heard Ronald Reagan talk about America as "the shining city on a hill," few knew it referred to Puritan John Winthrop's vision, much less that Winthrop invoked Matthew 5:14b. Still, Reagan's famous speech had a biblical "feel" that made the image inspiring.

From the start, Americans have taken from the "story above all stories" the template of a limited set of grand biblical themes. These narrative archetypes blended with political, economic and expansionist tendencies to create an enduring national myth. Readers will notice a recurrence of certain texts and biblical figures. Someone who had never seen a Bible and who tried to reconstruct it from American public discourse would come up with a relatively small book including Creation and Eden, Exodus, an apocalyptic end-time, the strange trio of Moses, Jesus, and Paul, and an idyllic picture of an early church. Other verses and figures appear in cameo roles, often to address particular social issues. Some of these bit parts would involve: Abraham to prove slavery; Lot and the people of Sodom (combined with a Levitical prohibition) to argue against homosexuality; the Good Samaritan to argue for gay/lesbian inclusion; Mary Magdalene and the women around Paul and Jesus to argue for women's rights.

Among the most enduring biblical archetypes in American culture has been the image of a return to Eden. America holds the possibility to restore a pure and primitive primordium said Thomas Paine, "we have it in our power to begin the world over again." Ronald Reagan cited this statement in a speech laced with biblical references to the annual convention of the National Association of Evangelicals on 8 March 1983. And, as we suggest, Barack Obama's first speech as President echoes nearly every other inaugural address by summoning the possibility to remake society, providing an example to the world, "a light to the peoples" (Isa 51:4). The paintings of the Hudson River School, especially Thomas Cole, depict America as the New Eden, an untamed and beautiful paradise. In *Illusions of Innocence*, Richard T. Hughes and C. Leonard Allen show the pull of the "myth of first times," noting that even the seal of the United States shows a nation emerging from an empty plain, as if nothing preceded it, and the motto *novus ordo seclorum*, "a new order of the ages" (1998: xvi, 1).

Hughes and Allen identify this archetype as a crucial part of a wider form of "restorationism" evident not only among the Puritans but also with the Baptists, Mormons, and many others. A familiar American theme has been the call to "restore" or "revive" corrupted religious traditions – and, more broadly, a fallen society – to its original promise and glory. Christian groups frequently look to the first Christian communities, the so-called "Primitive Church," as the model for a godly future. Some Reform Jews saw America as the place Judaism could be saved and renewed. In 1911, Kaufmann Kohler, the German-born president of Hebrew Union College, said:

Ever since I was privileged to imbibe the invigorating air of this God-blessed land of liberty, American Israel [Jewry] appeared to me as a new type of Joseph, "the prince among his brethren," whom Divine Providence entrusted with the mission of not merely preserving the *lives* of the tens of thousands who came to seek bread and shelter under the starry banner, but of reviving the *spirit* of God's chosen people, and of endowing them with a new hope and a wider outlook, with a deeper comprehension of their prophetic vision and their world-duty.

(Kohler 1916)

Whether in the figure of Eden, ancient Israel, or the Primitive Church, the cultural trope of a-return-to-the-past has been resolutely biblical in the American context.

Another archetypical theme within the American myth is the sustained narrative of the Exodus from Egypt, Israel's wandering in the wilderness sustained by God's favor and Moses' imperfect and sometimes unheeded leadership, the claim of chosenness that is revealed at Sinai, and Israel's entrance into the Promised Land. As Chapter 2 shows, many early settlers had no plans to found an interfaith Utopia but instead intended to inculcate the new settlements with their own brand of Christianity. Perry Miller's influential book, *Errand into the Wilderness* (the phrase taken from a 1670 sermon of Samuel Danforth) delineates the Puritan self-definition of themselves as the new Israel, venturing into the wilderness of a new continent, to build a new Zion under divine Providence. Westward expansion in the 1800s, fueled by nationalism, desire for land, the fur trade and, in 1848, the discovery of gold, nevertheless could be couched in religious terms. Journalist John O'Sullivan, who is credited with coining the term "Manifest Destiny," wrote in 1839 in *The United States Magazine and Democratic Review*:

We have no interest in the scenes of antiquity, only as lessons of avoidance of nearly all their examples. The expansive future is our arena, and for our history. We are entering on its untrodden space, with the truths of God in our minds, beneficent objects in our hearts, land with a clear conscience unsullied by the past. We are a nation of human progress, and who will, what can, set limits to our onward march? Providence is with us, and no earthly power can.

However, the prevalence of the Exodus narrative as an American archetype serves as a powerful reminder that many individuals and communities have variously challenged the predominant interpretations of the Bible along with "the American myth" more generally.

African Americans under slavery also adopted the Exodus story with its message of God's liberation of the oppressed and escape to freedom. As Albert Raboteau has shown, the slaves and other African Americans saw themselves as reliving a different part of the narrative than did the Puritans. If the Puritans thought of themselves as new Israelites arriving at the Promised

Land after a period of tortuous wandering, African Americans identified with the Israelites in Egypt, awaiting liberation from slavery and redemption from suffering (Raboteau 1994). A later, unforgettable image from the Civil Rights movement evokes another moment in the story of Exodus. In his last speech, delivered on 3 April 1968, Martin Luther King eerily echoed Moses, before his death, looking at the Promised Land that he would never enter: "And He's allowed me to go up to the mountain. And I've looked over. And I've seen the Promised Land. I may not get there with you. But I want you to know tonight, that we, as a people, will get to the Promised Land."

A third major biblical archetype – the theme of living in the end-times – also conveys the myth of American distinction. Especially prevalent in the nineteenth century among millennialist and utopian groups, this narrative theme evokes the idea of the small minority of the saved. The idea of a "saved remnant" appears in the Hebrew Bible (Isa 10:21–22) but especially dominates Revelation, the last book of the New Testament, with concepts like the "144,000" (Rev 7:1–4; 14:1–3).

Like the other major themes of Eden and Exodus, the figure of the Saved has both reinforced and unsettled the "American myth." While Americans might imagine themselves collectively as the Saved, the same biblical passages have enabled other groups that feel marginalized from the mainstream to make sense of their experience on inverse terms. They can identify themselves as the sanctified few within a corrupted American society. In some form, the notion of a unique community in the world, but not completely continuous with it, is foundational for most religious groups, but certainly for the peoples of the Book. Early groups like the Shakers established their own communities according to a radically different social and economic order from the culture around them and felt themselves the seed of the godly kingdom foretold in the Bible, and in later decades of the nineteenth century other groups like the Seventh-Day Adventists and Jehovah's Witnesses followed a similar line of thinking in different directions. In the twentieth century groups like Jim Jones' People's Temple and the Branch Davidians, at their beginning under Victor Houteff and around David Koresh at their end, exhibited the same tendencies in organizing unique communities in deliberate contrast to the majority.

HOW THE BIBLE IS INTERPRETED

Beyond engagement with broad themes and symbols, Americans have employed specific rhetorical strategies to represent themselves and others. In the sources here readers will come upon a variety of methods for using the Bible. Some recurring modes of usage include proof-texting; typology; adopting biblical narratives as alternative accounts of development; deriving inspiration; and seeing the Bible as adversary.

In proof-texting, individual verses are pulled out and brought to bear on contemporary issues. Familiar uses include the use of Gen 1:27 ("male and female he created them") to prove women's equality, or Exodus 20:15 ("You shall not steal") to argue against slavery as "man-stealing." Typology is frequently at work when biblical people are invoked as representative of later people or groups. We have seen that the early settlers saw themselves as the chosen nation, a new Israel in the wilderness, while women matriarchs in the Hebrew Bible and disciples in the New Testament become models for women preachers and teachers in the church. Individual people could become biblical types. At his death George Washington was compared to everyone from Abel to David, while Lincoln, too, was compared to Moses, David, and, after his assassination during Holy Week, to Jesus. Southerners, on the other hand, likened him to Pharaoh (Noll 1982: 43–4).

The tactic of presenting biblical narrative as an alternative account of development is most obvious in the social justice movements, civil rights, social reform, and among religious separatists who argue that the majority does not comprehend the acting out of the biblical story in our own time. Similarly too, many individuals and groups who claim direct experience of the divine derive particular inspiration from and see themselves following in the footsteps of the earliest generations of the church, who received the Holy Spirit at Pentecost in Acts 2. The idea of the Bible as a source of inspiration pervades much of our material but is essential to the last chapter, where artists, poets, and writers draw on its powerful images.

Others work from the opposite standpoint, posing the Bible as adversary. *The Woman's Bible*, while a feminist commentary on the Bible, sees much of the book as a stumbling block to equal rights for women. Some selections in Chapter 4 of this book use the adversarial mode in a unique but effective way: they hold scripture to its fundamental value as a teacher of liberation and justice in order to demonstrate how the Bible has been used to bar justice and progress.

WHAT IS THE BIBLE?

In its most familiar connotation today, the Bible refers to a collection of sacred writings of Judaism or Christianity. The term "Bible" derives from the Greek *ta biblia* (the books) suggesting a multiplicity of texts rather than a singular, cohesive "Book." The Hebrew Bible, or Old Testament, originally consisted of works on separate scrolls, and the earliest works of the New Testament were written on papyri. The earliest collection of the Bible as a single book that is extant is *Codex Sinaiticus*, from the fourth century. A codex consists of sheets of writing bound on one end.

Because scripture originally was a plurality of texts, groups often disagreed on exactly which of the "books" belonged in the authoritative collection. Questions about which texts are sacred, and why, surround the debates over canon. Most obviously, differences divide Jews and Christians, all "People of the Book" (along with Muslims) who lay claim to the legacy of Abraham's ancient covenant with a singular God. For Christians, the Bible includes the books of the Old Testament and the New Testament. For Jews, who (except for messianic Jews) do not recognize the messianic status or divinity of Jesus, the New Testament is not included. There is no "old" or "new" testament but simply the Bible or, as Jews traditionally call it, the "Tanakh." In their unique historical perspective, Muslims traditionally recognize the divine origins of both the Christian as well as the Jewish "Bible." However, the founding of Islam presupposes the misunderstandings and misinterpretations inherent in Jewish and Christian scripture that necessitated a subsequent and final divine "recitation" (*qur'ān*) through Muhammad.

But even within each of the biblically based traditions, divergent views of canon arise. Differences have been especially significant within Christianity. The Catholic Bible is larger, because Catholics accept as scripture certain books (like 1, 2 Maccabees) that Protestants do not. Protestants gather a number of these extra books in a section called the Apocrypha. In 2010, the Westar Institute released the fourth edition of *The Complete Gospels*, which includes the canonical four gospels with non-canonical works like *The Gospel of Thomas*, as well as other gospels not considered scripture by any authoritative body. Even a text as seemingly immutable as the Ten Commandments appears in three versions: Jewish, Protestant, and Catholic (recognized as well in Lutheran, Episcopal and Orthodox traditions). As indicated in our Chapter 4, the insistence on supplements to scripture and the expansion of the Bible has recurred throughout American history.

Not only the content and organization but also the translations of the Bible differed. The Protestant Authorized Version (best known as the King James Version: KJV) was the dominant version in the early period of US history. Published originally in 1611, its language reflects its origins, and it could not take into account later manuscript discoveries. Many still prefer it today. When a revision of the King James was taken up, correcting errors in translation and bringing in the results of more recent manuscript discoveries, it was published as the Revised Version (RV; 1881 for the NT, 1885 for OT). Americans from the same committee produced their own version of the RV, first published as the American Standard Version in 1901 and subsequently updated in 1952 in a "Revised Standard Version" (RSV) and again in 1989 as "the New Revised Standard Version". Dissatisfaction with both of these products opened the door to the many translations we have today (discussed in Chapter 1). Elizabeth Cady Stanton's *The Woman's Bible* is in part a reaction against the RV. Jews and Catholics understandably were motivated to produce their own translations to counter Protestant dominance in translation.

CRITERIA FOR SELECTION

A book like ours, in spite of its length, must leave out more than it puts in. Our guiding principle has been to present texts that represent significant strains in American public life. Readers will note a decidedly Christian tilt to our selection. This proceeds from our recognition of the predominant legacies of Protestant, especially evangelical, Christianity, as described by Mark Noll (2002), John Lardas Modern (2008), and others. To give every group that adheres to the Bible equal space would misrepresent American public culture.

Readers will notice, too, that time periods are not all represented equally within every section or chapter. We consider moments or movements where the Bible played a significant part. The section that deals with the relationship between church and state, "The Bible and the Republic," quite naturally favors the seventeenth and eighteenth centuries, the period of early settlement through the founding of the state, and considers several contemporary issues, but does not deal much with the nineteenth century. That century, on the other hand, was unbelievably fertile for missionizing, spiritual enthusiasm, and millennialism, so it is well represented in "Spreading the Word," the chapter on mission and distribution of the Bible, as well as in "Reading in the margins," the chapter that most directly represents different utopian and millennialist groups. The nineteenth century also saw foundational debates over issues of slavery and women's rights and thus figures prominently in the chapter, "The Bible and America's great debates." African American experience has been so thoroughly bound up with the Bible that its expression appears prominently throughout the book.

Since history and experience do not fit categories neatly, there is overlap. Discussions of issues that play out on the civic or legal stage often have religious ramifications. Religiously based conflicts make their way to the public arena. Feminism in the nineteenth century coalesced over the right to vote, took place in the context of Victorian images of womanhood, and appears in the chapter on America's great debates over social issues. Contemporary feminist theology, however, appears in the section on restoring marginalized meanings, "Reading in the margins." Similarly, the discussion of gay marriage within the Presbyterian Church arises in our chapter on great debates on social issues, while two offerings from gay theology appear in the chapter on reading in the margins. Artistic expression holds a mirror up to experience, so is, in some ways, the most comprehensive category of all. Readers are encouraged to cross-reference across the chapters and relate sources to one another rather than simply to read the book serially.

We have, perhaps, over-represented the New England Puritans and their successors, but that is because they were the most overtly biblical of the European settlers. Patricia Seed (1995) explains how seizing of the New World took place through different activities. The Dutch drew maps, the Spanish gave speeches before military actions, and the French had processions. The English, however, planted gardens, built homes, and put up fences in imitation of their homeland, consciously carrying out the command of Gen 1:28, "Be fruitful and multiply." We have already noted the prominent themes of Eden, Exodus and Promised Land with which the Puritans identified.

OVERVIEW OF CHAPTERS

We have identified five general fields of activity in which the far-reaching presence of the Bible surfaces most clearly. Chapter 1, "Spreading the Word," explains how and why the Bible became so widely dispersed in our culture. A drive to missionize, embedded in the Great Commission in Matt 28:19, innovations in production and distribution, and the production of translations that reflect particular denominations and orientations, combined to place the Bible at the center of much of American public life. Bercovitch, citing Washington Irving, identifies the great outpouring of words that characterized America in its early days as a "logocracy," a society ruled by words. (With today's talk radio, Twitter, and blogosphere, the logocracy continues.) Indeed, there were productions of tracts, sermons, and treatises in the early period. Enthusiasm for the biblical word also spread through revival movements, from the First Great Awakening, associated with George Whitefield and others in the mid-eighteenth century, the Second Great Awakening in the nineteenth century, up to contemporary televised revivals.

While the King James translation held sway for the first part of the country's history, after the Revised Version of 1881–5, which in America became the American Standard Version (1901), a multiplicity of translations followed. Jews and Catholics produced their own versions to serve their communities and to reflect particular values. Today's Bible industry offers audience-specific editions and value-specific translations. Young people can pick up glossy magazines or comic-book versions. Environmentalists can turn to the Green Bible. Gullah speakers from the seacoast towns and islands of Georgia and North Carolina helped to produce the Gullah New Testament. A current online effort, the Conservative Bible Project, attempts to restore an understanding of the Bible that its creators feel has been lost in modern translations.

In Chapter 2, "The Bible and the Republic," we consider the effect of a biblical culture on civic matters. Illuminating two enduring strains of American public life, biblicism and republicanism, the sources in the chapter convey the significant influence of and distinctions between groups that Frank Lambert (2003) has called the Planting Fathers and the Founding Fathers. The former sought to found religiously based societies, while the latter crafted an alternative to the European models, a state that guaranteed free expression of religion to all, but did not promote any single religion. The implications of the Constitution's Establishment Clause continue to play out in many contemporary debates related to public expression of religion, often surrounding the question of the real intention of the Founders.

As the Bible occupied a central position in public space, it could not fail to be part of the many debates over social questions. In Chapter 3, "The Bible and America's great debates," we begin with what Mark Noll calls the "tragedy" of the biblical defense of slavery (2002: 17), a uniquely American phenomenon. Abolitionists who used the Bible were in a defensive posture, despite the reality that in the rest of the English-speaking world no Protestants thought the Bible sanctioned slavery. Discussions of literal meanings of individual words, distance between ancient and current societies and their mores, pointing to biblical figures, divining what Jesus meant, or what Paul said, all engaged the people on both sides. Similar arguments took place over women's rights.

Such debates connected with discussions that began to undermine straight literal understanding of the text. The emergence of new scholarly methods unsettled claims about the Bible's historical accuracy and eventually led to a deep division between "fundamentalist" and "modernist" positions. The debate over evolution carried the arguments out in a very public way. Some groups laid these questions to the side. The underlying liberationist message, God's favor for the poor and oppressed, emerged as the underpinning of the Social Gospel movement and later influenced the Civil Rights movement. The disputes over gay marriage and ordination combine both impulses. Some pull out particular words and verses, analyzing them for meaning, which is still applicable, while others draw on the themes of love and justice that pervade both testaments.

Chapter 4, "Reading in the margins," demonstrates how discussions over political and social life played out directly in religious ideas and practices. In these selections, people draw from their own experience to conclude that something has gone badly wrong in the way the Bible has been interpreted, taught, and applied. They seek to restore aspects of the Bible that have been forgotten, covered up, or misunderstood. While as individuals the writers may live relatively comfortable lives, they are in some way marginalized in traditional readings of the Bible. It is an eclectic group, with three main parts. The first includes feminist biblical scholars and theologians like Phyllis Trible, Rosemary Radford Ruether, and Elisabeth Schüssler Fiorenza, gay theologians Richard Cleaver and Gary Comstock, and African American theologian Jacquelyn Grant.

A second group in this section encompasses those who claim a direct experience of the Spirit. While operating within churches, and devoted to the Bible, their experience is self-authenticating. Jarena Lee, an early African American preacher, Phoebe Palmer, Catholic charismatic Patti Gallagher Mansfield, and the Pentecostals see their experience as a restoration of the same experience of the Spirit that came upon the Apostles in the upper room, described in Acts 2.

Selections in our third group could not seem more different from the other two groups and from each other. However, contemporary millennialist groups, like the Branch Davidians, share with the early Shakers and with many nineteenth-century millennialist groups the conviction that something has gone badly wrong in contemporary society. They attempt to build a new, separatist society, building on the cryptic messages of the book of Revelation.

Our last chapter, "The Bible and artistic expression," shows material that is different in kind from our other documents. Yet its works represent a simultaneous loyalty and freedom relative to the biblical text that is at work throughout the selections in this book. Scholar Herbert Schneidau (1983) calls it "the antinomian strain" in American arts and letters. It can range from a relatively benign image of Hagar, sculpted by Edmonia Lewis, to express her own marginalization, to the more pointed implicit critique by Herman Melville in *Moby Dick*. In showing patterns of diffusion, innovation, and inspiration, this section illuminates most pointedly patterns we have observed in all our chapters.

THE BIBLE AS TEXT

While the sources in this volume reveal myriad approaches to scripture throughout American history, one fact always shapes the uses of and debates about the Bible: in every case the Bible stands most immediately as a book, even when considered *the* Book; it remains "scripture," or a body of text. As such, the Bible bears a physical presence while it also invites interpretation, an imputation of meaning and purpose. These two co-existing characteristics – what we can refer to as the "materiality" and "textuality" of any book – carry significant implications for the Bible's place in American history and culture.

As Colleen McDannell (1986, 1995) has demonstrated forcefully in a range of studies, the Bible's role in American life has much to do with its physicality. The Bible's heft as a book has lent it respectability and authenticity, while the portability that accompanied changes in printing technology eventually made the book an available and flexible companion. The physical impact of the Bible has become more complicated as it has moved increasingly from print into electronic forms, but that shift only heightens the issues surrounding scripture's physical existence rather than erasing them.

Thus, materiality is bound to issues of authority. Along with the fact of its physical presence comes the issue of the Bible's status. The relation between the Bible's material existence and its relevance has been and perhaps always will be a fundamental point of theological reflection. Americans engage fiercely in the millennia-old discussion of relations between words and their ultimate source (as John's Gospel asserts, "In the beginning was the Word …"). For instance, these debates frame the emergence of the Holiness and Pentecostal movements in the late nineteenth- and early twentieth-century American contexts. That development reverberates strongly today as those traditions experience rapid and global expansion.

In any of its recognized forms, the Bible is defined inherently not only by its materiality but also by its textuality. As "scripture," it contains words that do not accumulate randomly. They take shape as ideas, teachings, command-ments, genealogies, and stories. As examined at great length and in profound depth by Paul Ricoeur, the renowned theologian and leading figure in the field of hermeneutics, the insistence on the Bible's status as sacred literature only heightens the paradox that inhabits any text (Lacocque and Ricoeur 1998; Ricouer and Ihde 2007). On one hand, writing, or "inscription," conveys a sense of permanence; on the other hand, meaning can be fluid as inscribed texts continually undergo interpretation. That process of interpretation becomes fraught with further implications with a text like the Bible, ostensibly inscribed by a permanent, divine force. Ricouer's analysis also serves as an important reminder that, at surface level, control over the interpretation of the Bible and other sacred texts typically translates into religious authority and, potentially, into social, political, and economic power as well.

Discussion of the Bible's nature as a defining text inevitably leads to consid-eration of its relation to the other sacrosanct document in American life: the Constitution. In a November 2009 speech on "Living with the Constitution,"

Senator Sheldon Whitehouse of Rhode Island used a telling image and expressed a wider sentiment, proclaiming that he "revere[s] the Constitution like a secular Bible" (Whitehouse 2009). As he explained, the Constitution also provides moral grounding and an overarching code of action. It establishes the philosophical foundations as well as the legal scaffolding that hold together American civic life. The Constitution is approached like the Bible in many ways. While Americans generally recognize the Constitution as humanly constructed words open to amendment through a process agreed upon by "We the People," the document still stands over society as a "fixed" text by which residents are bound. In a familiar and ongoing process of public exegesis (mediated by federal judges, the legal ministers of the court system) Americans debate the meaning of the Constitution's words and the intentions of its authors. In these discussions, Americans often bring the Bible directly into the conversation. Even in the Constitutional Congress where the document was drafted, questions arose as to the manner in which the Constitution would or should be based on biblical precepts. Those issues have not abated. Warring groups call each other "unconstitutional," just as some label each other "unbiblical."

The juxtaposition of the Constitution and the Bible brings us back, in conclusion, to the forceful images with which this introduction began. In the first impression, the president speaks for the nation, assuring a vital ally about "the ideals and a set of values" that bind Americans; in the second take, the same president speaks to the nation, articulates those ideals through reference to a biblical passage and invocation of God's favor over a nation. To better understand that president's claims, one only has to think back minutes before that speech when the country's new chief executive was sworn into office. A president stands tall and proud and – with a right hand on the Bible – pledges to uphold the Constitution of the United States. In that moment, we see most clearly the relationship between the documents that animate American life. The Constitution structures civic life, but the Bible remains vividly present. The USA remains a "logocracy" animated by sets of sacred words.

REFERENCES

Albanese, Catherine L. 1999. *America, Religions, and Religion*. 3rd edn. Belmont, CA: Wadsworth.

Barr, David L., and Nicholas Piediscalzi, eds. 1982. *The Bible in American Education: From Source Book to Textbook*. Philadelphia, PA and Chico, CA: Fortress Press and Scholars Press.

Bercovitch, Sacvan. 1983. "The Biblical Basis of the American Myth." In G. B. Gunn, ed., *The Bible and American Arts and Letters*. Philadelphia, PA and Chico, CA: Fortress Press and Scholars Press, 219–29.

Frerichs, Ernest S. 1988. *The Bible and Bibles in America*. Atlanta, GA: Scholars Press.

Gunn, Giles B., ed. 1983. *The Bible and American Arts and Letters*. Philadelphia, PA and Chico, CA: Fortress Press and Scholars Press.

Hatch, Nathan O., and Mark A. Noll, eds. 1982. *The Bible in America: Essays in Cultural History*. New York: Oxford University Press.

Hughes, Richard T., and Crawford Leonard Allen. 1988. *Illusions of Innocence: Protestant Primitivism in America, 1630–1875*. Chicago: University of Chicago Press.

Johnson, James Turner, ed. 1985. *The Bible in American Law, Politics, and Political Rhetoric*. Philadelphia, PA and Chico, CA: Fortress Press and Scholars Press.

Kohler, Kaufman. 1916. "American Israel." In *Hebrew Union College and Other Addresses*. Cincinnati, OH: Ark Press.

Lacocque, André, and Paul Ricœur. 1998. *Thinking Biblically: Exegetical and Hermeneutical Studies*. Chicago: University of Chicago Press.

Lambert, Frank. 2003. *The Founding Fathers and the Place of Religion in America*. Princeton, NJ: Princeton University Press.

McDannell, Colleen. 1986. *The Christian Home in Victorian America, 1840–1900*. Bloomington: Indiana University Press.

—— 1995. *Material Christianity: Religion and Popular Culture in America*. New Haven, CT: Yale University Press.

Miller, Perry. 1956. *Errand into the Wilderness*. Cambridge, MA: Belknap Press.

Modern, John Lardas. 2008. "Evangelical Secularism and the Measure of Leviathan." *Church History* 77: 801–76.

Noll, Mark A. 1982. "The Image of the United States as a Biblical Nation, 1776–1865." In N. O. Hatch and M. A. Noll, eds, *The Bible in America: Essays in Cultural History*. New York: Oxford University Press, 39–58.

—— 2002. *America's God: From Jonathan Edwards to Abraham Lincoln*. New York: Oxford University Press.

Pasha, Kamran. 2009. "Obama Extends Hand of Friendship to Islam." Huffington Post: www.huffingtonpost.com/kamran-pasha/obama-extends-a-hand-of-f_b_183780.html.

Phy-Olsen, Allene. 1985. *The Bible and Popular Culture in America*. Philadelphia, PA and Chico, CA: Fortress Press and Scholars Press.

Raboteau, Albert J. 1994. "African Americans, Exodus, and the American Israel." In P. E. Johnson, ed., *African-American Christianity: Essays in History*. Berkeley: University of California Press, 1–17.

Ricoeur, Paul, and Don Ihde. 2007. *The Conflict of Interpretations*. Evanston, IL: Northwestern University Press. Original edition, 1974.

Sandeen, Ernest Robert, ed. 1982. *The Bible and Social Reform*. Philadelphia, PA and Chico, CA: Fortress Press and Scholars Press.

Schneidau, Herbert. 1983. "The Antinomian Strain: The Bible and American Poetry." In G. B. Gunn, ed., *The Bible and American Arts and Letters*. Philadelphia, PA and Chico, CA: Fortress Press and Scholars Press, 11–32.

Seed, Patricia. 1995. *Ceremonies of Possession in Europe's Conquest of the New World, 1492–1640*. Cambridge and New York: Cambridge University Press.

Whitehouse, Sheldon. 2009. "Living up to Our Constitution." Brennan Center for Justice: www.brennancenter.org/content/resource/living_up_to_our_constitution/.

1 Spreading the Word

In August 2009, the conservative commentator Andrew Schlafly announced the launch of the Conservative Bible Project. Schlafly set as the project's goal "a fully conservative translation of the Bible" (Conservapedia 2010). Through Conservapedia, a USA-based online encyclopedia that Schlafly founded, everyone was invited to collaborate on the production. According to Schlafly, the Conservative Bible Project's group-directed format would enable the restoration of the Bible's original character and meaning in the face of "a liberal bias that has become the single biggest distortion in modern Bible translations" (Beato 2010: 14).

In its labors, the Conservative Bible Project is both original and familiar. On one hand, the project's ends and means are unique. Never before has an explicitly "conservative" English translation of the Bible appeared, much less as an openly collaborative production in electronic form. On the other hand, the Conservative Bible Project stands as the latest embodiment of three long-running patterns in American culture with respect to "spreading the Word." First, in trying to make the Bible widely available the Conservative Bible Project reinforces a familiar precedent in American history for acting on Jesus' commission to his followers to "make disciples of all nations" (Matt 28:19). Even if the Project renders the passage in a new way ("So go and make students from all ethnic groups, baptizing them in the Name of the Father, and of the Son, and of the Divine Guide"), the drive to missionize is familiar. So too is the search for efficient and effective means of the Bible's production and distribution. The Project's move to the internet reflects new-media trends, but also reflects the second pattern, a centuries-old American effort to make the Bible more widely accessible. The same combination of innovation and custom characterizes the Project's turn to user-defined content. As a web-hosted collaboration it represents another form of the third common trend: the development of new audience-specific translations of the Bible rooted in a particular set of values. The documents in this chapter bear out these three patterns in the American history of "spreading the Word."

Missionizing

The biblical injunction to "spread the Word" inspired and justified ongoing settlement of the Americas as territory where, among other activities, biblical teachings would be disseminated, studied, and potentially fulfilled. The First Charter of Virginia (1606) offers a clear reminder that, from the start, powerful validation for colonial efforts in the Americas came from the expressed task of "propagating of Christian Religion to such People, as yet live in Darkness and miserable Ignorance of the true Knowledge and Worship of God" (see "First Charter of Virginia" in Chapter 2).

Nor did the impulse to propagate biblical teachings die out once colonies were established. John Eliot produced the first new edition of a bible in North America – his famous "Indian Bible" of 1670 – by learning the languages of natives in the Massachusetts region and then translating and printing the Christian Bible in their idiom. Virginia, originally chartered to stamp out "miserable Ignorance" of God's teachings, pioneered other approaches to spreading the Word to America's natives. The 1693 charter of the College of William and Mary reveals that the college's namesakes authorized the new institution as a place to educate Native Americans, principally in Christian scripture and Anglican tradition.

A few decades later, a Congregational minister named Eleazar Wheelock pursued a similar objective in the northern colonies. After establishing Moor's Charity School in Lebanon, Connecticut, with the intent of educating Native Americans in Bible and other subjects, Wheelock relocated the school to Hanover in New Hampshire Province. The colony's Royal Governor provided the land and, in December 1769, conveyed the charter from King George III to establish Dartmouth College "to encourage the laudable and charitable design of spreading Christian knowledge among the savages of our American wilderness … and also of English Youth and any others."

Despite their stated objective of educating Native Americans, the actual development of both William and Mary and Dartmouth reflects a more common pattern in American higher education. Very few Native Americans matriculated to either school and, like most of America's oldest and most venerable colleges, William and Mary and Dartmouth took shape as training grounds for promising young men to study the Bible and to prepare for ministry. The legislature of the Massachusetts Bay Colony established the first college in North America in 1636, Harvard College, under the motto *Veritas Christo et Ecclesiae*, "Truth for Christ and the Church," to produce New England's prominent Puritan ministers. Other colonial bodies followed suit: Congregational ministers laid the foundations for Yale in 1701; the University of Pennsylvania took root in 1740 under Quaker influence; Princeton, chartered by King George II in 1746 for "any Person of any religious Denomination whatsoever," focused on ecclesiastical training and developed strong Presbyterian ties.

The American system of higher education, germinating from the establishment of religiously oriented institutions which centered on bible study, came in waves with expanding and shifting settlement. During the nineteenth century scores of religiously affiliated schools sprang up across the territories of the American heartland: Knox (1837) and Grinnell (1847) as Congregational colleges; Methodist schools such as De Pauw (1837) and Ohio Wesleyan (1842); Baptist institutions like Denison (1831); the Catholic universities of the Midwest, beginning with St. Louis (1818) and Notre Dame (1842); Kenyon (1824) and University of the South (1857), both with Episcopal ties; and the first Mormon university, Brigham Young (1875). Wheaton College, established in 1860 in Illinois as an interdenominational evangelical institution, foreshadowed the growth of biblically directed education in the United States during the twentieth and early twenty-first centuries.

If Puritans figured their seventeenth-century colonial efforts in North America as "an errand into the wilderness," others saw their later missionary efforts as "an errand into the world." Especially in the latter part of the nineteenth century and in fluctuating intervals since, Americans fanned across the globe in substantial numbers with a sense of their "Great Commission," a belief in their divine calling *as Americans* to carry out a redemptive destiny figured in biblical prophecy. The Student Volunteer Movement, which sprang to life in the last decade of the nineteenth century, stands as one formidable example of the pioneering role of young Americans in issuing and heeding the call to active venture into unfamiliar territory to turn the ostensible tides of sin toward a biblically foretold Kingdom of God.

Yet, wherever the drive to carry biblically inspired teachings has carried them, ministers of "the Word" have confronted recurring questions about the precise role of scripture. As discussed in the introduction to this volume, claims about the Bible often reinforce an inherent tension between the scriptural text as object and its relation to the divine presence ostensibly revealed through the text. This friction between Word and Spirit (to cast the issue in Christianity's familiar terms) plays out throughout the history and traditions of all religions of "the Book." Just as questions about the status of scripture fostered much of the Reformation critique that gave rise to Protestant traditions, the issues arose almost immediately among the Protestant settlers in the American colonial contexts. For example, the conflict over access to God through Word or Spirit structures the theological debate at the heart of the 1637 Examination of Anne Hutchinson (see Chapter 2, "The Bible and the Republic"). The issue has yet to dissipate.

Nowhere are the issues more pronounced than in the "revival" movements that began with the so-called First Great Awakening. In a foundational 1733 sermon, "A Divine and Supernatural Light," Jonathan Edwards provided theological reasoning for the popular revivals that subsequently sprang up around his friend, George Whitefield, and others during the 1740s. In the sermon, Edwards emphasizes that God is most immediately a *living* presence, continually and actively manifested in "the Holy Spirit." Although Edwards refers to the Bible throughout his discourse, he relates the written "Word" to "divine and supernatural light, immediately imparted." In turn, the proliferation of "the Word" – in what became the hallmark of revival tradition – depends upon spiritual and visceral response to the present Spirit rather than to, or through, the inscribed text.

A similar dynamic emerges in different cultural contexts and at various points in American history. The Holiness/Pentecostal movements that emerged in the late 1800s and early 1900s, and the televised "revivals" of the late twentieth century, all claim allegiance to the Bible, while promoting an independent experience of the Spirit. In his 1819 sermon, "Unitarian Christianity," William Ellery Channing offers another approach to the questions about the relationship between Word and Spirit. In responding to popular developments during the "Second Great Awakening," Channing articulates the liberal Christians' position that their principles were also derived from Scripture. He argues for the rejection of the Trinity and the Atonement, and belief in human goodness, from the biblical texts.

Production and distribution

In any effort related to the Bible, issues of media are ever-present: *How* and in *what form* are the scriptures circulated? As an open, online resource instantly available to anyone with an internet connection, the Conservative Bible Project radically advances an evangelical ideal deeply rooted and fiercely pursued in North America: convenient, free, and universal access to the Bible.

The English Parliament set a precedent in 1649 by chartering the Society for the Propagation of the Gospel in New England. The expressed purpose of the Cambridge, England-based "New England Company," as it was commonly called, was production of bibles and related texts for the American colonies. It provided the resources, skill, and technology – all in limited and concentrated supply – to produce and distribute Eliot's "Indian Bible." Other organizations followed suit, including the Anglican Church's influential Society for the Propagation of the Gospel in Foreign Parts (founded 1701). Nevertheless, according to imperial law copies of the Bible circulated in the colonies could only be printed in Britain with Royal Copyright. The quest for a domestically produced Bible did not begin officially until 1777, after the colonies had broken with the monarchy and the new Continental Congress encouraged the effort.

The realities of independence, including the severing of ties with the royal publishers, unleashed a flurry of activity. Demand for scriptures, as well as the desire to circulate the Bible more widely, intensified in the midst of the post-independence religious revivalism of the Second Great Awakening. The formation of the Philadelphia Bible Society in 1808 was the first in a wave of similar organizations established in the Atlantic region. At a May 1816 general meeting in New York, representatives from 28 of those local societies drew up a constitution for a national organization "of which the sole object shall be to encourage a wider circulation of the Holy Scriptures, without note or comment." The organization's commitment to that mission is now legendary. In just over three decades, the American Bible Society managed to produce and distribute nearly six million partial or full copies of the Christian scriptures in multiple languages all over the globe. The Society's work continues, and countless other organizations in the United States have taken up the cause, like the Wisconsin-based Gideons International, which has provided bibles free of charge to hotel rooms around the world since 1899.

Developments in technology and in management have profoundly impacted the commitment to mission. David Paul Nord, an American cultural historian, delineates the ways in which the bible societies – and the American Bible Society, in particular – helped pioneer the modern mass media by making use of emerging print technologies, by developing highly organized distribution networks, and by adapting quickly to target new audiences. Nord insists that the bible societies' efforts generated an extensive "charity marketplace" that paralleled – and in many ways, deliberately challenged – the rapidly growing commercial marketplace.

Nord also shows that the societies helped create a "bible industry" that over the last two centuries has developed into one of the United States' largest media spheres – and into one of the nation's biggest money-makers. By rapidly adapting emerging media forms to serve new target audiences, the American Bible Society helped forge "niche" publishing. The Bible – and related accessories – now come in every possible format to appeal in the open market to every possible consumer. There are a range of glossy "bible 'zines" for socially curious adolescents, audio dramatizations for one's car ride, illustrated and comic-book versions, coffee-table bibles, the Green Bible for the environmentally conscious, the Patriot's Bible for the nation-loving American, the new online, "wiki" option for conservatives, and more.

Translation

The third issue in the long-running effort to "spread the Word" is the question of translation. Not only do the medium and format vary, but the text itself often differs in language, structure, and length, according to different groups. As compellingly demonstrated by Peter Thuesen (1999) in his study of critical "battles" over translation, the process of developing new versions of scripture has been an ongoing and fundamental part of Americans' debates over values and identity. The Conservative Bible Project, for example, aims to restore the "true" meaning of the Bible in the wake of scriptural "distortion" from a "liberal" drift in modern translations. As with production, biblical translation did not comprise an open and varied field of activity before the American Revolution. From the beginning of exploration and settlement, most readers or listeners in North America encountered the Bible in the predominant English form: the Authorized Translation of 1611, better known as the King James Version. Some made use of the 1560 "Geneva" version, so-called because the English translation was carried out by English Protestants who fled to Geneva during the reign of Mary Tudor (1553–58). A handful of early Catholic settlers utilized the early seventeenth-century Douay College translation of the authorized Latin Vulgate.

The King James Version continued to hold sway well through the eighteenth century. With the era of independence, however, new approaches to the biblical texts emerged. In a landscape of radically shifting religious configurations as well as political, social, and economic change, individuals and groups began to offer renderings of the Bible that represented their own particular perspectives. Thomas Jefferson, an Enlightenment thinker, began working on his rationalist study of the gospels in 1803, while in the White House. Excising all supernatural aspects, including Jesus' miracles and resurrection, as well as perceived distortions by the writers, he finished his unique version, "The Life and Morals of Jesus of Nazareth," around 1820, but refused to publish it.

Three decades later, a group of conservative Baptists working through the American Bible Union of New York prepared their own translation of the New Testament (underscoring the significance of the translation "immerse" over "baptize"). Continuing John Eliot's early missionary efforts, the Bible was translated into many Native American languages. A 26-year project to translate the New Testament into Gullah, the language of the seacoast towns and islands off South Carolina and Georgia, was completed in 2005. Environmentalist scholars published the Green Bible in 2008, raising awareness of the relation of God, humanity, and nature by highlighting in green ink the biblical passages that speak to that relation.

Textual criticism and archaeological discoveries, part of the development of historical-critical methods in the nineteenth century, forced scholars to reconsider the meanings and translations of early biblical texts. During the first half of the nineteenth century a handful of individuals, beginning with Charles Thomson (1729–1824), produced partial or full translations by working on the early Greek manuscripts. In 1881 the first committee-based "Revised Translation" of the venerable King James Version of the New Testament appeared, creating a sensation on both sides of the Atlantic. The Revised Version Old Testament was published in 1885. A host of other widely used translations have followed. One reaction to the Revised Translation was Elizabeth Cady Stanton's *The Woman's Bible* (see Chapter 3). Two different Protestant groups took up revision of the American Standard Version, originally released in 1901. The first group produced the Revised Standard Version (1946) and the New Revised Standard Version (1989), while the second line of revision eventually led to the New American Standard Bible (1971). Similarly, the International Bible Society and the American Bible Society eventually produced their own translations – the New International Version (1973) and Today's English Version (1968), respectively – by working from original languages. In 1961 the Jehovah's Witnesses produced the first edition of their own version, the New World Translation.

The effort of the Witnesses to produce a denominationally specific edition of the Bible, as the conservative Baptists had more than a century earlier, calls attention to the fact that much of the effort of translation has been carried out against the prevailing influence in American culture of the King James Version. Jews and Catholics especially have worked to establish English translations that more accurately represent their traditions. That effort took on greater urgency in the mid-1800s because of the success of the American

Bible Society. With easy and cheap access to portable copies provided by ABS, many Jews and Catholics during that period relied on the King James Version, despite clear biases in that edition toward Protestantism and against Judaism and Catholicism.

Accordingly, the influential Jewish leader Isaac Leeser took up the task in the 1840s and 1850s of producing an English translation from the Hebrew texts. During roughly the same period Francis Kenrick, who became Archbishop of Baltimore, labored on a new edition of the Douay translation so that English-speaking Catholics in the United States and elsewhere could have a version of the Bible that in language and structure better represented Catholicism. New church-supported endeavors eventually led to the interdenominational production of the New American Bible in 1970 under the auspices of the United States Conference of Catholic Bishops. The text has received ongoing updates, including incorporation of gender-neutral and gender-inclusive language in 1986 and 1991 editions. A complete revision of the Old Testament, begun in 1994, was accepted by the American bishops in 2008, paving the way in 2010 for the fourth edition of the New American Bible.

The Jewish Publication Society, founded in 1888 to serve the children of the waves of Jewish immigrants coming from Europe, has produced two translations of the Hebrew Bible, the Tanakh. The second, a 30-year project finished in 1985 and translated directly from the Hebrew text, bypasses English translations. JPS states on its website that, in light of "new advances in scholarship, archaeology, and literary translation theory, the 28-year-old translation is ready for revision." In the meantime, JPS is developing an interactive site to learn and discuss the Bible, and producing an audio version with the Jewish Braille Institute.

The Book among books?

The ongoing and multifaceted efforts to "spread the Word" through missionizing, production, distribution, and translation reflect – and ensure – the Bible's ubiquity in the lives of Americans. More than five centuries after European explorers arrived in the Americas with "the Word" in hand, the Bible remains arguably the single most familiar and influential book in American culture. Still, the documents in this chapter speak to how the Bible's familiarity and influence continue to change. No longer does "the Word" necessarily circulate as words, nor "the Book" as a book. It is also now one book among many. With all of the different versions and formats, new questions arise. After all, what exactly is the place of the Bible now among "a reading public" and in an ever-expanding universe of media that, as David Paul Nord suggests, bible production helped to spawn? The cultural historian Paul Gutjahr identifies a critical paradox in the story of the Bible's proliferation in American culture: With more versions of the Bible and more bibles continually available, efforts – such as the Conservative Bible Project – arise anew with the goal of creating a more definitive version of "the Book."

JOHN ELIOT'S *BRIEF NARRATIVE*

The Cambridge-trained minister John Eliot (1604–90) arrived in Boston in November 1631 to assume the position of "teaching elder" at the First Church of Roxbury. With a background in Greek, Latin, and Hebrew, around 1646 he set out to learn the Natick language of the Massachusetts Indians as a means for preaching to them. He engaged in several successful publishing ventures, none more difficult or monumental than his translation of the complete Christian Bible into Natick and production of scores of copies. With the help of various Indians and printers in England and Massachusetts, he completed the translation in 1658 and published the first sections of the Natick Bible in 1661. Eliot's "Indian Bible," as it became known, was the first bible printed in North America and remained one of the only domestic productions of the scriptures for more than a century. In a 1670 report to the Society for the Promoting and Propagating the Gospel in New England, the group chartered by British Parliament to assist missionary efforts and the primary benefactor of the Natick Bible and other missionary publications, Eliot describes the state of progress in "the Indian Work" and recommends the ordination of native ministers.

Source: *American Historical Documents, 1000–1904.* Vol. xliii. The Harvard Classics. New York: P.F. Collier & Son, 1909–14; Bartleby.com, 2001: www.bartleby.com/43/ © 2001 Bartleby.com, Inc. Used by permission.

To the Right Worshipful the Commissioners under his Majesties' Great-Seal, for Propagation of the Gospel amongst the poor blind Indians in New-England:

THAT brief Tract of the present state of the *Indian-Work* in my hand. … I shall begin with our last great motion in that Work done this Summer, because that will lead me to begin with the state of the *Indians* under the hands of my Brethren Mr. *Mahew* and Mr. *Bourn.*

… In as much as now we have ordained *Indian Officers* unto the Ministry of the Gospel, it is needed to add a word or two of Apology: I find it hopeless to expect *English* Officers in our *Indian* Churches; the work is full of hardship, hard labour, and chargeable also, and the *Indians* not yet capable to give considerable support and maintenance; and Men have bodies, and must live of the Gospel: And what comes from England is liable to hazard and uncertainties. On such grounds as these partly, but especially from the secret wise governance of Jesus Christ, the Lord of the Harvest, there is no appearance of hope for their souls feeding in that way: they must be trained up to be able to live of themselves in the ways of the Gospel of Christ; and through the riches of God's Grace and Love, sundry of themselves who are expert in the Scriptures, are able to teach each other: An *English* young man raw in that language, coming to teach among our Christian-*Indians*, would be much to their loss; there be of themselves such as be more able, especially being advantaged that he speaketh his own language, and knoweth their manners. Such *English* as shall hereafter teach them, must begin with a People that begin to pray unto God, (and such opportunities we have many) and then as they grow in knowledge, he will grow (if he be diligent) in ability of speech to communicate the knowledge of Christ unto them. And seeing they must have Teachers amongst themselves, they must also be taught to be Teachers: for which cause I have begun to teach them the Art of Teaching, and I find some of them very capable. And while I live, my purpose is, (by the grace of Christ assisting) to make it one of my chief cares and labours to teach them some of the Liberal Arts and Sciences, and the way how to analize, and lay out into particulars both the Works and Word of God; and how to communicate knowledge to others methodically and skilfully, and especially the method of Divinity. There be sundry Ministers who live in an opportunity of beginning with a People, and for time to come I shall cease my importuning of others, and onely fall to perswade such unto this service of Jesus Christ, it being one part of our Ministerial Charge to preach to the World in the Name of Jesus, and from amongst them to gather Subjects to his holy Kingdom. The Bible, and the Catechism drawn out of the Bible, are general helps to all parts and places about us, and are the ground-work of Community amongst all our *Indian*-Churches and Christians.

Thus I have briefly touched some of the chiefest of our present Affairs, and commit them to your Prudence, to do with them what you please; committing your Selves, and all your weighty Affairs unto the Guidance and Blessing of the Lord, I rest,

Your Worships to serve you in the Service of our Lord *Jesus.*

JOHN ELLIOT.

Roxbury, this 20th of the 7th month, 1670.

CHARTER OF COLLEGE OF WILLIAM AND MARY

As indicated in Virginia's First Charter, the colony's founding authorities considered the spread of the Christian gospel to Native Americans as a foundational component of the colonial mission. Rather than actively taking the message to the natives, the Virginia colonists focused more immediately on bringing natives to the message. In 1618, less than a decade after establishing the Jamestown settlement, the colony's leaders set up a provisional university at Henricus (near present-day Richmond) in order to educate natives and the sons of planters alike in Bible study and Church of England tradition. The school was wiped out with the settlement during a 1622 conflict with Indians, but the idea endured. In 1691 James Blair, the colony's main religious authority, returned to England at the urging of the House of Burgesses to petition for the monarchs' support of a revived endeavor. King William and Queen Mary II, after whom the college would be named, granted the royal charter in 1693. The excerpt below, from the charter, demonstrates the persistence of the original mission, even if the effort to educate natives at "the Indian school" remained weak until its official abandonment during the Revolutionary War.

Source: Special Collections Research Center, Royal Charter Collection, UA 77 (Williamsburg, VA: The College of William and Mary).

WILLIAM AND MARY, by the grace of God, of England, Scotland, France and Ireland, King and Queen, defenders of the faith, &c. To all to whom these our present letters shall come, greeting.

Forasmuch as our well-beloved and faithful subjects, constituting the General Assembly of our Colony of Virginia, have had it in their minds, and have proposed to themselves, to the end that the Church of Virginia may be furnished with a seminary of ministers of the gospel, and that the youth may be piously educated in good letters and manners, and that the Christian faith may be propagated amongst the Western Indians, to the glory of Almighty God; to make, found and establish a certain place of universal study, or perpetual College of Divinity, Philosophy, Languages, and other good Arts and Sciences, consisting of one President, six Masters or Professors, and an hundred scholars more or less, according to the ability of the said college, and the statutes of the same; to be made, increased, diminished, or changed there, by certain trustees nominated and elected by the General Assembly aforesaid …

JONATHAN EDWARDS, "A DIVINE AND SUPERNATURAL LIGHT"

The famed preacher and theologian Jonathan Edwards (1703–58) delivered the sermon from which the following excerpt is drawn in 1733 at his church in Northampton, Massachusetts. Upon hearing the oration, listeners urged Edwards to make it widely available in print. The sermon now stands as an early and influential theological foundation for the "revival" movement – subsequently labeled "the First Great Awakening" – that developed over the following decade. Despite Edwards' familiar insistence on "the scriptural proof" of his argument for recurring manifestations of "divine and supernatural light," some of his contemporaries – as well as critics ever since – still wondered what his theology suggested about the actual role of the Bible in the process of "spreading the Word."

Source: *The Works of President Edwards* (NY: Leavitt, Trow & Co., 1844), iv, 439f.

All Moral Knowledge and business Skill from God.

God is the author of all knowledge and understanding whatsoever. He is the author of the knowledge that is obtained by human learning: he is the author of all moral prudence, and of the knowledge and skill that men have in their secular business. Thus it is said of all in Israel that were *wise-hearted*, and skilled in embroidering, that God had *filled* them *with the spirit of wisdom*, Exodus 28:3.

Yet Flesh and Blood Reveals It. God is the author of such knowledge; but yet not so but that *flesh and blood reveals it*. Mortal men are capable of imparting the knowledge of human arts and sciences, and skill in temporal affairs. God is the author of such knowledge by those means: *flesh and blood* is employed as the *mediate* or *second* cause of it; he conveys it by the power and influence of natural means.

God Alone the Author of Spiritual Knowledge. But this spiritual knowledge, spoken of in the text, is what God is the author of, and none else: he *reveals it,* and *flesh and blood reveals it not.* He imparts this knowledge immediately, not making use of any intermediate natural causes, as he does in other knowledge.

Doctrine

That there is such a thing as a spiritual and divine light immediately imparted to the soul by God, of a different nature from any that is obtained by natural means ...

Not "New Revelations" Apart From Scripture.

... 3. This spiritual light is not the suggesting of any new truths or propositions not contained in the word of God. This suggesting of new truths or doctrines to the mind, independent of any antecedent revelation of those propositions, either in word or writing, is inspiration; such as the prophets and apostles had, and such as some enthusiasts pretend to. But this spiritual light that I am speaking of, is quite a different thing from inspiration: it reveals no new doctrine, it suggests no new proposition to the mind, it teaches no new thing of God, or Christ, or another world, not taught in the Bible, but only gives a due apprehension of those things that are taught in the word of God ...

The Proof and Benefits of Divine Light

III. To show the truth of the doctrine; that is, to show that there is such a thing as that spiritual light that has been described, thus immediately let into the mind by God. And here I would show briefly, that this doctrine is both *scriptural* and *rational.*

The Scriptural Proof of this Doctrine

Saints Possess This Knowledge and Sight of God. First, It is scriptural. My text is not only full to the purpose, but it is a doctrine that the Scripture abounds in. We are there abundantly taught, that the saints differ from the ungodly in this, that they have the knowledge of God, and a sight of God, and of Jesus Christ. I shall mention but few texts of many. 1 John 3:6, "Whosoever sinneth, has not seen him, nor known him." 3 John 11, "He that doth good, is of God: but he that doth evil, hath not seen God." John 14:19, "The world seeth me no more; but ye see me." John 17:3, "And this is eternal life, that they might know thee, the only true God, and Jesus Christ whom thou hast sent." This knowledge, or sight of God and Christ, cannot be a mere speculative knowledge; because it is spoken of as a seeing and knowing, wherein they differ from the ungodly.

And by these Scriptures it must not only be a different knowledge in degree and circumstances, and different in its effects; but it must be entirely different in nature and kind ...

Those Possessing Divine Light Assured. The Apostle Peter mentions it as what gave them (the apostles) good and well grounded assurance of the truth of the gospel, that they had seen the divine glory of Christ. 2 Pet. 1:16, "For we have not followed cunningly devised fables when we made known unto you the power and coming of our Lord Jesus Christ, but were eyewitnesses of his majesty." The apostle has respect to that visible glory of Christ which they saw in his transfiguration: that glory was so divine, having such an ineffable appearance and semblance of divine holiness, majesty and grace, that it evidently denoted him to be a divine person. But if a sight of Christ's outward glory might give a rational assurance of his divinity, why may not an apprehension of his spiritual glory do so too? Doubtless Christ's spiritual glory is in itself as distinguishing, and as plainly showing his divinity, as his outward glory, and a great deal more: for his spiritual glory is that wherein his divinity consists; and the outward glory of his transfiguration showed him to be divine, only as it was a remarkable image or representation of that spiritual glory. Doubtless, therefore, he that has had a clear sight of the spiritual glory of Christ, may say, I have not followed cunningly devised fables, but have been an eyewitness of his majesty, upon as good grounds as the apostle, when he had respect to the outward glory of Christ that he had seen.

CONTINENTAL CONGRESS AUTHORIZES BIBLE PRINTING

Until the revolution, all bibles in the American colonies came from Britain. As territories within the United Kingdom, the colonies observed the imperial laws that granted Royal Copyright of scriptures to a handful of British publishers. Aside from legal prohibitions, practical considerations constricted domestic bible production in the colonies. Equipment and materials were expensive and scarce and the printing process required a combination of skills and time rare among American colonists. With their declaration of independence from the crown in 1776, colonial authorities quickly recognized a need for other sources of English-language bibles aside from Britain. In 1777, the Continental Congress began to look into importing bibles from Holland and elsewhere. With that option made nearly impossible by the ongoing war for independence, the Congress expressed support for individual efforts in domestic bible production. American printers managed partial editions over the following years until finally, in 1782, Robert Aitken's press in Philadelphia produced the complete Christian scriptures. Below, a report of the Continental Congress from September of that year reviews the achievement and issues the official congressional approval of "The Aitken's Bible."

Source: "Aitken's Bible," *Religion and the Founding of the American Republic*, special exhibit of the Library of Congress: www.loc.gov/exhibits/religion/.

THURSDAY, September 12, 1782

The committee, consisting of Mr. Duane, Mr. McKean and Mr. Witherspoon, to whom was referred a memorial of Robert Aitkin [sic], printer, dated January 21st, 1781, respecting an edition of the holy scriptures, report,

"That Mr. Aitkin has at a great expence now finished an American edition of the holy scriptures in English; that the committee have from time to time attended to his progress in the work; that they also recommended it to the two chaplains of Congress to examine and give their opinion of the execution, who have accordingly reported thereon.

The recommendation and report being as follows:

"Philadelphia, September 1st, 1782.

Reverend gentlemen,

Our knowledge of your piety and public spirit leads us without apology to recommend your particular attention to the edition of the holy scriptures publishing by Mr. Aitkin. He undertook this expensive work at a time, when from the circumstances of the war an English edition of the bible could not be imported, nor any opinion formed how long the obstruction might continue. On this account particularly he deserves applause and encouragement. We therefore wish you, reverend gentlemen, to examine the execution of the work, and if approved to give it the sanction of your judgment and the weight of your recommendation. We are, with very great respect, your most humble servants,

(Signed.) JAMES DUANE, chairman, in behalf of a committee of Congress on Mr. Aitkin's memorial.

Reverend doctor White and reverend Mr. Duffield, chaplains of the United States in Congress assembled."

Report.

"Gentlemen,

Agreeably to your desire we have paid attention to Mr. Robert Aitkin's impression of the holy scriptures of the old and new testament. Having selected and examined a variety of passages throughout the work, we are of opinion that it is executed with great accuracy as to the sense, and with as few grammatical and typographical errors as could be expected in an undertaking of such magnitude. Being ourselves witnesses of the demand for this invaluable book, we rejoice in the present prospect of a supply, hoping that it will prove advantageous as it is honourable to the gentleman, who has exerted himself to furnish it at the evident risque of private fortune. We are, gentlemen, your very respectful and humble servants,

(Signed.) William White,

George Duffield.

Honourable James Duane, esquire, chairman, and the other honourable gentlemen of the committee of Congress on Mr. Aitkin's memorial.

Philadelphia, September 10, 1782.

Whereupon,

Resolved, That the United States Congress assembled highly approve the pious and laudable understaking of Mr. Aitkin, as subservient to the interest of religion as well as an instance of the progress of arts in this country, and being

satisfied from the above report, of his care and accuracy in the execution of
the work, they recommend this edition of the bible to the inhabitants of the
United States, and hereby authorize him to publish this recommendation in
the manner he shall think proper.

THE JEFFERSON BIBLE

During his presidency, Thomas Jefferson (1743–1826) cut and pasted
materials from the gospels to create his "wee-little" book, "the Philosophy
of Jesus." He said it would prove he was "a real Christian" or a "disciple
of the doctrines of Jesus." This material from the beginning, middle, and
end of the book, shows Jefferson's rejection of the supernatural, including
Jesus' miracles and resurrection.

Source: Reprinted by permission of Princeton University Press and the Papers of
Thomas Jefferson, Second Series. From the work: *Jefferson's Extracts from the Gospels:
"The Philosophy of Jesus" and "The Life and Morals of Jesus,"* Dickinson W. Adams, ed.;
Ruth W. Lester, ass. ed.; intro. by Eugene R. Sheridan (1983), 60, 77, 83, 104–5.

CHAPTER II

And it came to pass in those days, that there went out a decree from Caesar
Augustus, that all the world should be taxed.

2 (And this taxing was first made when Cyrenius was governor of Syria).

3 And all went to be taxed, every one in his own city.

4 And Joseph also went up from Galilee, out of the city of Nazareth, into
Judaea, unto the city of David, which is called Bethlehem, (because he was of
the house and lineage of David,)

5 To be taxed with Mary his espoused wife, being great with child.

6 And so it was, that, while they were there, the days were accomplished
that she should be delivered.

7 And she brought forth her firstborn son, and wrapped him in swaddling
clothes, and laid him in a manger; because there was no room for them in the
inn ...

CHAPTER VI

[...]

25 Therefore I say unto you, Take no thought for your life, what ye shall
eat, or what ye shall drink; nor yet for your body, what ye shall put on. Is not
the life more than meat, and the body more than raiment?

26 Behold the fowls of the air for they sow not, neither do they reap, nor
gather into barns; yet your heavenly Father feedeth them. Are ye not much
better than they?

27 Which of you by taking thought can add one cubit unto his stature?

[...]

CHAPTER VII

1 Judge not, that ye be not judged.

2 For with what judgment ye judge, ye shall be judged: and with what
measure ye mete, it shall be measured to you again [...]

CHAPTER XV

35 A good man out of the good treasure of the heart bringeth forth good things; and an evil man out of the evil treasure bringeth forth evil things [...]

CHAPTER XXVII

17 And he bearing his cross went forth into a place called the place of a skull, which is called in the Hebrew, Golgotha:

33 And when they were come to the place which is called Calvary, there they crucified him, and the malefactors: one on the right hand, and the other on the left.

34 Then said Jesus, Father forgive them; for they know not what they do. And they parted his raiment, and cast lots.

CHAPTER XXIII

25 Now there stood by the cross of Jesus his mother, and his mother's sister, Mary *the wife* of Cleophas, and Mary Magdalene.

26 When Jesus therefore saw his mother, and the disciple standing by, whom he loved, he saith unto his mother, Woman, behold they son!

27 Then saith he to the disciple, Behold thy mother! And from that hour that disciple took her into his own home.

28 After this, Jesus knowing that all things were accomplished that the Scripture might be fulfilled, saith, I thirst.

29 Now there was a vessel full of vinegar: and they filled a sponge with vinegar, and put it upon hyssop, and put it to his mouth.

46. And about the ninth hour Jesus cried with a loud voice, saying, Eli, Eli, lama sabachthani? that is to say, My God, my God, why hast thou forsaken me?

30 When Jesus therefore had received the vinegar, he said, It is finished: and he bowed his head, and gave up the ghost.

THE AMERICAN BIBLE SOCIETY

The turn of the nineteenth century saw a renewal of Protestant energies in spreading the faith in central and western New York, New England, the South, and Pennsylvania and Ohio. As great numbers flocked to settle the West, societies formed to Christianize the Frontier. Camp meetings, revivals, and missionary societies were evidence of a Second Awakening of religious fervor. The American Bible Society was formed in 1816 to distribute Bibles, especially to the Bible-impoverished Western settlements. The first selection is Article I of its Constitution, adopted at the founding of the society in Philadelphia in 1816, and the second (1865) reports on its initiative during the Civil War, to distribute a Bible to every Union soldier.

Sources: Creighton Lacy, *The Word-Carrying Giant* (Pasadena: William Carey Library, 1977), 10; *Forty-sixth Annual Report of the American Bible Society*, May 16, 1862 (New York: American Bible Society, 1862), 30–32.

I. This society shall be known by the name of the AMERICAN BIBLE SOCIETY, of which the sole object shall be, to encourage a wider circulation of the Holy

Scripture without note or comment. The only copies in the English language to be circulated by the Society, shall be of the version now in common use.

II. The unhappy events taking place in our country have thrown a new care upon the American Bible Society. About the commencement of the Society's year, it became evident that a large number of citizens would be drawn from their homes to engage in the fearful conflict of arms. The Board, aware of the dangers to morals as well as to life, involved in the impending conflict, and anxious for the well being, temporal and spiritual, of the many thousands who would be thus exposed, lost no time in offering such provision as was needed, and as the Society was under obligation to afford. Accordingly, at the meeting of the Managers on the 2d day of May, the following resolution was adopted:

Resolved, That a circular be prepared by the Secretaries, and sent to each Agent and Auxiliary throughout the country, reminding them of the peculiar need of the Word of God which all persons have who are in circumstances of danger, and exposed to sudden death; and urging them to see that every soldier enlisted within their bounds is supplied with a copy of the Scriptures in whole or in part; and encouraging them, if unable without assistance to attend to this important duty, to apply for such assistance to the Parent Society.

The effect of this measure was very great. Steps were immediately taken by Agents and auxiliaries all over the country to supply the soldiers in companies and regiments, at their places of rendezvous, and in their encampments at the seat of war. The demand for books became very large, in one single month being something over 125,000 volumes, and making the entire number in the course of the year far beyond any former issues of this Society … It was the desire of the Board, nobly seconded by the auxiliaries throughout the country, that no soldier willing to receive one should go to the battlefield without a copy of the Word of God.

… The Managers have as far as possible kept an eye upon the books thus distributed, and sought information as to the effects produced. Although some of the books, like the seed which in sowing broadcast falls by the wayside, may return no fruit, yet on the whole, satisfactory evidence has been given that the effect was most salutary. They have been eagerly received, and for the most part carefully preserved and diligently read. Such is the testimony of Agents of this Society, chaplains in the army, and pious officers who have taken an interest in supplying their men. One Agent writes, that "when in a camp it was known that he had Testaments in a basket to distribute, he was surrounded so that he could scarcely move till they were gone. In a tent, some men, for want of something to do, were playing cards; but as soon as they found that he had Testaments, they ceased reading their books [the cards] and began to read his." In Missouri, a Testament was about being thrown away by a Catholic soldier, but was given on request to his comrade, and the next day it saved his life. Pious soldiers have persisted in reading their books uniformly and offering prayer on retiring at night, and the example has been blessed to the awakening and conversion of the ungodly messmates. Many soldiers, after diligently reading the Testament during their lives, have died clasping it in their hands, or have sent it home, after being pierced with a ball, as a memento, to their friends. It is the testimony of many that there has been more reading of the Scriptures in the country during the past year than was ever known before, and that many began the practice in camp who had previously been strangers to it.

LIBERAL RESPONSES TO CALVINISM

Some Christians reacted against Calvinist ideas of God and human nature as excessively negative. Universalism, a North American phenomenon, taught that God's love will redeem all. It joined with Unitarianism, a movement that began in Transylvania in the 16th century, which emphasized God's unity and desire to bring salvation to all his creatures. William Ellery Channing (1780–1842) gave his 1½-hour sermon, "Unitarian Christianity," at the ordination of Jared Sparks on May 5, 1819 in Baltimore. Enunciating the principles of liberal Christianity, it was widely read, and showed the growing strength of Unitarianism, Transcendentalism, and liberal Christian thought. In this excerpt, from the beginning of the sermon, Channing shows the scriptural basis of Unitarian ideas, including the rejection of the doctrines of the Trinity and the Atonement. This discourse revived issues and controversies that surfaced almost a century before, during the "First Great Awakening," regarding the role of scripture in the spread of religious commitment (see Jonathan Edwards selection above). Channing's sermon also hints at some of the new debates during the period about the relationship of the Bible and ministry.

Source: William Ellery Channing, "Unitarian Christianity," in *Unitarian Christianity and Other Essays*, ed. Irving H. Bartlett (New York: The Liberal Arts Press, 1957), 3–38.

1 Thes. v. 21: *"Prove all things; hold fast that which is good"*

The peculiar circumstances of this occasion not only justify, but seem to demand a departure from the course generally followed by preachers at the introduction of a brother into the sacred office. It is usual to speak of the nature, design, duties, and advantages of the Christian ministry; and on these topics I should now be happy to insist, did I not remember that a minister is to be given this day to a religious society, whose peculiarities of opinion have drawn upon them much remark, and may I not add, much reproach. Many good minds, many sincere Christians, I am aware, are apprehensive that the solemnities of this day are to give a degree of influence to principles which they deem false and injurious. The fears and anxieties of such men I respect; and, believing that they are grounded in part on mistake, I have thought it my duty to lay before you, as clearly as I can, some of the distinguishing opinions of that class of Christians in our country, who are known to sympathize with this religious society. I must ask your patience, for such a subject is not to be despatched in a narrow compass. I must also ask you to remember, that it is impossible to exhibit, in a single discourse, our views of every doctrine of

Revelation, much less the differences of opinion which are known to subsist among ourselves. I shall confine myself to topics, on which our sentiments have been misrepresented, or which distinguish us most widely from others. May I not hope to be heard with candor? God deliver us all from prejudice and unkindness, and fill us with the love of truth and virtue.

There are two natural divisions under which my thoughts will be arranged. I shall endeavour to unfold, 1st, The principles which we adopt in interpreting the Scriptures. And 2dly, Some of the doctrines, which the Scriptures, so interpreted, seem to us clearly to express.

I. We regard the Scriptures as the records of God's successive revelations to mankind, and particularly of the last and most perfect revelation of his will by Jesus Christ. Whatever doctrines seem to us to be clearly taught in the Scriptures; we receive without reserve or exception. We do not, however, attach equal importance to all the books in this collection. Our religion, we believe, lies chiefly in the New Testament. The dispensation of Moses, compared with that of Jesus, we consider as adapted to the childhood of the human race, a preparation for a nobler system, and chiefly useful now as serving to confirm and illustrate the Christian Scriptures. Jesus Christ is the only master of Christians, and whatever he taught, either during his personal ministry, or by his inspired Apostles, we regard as of divine authority, and profess to make the rule of our lives.

This authority, which we give to the Scriptures, is a reason, we conceive, for studying them with peculiar care, and for inquiring anxiously into the principles of interpretation, by which their true meaning may be ascertained. The principles adopted by the class of Christians in whose name I speak, need to be explained, because they are often misunderstood. We are particularly accused of making an unwarrantable use of reason in the interpretation of Scripture. We are said to exalt reason above revelation, to prefer our own wisdom to God's. Loose and undefined charges of this kind are circulated so freely, that we think it due to ourselves, and to the cause of truth, to express our views with some particularity.

Our leading principle in interpreting Scripture is this, that the Bible is a book written for men, in the language of men, and that its meaning is to be sought in the same manner as that of other books. We believe that God, when he speaks to the human race, conforms, if we may so say, to the established rules of speaking and writing. How else would the Scriptures avail us more, than if communicated in an unknown tongue?

Now all books, and all conversation, require in the reader or hearer the constant exercise of reason; or their true import is only to be obtained by continual comparison and inference. Human language, you well know, admits various interpretations; and every word and every sentence must be modified and explained according to the subject which is discussed, according to the purposes, feelings, circumstances, and principles of the writer, and according to the genius and idioms of the language which he uses. These are acknowledged principles in the interpretation of human writings; and a man, whose words we should explain without reference to these principles, would reproach us justly with a criminal want of candor, and an intention of obscuring or distorting his meaning.

Were the Bible written in a language and style of its own, did it consist of words, which admit but a single sense, and of sentences wholly detached from each other, there would be no place for the principles now laid down. We could not reason about it, as about other writings. But such a book would be of little worth; and perhaps, of all books, the Scriptures correspond least to this description. The Word of God bears the stamp of the same hand, which we see in his works. It has infinite connexions and dependences. Every proposition is linked with others, and is to be compared with others; that its full and precise import may be understood. Nothing stands alone. The New Testament is built on the Old. The Christian dispensation is a continuation of the Jewish, the completion of a vast scheme of providence, requiring great extent of view in the reader. Still more, the Bible treats of subjects on which we receive ideas from other sources besides itself; such subjects as the nature, passions, relations, and duties of man; and it expects us to restrain and modify its language by the known truths, which observation and experience furnish on these topics.

We profess not to know a book, which demands a more frequent exercise of reason than the Bible. In addition to the remarks now made on its infinite connexions, we may observe, that its style nowhere affects the precision of science, or the accuracy of definition. Its language is singularly glowing, bold, and figurative, demanding more frequent departures from the literal sense, than that of our own age and country, and consequently demanding more continual exercise of judgment. – We find, too, that the different portions of this book, instead of being confined to general truths, refer perpetually to the times when they were written, to states of society, to modes of thinking, to controversies in the church, to feelings and usages which have passed away, and without the knowledge of which we are constantly in danger of extending to all times, and places, what was of temporary and local application. – We find, too, that some of these books are strongly marked by the genius and character of their respective writers, that the Holy Spirit did not so guide the Apostles as to suspend the peculiarities of their minds, and that a knowledge of their feelings, and of the influences under which they were placed, is one of the preparations for understanding their writings. With these views of the Bible, we feel it our bounden duty to exercise our reason upon it perpetually, to compare, to infer, to look beyond the letter to the spirit, to seek in the nature of the subject, and the aim of the writer, his true meaning; and, in general, to make use of what is known, for explaining what is difficult, and for discovering new truths.

Need I descend to particulars, to prove that the Scriptures demand the exercise of reason? Take, for example, the style in which they generally speak of God, and observe how habitually they apply to him human passions and organs. Recollect the declarations of Christ, that he came not to send peace, but a sword; that unless we eat his flesh, and drink his blood, we have no life in us; that we must hate father and mother, and pluck out the right eye; and a vast number of passages equally bold and unlimited. Recollect the unqualified manner in which it is said of Christians, that they possess all things, know all things, and can do all things. Recollect the verbal contradiction between Paul and James, and the apparent clashing of some parts of Paul's writings with the general doctrines and end of Christianity. I might extend the enumeration indefinitely; and who does not see, that we must limit all these passages by the known attributes of God, of Jesus Christ, and of human nature, and by the circumstances under which they were written, so as to give the language a quite different import from what it would require, had it been applied to different beings, or used in different connexions.

Enough has been said to show, in what sense we make use of reason in interpreting Scripture. From a variety of possible interpretations, we select that which accords with the nature of the subject and the state of the writer, with the connexion of the passage, with the general strain of Scripture, with the known character and will of God, and with the obvious and acknowledged laws of nature. In other words, we believe that God never contradicts, in one part of scripture, what he teaches in another; and never contradicts, in revelation, what he teaches in his works and providence. And we therefore distrust every interpretation, which, after deliberate attention, seems repugnant to any established truth. We reason about the Bible precisely as civilians do about the constitution under which we live; who, you know, are accustomed to limit one provision of that venerable instrument by others, and to fix the precise import of its parts, by inquiring into its general spirit, into the intentions of its authors, and into the prevalent feelings, impressions, and circumstances of the time when it was framed. Without these principles of interpretation, we frankly acknowledge, that we cannot defend the divine authority of the Scriptures. Deny us this latitude, and we must abandon this book to its enemies.

We do not announce these principles as original, or peculiar to ourselves. All Christians occasionally adopt them, not excepting those who most vehemently decry them, when they happen to menace some favorite article of their creed. All Christians are compelled to use them in their controversies with infidels. All sects employ them in their warfare with one another. All willingly avail themselves of reason, when it can be pressed into the service of their own party, and only complain of it, when its weapons wound themselves. None reason more frequently than those from whom we differ. It is astonishing what a fabric they rear from a few slight hints about the fall of our first parents; and how ingeniously they extract, from detached passages, mysterious doctrines about the divine nature. We do not blame them for reasoning so abundantly, but for violating the fundamental rules of reasoning, for sacrificing the plain to the obscure, and the general strain of Scripture to a scanty number of insulated texts.

We object strongly to the contemptuous manner in which human reason is often spoken of by our adversaries, because it leads, we believe, to universal skepticism. If reason be so dreadfully darkened by the fall, that its most decisive judgments on religion are unworthy of trust, then Christianity, and even natural theology, must be abandoned; for the existence and veracity of God, and the divine original of Christianity, are conclusions of reason, and must stand or fall with it. If revelation be at war with this faculty, it subverts itself, for the great question of its truth is left by God to be decided at the bar of reason. It is worthy of remark, how nearly the bigot and the skeptic approach. Both would annihilate our confidence in our faculties, and both throw doubt and confusion over every truth. We honor revelation too highly to make it the antagonist of reason, or to believe that it calls us to renounce our highest powers.

We indeed grant, that the use of reason in religion is accompanied with danger. But we ask any honest man to look back on the history of the church, and say, whether the renunciation of it be not still more dangerous. Besides, it is a plain fact, that men reason as erroneously on all subjects, as on religion. Who does not know the wild and groundless theories, which have been framed in physical and political science? But who ever supposed, that we must cease to exercise reason on nature and society, because men have erred for ages in explaining them? We grant, that the passions continually, and sometimes fatally, disturb the rational faculty in its inquiries into revelation. The ambitious contrive to find doctrines in the Bible, which favor their love of dominion. The timid and dejected discover there a gloomy system, and the mystical and fanatical, a visionary theology. The vicious can find examples or assertions on which to build the hope of a late repentance, or of acceptance on easy terms. The falsely refined contrive to light on doctrines which have not been soiled by vulgar handling. But the passions do not distract the reason in religious, any more than in other inquiries, which excite strong and general interest; and this faculty, of consequence, is not to be renounced in religion, unless we are prepared to discard it universally. The true inference from the almost endless errors, which have darkened theology, is, not that we are to neglect and disparage our powers, but to exert them more patiently, circumspectly, uprightly. The worst errors, after all, having sprung up in that church, which proscribes reason, and demands from its members implicit faith. The most pernicious doctrines have been the growth of the darkest times, when the general credulity encouraged bad men and enthusiasts to broach their dreams and inventions, and to stifle the faint remonstrances of reasons, by the menaces of everlasting perdition. Say what we may, God has given us a rational nature, and will call us to account for it. We may let it sleep, but we do so at our peril. Revelation is addressed to us as rational beings. We may wish, in our sloth, that God had given us a system, demand of comparing, limiting, and inferring. But such a system would be at variance with the whole character of our present existence; and it is the part of wisdom to take revelation as it is given to us, and to interpret it by the help of the faculties, which it everywhere supposes, and on which founded.

To the views now given, an objection is commonly urged from the character of God. We are told, that God being infinitely wiser than men, his discoveries will surpass human reason. In a revelation from such a teacher, we ought to expect propositions, which we cannot reconcile with one another, and which may seem to contradict established truths; and it becomes us not to question or explain them away, but to believe, and adore, and to submit our weak and carnal reason to the Divine Word. To this objection, we have two short answers. We say, first, that it is impossible that a teacher of infinite wisdom should expose those, whom he would teach, to infinite error. But if once we admit, that propositions, which in their literal sense appear plainly repugnant to one another, or to any known truth, are still to be literally understood and received, what possible limit can we set to the belief of contradictions? What shelter have we from the wildest fanaticism, which can always quote passages, that, in their literal and obvious sense, give support to its extravagances? How can the Protestant escape from transubstantiation, a doctrine most clearly taught us, if the submission of reason, now contended for, be a duty? How can we even hold fast the truth of revelation, for if one apparent contradiction may be true, so may another, and the proposition, that Christianity is false, though involving inconsistency, may still be a verity?

We answer again, that, if God be infinitely wise, he cannot sport with the understandings of his creatures. A wise teacher discovers his wisdom in adapting himself to the capacities of his pupils, not in perplexing them with what is unintelligible, not in distressing them with apparent contradictions, not in filling them with a skeptical distrust of their own powers. An infinitely wise teacher, who knows the precise extent of our minds, and the best method of enlightening them, will surpass all other instructors in bringing down truth to our apprehension, and in showing its loveliness and harmony. We ought, indeed, to expect occasional obscurity in such a book as the Bible, which was written for past and future ages, as well as for the present. But God's wisdom is a pledge, that whatever is necessary for US, and necessary for salvation, is revealed too plainly to be mistaken, and too consistently to be questioned, by a sound and upright mind. It is not the mark of wisdom, to use an unintelligible phraseology, to communicate what is above our capacities, to confuse and unsettle the intellect by appearances of contradiction. We honor our Heavenly Teacher too much to ascribe to him such a revelation. A revelation is a gift of light. It cannot thicken our darkness, and multiply our perplexities.

II. Having thus stated the principles according to which we interpret Scripture, I now proceed to the second great head of this discourse, which is, to state some of the views which we derive from that sacred book, particularly those which distinguish us from other Christians …

THE STUDENT VOLUNTEER MOVEMENT

Popular American interest in foreign missions surged at the very end of the nineteenth century and continued through the 1920s. Millions of Americans participated in the effort domestically, supporting tens of thousands of compatriots who took up the effort to spread their religion abroad. The movement was driven overwhelmingly by Protestants, and most of the foreign missionaries were males with college degrees or beyond. The Student Volunteer Movement represented the vanguard of the effort, for reasons suggested in the selection below. The organization took shape in July 1886 at a religious conference for students held at the Mount Hermon School in Northfield, Massachusetts. The first group of student missionaries formed at Princeton in 1888. In the following excerpt, taken from the proceedings of the organization's first major gathering in 1891, one of the missionary pioneers outlines the ideals – as well as some practical considerations – needed for missions to China.

Source: Student Volunteer Movement for Foreign Missions, *Report of the First International Convention of the Student Volunteer Movement for Foreign Missions, held at Cleveland, Ohio, U.S.A., February 26, 27, 28 and March 1, 1891* (Boston: T. O. Metcalf, 1891), 49–51.

Proceedings of convention day 2 (Feb 27, 1891), afternoon session

The Rev. F. A. Steven, of the China Inland Mission, spoke as follows: –

What is required in candidates for the China Inland Mission? We may remind ourselves in the first instance – we cannot remind ourselves too often – that unmistakable evidence of the new birth is the first essential for a missionary. No amount of culture can possibly take the place of this. Zeal for God's glory in the preaching of the Gospel among the heathen is the next essential. That a man should go out to represent a missionary society, or to represent a church or denomination, and not put God first, not live wholly for God among the heathen, is a deplorable thing indeed. The heathen are sunken in idolatry, and unless we represent a pure, simple, joyous, powerful Christianity among them, we shall never be able to move them from their heathenism.

A fair acquaintance with God's word, and a real deep love for it, is a requisite that cannot possibly be dispensed with. I say a fair acquaintance with God's word, because a man is always learning, and if he have a deep love for the word of God will go on perfecting himself in the knowledge of it when he is in the field. Let us remember that a man's training by no means ceases when he leaves these shores. In the China Inland Mission a man's training begins then, or rather a very important part of his training and fitness for his work begins after he leaves these shores. We have, I thank God for it, established two training homes in connection with the mission, one for ladies and one for gentlemen, and at the present time there are I suppose somewhere about thirty young men at the training home, and about the same number of ladies, studying the Chinese language and the Bible under competent teachers. This is a very, very great advantage in the carrying on of the work ...

Soundness in the faith is most essential. We do not want any to go to China to teach heresy. There is plenty of heathenism, plenty of wandering from God, in China already, without adding to the confusion of the people by new heresies. Let me read from the "Principles and Practice" of the mission: "Candidates are expected to satisfy the Directors and Home Council as to their soundness in the faith on all fundamental truths by handing in, together with the schedule of application, a written statement of their views as to the inspiration of the Scriptures, the Trinity, the fall of man and his state by nature, the atonement, the eternal salvation of the redeemed, and the everlasting punishment of the lost." If a man is shaky upon that last point we don't want him. They must be catholic in their views, and able to have fellowship at work and at the Lord's table with all believers holding these fundamental truths, even if widely differing in their judgment as to the points of church government ...

God has been faithful to His promises. Not one iota of all His pledge of love to His children has ever failed. I have been in connection with the mission about eight years, and in journeying right across China from side to side and over into Burmah, and for three years and a half I have never lacked any good thing. To the praise of God be it spoken, His right hand has supplied after His own bountiful fashion.

I must say here that in the China Inland Mission we wear the native dress and live in native houses, which, however, we can accommodate to our requirements by internal changes. We do not make external changes in the interior provinces of China, in order to avoid prejudice in the people. Wearing the native dress and living upon the food available in the districts, we are able to live comfortably and well upon $300 per annum, including traveling expenses. I have never found it either necessary or advantageous to use so much as the figure I have mentioned ...

A fair English education is desirable for all who go to China, and without that we should advise a time of further training in this country as a test of the ability and perseverance that would be necessary for the acquirement of the Chinese language. Yet we do not ask that all should be highly educated. If a man were to say: "My house that I am to build is to be such as none ever was before. Not a man shall touch trowel or carry mortar on that house but who has been bred as an architect and passed his examination," we should say that the man would be a long, long time before he got his house built. In the China Inland Mission we recognize that God calls men of different qualifications for different fields of labor. I rejoice that most of the Boards also recognize this. I believe that the time is coming when men of capable business habits and ability will do a still larger share of the work of foreign missions than heretofore. Send us the best, send us the most highly educated; but oh! do not forget to send us the competent, clear-headed, common sense business men, who give up all for Christ and come to preach the Gospel to the heathen.

ISAAC LEESER AND THE TRANSLATION OF HEBREW SCRIPTURE

The Prussian-born Isaac Leeser (1806–68) immigrated to Richmond, Virginia at seventeen and soon became an active and outspoken member of the local Jewish community. Leeser's published response to an 1828 critique of Judaism in *The London Quarterly* gained the attention of a congregation in Philadelphia, where he moved the following year and remained for the rest of his life. In a city known for its political, religious, and cultural ferment – the place where Robert Aitken produced a new, congressionally authorized American bible during the Revolutionary War (see earlier selection) – Leeser emerged in his own right as an influential political activist, spiritual leader, and publisher. He remains a key figure in the development of American Judaism, and one of his most significant accomplishments was the first domestically produced English translation of the Jewish scriptures, carried out almost entirely on his own time and at his own expense. Working directly from the Hebrew texts and relying on earlier Jewish commentators, Leeser completed his full translation in 1853. In the preface to the edition, Leeser explains the methods and motivations for producing "a version of the Bible which has not been made by the authority of churches."

Source: Isaac Leeser, *The Twenty-four Books of the Holy Scriptures, Carefully Translated According to the Massoretic Text, on the Basis of the English Version, After the Best Jewish Authorities and Supplied with Short Explanatory Notes by Isaac Leeser* (Philadelphia, PA: A. De Sola, 1853), iii–iv.

In presenting this work to the public, the translator would merely remark, that is it not a new notion by which he was seized of late years which impelled him to the task, but a desire entertained for more than a quarter of a century, since the day he quitted school in his native land to come to this country, to present to his fellow-Israelites an English version, made by one of themselves, of the Holy Word of God. From early infancy he was made conscious how much persons differing from us in religious ideas make use of Scripture to assail Israel's hope and faith, by what he deems, in accordance with the well-settled opinions of sound critics, both Israelites and others, a perverted and hence erroneous rendering of the words of the original Bible. Therefore he always entertained the hope to be one day permitted to do for his fellow Hebrews who use the English as their vernacular, what has been done for the Germans by some of the most eminent minds whom the Almighty has endowed with the power of reanimating in us the almost expiring desire for critical inquiry into the sacred text.

  … It must be left to those acquainted with the subject, to decide whether he has taken due advantage of the materials in his hand; but he trusts that the judgment will be in his favour, at least so far, that he has been honest and faithful.

  The translator is an Israelite in faith, in the full sense of the word: he believes in the Scriptures as they have been handed down to us; in the truth and authenticity of prophecies and their ultimate literal fulfillment. He has always studied Scriptures to find a confirmation for his faith and hope; nevertheless, he asserts fearlessly, that in his going through this work, he has thrown aside all bias, discarded every preconceived opinion, and translated the text before him without regard to the result thence arising for his creed. But no perversion or forced rendering of any text was needed to bear out his opinions or those of Israelites in general; and he for one would place but little confidence in them, if he were compelled to change the evident meaning of the Bible to find support for them. He trusts, therefore, that to those who agree with him in their religious persuasion, he has rendered an acceptable service;

as they will now have an opportunity to study a version of the Bible which has not been made by the authority of churches in which they can have no confidence; and that to those also who are a different persuasion, his labours will not be unacceptable, as exhibiting, so far as he could do it, the progress of biblical criticism among ancient and modern Israelites – a task utterly beyond the power of any but a Jew by birth and conviction.

... With these few remarks the translator surrenders a labour in which he has been engaged, occasionally, for more than fifteen years, to the kindness of the public, trusting that, by the blessing of the Father of all, it may be made instrumental in diffusing a taste for Scripture reading among the community of Israelites, and be the means of a better appreciation of the great treasures of revelation to many who never have had the opportunity of knowing what the Hebrews have done for mankind, not alone in preserving the sacred books, but by labouring to make them intelligible to the world at large.

Philadelphia, Elul 17th, 5613/Sept. 20th, 1853

FRANCIS KENRICK'S TRANSLATION OF THE PENTATEUCH

Just as Isaac Leeser saw a need for a Jewish-centered translation of Hebrew scriptures, his Philadelphia contemporary Francis Kenrick (1796–1863) recognized the necessity of an updated English translation to better serve American Catholics. Born in Ireland and trained in Rome, Kenrick came to the USA in 1821 to join a diocese in Kentucky. Widely respected as a theologian as well as for his pastoral activities, Kenrick was appointed as a bishop of Philadelphia in 1830 and eventually rose in 1851 to Archbishop of Baltimore. In the midst of fierce, at times violent conflicts in Philadelphia over versions of the Bible made available to Catholic schoolchildren, Kenrick embarked in 1843 on a new edition of the traditional Catholic Douay translation of the Bible. His work appeared in separate sections published between 1849 and 1860. As Kenrick explains in the selection below – excerpted from the 1860 preface to his next-to-last volume, the translation of the Bible's first five books – he worked from the original languages and compared them to the Latin Vulgate to determine appropriate English renderings. This approach, in drawing on emerging historical critical methods, was a significant and novel development among Catholic theologians of the period.

Source: Francis Patrick Kenrick, trans. and ed., *The Pentateuch* (Baltimore, MD: Kelly, Hedian, and Piet, 1860), vii–x.

The first five books of Scripture are called the Pentateuch, from Greek terms expressive of that number. They are the work of Moses, the celebrated leader, under whom the Israelites went forth from Egypt. The latter four books, which contain his biography, with an account of his government and the code of laws which he delivered, furnish strong intrinsic evidence that he is their author: and the first book is so intimately connected with them, that it also must have proceeded from his pen, or have been kept in view in their composition. It is a favorite opinion with modern critics, especially of the Rationalistic school, that it was formed of a variety of ancient records, which Moses combined with very little change. In support of this conjecture, they point to the marked difference which is found in the names given to the Supreme Being, in various portions of the first chapters, as also to various repetitions and apparent discrepancies, which betray different sources: but although the supposition that Moses availed himself of such records is not irreconcilable with the authority, or even the inspiration of the work, the venerable tradition of Christians, as well as Jews, point to him as the first inspired writer. St. Justin, in his exhortation to the Greeks (No. 28), ascribes to Moses the history of the creation, quotes in his name the opening words of Genesis, styles him the first prophet, and calls his history divine. St. Basil tells us that we should assent to the history of the creation on the authority of Moses, who narrates it (In Hexa, meron hom. 1.), and who himself was instructed by God (Ibidem. Hom. 6). Whatever, then, may be thought of such critical observations, we should hold Moses to be the inspired author, by whom the whole Pentateuch was composed. Eichhorn and others who regard it as a compilation, are forced to admit many things which it requires great ingenuity to reconcile with their theory.

The Pentateuch, as the most ancient history and code of laws extant, is deserving of most serious attention, even if regarded as a mere human production; but as a divinely inspired work, such as the tradition of the Christian Church supported by the testimony of the Jewish nation, declares it to be, it claims our profound homage. It is believed that Moses was specially moved by God to record the facts within his own knowledge, divinely enlightened to discern truth from falsehood in regard to all that he received on the testimony of others or learned from monuments of past ages, and immediately instructed by the Holy Spirit in what could only be known to him from divine revelation. St. Chrysostom remarks, that in undertaking to describe the creation of the world, he tacitly affirms, that he was instructed by God (De. Gen. hom. 2). Tertullian speaks of Genesis as composed under the influence of the Divine Spirit (De Oratione, n. 17). St. Irenus (L. 1 adv. h … r. c.45, 46) and St. Justin (Dial. Cum Tryphone) consider the words of Moses as those of Christ. This constant belief of Jews and Christians is corroborated by the contents of the books themselves. The narrative of the sacred author solves the problems which puzzled all the philosophers, how to account for the origin of all things, and warrants the inference, that the solution was derived from supernatural illumination. The facts which he records as occurring under his own eyes, were of so public a character, that they could not be invented without certainty of contradiction and exposure; and were so extraordinary, that they could not find credit unless on the most satisfactory evidence. The candor of the historian is manifest from the whole tenor of his work, and his veracity and integrity may safely be inferred from the calm tone of his writing, and the circumstantial details into which he enters. The acceptance of the work by his contemporaries, who were interested in denying many of his statements, is the seal of its truth; and the veneration with which it has ever since been regarded by the Jewish nation, leaves no room to question its high authority. Christ our Lord referred to Moses as a prophet who had spoken of Him (John 5:46).

The simplicity of ancient style gives to the Pentateuch a character of abruptness from the conciseness of the phrases, and the perpetual recurrence of the simple conjunction, in a great variety of meanings. To give smoothness to the narrative the Latin interpreter varied the conjunctive particles, avoided the frequent repetition of the noun, and otherwise modified the sentence, especially by abridging descriptions wherein repetitions abound. This freedom of interpretation, in the judgment of Geddes, a learned Scottish critic, gives the Vulgate an advantage over the Protestant version. "The chief study of the English translators," he observes, "was to give a strictly literal version, at the expense of almost every other consideration, whilst the author of the Vulgate endeavored to render his originals equivalently into such Latin as was current in his age. I perceived a considerable difference between it and the English translation. The latter appeared to me rugged, constrained, and often obscure, where the former was smooth, easy, and intelligible." The enthusiastic admirers of the Protestant version will not easily subscribe to this judgment. For my own part, where no doctrinal bias betrays itself, I have no disposition to detract from its literary excellence, especially as regards its close adherence to the text. In revising the Douay translation I have constantly had in view the Hebrew original, which, however, I did not always feel at liberty to render closely, when it would imply a departure from the Vulgate, since this is the standard of all vernacular versions for general use, according to the settled usage of the Holy See. In endeavoring to express the meaning of the text without abandoning the Vulgate, I may occasionally have used terms in a sense somewhat forced. In cases when the Vulgate offers a reading different from the actual Hebrew, it is quite probable that it may be derived from some manuscript of high antiquity; but when the Latin interpreter manifestly had the same reading as that which is now received, although he rendered it somewhat freely, I think it desirable that the English translation should approach as nearly as possible to the original. I have conformed in many instances to the received appellations of objects, the mode of spelling certain names of more frequent recurrence, and have otherwise deferred to usage, although of Protestant origin, feeling that, in things indifferent, conformity is desirable, and that every approach to uniformity in the rendering of the inspired word, without sacrifice of principle, or violation of disciplinary rules, is a gain to the common cause of Christianity. To many I may appear bold, in the emendations which I have suggested; but as my work is in the nature of a literary essay, for examination by my venerable colleagues, I hope I shall escape the censure of temerity. To the judgment of the Chief Bishop it is most unreservedly submitted.

BALTIMORE, Ascension Day, 1860.

THE JEWISH PUBLICATION SOCIETY

Nineteenth-century figures like Isaac Leeser and Francis Kenrick pioneered the movement toward tradition-specific, American English bible translations. By the twentieth century, developments in language and scholarship pushed American religious organizations to undertake updated translations to serve their communities. Already by 1892 the Jewish Publication Society, one of a number of Jewish organizations established in the USA during the late nineteenth-century wave of Jewish emigration from Europe, began working toward a replacement of Isaac Leeser's translation (see earlier selection) commonly used among American Jews. The process encountered various challenges and delays, but 25 years later a committee of leading scholars finished the translation of the Hebrew scriptures that would remain the standard for American Jews until the Society's revised version appeared in 1985. With notable echoes of and responses to the preface to Leeser's 1853 translation of the Jewish scriptures, the editors of JPS's 1917 version explain in their own preface the process and rationale for an updated English text.

Source: Max Leopold Margolis, ed., *The Holy Scriptures According to the Masoretic Text* (Philadelphia, PA: Jewish Publication Society of America, 1917), iii–viii, xii.

The sacred task of translating the Word of God, as revealed to Israel through lawgiver, prophet, psalmist, and sage, began at an early date. According to an ancient rabbinic interpretation, Joshua had the Torah engraved upon the stones of the altar (Joshua viii. 32) not in the original Hebrew alone, but in all the languages of mankind, which were held to be seventy, in order that all men might become acquainted with the words of the Scriptures. This statement, with its universalistic tendency, is, of course, a reflex of later times, when the Hebrew Scriptures had become a subject of curiosity and perhaps also of anxiety to the pagan or semi-pagan world.

While this tradition contains an element of truth, it is certain that the primary object of translating the Bible was to minister to a need nearer home. Upon the establishment of the Second Commonwealth under Ezra and Nehemiah, it became imperative to make the Torah of God 'distinct and giving sense' through the means of interpretation (Nehemiah viii. 8 and xiii. 24). ... Israel had forgotten the sacred language, and spoke the idiom current in a large part of western Asia. All this, however, is veiled in obscurity, as is the whole inner history of the Jews during the Persian rule.

The historic necessity for translation was repeated with all the great changes in Israel's career. It is enough to point to the Septuagint, or the Greek translation of the Scriptures, the product of Israel's contact with the Hellenistic civilization dominating the world at that time; to the Arabic translation by the Gaon Saadya, when the great majority of the Jewish people came under the sceptre of Mohammedan rulers; and to the German translation by Mendelssohn and his school, at the dawn of a new epoch, which brought the Jews in Europe, most of whom spoke a German dialect, into closer contact with their neighbours. These translations are all historical products intimately connected with Israel's wanderings among the nations and with the great events of mankind in general.

Ancient and continuous as this task of translation was, it would be a mistake to think that there were no misgivings about it. At least it is certain that opinions were divided as to the desirability of such undertakings. While Philo and his Alexandrian coreligionists looked upon the translation of the Seventy as a work of inspired men, the Palestinian Rabbis subsequently considered the day on which the Septuagint was completed as one of the most unfortunate in Israel's history, seeing that the Torah could never be adequately translated …

The greatest change in the life of Israel during the last two generations was his renewed acquaintance with English-speaking civilization. Out of a handful of immigrants from Central Europe and the East who saw the shores of the New World, or even of England and her colonies, we have grown under Providence both in numbers and in importance, so that we constitute now the greatest section of Israel living in a single country outside of Russia. We are only following in the footsteps of our great predecessors when, with the growth of our numbers, we have applied ourselves to the sacred task of preparing a new translation of the Bible into the English language, which, unless all signs fail, is to become the current speech of the majority of the children of Israel.

The need of such a translation was felt long ago. Mention may here be made of the work of Isaac Leeser in America, which was both preceded and followed by two translations produced in England: the one by Dr. A. Benisch, the other by Dr. Michael Friedlander. The most popular, however, among these translations was that of Leeser, which was not only the accepted version in all the synagogues of the United States, but was also reproduced in England. Its great merit consisted in the fact that it incorporated all the improvements proposed by the Mendelssohn School and their successors, whose combined efforts were included and further developed in the so-called Zunz Bible, which enjoyed a certain authority among German Jews for several generations. With the advance of time and the progress made in almost all departments of Bible study, it was found that Leeser's translation would bear improvement and recasting …

In 1908 the Jewish Publication Society of America and the Central Conference of American Rabbis reached an agreement to co-operate in bringing out the new translation upon a revised plan of having the entire work done by a Board of Editors instead of endeavoring to harmonize the translations of individual contributors …

The present translation is the first for which a group of men representative of Jewish learning among English-speaking Jews assume joint responsibility, all previous efforts in the English language having been the work of individual translators. It has a character of its own. It aims to combine the spirit of Jewish tradition with the results of biblical scholarship, ancient, mediaeval, and modern. It gives to the Jewish world a translation of the Scriptures done by men imbued with the Jewish consciousness, while the non-Jewish world, it is hoped, will welcome a translation that presents many passages from the Jewish traditional point of view.

The repeated efforts by Jews in the field of biblical translation show their sentiment toward translations prepared by other denominations. The dominant feature of this sentiment, apart from the thought that the christological interpretations in non-Jewish translations are out of place in a Jewish Bible, is and was that the Jew cannot afford to have his Bible translation prepared for him by others. He cannot have it as a gift, even as he cannot borrow his soul from others. If a new country and a new language metamorphose him into a new man, the duty of this new man is to prepare a new garb and a new method of expression for what is most sacred and most dear to him.

We are, it is hardly needful to say, deeply grateful for the works of our non-Jewish predecessors, such as the Authorised Version with its admirable diction, which can never be surpassed, as well as for the Revised Version with its ample learning – but they are not ours ...

As to the text and order of the biblical books, the present translation follows Jewish tradition, the Sacred Scriptures having come down in a definite compass and in a definite text. They are separated into three divisions: Law (Torah, Pentateuch), Prophets (Nebi'im), Writings (Ketubim) ...

In all humility their co-workers submit this version to the Jewish people in the confident hope that it will aid them in the knowledge of the Word of God.

DEI VERBUM

Pope Paul VI (1897–1978) promulgated the "Dogmatic Constitution on Divine Revelation," otherwise known as *Dei Verbum* (Word of God), on November 18, 1965 following the overwhelming approval in a vote by Catholic bishops. The document was a central component of the Second Vatican Council. Most immediately, *Dei Verbum* solidified the Church's evolving position on ritual and non-ritual use of scripture in the vernacular. The document also authorized application of developing historical-critical methods to produce new translations of the Bible based on original manuscripts instead of the traditional Latin Vulgate. Pope Pius XII had encouraged those steps in a famous 1943 encyclical (referenced at the beginning of the next selection) and *Dei Verbum* formalized the changes, with both symbolic and practical effects.

Source: *The Dogmatic Constitution Dei Verbum, promulgated by His Holiness Pope Paul VI, Chapter vi, Paragraphs xxii and xxiii.* © Libreria Editrice Vaticana, 1965. Used by permission.

CHAPTER VI
SACRED SCRIPTURE IN THE LIFE OF THE CHURCH

22. Easy access to Sacred Scripture should be provided for all the Christian faithful. That is why the Church from the very beginning accepted as her own that very ancient Greek translation; of the Old Testament which is called the Septuagint; and she has always given a place of honor to other Eastern translations and Latin ones especially the Latin translation known as the vulgate. But since the word of God should be accessible at all times, the Church by her authority and with maternal concern sees to it that suitable and correct translations are made into different languages, especially from the original texts of the sacred books. And should the opportunity arise and the Church authorities approve, if these translations are produced in cooperation with the

separated brethren as well, all Christians will be able to use them.

23. The bride of the incarnate Word, the Church taught by the Holy Spirit, is concerned to move ahead toward a deeper understanding of the Sacred Scriptures so that she may increasingly feed her sons with the divine words. Therefore, she also encourages the study of the holy Fathers of both East and West and of sacred liturgies. Catholic exegetes then and other students of sacred theology, working diligently together and using appropriate means, should devote their energies, under the watchful care of the sacred teaching office of the Church, to an exploration and exposition of the divine writings. This should be so done that as many ministers of the divine word as possible will be able effectively to provide the nourishment of the Scriptures for the people of God, to enlighten their minds, strengthen their wills, and set men's hearts on fire with the love of God. The sacred synod encourages the sons of the Church and Biblical scholars to continue energetically, following the mind of the Church, with the work they have so well begun, with a constant renewal of vigor.

THE NEW AMERICAN BIBLE

The Catholic Church's new approaches to translation and vernacular use of the Bible, announced in 1943 by Pius XII and formalized in 1965 by Vatican II, produced material results by 1970. That year, the Church released the New American Bible. In the preface to the text (excerpted below), the editors reviewed the history of Catholic translations of the Bible into English in order to reinforce the need for and process of producing a new, Church-supported version. As also noted in the preface, the New American Bible fulfilled an expectation outlined in Pius XII's encyclical and reiterated in the Vatican II constitution (*Dei Verbum*): that in producing new translations Catholic scholars should collaborate with Protestant colleagues who shared the same Christian heritage. The American bishops who oversaw the production of the New American Bible also emphasized the importance of a shared national heritage that would enable the collaboration to speak most effectively to Catholic and Protestant compatriots alike.

Source: *New American Bible* (Washington, DC: Confraternity of Christian Doctrine, 1970).

On September 30, 1943, His Holiness Pope Pius XII issued his now famous encyclical on scripture studies, *Divino afflante Spiritu*. He wrote: "We ought to explain the original text which was written by the inspired author himself and has more authority and greater weight than any, even the very best, translation whether ancient or modern. This can be done all the more easily and fruitfully if to the knowledge of languages be joined a real skill in literary criticism of the same text."

Early in 1944, in conformity with the spirit of the encyclical, and with the encouragement of Archbishop Cicognani, Apostolic Delegate to the United

States, the Bishops' Committee of the Confraternity of Christian Doctrine requested members of The Catholic Biblical Association of America to translate the sacred scriptures from the original languages or from the oldest extant form of the text, and to present the sense of the biblical text in as correct a form as possible.

The first English Catholic version of the Bible, the Douay-Rheims (1582–1609/10), and its revision by Bishop Challoner (1750) were based on the Latin Vulgate. In view of the relative certainties more recently attained by textual and higher criticism, it has become increasingly desirable that contemporary translations of the sacred books into English be prepared in which due reverence for the text and strict observance of the rules of criticism would be combined.

The New American Bible has accomplished this in response to the need of the church in America today. It is the achievement of some fifty biblical scholars, the greater number of whom, though not all, are Catholics. In particular, the editors-in-chief have devoted twenty-five years to this work. The collaboration of scholars who are not Catholic fulfills the directive of the Second Vatican Council, not only that "correct translations be made into different languages especially from the original texts of the sacred books," but that, "with the approval of the church authority, these translations be produced in cooperation with separated brothers" so that "all Christians may be able to use them."

The text of the books contained in *The New American Bible* is a completely new translation throughout. From the original and the oldest available texts of the sacred books, it aims to convey as directly as possible the thought and individual style of the inspired writers. The better understanding of Hebrew and Greek, and the steady development of the science of textual criticism, the fruit of patient study since the time of St. Jerome, have allowed the translators and editors in their use of all available materials to approach more closely than ever before the sense of what the sacred authors actually wrote …

The work of translating the Bible has been characterized as "the sacred and apostolic work of interpreting the word of God and of presenting it to the laity in translations as clear as the difficulty of the matter and the limitations of human knowledge permit" (A. G. Cicognani, Apostolic Delegate, in *The Catholic Biblical Quarterly*, 6, [1944], 389–90). In the appraisal of the present work, it is hoped that the words of the encyclical *Divino afflante Spiritu* will serve as a guide: "Let all the sons of the church bear in mind that the efforts of these resolute laborers in the vineyard of the Lord should be judged not only with equity and justice but also with the greatest charity; all moreover should abhor that intemperate zeal which imagines that whatever is new should for that very reason be opposed or suspected."

THE GULLAH BIBLE

In November 2005 a team of translators finished a 26-year project of translating the New Testament into Gullah, a language spoken on the Sea Islands off the coast of South Carolina and Georgia and in cities on the seacoast. The islands were the first stops for the slave ships from West Africa. After the Civil War, emancipated slaves created communities on the islands, which included schools promoting free education and religious expression. The translation project was jointly sponsored by the American Bible Society, the Summer Institute of Linguistics, Wycliffe Bible Translators, the United Bible Societies, and the Penn Center on St. Helena Island.

Source: www.gullahbible.com; ©2005 Wycliffe Bible Translators.

The Lord's Prayer, Matthew 6:9b–13, in Gullah

We Fada wa dey een heaben
Leh ebrybody hona ya name.
We pray dat soon ya gwine
Rule oba de wol.
Wasoneba ting ya wahn,
leh um be so een dis wol
same like dey een heaben.
Gii we de food wa we need
dis day yah an ebry day.
Fagib we fa we sin,
same like we da fagib dem people
wa do bad ta we.
Leh we dohn hab haad test
wen Satan try we.
Keep we fom ebil.

1 Corinthians 13:1- 7. Paul's Discourse on Love, in Gullah

Eben ef A kin taak een all de language dem wa people da taak an wa de angel dem da taak, ef A ain lob oda people, all wa A da say ain mount ta nottin. E jes like de nise wen somebody da beat a bucket or wen a cymbal da soun too loud. Eben ef A got powa fa tell people wod wa God tell me fa say, an ef A kin ondastan all God plan wa e ain tell oda people an A know all ting, an ef A bleebe God sommuch dat e da gii me powa fa moob mountain, eben ef A able fa do all dem ting yah, ef A ain lob oda people, A ain wot nottin. Eben ef A gii way ebryting A got an A gree fa leh um bun me body, ef A ain lob oda people, all dat ain do me no good.

Ef oona lob oda people, oona gwine beah wid um. Oona gwine be kind ta um. Oona ain gwine all de time wahn wa dey got, an oona ain gwine brag on oonasef an be oppity. Ef oona lob people, oona gwine be manisable all de time an oona ain gwine wahn ya own way. Oona ain gwine git bex, an oona ain gwine keep ting een oona haat ginst oda people wa do oona wrong. Ef oona lob oda people, oona ain gwine rejaice oba no ebil ting, bot oona gwine rejaice oba wa true. Ef oona lob people, oona gwine beah op onda ebryting wa people do ta oona. Oona gwine be ready fa bleebe good ting bout people.

Oona gwine hope fa de betta bout um, an oona gwine pit op wid people an lob um eben wen oona da suffa.

THE GREEN BIBLE

In 2008 a group of scholars and environmentalists published an edition of the New Revised Standard Version that highlighted passages related to the environment. Passages that emphasized God's and Jesus' interaction with the earth, the interdependence of nature, the natural world's response to God, and the obligation to care for the world, are highlighted in green lettering (here represented in bold type). Printed on partially recycled paper, with soy-based ink, the bible's introduction includes St. Francis' "Canticle of the Creatures," and an essay "The Power of a Green God."

Source: *The Green Bible* (San Francisco: HarperCollins, 2008).

Genesis 4:1–16

Now the man knew his wife Eve, and she conceived and bore Cain, saying, "I have produced a man with the help of the Lord." Next she bore his brother Abel. Now Abel was a keeper of sheep, and Cain a tiller of the ground. In the course of time Cain brought to the Lord an offering of the fruit of the ground, and Abel for his part brought of the firstings of his flock, their fat portions. And the Lord had regard for Abel and his offering, but for Cain and his offering he had no regard. So Cain was very angry, and his countenance fell. The Lord said to Cain, "Why are you angry, and why has your countenance fallen? If you do well, will you not be accepted? And if you do not do well, sin is lurking at the door; its desire is for you, but you must master it." Cain said to his brother Abel, "Let us go out to the field." And when they were in the field, Cain rose up against his brother Abel, and killed him. Then the Lord said to Cain, "Where is your brother Abel?" He said, "I do not know; am I my brother's keeper? **And the Lord said, "What have you done? Listen: your brother's blood is crying out to me from the ground! And now you are cursed from the ground, which has opened its mouth to receive your brother's blood from your hand. When you till the ground, it will no longer yield to you its strength; you will be a fugitive and a wanderer on the earth. Cain said to the Lord, "My punishment is greater than I can bear! Today you have driven me away from the soil, and I shall be hidden from your face; I shall be a fugitive and a wanderer on the earth, and anyone who meets me may kill me."** Then the Lord said to him, "Not so! Whoever kills Cain will suffer a sevenfold vengeance." And the Lord put a mark on Cain, so that no one who came upon him would kill him. Then Cain went away from the presence of the Lord, and settled in the Land of Nod, east of Eden.

Jeremiah 9: 7–12

Therefore thus says the Lord of hosts:
I will now refine and test them,
for what else can I do with my sinful people?
Their tongue is a deadly arrow;
it speaks deceit through the mouth.
They all speak friendly words to their neighbors,
But inwardly are planning to lay an ambush.
Shall I not punish them for these things?
says the Lord;
and shall I not bring retribution
on a nation such as this?
Take up weeping and wailing for the mountains,
and a lamentation for the pastures of the wilderness,
because they are laid waste so that no one passes through,
and the lowing of cattle is not heard,
both the birds of the air and the animals have fled and are gone.
I will make Jerusalem a heap of ruins, a lair of jackals;
And I will make the towns of Judah a desolation, without inhabitant.
Who is wise enough to understand this? To whom has the mouth
of the Lord spoken, so that they may declare it? Why is the land
ruined and laid waste like a wilderness, so that no one passes
through?

John 6:25–35

When they found him on the other side of the sea, they said to him, "Rabbi,
when did you come here?" Jesus answered them, "Very truly, I tell you, you
are looking for me, not because you saw signs, but because you ate your fill of
the loaves. **Do not work for the food that perishes, but for the food**
that endures for eternal life, which the Son of Man will give you.
For it is on him that God the Father has set his seal." Then they
said to him, "What must we do to perform the works of God?"
Jesus answered them, "This is the work of God, that you believe in him whom
he has sent." So they said to him, "What sign are you going to give us then,
so that we may see it and believe you? What work are you performing? **Our**
ancestors ate the manna in the wilderness; as it is written, 'He
gave them bread from heaven to eat.'" Then Jesus said to them, "Very
truly, I tell you, it was not Moses who gave you the bread from heaven, but it
is my Father who gives you the true bread from heaven. **For the bread of**
God is that which comes down from heaven and gives life to the
world." They said to him, "Sir, give us this bread always." **Jesus said to**
them, "I am the bread of life. Whoever comes to me will never be
hungry, and whoever believes in me will never be thirsty.

BIBLEZINES

Copies of the New Testament, New Century Version, are published in the style of magazines to appeal to young women. In *Revolve*, the biblical text appears with short introductions, and includes sidebars on fashion, diet, make-up, and dating. The 2010 version also includes Old Testament verses translated into a format for texting, for example, "sum trust n chariots, othas n GGs, but we trust d Lord r God//ps20:7." Below is a picture of the magazine cover and two of the sidebars. A similar magazine for young men is published as *Refuel*.

Source: *Revolve* (Nashville, TN: Thomas Nelson, 2003), 175, 184. Reproduced by permission Thomas Nelson Publishers.

Figure 1.1 Revolve

Body Language. Run With God

Turn your morning jog into your morning praise time. Instead of gossiping with a girlfriend, talk to Jesus about your worries and heartaches. Or just tell him all the great things you love about your life! Take your iPod and listen to praise music, and pray over your day to come. Download sermons from your church and get reminded of God's truth before you get into the real path of Satan's tricks. Or if you prefer the peace and quiet of a new morning, just spend time in prayer and refection. It's super easy to get swamped with responsibilities as the day goes on, and it's easy to forget to make time for God. But if you start each day by having a great conversation with him, you'll feel more centered and focused as you face the tough temptations of your day.

Dudes Decoded

The truth is, what a guy wants most in a girl is a friend. The media blast messages that say this isn't true. But the basis of any good relationship is the ability to be a good friend. You just need to realize what it takes to be one. Real friends have the ability to challenge, change, and inspire you. Are you willing to let those things happen? Friends care enough to be honest with you, even when they know your faults. Friends will call to see how you're doing – not just check up on what you're doing. Friends know when you're hurting and will be there to listen – without expecting anything in return. Real friends don't look to get stuff out of the relationship for themselves. They're willing to put your needs above their own.

REFERENCES

Beato, Greg. 2010. "The Greatest Business Story Ever Told." *Reason*, February 1: 14–15.

Conservapedia. 2010. The Conservative Bible Project. Available from http://www.conservapedia.com/Conservative_Bible_Project.

Gutjahr, Paul C. 1999. *An American Bible: A History of the Good Book in the United States, 1777–1880*. Stanford, CA: Stanford University Press.

Nord, David Paul. 2004. *Faith in Reading: Religious Publishing and the Birth of Mass Media in America*. New York: Oxford University Press.

Thuesen, Peter J. 1999. *In Discordance with the Scriptures: American Protestant Battles over Translating the Bible*. New York: Oxford University Press.

SUGGESTIONS FOR FURTHER RESEARCH

Bailey, Lloyd R. 1982. *The Word of God: A Guide to English Versions of the Bible*. Atlanta, GA: John Knox Press.

Fogarty, Gerald P. 1982. "The Quest for a Catholic Vernacular Bible in America." In N. O. Hatch and M. A. Noll, eds, *The Bible in America: Essays in Cultural History*. New York: Oxford University Press, 163–80.

Foote, Henry Wilder. 1960. *The Religion of Thomas Jefferson*. Boston: Beacon Press.

Frerichs, Ernest S. 1988. *The Bible and Bibles in America*. Atlanta, GA: Scholars Press.

Goldman, Shalom. 1993. *Hebrew and the Bible in America: The First Two Centuries.* Hanover: Published for Brandeis University Press and Dartmouth College by University Press of New England.

Hall, David D. 1996. *Cultures of Print: Essays in the History of the Book.* Amherst: University of Massachusetts Press.

Hills, Margaret Thorndike, and American Bible Society. 1962. *The English Bible in America: A Bibliography of Editions of the Bible and the New Testament Published in America, 1777–1957.* New York: American Bible Society.

Hutchison, William R. 1987. *Errand to the World: American Protestant Thought and Foreign Missions.* Chicago: University of Chicago Press.

Kupperman, Karen Ordahl. 2000. *Indians and English: Facing Off in Early America.* Ithaca, NY: Cornell University Press.

Lacy, Creighton. 1977. *The Word-Carrying Giant: The Growth of the American Bible Society (1816–1966).* South Pasadena, CA: William Carey Library.

Lehmann-Haupt, Hellmut, in collaboration with Lawrence C. Wroth, Rollo G. Silver, and Hellmut Lehmann-Haupt. 1951. *The Book in America: A History of the Making and Selling of Books in the United States.* 2nd edn. New York: R.R. Bowker Co. Original edition, 1939.

Lewis, Jack P. 1982. *The English Bible: From KJV to NIV.* Grand Rapids, MI: Baker.

McDannell, Colleen. 1995. *Material Christianity: Religion and Popular Culture in America.* New Haven, CT: Yale University Press.

Modern, John Lardas. 2008. "Evangelical Secularism and the Measure of Leviathan." *Church History* 77 (4): 801–76.

Moore, R. Laurence. 1994. *Selling God: American Religion in the Marketplace of Culture.* New York: Oxford University Press.

Orlinsky, Harry Meyer. 1974. *Essays in Biblical Culture and Bible Translation.* New York: Ktav Publishing.

Simms, Paris Marion. 1936. *The Bible in America; Versions that have Played Their Part in the Making of the Republic.* New York: Wilson-Erickson, Inc.

Wosh, Peter J. 1994. *Spreading the Word: The Bible Business in Nineteenth-Century America.* Ithaca, NY: Cornell University Press.

2 The Bible and the Republic

Since its ratification in 1787, the Constitution has served as the official scaffold for civic life in the United States. Yet well before, during, and after the drafting of the Constitution, Americans have disagreed over the proper balance between various frameworks of governance. Debates about the relations between religious and civil law – including questions surrounding the Bible's place in political life – took hold in the American colonies from the start and have yet to dissipate.

Many of the Europeans who first set out for and established settlements in the American territories did so because they found untenable the dynamics between church and state in the places they lived and hoped to strike a new balance of power. Most of the emigrants made their way into American lands under the banner of a mission to establish Christian societies. Accordingly, a primary impulse guided many of the first settlers, whom historian Frank Lambert identifies as the "Planting Fathers." Those pioneers often sought to establish societies explicitly built on and around a particular religious institution. Most famously, the Puritan settlers of New England sought religious freedom for themselves in order to construct a society that manifested a "purified" and "restored" Christianity that was governed by the church. For this band of Planting Fathers, the Bible provided the template for their experience. They saw themselves as the remaining remnant of the ancient Israelites who also wandered the wilderness and struggled against all odds to uphold their covenant with God. This God had long ago promised a prosperous earthly kingdom in exchange for loyalty and righteousness.

Competing impulses played out among early settlers. The mission to create new Christian societies generated the seemingly paradoxical idea of deliberately separating institutions of religion from the mechanisms of civic governance. The rationales behind the possible division of influences were varied, encompassing theological and philosophical conceptions of the free reign of individual conscience, conflicts of economic powers, and political pragmatism. And while the inclination toward the convergence of religious and political institutions predominated among the Planting Fathers, the latter, separationist impulse assumed precedence less than two centuries later among another generation of patriarchs, the celebrated "Founding Fathers" of the late eighteenth century who scripted the Constitution and founded the Republic.

The documents in this chapter illustrate how these two impulses – toward church–state integration, on one hand, or church–state separation, on the other – have played out in different ways from colonial settlement through the establishment of the Republic and into the present day. Some sources (e.g. the First Charter of Virginia, John Winthrop's "Model of Christian Charity," the Fundamental Orders of Connecticut) offer reminders that most of the colonies established biblically based state churches. The First Charter paved the way for the Anglican Churches of Virginia and other southern colonies, while the Orders and Winthrop's sermon represent the Congregationalist churches' central place in Connecticut, Massachusetts, and other Puritan colonies of New England. Similarly, the Catholic Church had an official role in the government of Maryland, as did the Quakers in Pennsylvania.

Yet the documents here also show that the realities of building new biblically informed societies were always more easily imagined than executed. As the colonial experiments unfolded, settlers in every colony invoked the Bible as the basis of unity and went to varying lengths to institute new religious, political, and social orders. Yet in every territory colonial leaders faced dissent, and frequently the Bible exacerbated rather than bridged divisions.

The tensions that developed as colonists sought to work out church–state relations surfaced in especially forceful and illuminating ways in the New England Puritan communities. Despite their status in Europe primarily as religious, social, and political renegades, those self-proclaimed reformers emerged in the colonies as resilient and successful governors. Their settlements endured against great odds largely because, now in positions of authority, they perpetuated a tightly regulated religious, political, and social order that discouraged the kind of dissent from which their own Puritanism sprang. The concord of their communities depended on authoritative interpretations of and theological attitudes toward the Bible that, paradoxically, generated fierce dissent. Some members of these communities challenged the authorities by invoking the traditional Puritan emphasis on each individual's direct relation with the divine through the scriptures. Roger Williams stands as a famous and significant example: his dissenting claim to authority of biblical interpretation unsettled the leaders of the Massachusetts colony and led to his exile, by which he founded Rhode Island as a home for dissenters and a haven for Jews and other minority groups.

Anne Hutchinson emerged as another powerful dissident. She too was excommunicated from the Puritan Church and exiled from Massachusetts for appealing to her own powers of biblical interpretation. As a woman, Hutchinson's assertion profoundly threatened the colony's authoritative order and even created trouble for her when she made her way to Rhode Island. Some of her original sympathizers soon questioned Hutchinson's religious vision and challenged the political structure of the community. Hutchinson and her family decided to set out yet again, this time for Dutch settlements in the present-day Bronx. Hutchinson's situation was indicative of a larger problem: because Williams and other founders rooted the government of Rhode Island in the anti-authoritarian principle of heterogeneous biblical interpretation – in direct contrast to the tightly regulated theocracy they left behind in Massachusetts – a plethora of competing claims to religious and political power plagued the colony in the years after its establishment.

Similarly, the founding denomination of Pennsylvania – the Quakers – rooted the government of the colony in a profoundly anti-authoritarian Puritan vision of religious tolerance through which every individual could pursue in his or her own way communion with God through the inner manifestations of the Holy Spirit. Yet the vacuum of political authority made practical governance difficult and factionalism rampant. Those tensions surface in a document from the 'Keithian Schism' of the 1690s, when one prominent Quaker began to critique other leaders' views of scripture in an effort to constitute another theological position and an ideal worldly order.

The ongoing challenges to establishing a definitive biblically inspired, church-centered society help explain why, as the seventeenth and eighteenth centuries unfolded, the impulse toward church–state integration waned and the separationist impulse gained steam. When the Constitutional Convention met in Philadelphia in mid-1787 to draft a Constitution, the Founders took the unusual step of jettisoning the idea of a state religion. James Madison in particular, promoted the idea of a secular state, arguing that it would benefit both religion and government. Religion could flourish without state intervention, and the healthy competition of religious ideas and practices in the public sphere and in each individual's conscience would promote excellence and discourage extremism. The state, too, would be restrained from the unchecked power that, throughout history, had marred regimes that combined religious and political power; the government would protect religious rights of all.

This logic assumed reality in the Constitution. First, no religious test was required to become president or serve in the government. Although all US presidents have been Christian (and with one exception, Protestant), no legal bar prevents someone of another religion, or no religion, from assuming the office. When Barack Obama ran for president in 2008, some opponents spread the false rumor that he was a Muslim, hoping to use anti-Muslim sentiment against him. Former Secretary of State Colin Powell responded by saying, "The real question is, 'What if he were [Muslim]?'" In other words, not only were the claims about Obama untrue but they were of no constitutional relevance. Interestingly, as early as 1797, in the Treaty of Tripoli, article 11, President John Adams reassured the Barbary state of America's friendliness to the Muslim government, since "the United States is not in any sense founded on the Christian religion."

Second, the First Amendment, part of the Bill of Rights passed by Congress in 1789, guarantees freedom of religious expression, along with freedom of the press and assembly: "Congress shall make no law respecting an establishment of religion, or prohibiting the free exercise thereof; or abridging the freedom of speech, or of the press; or the right of the people to assemble, and to petition the government for a redress of grievances." The non-establishment of state religion and the free exercise clauses have sometimes been put in opposition, but they are intended to complement each other. The first, by rejecting any official religion, guarantees the second, the free choice and practice of any or no religion. The two poles of the government's so-called "disestablishment" of religion and freedom of religion have resulted in many cases of testing the boundaries of and between the government's non-endorsement and the individual's right to openly express religious views. For example, Judge Roy Moore argued that his display of a Ten Commandments monument was legal by virtue of the Founders' guarantee of free expression. The courts disagreed, saying that by displaying biblical passages in the rotunda of the state courthouse, Moore was violating the Constitution's disestablishment clause and trampling on the rights of others who did not share his religious views and were forced to confront the monument. Still, a less conspicuous and more easily avoided monument remains on the grounds of the State Capital in Austin, Texas.

Even before the recent cases involving display of biblical passages in civic buildings, the courts have weighed in on ongoing disputes over the place of the Bible in another contested public space: the nation's schools. In 1940, the Supreme Court specified that the due process clause of the Fourteenth Amendment also applied to issues of religious freedom, limiting the power of the states. Accordingly, cases involving religion increased exponentially in the following decades as Americans called on the First Amendment more frequently and more openly not only with respect to federal edicts but also regarding laws at all levels of government. Many of the legal proceedings centered on the purview of the states and of local municipalities with regard to religion in the schools. In a cluster of important decisions in the early 1960s, the Supreme Court ruled – in varying directions – on a set of swirling questions regarding the place of the Bible in American education: *can* (or *should*) the Bible be read in public schools? If so, *how* can (or should) it be read? In the 1963 ruling in *Abington v. Schempp* (1963), the Court established a critical distinction between secular and religious study of the Bible that has continuing ramifications.

In the wake of those cases, the Bible has repeatedly entered into athletics, a particular domain of school life where familiar questions about religion's role have surfaced in new ways. For example, cheerleaders at a public school in Georgia were told to remove their signs quoting biblical verses during high school football games, while the well-decorated and wildly popular college football player Tim Tebow openly proclaimed his faith during nationally televised games by sporting a different biblical reference in his eye-black for each broadcast. In 2010, however, the NCAA banned any writing in eye-black.

Madison's intent to protect free public and personal expression of religious faith, by keeping it out of governmental control, has allowed religion to flourish. Compare, for example, former French president Jacques Chirac, who, in explaining an effort to ban personal religious symbols in schools, like Muslim headscarves, large crosses, skullcaps, and Sikh turbans, shows that religious expression is seen as inimical to French culture, "The decision to ban conspicuous signs (of religion) in school is a decision that respects our history, our customs, and our culture." One can hardly imagine an American making such a statement.

The separation between church and state is rarely absolute, in part because of the dual heritage of Planters and Fathers. While the legacy of the Founding Fathers continues to predominate through the constitutional separation of church and state, the heritage of the Planting Fathers lives on in real, even if less codified, forms. The shifting interplay over the past four centuries between the integrationist and separationist impulses reveals that the division of church and state is far from absolute and that the Bible is rarely out of American politics. No presidents have failed to quote or allude to the Bible, and some, like FDR, use it freely, acting at times like the nation's spiritual leader. Few, if any, inaugural speeches have avoided using it, and some, like Lincoln's Second Inaugural, have become legendary.

SETTLEMENT AND GOD'S PROVIDENCE

THE FIRST CHARTER OF VIRGINIA (1606)

On 10 April 1606, King James I granted the first charter to the Virginia Company, a group of London entrepreneurs inspired by the prospects of finding in "The New World" both gold and a water-based route to the Orient. The group proposed to establish "Jamestown Colony" in the Virginia territory as a foothold for the broader endeavor of exploration and discovery. Of course, the whole undertaking was framed as more than a commercial affair, as the lines below from the 1606 charter proclaim. The Company's mandate also included the task of "propagating of Christian religion" and establishing "a settled and quiet Government" on that basis. The charter proclaims a Christian mission. Its brevity and style stand in stark contrast to the sources that immediately follow, indicative of significantly different priorities for the Virginia Company's and the New England Puritans' New World colonies.

Source: The Avalon Project, Lillian Goldman Law Library, Yale Law School: http://avalon.law.yale.edu.

We, greatly commending and graciously accepting of their Desires for the Furtherance of so noble a Work, which may, by the Providence of Almighty God, hereafter tend to the Glory of His Divine Majesty, in propagating of Christian Religion to such People, as yet live in Darkness and miserable Ignorance of the true Knowledge and Worship of God, and may in time bring the Infidels and Savages, living in those Parts, to human Civility, and to a settled and quiet Government …

JOHN WINTHROP, "A MODEL OF CHRISTIAN CHARITY"

Few, if any, documents from the period of early colonial migration hold as much significance or carry as enduring a legacy as the selection below. According to legend, Winthrop (1588–1649) – a Puritan lawyer, lay minister, and eventual first Governor of the Massachusetts colony – delivered the following sermon aboard the *Arbella*, the flagship of the 1630 transports that came to be known as the "Winthrop Fleet" and which significantly increased the population of the Massachusetts settlements first established in 1620. Determined to escape the religious and political pressures of England after Charles I's effort to unsettle growing Puritan influence with his 1629 declaration of "Personal Rule" to bypass Parliament, Winthrop and his fellow travelers identified themselves and their place in history in clear and definitive biblical terms. The Puritan emigrants considered themselves contemporary Israelites who, like their ancient ancestors of the Old Testament, had undertaken an Exodus toward a "New Zion." In a legendary final image, Winthrop imagines a future in which the settlement appears as a divinely ordained "city upon a hill" for the rest of world to see and to emulate. His sermon outlined what the Puritans must do to achieve that end.

Source: Excerpted and modernized from John Winthrop, "A Modell of Christian Charity," *Collections of the Massachusetts Historical Society*, 3rd ser. (Boston: Massachusetts Historical Society, 1838), 7: 31–48. Reprinted by permission of the publisher from *The Journal of John Winthrop: 1630–49*. Abridged edn, ed. Richard Dunn, James Savage and Laetitia Yeandle, pp. 1–12. Cambridge, MA: The Belknap Press of Harvard University Press. © 1996 The President and Fellows of Harvard College.

God Almighty in His most holy and wise providence, hath so disposed of the condition of mankind, as in all times some must be rich, some poor, some high and eminent in power and dignity; others mean and in submission.

The Reason hereof: … That every man might have need of others, and from hence they might be all knit more nearly together in the bonds of brotherly affection. From hence it appears plainly that no man is made more honorable than another or more wealthy etc., out of any particular and singular respect to himself, but for the glory of his Creator and the common good of the creature, man.

… There is likewise a double Law by which we are regulated in our conversation towards another. In both the former respects, the Law of Nature and the Law of Grace (that is, the moral law or the law of the gospel) to omit the rule of justice as not properly belonging to this purpose otherwise than it may fall into consideration in some particular cases. By the first of these laws, man as he was enabled so withal is commanded to love his neighbor as himself. Upon this ground stands all the precepts of the moral law, which concerns our dealings with men. To apply this to the works of mercy, this law requires two things. First, that every man afford his help to another in every want or distress. … When there is no other means whereby our Christian brother may be relieved in his distress, we must help him beyond our ability rather than tempt God in putting him upon help by miraculous or extraordinary means. This duty of mercy is exercised in the kinds: giving, lending and forgiving (of debt).

… The definition which the Scripture gives us of love is this: Love is the bond of perfection. First it is a bond or ligament. Secondly, it makes the work perfect. There is no body but consists of parts and that which knits these parts together, gives the body its perfection, because it makes each part so contiguous to others as thereby they do mutually participate with each other, both in strength and infirmity, in pleasure and pain. To instance in the most perfect of all bodies: Christ and his Church make one body. The several parts of this body considered a part before they were united, were as disproportionate and as much disordering as so many contrary qualities or elements, but when Christ comes, and by his spirit and love knits all these parts to himself and each to other, it is become the most perfect and best proportioned body in the world (Eph. 4:15–16). Christ, by whom all the body being knit together by every joint for the furniture thereof, according to the effectual power which is in the measure of every perfection of parts, a glorious body without spot or wrinkle; the ligaments hereof being Christ, or his love, for Christ is love (1 John 4:8). So this definition is right. Love is the bond of perfection.

… It rests now to make some application of this discourse, by the present design, which gave the occasion of writing of it …

First, for the persons. We are a company professing ourselves fellow members of Christ, in which respect only, though we were absent from each other many miles, and had our employments as far distant, yet we ought to account ourselves knit together by this bond of love and live in the exercise of it, if we would have comfort of our being in Christ …

Secondly for the work we have in hand. It is by a mutual consent, through a special overvaluing providence and a more than an ordinary approbation of the churches of Christ, to seek out a place of cohabitation and consortship under a due form of government both civil and ecclesiastical. In such cases as this, the care of the public must oversway all private respects, by which, not only conscience, but mere civil policy, doth bind us. For it is a true rule that particular estates cannot subsist in the ruin of the public.

Thirdly, the end is to improve our lives to do more service to the Lord; the comfort and increase of the body of Christ, whereof we are members, that ourselves and posterity may be the better preserved from the common corruptions of this evil world, to serve the Lord and work out our salvation under the power and purity of his holy ordinances.

Fourthly, for the means whereby this must be effected. They are twofold, a conformity with the work and end we aim at. These we see are extraordinary, therefore we must not content ourselves with usual ordinary means. Whatsoever we did, or ought to have done, when we lived in England, the same must we do, and more also, where we go. That which the most in their churches maintain as truth in profession only, we must bring into familiar and constant practice; as in this duty of love, we must love brotherly without dissimulation, we must love one another with a pure heart fervently. We must bear one another's burdens. We must not look only on our own things, but also on the things of our brethren.

… When God gives a special commission He looks to have it strictly observed in every article. … Thus stands the cause between God and us. We are entered into covenant with Him for this work. We have taken out a commission. The Lord hath given us leave to draw our own articles. We have professed to enterprise these and those accounts, upon these and those ends. We have hereupon besought Him of favor and blessing. Now if the Lord shall please to hear us, and bring us in peace to the place we desire, then hath He ratified this covenant and sealed our commission, and will expect a strict performance of the articles contained in it; but if we shall neglect the observation of these articles which are the ends we have propounded, and, dissembling with our God, shall fall to embrace this present world and prosecute our carnal intentions, seeking great things for ourselves and our posterity, the Lord will surely break out in wrath against us, and be revenged of such a people, and make us know the price of the breach of such a covenant.

Now the only way to avoid this shipwreck, and to provide for our posterity, is to follow the counsel of Micah, to do justly, to love mercy, to walk humbly with our God. For this end, we must be knit together, in this work, as one man. We must entertain each other in brotherly affection. We must be willing to abridge ourselves of our superfluities, for the supply of others' necessities. We must uphold a familiar commerce together in all meekness, gentleness, patience and liberality. We must delight in each other; make others' conditions our own; rejoice together, mourn together, labor and suffer together, always having before our eyes our commission and community in the work, as members of the same body. So shall we keep the unity of the spirit in the bond of peace. The Lord will be our God, and delight to dwell among us, as His own people, and will command a blessing upon us in all our ways, so that we shall see much more of His wisdom, power, goodness and truth, than formerly we have been acquainted with. We shall find that the God of Israel is among us, when ten of us shall be able to resist a thousand of our enemies; when He shall make us a praise and glory that men shall say of succeeding plantations, "may the Lord make it like that of New England." For we must consider that we shall be as a city upon a hill. The eyes of all people are upon us. So that if we shall deal falsely with our God in this work we have undertaken, and so cause Him to withdraw His present help from us, we shall be made a story and a by-word through the world. We shall open the mouths of enemies to speak evil of the ways of God, and all professors for God's sake. We shall shame the faces of many of God's worthy servants, and cause their prayers to be turned into curses upon us till we be consumed out of the good land whither we are going.

And to shut this discourse with that exhortation of Moses, that faithful servant of the Lord, in his last farewell to Israel, Deut. 30. "Beloved, there is now set before us life and death, good and evil," in that we are commanded this day to love the Lord our God, and to love one another, to walk in his ways and to keep his Commandments and his ordinance and his laws, and the articles of our Covenant with Him, that we may live and be multiplied, and that the Lord our God may bless us in the land whither we go to possess it. But if our hearts shall turn away, so that we will not obey, but shall be seduced, and worship other Gods, our pleasure and profits, and serve them;

it is propounded unto us this day, we shall surely perish out of the good land whither we pass over this vast sea to possess it.

Therefore let us choose life, that we and our seed may live, by obeying His voice and cleaving to Him, for He is our life and our prosperity.

FUNDAMENTAL ORDERS OF CONNECTICUT

In 1959, the Connecticut General Assembly approved "The Constitution State" as an official state nickname. The Assembly's move rested on long-running claims that Connecticut's "Fundamental Orders," adopted by a body of the colony's leaders on January 14, 1639, served as the first constitution of its kind written in North America. The Orders outlined the "social compact" by which a new and independent commonwealth would be established and governed. Roger Ludlow began drafting the Orders in 1638. He credited the preaching of Thomas Hooker, the powerful Puritan minister of one of the colony's founding congregations, as a primary inspiration. The Orders clearly – and famously – situate the "direction and government of all men in all duties" on scriptural foundations. As an early and biblically based colonial political model, Connecticut's Orders subsequently have served as an important point of consideration for others engaged in the process of drafting frameworks for governance at all levels.

Source: The Avalon Project, Lillian Goldman Law Library, Yale Law School: http:// avalon.law.yale.edu.

The committee convened to frame the orders was charged to make the laws:
As near the law of God as they can be.

The Connecticut towns of Hartford, Wethersfield, and Windsor adopted the constitution, January 14, 1639, which stated in its Preamble:

Forasmuch as it has pleased the Almighty God by the wise disposition of His divine providence so to order and dispose of things that we the inhabitants and residents of Windsor, Hartford and Wethersfield and now cohabiting and dwelling in and upon the River Connecticut and the lands thereunto adjoining; and well knowing when a people are gathered together the Word of God requires, that to maintain the peace and union of such a people, there should be an orderly and decent government established according to God, to order and dispose of the affairs of all the people at all seasons as occasion shall require; do therefore associate and conjoin ourselves to be as one public State or Commonwealth, and do, for ourselves and our successors and such as shall be adjoined to us at any time hereafter, enter into Combination and Confederation together, to maintain and preserve the liberty and purity of the Gospel of our Lord Jesus which we now profess ... which, according to the truth of the said Gospel, is now practiced amongst us; as also, in our civil affairs to be guided and governed according to such laws, rules, orders, and decrees.

Articles of the Constitution of Connecticut

Article I That the Scriptures hold forth a perfect rule for the direction and government of all men in all duties which they are to perform to God and men, as well in families and commonwealths as in matters of the church.

Article II That as in matters which concern the gathering and ordering of a church, so likewise in all public offices which concern civil order, – as the choice of magistrates and officers, making and repealing laws, dividing allotments of inheritance, and all things of like nature, – they would all be governed by those rules which the Scripture held forth to them.

Article III That all those who had desired to be received free planters had settled in the plantation with a purpose, resolution, and desire that they might be admitted into church fellowship according to Christ.

Article IV That all the free planters held themselves bound to establish such civil order as might best conduce to the securing of the purity and peace of the ordinance to themselves, and their posterity according to God.

DISSENT AMONG THE DISSENTERS: THE BIBLE AND THE CHALLENGES OF COLONIAL GOVERNANCE

THE EXAMINATION OF ANNE HUTCHINSON AT THE COURT AT NEWTON

The Massachusetts Bay Colony survived, against unlikely odds, under John Winthrop's leadership. However, theological differences spurred ongoing challenges to the colony's political as well as religious authorities. Roger Williams presented early and fierce critiques that forced him out of Massachusetts and toward the founding of Rhode Island. In Williams' wake, Anne Hutchinson (1591–1643) presented new challenges to the colony's authorities. She left with her family for Massachusetts from England in 1634 in order to follow her minister, John Cotton. After her arrival in Massachusetts Hutchinson began Bible study meetings for women, and the originality of her approach to and interpretations of the scriptures quickly attracted groups – eventually including men – of eighty or more. Hutchinson challenged the authority of both the ministers and magistrates by forgoing their accepted biblical and civic teachings and encouraging her compatriots – especially women – to develop their own views guided by divine inspiration. In November 1637 she was brought before the General Court of the colony, accused of inciting social and religious disorder by calling the ministers' authority into question and by pulling women away from domestic responsibilities. Her judgers – headed by John Winthrop as Massachusetts' Governor – found her guilty, punishable by banishment from the colony. The selection below is adapted from the record of the proceedings first published in a 1767 history of Massachusetts by Thomas Hutchinson, Anne's great-great-grandson and an important pre-revolutionary political figure. After a separate religious trial in March 1638 excommunicated Hutchinson from the Puritan Church as a heretic, she and a band of sympathizers resettled at Williams' invitation in Rhode Island. Facing ongoing tensions there, they moved again in 1642 to the Pelham Bay region (now part of the Bronx) of New Netherland. Hutchinson and her entire family (with the exception of her youngest daughter) were killed the following year by a band of local Native Americans at odds with the region's Dutch settlers.

Source: David D. Hall, ed. *The Antinomian Controversy, 1636–1638*, 2nd edn (Durham, NC: Duke University Press, 1990), 312, 314, 317–18, 320–1, 324, 336–7, 338, 343, 348.

[*Description: The General Court, highest in authority in Massachusetts Bay Colony, consisted of the Governor as Chair of the Court, the Deputy Governor, five assistants, and five deputies. Several other ministers were in attendance including Rev. John Cotton, Mrs. Hutchinson's minister, and the person who inspired her basic theological position.*]

MR. JOHN WINTHROP, GOVERNOR: Mrs. Hutchinson, you are called here as one of those that have troubled the peace of the commonwealth and the churches here; you are known to be a woman that hath had a great share in the promoting and divulging of those opinions that are the cause of this trouble, and to be nearly joined not only in affinity and affection with some of those the court had taken notice of and passed censure upon, but you have spoken divers things, as we have been informed, very prejudicial to the honour of the churches and ministers thereof, and you have maintained a meeting and an assembly in your house that hath been condemned by the general assembly as a thing not tolerable nor comely in the sight of God nor fitting for your sex, and notwithstanding that was cried down you have continued the same. Therefore we have thought good to send for you to understand how things are, that if you be in an erroneous way we may reduce you that so you may become a profitable member here among us. Otherwise if you be obstinate in your course that then the court may take such course that you may trouble us no further ...

GOV. WINTHROP: Why do you keep such a meeting at your house as you do every week upon a set day?

HUTCHINSON: It is lawful for me to do so, as it is all your practices, and can you find a warrant for yourself and condemn me for the same thing? The ground of my taking it up was, when I first came to this land because I did not go to such meetings as those were, it was presently reported that I did not allow of such meetings but held them unlawful and therefore in that regard they said I was proud and did despise all ordinances. Upon that a friend came unto me and told me of it and I to prevent such aspersions took it up, but it was in practice before I came. Therefore I was not the first. [... Furthermore,] I conceive there lies a clear rule in Titus that the elder women should instruct the younger and then I must have a time wherein I must do it ...

THOMAS DUDLEY, DEPUTY GOVERNOR: I would go a little higher with Mrs. Hutchinson. About three years ago we were all in peace. Mrs. Hutchinson, from that time she came hath made a disturbance, and some that came over with her in the ship did inform me what she was as soon as she was landed. I being then in place dealt with the pastor and teacher of Boston and desired them to enquire of her, and then I was satisfied that she held nothing different from us. But within half a year after, she had vented divers of her strange opinions and had made parties in the country, and at length it comes that Mr. Cotton and Mr. Vane were of her judgment, but Mr. Cotton had cleared himself that he was not of that mind. But now it appears by this woman's meeting that Mrs. Hutchinson hath so forestalled the minds of many by their resort to her meeting that now she hath a potent party in the country. Now if all these things have endangered us as from that foundation and if she in particular hath disparaged all our ministers in the land that they have preached a covenant of works, and only Mr. Cotton a covenant of grace, why this is not to be suffered, and therefore being driven to the foundation and it being found that Mrs. Hutchinson is she that hath depraved all the ministers and hath been the cause of what is fallen out, why we must take away the foundation and the building will fall.

HUTCHINSON: Did I ever say they preached a covenant of works then?

DEP. GOV. DUDLEY: If they do not preach a covenant of grace clearly, then they preach a covenant of works.

HUTCHINSON: No, Sir. One may preach a covenant of grace more clearly than another, so I said …

DEP. GOV. DUDLEY: When they do preach a covenant of works do they preach truth?

HUTCHINSON: Yes, Sir. But when they preach a covenant of works for salvation, that is not truth …

[*Six ministers then testify to the particular charges and that she was "not only difficult in her opinions, but also of an intemperate spirit"*]

MR. HUGH PETERS: [I asked her,] What difference do you conceive to be between your teacher and us? … Briefly, she told me there was a wide and broad difference … He preaches the covenant of grace and you the covenant of works, and that you are not able ministers of the New Testament and know no more than the apostles did before the resurrection of Christ. I did then put it to her, What do you conceive of such a brother? She answered he had not the seal of the spirit …

DEP. GOV. DUDLEY (TO HUTCHINSON): I called these witnesses and you deny them. You see they have proved this and you deny this, but it is clear. You say they preached a covenant of works and that they were not able ministers of the New Testament; now there are two other things that you did affirm which were that the scriptures in the letter of them held forth nothing but a covenant of works and likewise that those that were under a covenant of works cannot be saved …

HUTCHINSON: If you please to give me leave I shall give you the ground of what I know to be true. Being much troubled to see the falseness of the constitution of the Church of England, I had like to have turned Separatist. Whereupon I kept a day of solemn humiliation and pondering of the thing; this scripture was brought unto me – he that denies Jesus Christ to be come in the flesh is antichrist. This I considered of and in considering found that the papists did not deny him to be come in the flesh, nor we did not deny him – who then was antichrist? Was the Turk antichrist only? The Lord knows that I could not open scripture; he must by his prophetical office open it unto me. So after that being unsatisfied in the thing, the Lord was pleased to bring this scripture out of the Hebrews. He that denies the testament denies the testator, and in this did open unto me and give me to see that those which did not teach the new covenant had the spirit of antichrist, and upon this he did discover the ministry unto me; and ever since, I bless the Lord, he hath let me see which was the clear ministry and which the wrong. Since that time I confess I have been more choice and he hath left me to distinguish between the voice of my beloved and the voice of Moses, the voice of John the Baptist and the voice of antichrist, for all those voices are spoken of in scripture. Now if you do condemn me for speaking what in my conscience I know to be truth I must commit myself unto the Lord.

MR. NOWEL [ASSISTANT TO THE COURT]: How do you know that was the spirit?

HUTCHINSON: How did Abraham know that it was God that bid him offer his son, being a breach of the sixth commandment?

DEP. GOV. DUDLEY: By an immediate voice.

HUTCHINSON: So to me by an immediate revelation.

DEP. GOV. DUDLEY: How! an immediate revelation …

HUTCHINSON: But now having seen him which is invisible I fear not what man can do unto me.

GOV. WINTHROP: Daniel was delivered by miracle; do you think to be deliver'd so too?

HUTCHINSON: I do here speak it before the court. I look that the Lord should deliver me by his providence …

GOV. WINTHROP: I am persuaded that the revelation she brings forth is delusion.

ALL THE COURT BUT SOME TWO OR THREE MINISTERS CRY OUT, we all believe it – we all believe it …

GOV. WINTHROP: Mrs. Hutchinson, the sentence of the court you hear is that you are banished from out of our jurisdiction as being a woman not fit for our society, and are imprisoned till the court shall send you away.

HUTCHINSON: I desire to know wherefore I am banished?

GOV. WINTHROP: Say no more, the court know wherefore and is satisfied.

THE MASSACHUSETTS WITCHCRAFT TRIALS

Fifty-five years after the legendary "examination" of Anne Hutchinson, some residents of the Massachusetts Bay Colony took to the courts once again to confront some female elements who threatened the stability of the community with behaviors apparently unbecoming to biblically inclined Puritans. The events leading to what would become known as "the Salem Witch Trials" began in Salem Village in 1692 when Betty Parris (age 9) and Abigail Williams (11), the daughter and niece, respectively, of village minister Samuel Parris began to have sudden and strange fits. When other young women of Salem Village began to manifest similar episodes, the community's rumor mill fed suspicions about three women on the fringes of the community – the poor beggar Sarah Good, the irregular churchgoer Sarah Osborne, who was reportedly in a sexual affair with her indentured servant, and the slave girl Tituba. Around March 1, all three were brought before local magistrates on charges of witchcraft, put in jail, and interrogated for several days. In the months that followed, accusations of other women ensued and spread to larger, neighboring towns, involving the colony's Governing Council and engulfing respected church members. Formal trials began in June and continued into May of the following year. Along the way, fourteen women and five men were hanged, a number of others died in prison, and one elderly man was pressed to death for refusal to enter a plea. The three selections that follow come from men who played a part in the initial events in Salem Village in early 1692.

COTTON MATHER, FROM *MEMORABLE PROVIDENCES RELATING TO WITCHCRAFTS AND POSSESSIONS*

In matters of Puritan ministerial pedigree, few could challenge Cotton Mather (1663–1728). The son of Increase Mather and grandson of Richard Mather and John Cotton – important ministers all – Cotton Mather earned further recognition on his own as Pastor at Boston's North Church and prolific commentator on various matters religious, social, and political. His books and pamphlets were widely disseminated, read, and discussed around Massachusetts and beyond. The work that includes the following excerpt addressed the case of a "possessed" Irish washerwoman named Goody Glover. As illustrated in the selection below, Mather's study operates according to a familiar assumption among Massachusetts Puritans: that the Bible, filled with references to demonic possessions, proves the reality of witches and demons and serves as a powerful weapon against them.

Source: Cotton Mather, *Memorable Providences Relating to Witchcrafts and Possessions* (Boston: R. Pierce, 1689).

Sect. **XXIX.** Devotion was now, as formerly, the terriblest of all the provocations that could be given her. I could by no means bring her to own, That she desired the mercies of God, and the prayers of good men. I would have obtained a Sign of such a Desire, by her Lifting up of her hand; but she stirr'd it not: I then lifted up her hand my self, and though the standers-by thought a more insignificant thing could not be propounded, I said, "Child, If you desire those things, let your hand fall, when I take mine away:" I took my hand away, and hers continued strangely and stiffly stretched out, so that for some time, she could not take it down. During these two dayes we had Prayers oftener in our Family than at other times; and this was her usual Behavior at them. The man that prayed, usually began with Reading the Word of God; which once as he was going to do, she call'd to him, "Read of Mary Magdelen, out of whom the Lord cast seven Devils." During the time of Reading, she would be laid as one fast asleep; but when Prayer was begun, the Devils would still throw her on the Floor, at the feet of him that prayed. There would she lye and Whistle and sing and roar, to drown the voice of the Prayer; but that being a little too audible for Them, they would shutt close her Mouth and her ears, and yet make such odd noises in her Threat as that she her self could not hear our Cries to God for her. … Once lying thus, as he that was praying was alluding to the words of the Canaanites, and saying, "Lord, have mercy on a Daughter vexed with a Devil;" there came a big, but low voice from her, saying, "There's Two or Three of them" (or us!) and the standers-by were under that Apprehension, as that they cannot relate whether her mouth mov'd in speaking of it. When Prayer was ended, she would Revive in a minute or two, and continue as Frolicksome as before. … The others kept close to their good Books which then called for their Attention. When she saw that, immediately she fell asleep; and in two or three hours, she waked perfectly her self; weeping bitterly to remember (for as one come out of a dream she could remember) what had befallen her.

SAMUEL PARRIS, "CHRIST KNOWS HOW MANY DEVILS THERE ARE"

> Samuel Parris delivered the sermon below at the beginning of the legal proceedings against suspected witches. Influenced by Cotton Mather's "providences relating to witchcrafts and possessions"(above), Parris here speaks to the Bible's recognition of "devils" that threaten the solidarity and righteousness of every community, including even Jesus' inner circle. As noted above, the unsettling fits of Parris's daughter and niece set off the witchcraft frenzy in Massachusetts.
>
> Source: Samuel Parris, "Christ Knows How Many Devils There Are," by permission, The Connecticut Historical Society, Hartford, Connecticut.

27 March 1692, Sacrament day.

Occasioned by dreadful Witchcraft broke out here a few weeks past, and one Member of this Church, and another of Salem, upon public examination by Civil Authority vehemently suspected for she-witches, and upon it committed.

John 6: 70. "Have not I chosen you twelve, and one of you is a Devil."

This Chapter consists of 3 principal parts:

Part 1 consists of a declaration of Christ's miraculous feeding of 5,000 with 5 loaves and 2 small fishes (verses 1–15).

Part 2 treats of Christ's miraculous walking upon the sea (v. 15–22).

Part 3 consists of Christ's sermon to the Capernates (v. 22–end) concerning the heavenly, or truly vivified, bread …

Whereupon note: 1. Our Lord takes occasion to ask his disciples whether they also would desert him (v. 67). 2. Peter in the name of the rest answers by confessing the excellency both of Christ's doctrine and his person (v. 68~69). 3. (Last) This confession Christ so approves of that in the meanwhile he doth admonish them that there is an hypocrite among them, a Devil among them (v. 70–71) …

Doctrine: *Our Lord Jesus Christ knows how many Devils there are in his Church, and who they are.*

1. There are devils as well as saints in Christ's Church.

2. Christ knows how many of these devils there are.

3. Christ knows who these devils are.

Proposition 1: … (1) … By devil is ordinarily meant any wicked angel or spirit. Sometimes it is put for the prince or head of the evil spirits, or fallen angels. Sometimes it is used for vile and wicked persons–the worst of such, who for their villainy and impiety do most resemble devils and wicked spirits. Thus Christ in our text calls Judas a devil: for his great likeness to the devil … (2). There are such devils in the church. Not only sinners, but notorious sinners; sinners more like to the devil than others. … Hypocrites are the sons and heirs of the devil, the free-holders of hell–whereas other sinners are but tenants. … (3). There are also true saints in the church. The church consists of good and bad: as a garden that has weeds as well as flowers, and as a field that has wheat as well as tares. Hence that gospel is compared to a net that taketh good and bad (Matth. 13: 47–50) …

Use 1. Let none then build their hopes of salvation merely upon this: that they are church members. This you and I may be, and yet devils for all that (Matth. 8: 11–12 – "Many shall come from the east and west, and shall sit down, etc. And however we may pass here, a true difference shall be made shortly, etc.").

Use 2. Let none then be stumbled at religion, because too often there are devils found among the saints. You see, here was a true church, sincere converts and sound believers; and yet here was a devil among them.

Use 3. Terror to hypocrites who profess much love to Christ but indeed are in with their lusts, which they prefer above Christ. Oh! remember that you are devils in Christ's account. Christ is lightly esteemed of you, and you are vilely accounted for by Christ. Oh! if there be any such among us, forbear to come this day to the Lord's table, lest Satan enter more powerfully into you–lest while the bread be between your teeth, the wrath of the Lord come pouring down upon you (Psalm 78: 30–31).

Use 4. Exhort in two branches:

(1). To be deeply humbled for the appearances of devils among our churches. If the church of Corinth were called to mourn because of one incestuous person among them (I Cor. 5: 1), how much more may New England churches mourn, that such as work witchcraft, or are vehemently suspected so to do, should be found among them.

(2). To be much in prayer that God would deliver our churches from devils; God would not suffer devils in the guise of saints to associate with us. One sinner destroys much good: how much more one devil. Pray we also that not one true saint may suffer as a devil, either in name or body. The devil would represent the best saints as devils if he could, but it is not easy to imagine that his power is of such extent, to the hazard of the church.

Use 5. Examine we ourselves well, what we are – what we church members are. We are either saints or devils: the Scripture gives us no medium. The Apostle tells us we are to examine ourselves (2 Cor. 13: 5). Oh! it is a dreadful thing to be a devil, and yet to sit down at the Lord's table (1 Cor. 10: 21). Such incur the hottest of God's wrath (as follows – v. 22). Now, if we would not be devils, we must give ourselves wholly up to Christ, and not suffer the predominancy of one lust – and particularly that of covetousness, which is made so light of, and which prevails in these perilous times. Why, this one lust made Judas a devil (John 12: 6, Matth. 26: 15). And no doubt it has made more devils than one. For a little pelf, men sell Christ to his enemies, and their souls to the devil. But there are certain sins that make us devils; see that we be not such:

1. A liar or murderer (John 8: 44)
2. A slanderer or an accuser of the godly
3. A tempter to sin
4. An opposer of godliness, as Elymos (Acts 13: 8 etc.)
5. Envious persons as witches
6. A drunkard (I Sam. 1: 15–16)
7. A proud person

JOHN HALE, "A MODEST INQUIRY INTO THE NATURE OF WITCHCRAFT"

Hale (1636–1700) was pastor at Church of Christ in Beverly, not far from Salem Village. He had been an enthusiastic prosecutor of suspected witches until his wife, Sarah Noyes Hale, was accused of witchcraft during the escalating frenzy of 1692. He became one of the most prominent and vocal opponents of the trials. After his wife's death in 1697, he wrote the book introduced by the selection below. In his "modest inquiry," Hale offered a retrospective and highly critical firsthand review of the proceedings. Like most of his contemporaries, he accepts the biblical recognition of devils and witches. However, in these introductory remarks Hale points to the scriptures' warnings against one of the devil's best tricks: providing fuel for a zealous rush to judgment that irrevocably cracks apart the community of believers.

Source: John Hale, "A Modest Inquiry into the Nature of Witchcraft," by permission, The Beverly Historical Society.

The Preface to the Christian Reader

The Holy Scriptures inform us that the Doctrine of Godliness is a great Mystery, containing the Mysteries of the Kingdom of Heaven: Mysteries which require great search for the finding out: And as the Lord hath his Mysteries to bring us to Eternal Glory; so Satan hath his Mysteries to bring us to Eternal Ruine: Mysteries not easily understood, whereby the depths of Satan are managed in hidden wayes. So the Whore of Babylon makes the Inhabitants of the Earth drunk with the Wine of her Fornication, by the Mystery of her abominations, Rev. 17. 2. And the man of Sin hath his Mystery of iniquity whereby he deceiveth men through the working of Satan in signes and lying wonders, 2 Thes. 2. 3, 7, 9.

And among Satan's Mysteries of iniquity, this of Witchcraft is one of the most difficult to be searched out by the Sons of men; as appeareth by the great endeavours of Learned and Holy men to search it out, and the great differences that are found among them, in the rules laid down for the bringing to light these hidden works of darkness. So that it may seem presumption in me to undertake so difficult a Theam, and to lay down such rules as are different from the Sentiments of many Eminent writers, and from the Presidents and practices of able Lawyers; yea and from the Common Law it self.

But my Apology for this undertaking is;

1. That there hath been such a dark dispensation by the Lord, letting loose upon us the Devil, *Anno.* 1691 and 1692, as we never experienced before: And thereupon apprehending and condemning persons for Witchcraft; and nextly acquitting others no less liable to such a charge; which evidently shew we were in the dark, and knew not what to do; but have gone too far on the one or other side, if not on both. Hereupon I esteemed it necessary for some person to Collect a Summary of that affair, with some *animadversions* upon it, which might at least give some light to them which come after, to shun those Rocks by which we were bruised, and narrowly escaped Shipwreck upon.

   And I have waited five years for some other person to undertake it, who might doe it better than I can, but find none; and judge it better to do what I can, than that such a work should be left undone. Better sincerely though weakly done, then not at all, or with such a byas of prejudice as will put false glosses upon that which was managed with uprightness of heart, though there was not so great a spirit of discerning, as were to be wished in so weighty a Concernment.

2. I have been present at several Examinations and Tryals, and knew sundry of those that Suffered upon that account in former years, and in this last affair, and so have more advantages than a stranger, to give account of these Proceedings.

3. I have been from my Youth trained up in the knowledge and belief of most of those principles I here question as unsafe to be used. The first person that suffered on this account in New-England, about Fifty years

since, was my Neighbour, and I heard much of what was charged upon her, and others in those times; and the reverence I bore to aged, learned and judicious persons, caused me to drink in their principles in these things, with a kind of Implicit Faith. *Quo semel est imbuta recens servabit odorem, Testa diu.*

A Child will not easily forsake the principles he hath been trained up in from his Cradle. But observing the Events of that sad Catastrophe, *Anno* 1692, I was brought to a more strict scanning of the principles I had imbibed, and by scanning, to question, and by questioning at length to reject many of them, upon the reasons shewed in the ensuing Discourse. It is an approved saying *Nihil certius, quam quod ex dubio fit certum.* No truth more certain to a man, than that which he hath formerly doubted or denied, and is recovered from his error, by the convincing evidence of Scripture and reason. Yet I know and am sensible, that while we know but in part, man is apt in flying from a discovered error, to run into the contrary extream.

Incidit in Scyllam qui vult vitare Charybdim.

The middle way is commonly the way of truth. And if any can shew me a better middle way than I have here laid down, I shall be ready to embrace it: But the conviction must not be by vinegar or drollery, but by strength of argument …

5. I observe the failings that have been on the one hand, have driven some into that which is indeed an extream on the other hand, and of dangerous consequences, *viz.* To deny any such persons to be under the New Testament, who by the Devil's aid discover Secrets, or do work wonders. Therefore in the latter part of this discourse, I have taken pains to prove the Affirmative, yet with brevity, because it hath been done already by Perkins of *Witchcraft*, Glanvil his *Saducismus Triumphatus*, Pt. 1. p. 1 to 90 and Pt. 2. p. 1 to 80. Yet I would not be understood to justify all his notions in those discourses, but acknowledge he hath strongly proved the being of Witches.

6. I have special reasons moving me to bear my testimony about these matters, before I go hence and be no more; the which I have here done, and I hope with some assistance of his Spirit, to whom I commit myself and this my labour, even that God whose I am and whom I serve: Desiring his Mercy in Jesus Christ to Pardon all the Errors of his People in the day of darkness; and to enable us to fight with Satan by Spiritual Weapons, putting on the whole Armour of God.

And tho' Satan by his Messengers may buffet God's Children, yet there's a promise upon right *Resisting, he shall flee from them,* Jam. 4. 7. *And that all things shall work together for the good of those that Love the Lord,* Rom. 8. 28. So that I believe God's Children shall be gainers by the assaults of Satan, which occasion'd this Discourse; which that they may, is the Prayer of, Thine in the Service of the Gospel.

John Hale.

Beverly, Decemb. 15th, 1697.

QUAKER PENNSYLVANIA AND "THE KEITHIAN SCHISM"

Guided by a unique brand of Puritanism, William Penn and other Quaker leaders looked to the Bible as the foundation for Pennsylvania, their "Holy Experiment" in building a new, godly society based on principles of brotherly love and the transforming power of the Holy Spirit through the workings of every person's "Inner Light." However, the Quakers' persistent rejection of a clerical hierarchy on grounds of the individual's spiritual authority resulted in numerous political, ethnic, and religious factions that nevertheless shared an anti-authoritarianism that resisted claims to power. This growing factionalism was enabled by and foreshadowed in fierce theological debates of the late 1600s. The most explosive of the disputes was the so-called "Keithian Schism" of the 1690s. In the first years of that decade, George Keith, a prominent Scottish Quaker who had taken over as head of Philadelphia's Friends School in 1689, began to criticize other Quaker leaders for stressing too greatly the notion of Inner Light at the expense of the Bible as spiritual guide. In the selection below, the English Quaker John Penington ferociously responds to Keith and his cohorts.

Source: John Penington, *An Apostate Exposed; or, George Keith Contradicting himself and his brother Bradford* (London: T. Sowle, 1695), 7–12.

I observe, that in the Year 1692 and before, the Quakers were found [by George Keith] in the Faith; then G.K. with others, labour to convince our Opposers, that our belief and expectation of Salvation by the Man Christ Jesus, that was outwardly Crucified without the Gates of Jerusalem, is and hath been constant and firm, whereas now he insinuates, the leading Men (as he terms them) viz. George Whitehead, William Penn, and John Whitehead are inconsistent, in their present late Answers to the express words and sentiments of their printed Books.

    … The vile Errors [Keith] ascribes to Friends' former Sayings, Sentiments, and printed Books; their Hypocrisie to their not acknowledging them; but referring to their Answers made publick, and yet allows some Reformation of Judgment, but not total, but that they are still under great Blindness, Darkness and Error. … How wide he will stretch [this Charge] to fetch in the rest, under the notion of credulous Followers and Admirers, himself best knows, if any. That these were not his Sentiments formerly, or at least that he hath declared otherwise, is what now lieth before me to evince … *Suo so jugulet gladio.*

    … In Pag. 3 G.K. and others (in order to vindicate the people called Quakers, from the *Calumnies of Christian Lodowick*) say, "Whereas divers of us, challenged by [Lodowick], declared sincerely their sincere Faith, as concerning the Lord Jesus Christ of Nazareth, and what the Holy Scriptures testifie of him, yet he did continue to accuse them still, as denying the true Christ, alledging, they had another Sense than the Scripture-Words did bear, and that his Sense was true, but their Sense was false, appealing to their Consciences, whether it was not so; thus making himself Judge over our Secret Thoughts, as having a secret Sense in our thoughts of Scripture-Words, contrary to the true sense of them, though we have not given him or any other occasion to judge so rashly, and uncharitably of us, and our Consciences bear us witness in the fight of God, that we do sincerely believe, and think as we speak, when we say according to the Holy Scripture, that Jesus of Nazareth is the true Christ of God, and the only true Saviour, and there is no other Name given under Heaven, whereby men must be saved ...

"Therefore hath this Accuser joined with Tho. Hicks, a Baptist Teacher at London, and divers others, to accuse us as denying the true Christ, because we believe and confess to Christ's inward and outward appearance."

George Keith hath [made the same accusation] since. ... This Charge was groundless then, how comes it to be true now?

FOUNDING THE REPUBLIC

PRAYER BEFORE THE FIRST CONTINENTAL CONGRESS

> When the Founders convened for the First Continental Congress on September 6, 1774, one member suggested they begin with a prayer. John Jay of New York and John Rutledge of South Carolina, both Episcopalians, objected on the grounds that there were many denominations in the group, and it would create strife. Samuel Adams brought a motion to hear the prayer, arguing that he could hear a prayer from any pious patriot. Sam Adams' motion carried. His cousin John describes the scene in a letter to his wife. Reverend Duché's prayer follows Adams' letter.
>
> Source: John Adams to Abigail Adams, 16 September 1774 (electronic edition), *Adams Family Papers: An Electronic Archive.* Massachusetts Historical Society: www.masshist. org/digitaladams/.

Letter from John Adams to Abigail Adams

Phyladelphia Septr. 16, 1774

Having a Leisure Moment, while the Congress is assembling, I gladly embrace it to write you a Line.

When the Congress first met, Mr. Cushing made a Motion, that it should be opened with Prayer. It was opposed by Mr. Jay of N. York and Mr. Rutledge of South Carolina, because we were so divided in religious Sentiments, some Episcopalians, some Quakers, some Anabaptists, some Presbyterians and some Congregationalists, so that We could not join in the same Act of Worship. Mr. S. Adams arose and said he was no Bigot, and could hear a Prayer from a Gentleman of Piety and Virtue, who was at the same Time a Friend to his Country. He was a Stranger in Phyladelphia, but had heard that Mr. Duche (Dushay they pronounce it) deserved that Character, and therefore he moved that Mr. Duche, an Episcopal Clergyman, might be desired, to read Prayers to the Congress, tomorrow Morning. The Motion was Seconded and passed in the Affirmative. Mr. Randolph, our President, waited on Mr. Duche, and received for Answer that if his Health would permit, he certainly would. Accordingly next Morning he appeared with his Clerk and in his Pontificallibus, and read several Prayers, in the established Form; and then read the Collect for the seventh day of September, which was the Thirty fifth Psalm.

– You must remember this was the next Morning after we heard the horrible Rumour, of the Cannonade of Boston. – I never saw a greater Effect upon an Audience. It seemed as if Heaven had ordained that Psalm to be read on that Morning.

After this Mr. Duche, unexpected to every Body struck out into an extempo-rary Prayer, which filled the Bosom of every Man present. I must confess I never heard a better Prayer or one, so well pronounced. Episcopalian as he is, Dr. Cooper himself never prayed with such fervour, such Ardor, such Earnestness and Pathos, and in Language so elegant and sublime – for America, for the Congress, for The Province of Massachusetts Bay, and especially the Town of Boston. It has had an excellent Effect upon every Body here.

I must beg you to read that Psalm. If there was any Faith in the sortes Virgilianae, or sortes Homericae, or especially the Sortes biblicae, it would be thought providential. It will amuse your Friends to read this Letter and the 35th. Psalm to them. Read it to your Father and Mr. Wibirt. – I wonder what our Braintree Churchmen would think of this? – Mr. Duche is one of the most ingenious Men, and best Characters, and greatest orators in the Episcopal order, upon this Continent – Yet a Zealous Friend of Liberty and his Country.

I long to see my dear Family. God bless, preserve and prosper it.

Adieu.

John Adams

THE PRAYER OF REV. DUCHÉ BEFORE THE CONTINENTAL CONGRESS

Jacob Duché, an Episcopal minister in Philadelphia, chose as one of his texts, a verse from Paul's letter to the Galatians. This excerpt, from a much longer sermon, applies the words to the colonies' conflict with Britain. Nearly two years before the Declaration of Independence, he shows hope of remaining part of Britain.

Source: Frank Moore ed., *The Patriot Preachers of the American Revolution* (New York: Charles T. Evans, 1862), 75, 84–6.

Stand fast, therefore, in the liberty wherewith Christ has made us free. Galatians v. 1.

GENTLEMEN OF THE FIRST BATTALION OF THE CITY AND LIBERTIES OF PHILADELPHIA: – Though I readily accepted of the invitation with which you were pleased to honor me, and am fully satisfied that there can be no impropriety in complying with your request, yet I confess, that I now feel such an uncommon degree of diffidence, as nothing but a sense of duty, and a sincere sympathy with you in your present trying circumstances could enable me to overcome. The occasion is of first importance; the subject in a great measure is new to me – throwing myself, therefore, upon your candor and indulgence, considering myself under the twofold character of a minister of Jesus Christ, and a fellow-citizen of the same state, and involved in the same public calamity with yourselves, and looking up for a counsel and direction to the source of all wisdom, "who giveth liberally to those that ask it," I have made choice of a passage of Scripture, which will give me an opportunity of addressing myself to you as freemen, both in the spiritual and temporal sense ...

Yet why this unreasonable and unrighteous jealousy? – We wish not to interfere with that commercial system which they have hitherto pursued. We have not even stretched our expectations beyond the line which they themselves had drawn. We wish not to possess the golden groves of Asia, to sparkle in the public eye with jewels torn from the brows of weeping nabobs, or to riot on the spoils of plundered provinces. We rather tremble for the parent state, and would fain keep off from our own borders those luxuries, which may perhaps already have impaired her constitutional vigor. We only wish, that what we have, we may be able to call our own; that those fruits of honest industry, which our ancestors had acquired, or those which have been, or may be added to them by the sweat of our own brows, should not be wrested from us by the hand of violence, but left to our own free disposal; satisfied as we are in our consciences, that when constitutionally called upon, we shall not give "grudgingly or of necessity," but cheerfully and liberally.

And as to any pretensions to, even desire of, independency, have we not openly disavowed them in all our petitions, representations, and remonstrances? Have we not repeatedly and solemnly professed an inviolable loyalty to the person, power, and dignity of our sovereign, and unanimously declared, that it is not with him we contend, but with an envious cloud of false witnesses, that surround his throne, and intercept the sunshine of his favour from our oppressed land?

If, notwithstanding all this, Britain, or rather some degenerate sons of Britain, and enemies to our common liberty, still persist in embracing *delusion*, and believing a lie – if the sword is still unsheathed against us, and *submit or perish* is the sanguinary decree – why then –. I cannot close the sentence –. Indulge a minister of Jesus! My soul shrinks back with horror from the tragic scene of fraternal slaughter – and the free spirit of the citizen is arrested by the tenderness of gospel love. Gracious God! Stop the precious effusion of British and American blood – too precious to be spared in any other cause than the joint interest of both against a common foe!

Pained as I am at this melancholy prospect, I mean not, however, to decline addressing you in your military capacity, and suggesting such a conduct for the preservation of your temporal rights as, by the blessing of heaven, will be most likely to insure you success.

"Stand fast," then.

THE CALL TO WAR, THE CHALLENGE OF PEACE

PATRICK HENRY'S CALL FOR REVOLUTION

Patrick Henry delivered this speech before the Virginia House of Burgesses, of which he was a member, on March 23, 1775. Coming only a few hours after the British marched on Concord, it marks the start of the revolution in Virginia. He invokes the God of nature, but also the God who cares about the fate of nations. The chapter and verse numbers of his many biblical references and allusions are added.

Source: University of Oklahoma College of Law: www.law.ou.edu.

No man thinks more highly that I do of the patriotism, as well as abilities, of the very worthy gentlemen who have just addressed the house. But different men often see the same subject in different lights; and therefore, I hope it will not be thought disrespectful to those gentlemen if, entertaining as I do opinions of a character very opposite to theirs, I shall speak forth my sentiments freely and without reserve. This is no time for ceremony. The question before the house is one of awful moment to this country. For my own part, I consider it as nothing less than a question of freedom or slavery; and in proportion to the magnitude of the subject ought to be the freedom of the debate. It is only in this way that we can hope to arrive at the truth, and fulfill the great responsibility which we hold to God and our county. Should I keep back my opinions at such a time, through fear of giving offense, I should consider myself as guilty of treason towards my country, and of an act of disloyalty toward the Majesty of Heaven, which I revere above all earthly kings.

Mr. President, it is natural to man to indulge in the illusions of hope. We are apt to shut our eyes against a painful truth, and listen to the song of that siren till she transforms us into beasts. Is this the part of wise men, engaged in a great or arduous struggle for liberty? Are we disposed to be of the numbers of those who, having eyes, see not, and having ears, hear not [Jer 5:21; Mark 8:18], the things which so nearly concern their temporal salvation for my part, whatever anguish of spirit it may cost, I am willing to know the whole truth, to know the worst, and to provide for it.

I have but one lamp by which my feet [Ps 119:105] are guided, and that is the lamp of experience. I know of no way of judging of the future but by the past. And judging by the past, I wish to know what there has been in the conduct of the British ministry for the last ten years to justify those hopes with which gentlemen have been pleased to solace themselves and the House. Is it that insidious smile with which our petition has been lately received?

Trust it not, sir; it will prove a snare to your feet. Suffer not yourselves to be betrayed with a kiss [Matt 26:48]. Ask yourselves how this gracious reception of our petition comports with those warlike preparations which cover our waters and darken our land. Are fleets and armies necessary to a work of love and reconciliation? Have we shown ourselves so unwilling to be reconciled that force must be called in to win back our love? Let us not deceive ourselves, sir. These are the implements of war and subjugation; the last arguments to which kings resort. I ask gentlemen, sir, what means this martial array, if its purpose be not to force us to submission? Can gentlemen assign any other possible motive for it? Has Great Britain any enemy, in this quarter of the world, to call for all this accumulation of navies and armies? No, sir, she has none. They are meant for us; they can be meant for no other. They are sent over to bind and rivet upon us those chains which the British ministry have been so long forging. And what have we to oppose to them? Shall we try argument? Sir, we have been trying that for the last ten years. Have we anything new to offer upon the subject? Nothing. We have held the subject up in every light of which it is capable; but it has been all in vain. Shall we resort to entreaty and humble supplication? What terms shall we find which have not been already exhausted? Let us not, I beseech you, sir, deceive ourselves. Sir, we have done everything that could be done to avert the storm which is now coming on. We have petitioned; we have remonstrated; we have supplicated; we have prostrated ourselves before the throne, and have implored its interposition to arrest the tyrannical hands of the ministry and Parliament. Our petitions have been slighted; our remonstrances have produced additional violence and insult; our supplications have been disregarded; and we have been spurned, with contempt, from the foot of the throne! In vain, after these things, may we indulge the fond hope of peace and reconciliation.

There is no longer any room for hope. If we wish to be free – if we mean to preserve inviolate those inestimable privileges for which we have been so long contending – if we mean not basely to abandon the noble struggle in which we have been so long engaged, and which we have pledged ourselves never to abandon until the glorious object of our contest shall be obtained – we must fight! I repeat it, sir, we must fight! An appeal to arms and to the God of hosts is all that is left us! They tell us, sir, that we are weak; unable to cope with so formidable an adversary. But when shall we be stronger? Will it be the next week, or the next year? Will it be when we are totally disarmed, and when a British guard shall be stationed in every house? Shall we gather strength by irresolution and inaction? Shall we acquire the means of effectual resistance by lying supinely on our backs and hugging the delusive phantom of hope, until our enemies shall have bound us hand and foot? Sir, we are not weak if we make a proper use of those means which the God of nature hath placed in our power. The millions of people, armed in the holy cause of liberty, and in such a country as that which we possess, are invincible by any force which our enemy can send against us. Besides, sir, we shall not fight our battle alone. There is a just God who presides over the destinies of nations, and who will raise up friends to fight our battles for us [2 Chron 32:8]. The battle, sir, is not to the strong alone [Ecc 9:11]; it is to the vigilant, the active, the brave. Besides, sir, we have no election. If we were base enough to desire it, it is now too late to retire from the contest. There is no retreat but in submission and slavery! Our chains are forged! Their clanking may be heard on the plains of Boston! The war is inevitable – and let it come! I repeat it, sir, let it come.

It is in vain, sir, to extenuate the matter. Gentlemen may cry, Peace, Peace – but there is no peace [Jer 6:14]. The war is actually begun! The next gale that sweeps from the north will bring to our ears the clash of resounding arms! Our brethren are already in the field! Why stand we here idle [Matt 20:6]? What is it that gentlemen wish? What would they have? Is life so dear, or peace so sweet, as to be purchased at the price of chains and slavery? Forbid it, Almighty God! I know not what course others may take; but as for me, give me liberty or give me death!

ABRAHAM LINCOLN'S SECOND INAUGURAL ADDRESS

> Lincoln's address on March 3, 1865 came at a time that the country was suffering the national trauma of the Civil War. He predicates his message on the belief that God is just, quoting Psalm 19:9. He speaks of the catastrophic loss of life using the language of atonement and ritual sacrifice, suggesting that the deaths of Union and Confederate soldiers is expiation for the sin of slavery.
>
> Source: The Avalon Project, Lillian Goldman Law Library, Yale Law School: http:// avalon.law.yale.edu.

At this second appearing to take the oath of the presidential office, there is less occasion for an extended address than there was at the first. Then a statement, somewhat in detail, of a course to be pursued, seemed fitting and proper. Now, at the expiration of four years, during which public declarations have been constantly called forth on every point and phase of the great contest which still absorbs the attention, and engrosses the energies of the nation, little that is new could be presented. The progress of our arms, upon which all else chiefly depends, is as well known to the public as to myself; and it is, I trust, reasonably satisfactory and encouraging to all. With high hope for the future, no prediction in regard to it is ventured.

On the occasion corresponding to this four years ago, all thoughts were anxiously directed to an impending civil war. All dreaded it – all sought to avert it. While the inaugural address was being delivered from this place, devoted altogether to *saving* the Union without war, insurgent agents were in the city seeking to *destroy* it without war – seeking to dissolve the Union, and divide effects, by negotiation. Both parties deprecated war; but one of them would *make* war rather than let the nation survive; and the other would *accept* war rather than let it perish. And the war came.

One-eighth of the whole population were colored slaves, not distributed generally over the Union, but localized in the Southern part of it. These slaves constituted a peculiar and powerful interest. All knew that this interest was, somehow, the cause of the war. To strengthen, perpetuate, and extend this interest was the object for which the insurgents would rend the Union, even by war; while the government claimed no right to do more than to restrict the territorial enlargement of it. Neither party expected for the war, the magnitude, or the duration, which it has already attained. Neither anticipated that the *cause* of the conflict might cease with, or even before, the conflict itself would cease. Each looked for an easier triumph, and as a result less fundamental and astounding. Both read the same Bible, and pray to the same God; and each invokes His aid against the other. It may seem strange that any men should dare to ask a just God assistance in wringing their bread from the sweat of other men's faces; but let us judge not that we be not judged. The prayers of both could not be answered; that of neither has been answered fully. The Almighty has His own purposes. "Woe unto the world because of offenses! For it must needs be that offenses come; but woe to that man by whom the offense cometh!" If we shall suppose that American slavery is one of those offenses which, in the providence of God, must needs come, but which, having continued through His appointed time, He now wills to remove, and that He gives to both North and South, this terrible war, as the woe due to those by whom the offense came, shall we discern therein any departure from those divine attributes which the believers in a Living God always ascribe to Him? Fondly do we hope – fervently do we pray – that this mighty scourge of war may speedily pass away. Yet, if God wills that it continue, until all the wealth piled by the bondman's two hundred and fifty years of unrequited toil shall be sunk, and until every drop of blood drawn with the lash, shall be paid by another drawn with the sword, as was said three thousand years ago, so still it must be said "the judgments of the Lord, are true and righteous altogether [Ps 19:9]."

With malice toward none; with charity for all; with firmness in the right, as God gives us to see the right, let us strive on to finish the work we are in; to bind up the nation's wounds; to care for him who shall have borne the battle, and for his widow, and his orphan – to do all which may achieve and cherish a just, and a lasting peace, among ourselves, and with all nations.

FRANKLIN D. ROOSEVELT AS THE NATION'S PASTOR

Franklin D. Roosevelt, who shepherded the country out of the Great Depression and through most of World War II, frequently used biblical references and ideas and spoke of God quite freely. On D-Day, June 6, 1944, he composed his own prayer which he broadcast to the nation. His attitude towards the Bible is explicit in this excerpt from a statement on October 6, 1935, the 400th anniversary of the printing of the English Bible.

Source: The American Presidency Project, University of California at Santa Barbara: www.presidency.ucsb.edu.

In the formative days of the Republic the directing influence the Bible exercised upon the fathers of the Nation is conspicuously evident …

The book continues to hold its unchallenged place as the most loved, the most quoted and the most universally read and pondered of all the volumes which our libraries contain. It has withstood assaults, it has resisted and survived the most searching microscopic examination, it has stood every test that could be applied to it and yet it continues to hold its supreme place as the Book of books. There have been periods when it has suffered stern and searching criticism, but the hottest flame has not destroyed its prevailing and persistent power.

We cannot read the history of our rise and development as a Nation, without reckoning with the place the Bible has occupied in shaping the advances of the Republic. Its teaching, as has been widely suggested, is ploughed into the very heart of the race.

Where we have been truest and most consistent in obeying its precepts we have attained the greatest measure of contentment and prosperity; where it has been to us as the words of a book that is sealed, we have faltered in our way, lost our range finders and found our progress checked ...

As literature, as a book that contains a system of ethics, of moral and religious principles, it stands unique and alone. I commend its thoughtful and reverent reading to all our people. Its refining and elevating influence is indispensable to our most cherished hopes and ideals.

CONGRESS DECLARES THE BIBLE "THE WORD OF GOD"

A joint resolution of the House and Senate called on President Ronald Reagan to proclaim 1983 the "Year of the Bible." Reagan authorized the measure by Proclamation 5018, making it a public law. President George H. W. Bush similarly followed a Congressional resolution by making 1990 the International Year of Bible Reading.

Source: "Public Laws," Thomas, Library of Congress: http://thomas.loc.gov.

[Senate Joint Resolution 165] 96 Stat. 1211. Public Law 97-280-October 4, 1982

Joint Resolution authorizing and requesting the President to proclaim 1983 as the "Year of the Bible."

Whereas the Bible, the Word of God, has made a unique contribution in shaping the United States as a distinctive and blessed nation and people;

Whereas deeply held religious convictions springing from the Holy Scriptures led to the early settlement of our Nation;

Whereas Biblical teachings inspired concepts of civil government that are contained in our Declaration of Independence and the constitution of he United States;

Whereas many of our great national leaders – among them Presidents Washington, Jackson, Lincoln, and Wilson – paid tribute to the surpassing influence of the Bible in our country's development, as the words of President Jackson that the Bible is "the rock on which our Republic rests";

Whereas the history of our Nation clearly illustrates the value of voluntarily applying the teachings of the Scriptures in the lives of individuals, families, and societies;

Whereas this Nation now faces great challenges that will test this Nation as it has never been tested before; and

Whereas that renewing our knowledge of and faith in God through Holy Scripture can strengthen us as a nation and a people; Now, therefore, be it

Resolved by the Senate and House of Representatives of the United States of America in Congress assembled, That the President is authorized and requested to designate 1983 as a national "Year of the Bible" in recognition of both the formative influence the Bible has been for our Nation, and our national need to study and apply the teachings of the Holy Scriptures.

Approved October 4, 1982

PUBLIC DISPLAY OF RELIGION

ABINGTON V. SCHEMPP

In 1940 the Supreme Court ruled that the states as well as the federal government were bound by constitutional rights, including First Amendment stipulations regarding religion. The issue of the Bible's place in public education surfaced regularly in the explosion of religion-related cases in the courts in the following decades. In 1962 the Supreme Court heard the case of *Engle v. Vitale,* which called into question the require-ment by the Regents of New York of a daily bible-based prayer in all of the state's public classrooms. When the Court ruled – with only one dissenting opinion – that New York's law was unconstitutional, the public outcry was loud and unrelenting. The next year, the Court took up a similar issue in *Abington School District v. Schempp.* A description of the land-mark case as well as the Court's decision is excerpted below from the majority opinion delivered by Justice Thomas Clark.

Source: www.FindLaw.com. *Abington Township School District v. Schempp,* 374 US 203 (1963).

Once again we are called upon to consider the scope of the provision of the First Amendment to the United States Constitution which declares that "Congress shall make no law respecting an establishment of religion, or prohibiting the free exercise thereof … " These companion cases present the issues in the context of state action requiring that schools begin each day with readings from the Bible. While raising the basic questions under slightly different factual situations, the cases permit of joint treatment. In light of the history of the First Amendment and of our cases interpreting and applying its requirements, we hold that the practices at issue and the laws requiring them are unconstitutional under the Establishment Clause, as applied to the States through the Fourteenth Amendment.

The Facts in Each Case: No. 142. The Commonwealth of Pennsylvania by law, 24 Pa. Stat. 15–1516, as amended, Pub. Law 1928 (Supp. 1960) Dec. 17, 1959, requires that "At least ten verses from the Holy Bible shall be read, without comment, at the opening of each public school on each school day. Any child shall be excused from such Bible reading, or attending such Bible reading, upon the written request of his parent or guardian." The Schempp family, husband and wife and two of their three children, brought suit to enjoin enforcement of the statute, contending that their rights under the Fourteenth Amendment to the Constitution of the United States are, have been, and will continue to be violated unless this statute be declared unconstitutional as violative of these provisions of the First Amendment ...

The appellees Edward Lewis Schempp, his wife Sidney, and their children, Roger and Donna, are of the Unitarian faith and are members of the Unitarian church in Germantown, Philadelphia, Pennsylvania, where they, as well as another son, Ellory, regularly attend religious services ... The [younger] children attend the Abington Senior High School, which is a public school operated by appellant district.

On each school day at the Abington Senior High School between 8:15 and 8:30 a.m., while the pupils are attending their home rooms or advisory sections, opening exercises [374 US 203, 207] are conducted pursuant to the statute. The exercises are broadcast into each room in the school building through an intercommunications system and are conducted under the supervision of a teacher by students attending the school's radio and television workshop. Selected students from this course gather each morning in the school's workshop studio for the exercises, which include readings by one of the students of 10 verses of the Holy Bible, broadcast to each room in the building. This is followed by the recitation of the Lord's Prayer, likewise over the intercommunications system, but also by the students in the various classrooms, who are asked to stand and join in repeating the prayer in unison. The exercises are closed with the flag salute and such pertinent announcements as are of interest to the students. Participation in the opening exercises, as directed by the statute, is voluntary. The student reading the verses from the Bible may select the passages and read from any version he chooses, although the only copies furnished by the school are the King James version, copies of which were circulated to each teacher by the school district. During the period in which the exercises have been conducted the King James, the Douay and the Revised Standard versions of the Bible have been used, as well as the Jewish Holy Scriptures. There are no prefatory statements, no questions asked or solicited, no comments or explanations made and no interpretations given at or during the exercises. The students and parents are advised that the student may absent himself from the classroom or, should he elect to remain, not participate in the exercises ...

At the first trial Edward Schempp and the children testified as to specific religious doctrines purveyed by a literal reading of the Bible "which were contrary to the religious beliefs which they held and to their familial teaching." 177 F. Supp. 398, 400. The children testified that all of the doctrines to which they referred were read to them at various times as part of the exercises. Edward Schempp testified at the second trial that he had considered having Roger and Donna excused from attendance at the exercises but decided against it for several reasons, including his belief that the children's relationships with their teachers and classmates would be adversely affected ...

It is true that religion has been closely identified with our history and government. ... The fact that the Founding Fathers believed devotedly that there was a God and that the unalienable rights of man were rooted in Him is clearly evidenced in their writings, from the Mayflower Compact to the Constitution itself. This background is evidenced today in our public life through the continuance in our oaths of office from the Presidency to the Alderman of the final supplication, "So help me God." ... This is not to say, however, that religion has been so identified with our history and government that religious freedom is not likewise as strongly imbedded in our public and private life. ... This freedom to worship was indispensable in a country whose people came from the four quarters of the earth and brought with them a diversity of religious opinion. Today authorities list 83 separate religious bodies, each with membership exceeding 50,000, existing among our people, as well as innumerable smaller groups. Bureau of the Census. op. cit., supra, at 46–47.

... The religious character of the exercise was admitted by the State. But even if its purpose is not strictly religious, it is sought to be accomplished through readings, without comment, from the Bible. Surely the place of the Bible as an instrument of religion cannot be gainsaid, and the State's recognition of the pervading religious character of the ceremony is evident from the rule's specific permission of the alternative use of the Catholic Douay version as well as the recent amendment permitting nonattendance at the exercises. None of these factors is consistent with the contention that the Bible is here used either as an instrument for nonreligious moral inspiration or as a reference for the teaching of secular subjects.

The conclusion follows that in both cases the laws require religious exercises and such exercises are being conducted in direct violation of the rights of the appellees and petitioners. ... It is insisted that unless these religious exercises are permitted a "religion of secularism" is established in the schools. We agree of course that the State may not establish a "religion of secularism" in the sense of affirmatively opposing or showing hostility to religion, thus "preferring those who believe in no religion over those who do believe." *Zorach v. Clauson*, supra, at 314. We do not agree, however, that this decision in any sense has that effect. In addition, it might well be said that one's education is not complete without a study of comparative religion or the history of religion and its relationship to the advancement of civilization. It certainly may be said that the Bible is worthy of study for its literary and historic qualities. Nothing we have said here indicates that such study of the Bible or of religion, when presented objectively as part of a secular program of education, may not be effected consistently with the First Amendment. But the exercises here do not fall into those categories. They are religious exercises, required by the States in violation of the command of the First Amendment that the Government maintain strict neutrality, neither aiding nor opposing religion.

THE TEN COMMANDMENTS IN THE ALABAMA COURTHOUSE

In the 1990s Judge Roy Moore, a circuit court judge in Alabama and committed Southern Baptist, began to display a plaque of the Ten Commandments in his courtroom and to begin his judicial proceedings with a Christian prayer. Suits brought against him were dismissed, and he enjoyed considerable public support. On the night of July 31, 2001, he ordered the placement of a granite monument with the Protestant version of the Ten Commandments set up in the rotunda of the Alabama Judicial Building. He reasoned that such a display did not violate the Establishment clause of the First Amendment. Moore's understanding of the relationship between public expression of religion and the First Amendment appears in an article published a few years earlier, excerpted here.

Source: "Religion in the Public Square." Adopted from 29 *Cumberland Law Review* (1999) by permission © 1999 by *Cumberland Law Review*, 29, 350–1, 354–5, 357–8.

… The legal argument used by courts to separate God from American public life rest upon the prohibition of an establishment of religion contained in the First Amendment to the United States Constitution. To begin to understand the role of the Establishment Clause, one must first examine the clause in relation to its companion provision, the Free Exercise Clause. The relationship between these two clauses has been the topic of much debate. In his dissent in *Edwards v. Aguillard*, Supreme Court Justice Scalia wrote:

> Our cases interpreting and applying the purpose test have made such a maze of the Establishment Clause that even the most conscientious government officials can only guess what motives will be held unconstitutional. We have said essentially the following: Government may not act with the purpose of advancing religion, except when forced to do so by the Free Exercise Clause (which is now and then); or when eliminating existing government hostility to religion (which exists sometimes) or even when merely accommodating governmentally uninhibited religious practices, except that at some point (it is unclear where) intentional accommodation results in the fostering of religion, which is of course unconstitutional.

As usual, Justice Scalia, in his unique but eloquent manner, captured the dilemma which the Court created for itself. For many years, members of the Court have described the struggle to navigate "a neutral course between the two religion clauses, both of which are cast in absolute terms, and either of which, if expanded to a logical extreme, would tend to clash with the other."

But do the clauses "clash"? To claim that they do so is to conclude that the Framers contradicted themselves in the first sixteen words of the First Amendment. What did our forefathers intend by prohibiting Congress from passing laws "prohibiting the free exercise thereof"? To answer this question, it is essential that we know how the drafters of the First Amendment defined the word "religion" …

… According to [James] Madison, all men are subject to God, and their duty to him is superior to that owed to civil government simply because government authority is ordained by God. Thus, civil government was not to become entangled in questions of religion, or the duties which we owe to our Creator and the manner of discharging those duties. For this reason our forefathers declared that Congress shall make no law respecting the establishment of the duties which we owe to our Creator and the manner of discharging those duties. As the framers understood the term religion, there is no clash between the Establishment Clause and the Free Exercise Clause. Indeed, there cannot be any such clash even when the clauses are expanded to their logical extreme. Civil society can have no interest in the form of one's worship or the articles of one's faith, because all assume that these rights were given by God …

… Succinctly stated, the First Amendment Establishment Clause was never intended to eliminate the necessary truth that government must recognize the sovereignty of God. To the contrary, God's sovereignty over nations is the very basis of the First Amendment religion guarantees, and without such sovereignty, these arguments could not exist.

Why has the modern Supreme Court never embraced a definition of religion under the Establishment Clause, even though the term was so well-defined by the historical antecedents of the First Amendment and the early Supreme Court cases involving that amendment? The answer is simply that to recognize the original meaning of religion would not conform to a secular world view of society that some seek to establish, and that any other definition, if adopted by the Court, would go against logic and established precedent.

Since the 1960s, the Supreme Court has discussed "religion" and "religious" practices in many cases, although the meaning of the term "religion" under the Establishment Clause has never been addressed. For example, in a series of cases in 1965 involving conscientious objectors to involuntary military service, the Court, found it necessary to determine the meaning of "religious training and belief." The court stated that "the test might be stated in these words: A sincere and meaningful belief which occupies in the life of its possessor a place parallel to that filled by the God of those admittedly qualifying for the exemption … " In other words, anything in which a person believed, or in which he professed a belief, which approximated a belief in God might qualify for an exemption – much different definition than the one controlling the term religion. Notwithstanding the clear textual difference between the language of the First Amendment and the Selective Service Act, the Court has acted as if the definitions are equivalent, giving rise to the dilemma that accommodating the free exercise of religion threatens a forbidden establishment of religion.

To avoid this dilemma, the current Supreme Court must once again recognize the original definition of "religion" under the Establishment clause. Should the Court redefine religion along the lines of Seeger, it would radically change the true meaning of the First Amendment provisions regarding religion without any supporting precedent. By leaving religion undefined, the Court has opened the door to the erroneous assumption that, under the Establishment Clause, religion could include Buddhism, Hinduism, Taoism, and whatever might occupy in man's life a place parallel to that filled by God, or even secular Humanism, which might be defined as man's belief in his own supremacy and sufficiency. In such a case, God and religion are no longer distinguished in meaning, permitting the First Amendment to be used to exclude the very object it was meant to protect, namely the sovereignty of God over civil government.

Separation of Church and State

Although the phrase "wall of separation between church and state" does not appear in the Constitution of the United States, Declaration of Independence, Articles of Confederation, or any other official American document, many Americans have been led to believe that the First Amendment Establishment Clause requires our government to separate itself from anything relating to God. Such an interpretation of the meaning of the religion clauses of the First Amendment is simply erroneous. Nevertheless, no discussion of religion in the public square could be complete without addressing the true meaning of the term "wall of separation between church and state." In 1947, the Supreme Court stated that "in the words of Jefferson, the clause against establishment of religion by law was intended to erect a wall of separation between Church and State ... That wall must be kept high and impregnable. We could not approve the slightest breach."

In an earlier case, the Court properly identified the origin of that phrase to be a letter dated January 1, 1802, sent by President Thomas Jefferson in reply to an inquiry from the Danbury Baptist Association. In that letter, Jefferson stated:

> Believing with you that religion is a matter which lies solely between man and his God: that he owes account to none other for his faith or his worship; that the legislative powers of the government reach actions only, and not opinions, I contemplate with sovereign reverence that act of the whole American people which declared that their legislature should make no law respecting an establishment of religion, or prohibiting the free exercise thereof, thus building a wall of separation between church and state.

Relying upon this phrase, which appears in no relevant legislative or constitutional document, the Court has construed the Establishment Clause to forbid a simple prayer acknowledging God that was required by the New York Board of Regents in public schools in 1962, the reading of the Bible in school classrooms in Maryland and Pennsylvania in 1963, a display of a crèche in the Allegheny County Courthouse in Pennsylvania during Christmas, and the inclusion of invocations and benedictions in the form of prayer in graduation ceremonies in Rhode Island public schools. Additionally, the Court declared unconstitutional a Rhode Island statute for the payment of salary supplements to teachers of secular subjects in non-public schools, an Alabama law providing for a daily period of silence in public schools for meditation of voluntary prayer, and a Louisiana statute providing for a balanced treatment of creation science and evolution science in public schools. Rather than protect individual freedom, these cases deny the right of individuals to voluntarily engage in an activity solely because of its "religious" content, even though no one is coerced to participate in the activity.

A distinguished lawyer once said that during closing arguments in every case a thread of truth could be found running throughout the evidence, and if one could only find that thread, one would then see the truth. The same can be said for these cases interpreting the Establishment Clause of the First Amendment. They have but one object in common – the removal of the knowledge of God from our society. Did Jefferson contemplate such a removal or separation of God and government? By choosing the phrase "wall of separation between church and state," did he truly mean that the government should in no way support religion?

LEGAL RESPONSES

Two civil actions were filed against Judge Moore, later combined into the case *Glassroth v. Moore*. A hearing on November 18, 2002, by the district court, determined that Moore had violated the Establishment Clause. On December 19, it entered a permanent injunction directing Moore to take down the monument. Moore appealed to the Eleventh Circuit Court of Appeals, which upheld the original judgment. Moore appealed to the Supreme Court, which refused to hear the case. The remaining eight chief justices of Alabama Supreme Court ordered the removal of the monument, and Moore was permanently removed from his position as Alabama chief justice. He later made an unsuccessful run for governor. The following is an excerpt from the November 18 ruling.

Source: www.FindLaw.com, *Glassroth v. Moore*, 11/18/02, 1–2, 18–19, 21–2, 27, 31–4.

The Establishment Clause of the First Amendment, made binding upon the States through the Fourteenth Amendment to the United States Constitution, provides that government "shall make no law respecting an establishment of religion." The question presented to this court is whether the Chief Justice of the Alabama Supreme Court violated the Establishment Clause when he placed a slightly over two-and-a-half ton granite monument – engraved with the Ten Commandments and other references to God – in the Alabama State Judicial Building with the specific purpose and effect, as the court finds from the evidence, of acknowledging the Judeo-Christian God as the moral foundation of our laws. To answer this question, the court applies two Supreme Court precedents: *Lemon v. Kurtzman*, 403 U. S. 602, 91 S. Ct. 2105 (1971), and *Marsh v. Chambers*, 463 U. S. 783, 103 S. Ct. 3330 (1983).

Based on the evidence presented during a week-long trial and for the reasons that follow, this court holds that the evidence is overwhelming and the law is clear that the Chief Justice violated the Establishment Clause. But, in announcing this holding today, the court believes it is important to clarify at the outset that the court does not hold that it is improper in all instances to display the Ten

Commandments in government buildings; nor does the court hold that the Ten Commandments are not important, if not one of the most important, sources of American law. Rather the court's limited holding, as will be explained below in more detail, is that the Chief Justice's actions and intentions in this case crossed the Establishment Clause line between the permissible and the impermissible.

With the standing issue resolved, the court moves to the heart of its Establishment Clause inquiry. For a practice to survive an Establishment Clause challenge, it "must have a secular legislative purpose, … its principal or primary effect must be one that neither advances nor inhibits religion, … [and it] must not foster 'an excessive government entanglement with religion.'" *Lemon v. Kurtzman*, 403 U. S. 602, 612–13, 91 S. Ct. 2105, 2111 (1971) (citations omitted). The plaintiffs contend that Chief Justice Moore's display of the monument fails this test, frequently called the *Lemon* test, in two ways: (1) his fundamental, if not sole, purpose in displaying the monument was non-secular; and (2) the monument's primary effect advances religion.

That Chief Justice Moore's purpose in displaying the monument was non-secular is self-evident. First, it is self-evident from his own words. At the monument's unveiling ceremony, the Chief Justice explained that the monument "serves to remind … that in order to establish justice we must invoke the favor and guidance of almighty God.'" He made clear that, in order to restore this moral foundation of law, "we must first recognize the source from which all morality springs … [by] recognizing the sovereignty of God" …

Chief Justice Moore's non-secular purpose is also evident from the monument itself. To be sure, "The Ten Commandments are undeniably a sacred text in the Jewish and Christian faiths, and no legislative recitation of a supposed secular purpose can blind us to that fact." *Stone v. Graham*, 449 U. S. 39, 41, 101 S. Ct. 192, 194 (1980) (per curiam). But, as the evidence in this case more than adequately reflected, the Ten Commandments have a secular aspect as well. Experts on both sides testified that the Ten Commandments were a foundation of American law, that America's founders looked to and relied on the Ten Commandments as a source of absolute moral standards. The second tablet, of course, is entirely secular – from "Thou shalt not kill" to "Thou shalt not covet" – but the first tablet also has secular aspects. As the Chief Justice pointed out in his speech unveiling the monument, Samuel Adams gave a speech, the day before signing the Declaration of Independence, referring to the King as a false idol, alluding to the Commandment that "Thou shalt have no other Gods before me."

While the secular aspect of the Ten Commandments can be emphasized, this monument, however, leaves no room for ambiguity about its religious appearance. Its sloping top and the religious air of the tablets unequivocally call to mind an open Bible resting on a podium. While the quotations on the monument's sides are non-Biblical, they still speak solely to non-secular matters, that is, to the importance of religion and the sovereignty of God in our society; these non-Biblical quotations are physically below and not on the same plane with the Biblical one. Further, there is the ineffable but still overwhelming sacred aura of the monument. As the court observed earlier, it was not surprising to learn that visitors and court employees found the monument to be an appropriate, and even compelling, place for prayer. The only way to miss the religious or non-secular appearance of the monument would be to walk through the Alabama State Judicial Building with one's eyes closed. The monument in the Alabama State Judicial Building is, therefore, dramatically different from other Ten Commandments displays in other government buildings and on other government land across the country.

... That the Ten Commandments monument's primary effect advances religion is also self-evident. To satisfy the second prong of the *Lemon* test, the challenged practice must have a "principal or primary effect ... that neither advances nor inhibits religion." *Lemon*, 403 US at 612, 91 S. Ct. at 2111.

... As discussed above, the monument's primary feature is the Ten Commandments, an "undeniably ... sacred text," *Stone v. Graham*, 449 U. S. 39, 41, 101 S. Ct. 192, 194 (1980), carved as tablets into the top of the monument. See *Indiana Civil Liberties Union v. O'Bannon*, 259 F. 3d 766, 772 (7th Cir. 2001) (recognizing additional religious significance when the Commandments are presented as tablet-shaped blocks), *cert. denied*, 534 US 1162, 122 S. Ct. 1173 (2002). The monument's sloping top and the religious air of tablets unequivocally call to mind an open Bible resting on a podium. While the quotations on the monument's sides are non-Biblical, the fact that they have been edited so as to emphasize the importance of religion and the sovereignty of God in our society fails to diminish, and even amplifies, the ineffable but still overwhelming holy aura of the monument ... Thus a reasonable observer, viewing this monument installed by the "Ten Commandments Judge" as a whole, would focus on the Ten Commandments, would find nothing on the monument to de-emphasize its religious nature, and would feel as though the State of Alabama is advancing or endorsing, favoring or preferring, Christianity ...

The Ten Commandments monument, viewed alone or in the context of its history, placement, and location, has the primary effect of endorsing religion. As such, the monument violates the second prong of the *Lemon* test, and it therefore violates the Establishment Clause.

SPORTING EVENTS AND RELIGIOUS EXPRESSION

High school cheerleaders in Fort Oglethorpe, Georgia regularly displayed signs with Bible verses on them as part of their rallying team spirit at football games. After a local resident voiced opposition, they were banned from the practice by the school system on September 28, 2009. Because the high school is a public school, any endorsement of religion is viewed as a violation of the First Amendment. This newspaper report is from Chattanooga, which is part of the same school district.

Source: *Chattanooga Times Free Press*: www.timesfreepress.com/news/2009/sep/29/cheerleaders-religious-signs-draw-fire/.

Community members are rallying around Lakeview-Fort Oglethorpe High School cheerleaders after they were banned from displaying signs with Bible verses urging fans and players to "commit to the Lord" and "take courage and do it."

The banners – the paper ones that football players crash through at the beginning of games – have been common sights in the school's football stadium since 2003, local officials say.

"The cheerleaders are not trying to push a religious cause, to shove religion down someone's throat," said local youth minister Brad Scott, who was LFO High's class president in 2004. "The cheerleaders are just using Scripture to show motivation and inspiration to the players and the fans."

Catoosa County Schools spokeswoman Marissa Brower said a Fort Oglethorpe resident lodged a verbal complaint to Superintendent Denia Reese last week, saying that the display of a Bible verse on the football field is a violation of federal law.

A school system statement released Monday said the message constitutes "a violation of the First Amendment of the Constitution for signs with Bible verses to be displayed on the football field."

Mr. Scott said the ban prompted a rally tonight in support of the cheerleaders outside the Chick-fil-A restaurant on Battlefield Parkway so people can show their support for the cheerleaders and their signs.

A Facebook page called "We support the LFO Cheerleaders! LET THEM HAVE THEIR SIGNS BACK!" has also been established.

Mrs. Reese lends her personal appreciation, if not her official support. "I regret that we had to ask the LFO cheerleaders to change the signs used in the stadium prior to football games," Mrs. Reese states, "Personally, I appreciate this expression of their Christian values; however, as superintendent, I have the responsibility of protecting the school district from legal action by groups who do not support their beliefs."

An area outside the stadium has been designated so the signs can be used there, she said.

"I rely on reading the Bible daily, and I would never deny our students the opportunity to express their religious beliefs," she said. "I appreciate that our community has rallied in support of this LFO tradition."

Fort Oglethorpe Mayor Ronnie Cobb vehemently disagrees with the ban and said he'll call on the City Council to support the cheerleaders and their signs.

"The signs don't infringe on anyone's religious rights and are good for school spirit. I'm totally against them doing away with it," Mr. Cobb said, adding that the cheerleaders' rights are being abused.

The mayor said football coach John Allen made the signs a tradition around 2003 and it has continued ever since.

"If it's offensive to anyone, let them go watch another football game," he said. "Nobody's forced to come there and nobody's forced to read the signs."

Current head football coach Todd Windham said the school system must obey the law, despite everyone's opinions.

"Just my standpoint, I thought the banners were unique," Mr. Windham said. "I really feel for the girls who prepare the banners and I think they really do a good job. They prepare a whole season's worth during the summer and they put in a lot of work on those."

However, officials say the school system's position centers on the trust between students' parents and what the system teaches.

"Families entrust public schools with the education of their children, but condition their trust on the understanding that the school activities will not purposely be used to advance religious views that may conflict with their religious beliefs," the system's release states. "As a result, the courts prohibit rabbi-led prayers at school sporting events, Wiccan posters in gymnasiums, reading the Quran over the school's public announcement system."

Catoosa officials say the US Supreme Court has "ruled that religious activities at high school football games create the 'inescapable conclusion' that the school endorses the religious activity."

Such violations open the system to "lawsuits resulting in injunctions, unnecessary legal costs and damages that have to be paid by the local taxpayers, and possibly the loss of federal funding," according to the statement.

Mr. Scott said the "separation of church and state" has nothing to do with cheerleaders who are not "part of the state" and simply want to offer an inspirational message with signs they made on their own time.

Mr. Scott, who ministers to some of the cheerleaders who attend his church, said the most recent sign he saw quoting from Timothy [sic] 1:7 could be considered inspirational in many settings.

"All those words; 'power, love, self-discipline' can be applied to the game, encourage other players and show school spirit," he said.

Local resident and 1992 LFO alum Jeremy Jones called the decision "premature."

"To act on the complaint of one person seems premature," Mr. Jones said. "The cheerleaders have raised their own money for this project and have worked hard to make these signs."

Several players were upset by the ruling and decided to hold a team prayer after they took the field last week, Mr. Windham said.

"That was something new, but it was something they wanted to do to show support for the cheerleaders," he said.

Following each game there is a player-led prayer, he said, but under their interpretation of the law, the coaches cannot lead a prayer.

VERSES IN EYE BLACK

During games throughout his college career, Tim Tebow, a football player for the University of Florida Gators, and winner of the Heisman trophy in 2007, referenced biblical verses in his eye black, which players wear to reduce glare. Fans tracked his successes and avidly searched the internet for each verse he displayed. Articles like "Evangelism Through Eye Black" (Wiley) appeared on the internet, matching each game to its biblical verse. The NCAA subsequently banned the practice. In his professional career, Tebow has worn plain eye black, minus any references.

Source: Phil Sandlin/AP/Press Association Images.

Figure 2.1 Tebow

REFERENCES

Wiley, Josh, "Evangelism Through Eye Black," www.associatedcontent.com/article/2546065/tim_tebow_bible_verses_game_by_game.html, 1/1/2010.

SUGGESTIONS FOR FURTHER RESEARCH

Barr, David L., and Nicholas Piediscalzi. 1982. *The Bible in American Education: From Source Book to Textbook*. Philadelphia, PA and Chico, CA: Fortress Press and Scholars Press.

Bellah, Robert. 1967. "Civil Religion in America." *Daedalus* 96: 1–21.

Bellah, Robert, and Phillip E. Hammond. 1980. *Varieties of Civil Religion*. San Francisco: Harper & Row.

Espinosa, Gastón. 2009. *Religion and the American Presidency: George Washington to George W. Bush*. New York: Columbia University Press.

Green, Steven K. 2010. *The Second Disestablishment: Church and State in Nineteenth-Century America*. New York: Oxford University Press.

Hall, David D., ed. 1990. *The Antinomian Controversy, 1636–1638: A Documentary History*. 2nd edn. Durham, NC: Duke University Press.

—— ed. 2004. *Puritans in the New World: A Critical Anthology*. Princeton, NJ: Princeton University Press.

Holmes, David L. 2006. *The Faiths of the Founding Fathers*. New York: Oxford University Press.

Hutson, James H. 2005. *The Founders on Religion: A Book of Quotations*. Princeton, NJ: Princeton University Press.

Johnson, James Turner. 1985. *The Bible in American Law, Politics, and Political Rhetoric*. Philadelphia, PA and Chico, CA: Fortress Press and Scholars Press.

Lambert, Frank. 2003. *The Founding Fathers and the Place of Religion in America*. Princeton, NJ: Princeton University Press.

Meacham, Jon. 2007. *American Gospel: God, the Founding Fathers, and the Making of a Nation*. New York: Random House.

Miller, Perry. 1956. *Errand into the Wilderness*. Cambridge, MA: Belknap Press.

Pottenger, John R. 2007. *Reaping the Whirlwind: Liberal Democracy and the Religious Axis*. Washington, DC: Georgetown University Press.

Seed, Patricia. 1995. *Ceremonies of Possession in Europe's Conquest of the New World, 1492–1640*. New York: Cambridge University Press.

Stout, Harry S. 1982. "Word and Order in Colonial New England." In N. O. Hatch and M. A. Noll, eds, *The Bible in America: Essays in Cultural History*. New York: Oxford University Press, 19–38.

Vowell, Sarah. 2008. *The Wordy Shipmates*. New York: Riverhead Books.

Wright, Louis B. 1943. *Religion and Empire: The Alliance Between Piety and Commerce in English Expansion, 1558–1625*. Chapel Hill: The University of North Carolina Press.

3   The Bible and America's great debates

When Fannie Lou Hamer (1917–77) is beaten in jail in 1963 for trying to register to vote, she tells her jailer it will be miserable for him when he has to face God, since Scripture says God "hath made of one blood all the nations of men for to dwell on all the face of the earth" (Acts 17:26 KJV). In denying her humanity because she is African American, he goes against Scripture. The jailer's only defense is to call it a lie, incorrectly attributing the verse to Abraham Lincoln. She also says that God sent a man to Mississippi to fight for their freedom, the same man that sent Moses to Egypt to bring out Israel. He would go down to Mississippi and tell Ross Barnett (the segregationist governor of Mississippi) to "Let my people go."

In weaving together her own experiences in the Civil Rights movement with biblical narratives and verses, Hamer shows some of the ways the Bible participates in the great social movements of American history. Above all, for her and others in the movement, it provides an alternative narrative to the one offered by a surrounding hostile society. Many of the groups discussed in this chapter understand themselves as a beleaguered and misunderstood minority, who nevertheless speak the truth. For these groups the Bible also provides a mine of proof-texts that can be brought out to bolster their claims. This means privileging of some texts and ignoring of others, creating a "canon within the canon." These claims often contain a sense of returning to origins, that their views reflect "the way it is supposed to be," as laid out in the creation stories in Genesis, the Exodus experience, the stories of the earliest church, or other founding narratives.

Not everyone feels the immediacy of Scripture. For some, like the opponents of slavery, or those who defend same-sex relationships, the distance between the ancient context and later society means the texts may not be read quite so literally. Individual words are scrutinized and parsed, to show that the meanings in the biblical context are not the same as in later usage. Finally, our selections show that the question "What would Jesus do?" is not a recent one. Many debates included attempts to prove Jesus' teaching on social issues like slavery, homosexuality, and women's rights, despite the absence of explicit statements. Paul, who seemed to have much more to say on many of these matters, could be a help or a hindrance, depending on one's argument, but he had to be accounted for.

As Americans struggled with social and political questions of their day, they looked to the Bible as an authoritative source of truth. To mine its riches, they used many methods: typology, or using a biblical person as a general character type, analyzing a certain word for multiple meanings, symbolism, comparison of different voices in the text, amplifying the teachings of Jesus and Paul from their examples, attributing unwelcome readings to the effects of culture on transmission and interpretation, and more. But the Bible did not simply speak to society and its problems: social movements affected the Bible. In bringing scriptural verses to bear on questions like slavery or the emancipation of women, a straight literalist reading could not stand. People questioned the Bible itself as a source of truth, wondered about the premises of interpretation, and compared it to the other repository of truth, science.

During the period of slavery, the Bible was invoked by both pro-slavery and anti-slavery advocates, while providing the tropes of liberation for the African Americans suffering under its yoke. Other factors, like racism, "scientific" inquiries into racial differences, belief in the inferiority of the African, patriarchalism, social and economic structures, mixed with biblical arguments to form a rationale for slavery. Fidelity to Scripture became associated with the pro-slavery position. It cited the patriarchs who owned slaves, laws of biblical slavery, and engaged in tortured exegesis of passages like Gen 9:20–28, where the curse of Canaan for his father Ham's sin becomes a permanent curse of servitude on the African race. Emancipation did not end the argument, as numerous pro- and anti-slavery tracts are written after the Civil War, some blaming the depressed social condition of blacks on Emancipation, others pinning responsibility on the legacy of slavery itself. A pernicious theory of polygenesis, or different origins as species of the different races, appears as late as 1902, in Charles Carroll's *The Tempter of Eve*. The serpent in the Garden of Eden is identified as a pre-human (therefore sub-human) ancestor of the African races, trying to seduce the nubile Eve. Both Carroll and A. Hoyle Lester, who appears below, are motivated by a horror of miscegenation, a mixing of the races.

Supporters of slavery argued that abolitionists were unbiblical. Indeed, some abolitionists, like William Lloyd Garrison, the editor of the anti-slavery newspaper *The Liberator*, saw slavery as such a moral evil that, if the Bible supported it, it meant the Bible was wrong. Most nineteenth-century people were not willing to go that far, however, and argued that Scripture rejected slavery. Their counter-arguments included the claims that biblical examples of slavery were not the same as American slavery, the word "slave" really means "servant," and that the spirit of the Bible rejects slavery even if the letter does not. Although Jesus did not preach against slavery, his radical egalitarian ethic was a "seed growing secretly" (a term of J. Albert Harrill's) that would eventually destroy the institution. Paul's statements that seem to accommodate slavery are overwhelmed by the principle of Gal 3:28, "there is no longer Jew or Greek, there is no longer slave or free, there is no longer male and female; for all of you are one in Christ Jesus."

While biblical verses that "proved" slavery were preached to the slaves on plantations by white missionaries, the slaves themselves drew on the root narrative of the Exodus, God's deliverance of the Hebrew slaves, his rescue of characters like Daniel, the motif of exile and wandering as analogue for escape to freedom, and the ultimate vanquishing of the evil-doers by Jesus in Revelation. Frederick Douglass describes the liberating power of learning to read the Bible, fulfilling his master's fear that "it will unfit him to be a slave."

Abolitionism brought feminism in its wake. Many of the same people who battled slavery with their public speaking, writing, and organizing quite naturally expanded the battle to women's rights, especially suffrage, the right to vote. Influenced by Enlightenment ideas of individual rights and Reason, at times filtered through reading the classic *A Vindication of the Rights of Women*, published by Mary Wollstonecraft in 1792, some rejected religion as an impediment to women, while others made the Bible central to their rhetoric. The extended commentary by Elizabeth Cady Stanton and others, *The Woman's Bible* (1895, 1898), for example, provoked criticism from both sides. Some found its critique of the Bible too severe, while others wondered why scripture was given a hearing at all.

Feminists used some of the same methods used by abolitionists: typology, philology, the scrutinizing of particular words, and the spirit over letter argument. They further identified different sources and underscored the negative effects of culture on interpretation. The Creation story in Gen 1 showed the essential equality of men and women, whereas the second version in Gen 2 belonged to some wily editor, or held Eve and Adam equally guilty. Every biblical woman of power is held up as a model. Jesus provides a powerful example in his positive treatment of the women around him. Frances Willard, below, argues some women are his disciples, an insight now accepted by most contemporary New Testament scholars. Paul, too, evidences women as fellow-preachers and teachers, while some of his more troubling statements are explained away. Even more than the abolitionists, the feminist interpreters often repaired to philological arguments and separated the inherent meaning of Scripture from the hands of the authors and editors. They partook of some of the newer historical-critical methods of the second half of the nineteenth century. They anticipated the debate over the inerrancy of Scripture that would flare up at the end of the nineteenth century and remain with us to this day.

In spite of the historic relationship between abolitionism and feminism, the battle to end slavery and extend the vote to African Americans and the battle to extend the vote to women sometimes worked against black women. They were excluded by virtue of their sex from the Fifteenth Amendment, which gave men of their race the right to vote, but excluded from parts of the suffrage movement by virtue of their race. Leaders like Mary Church Terrell, Ida Wells-Barnett, and Frances Harper formed the National Association of Colored Women in 1896 to improve the situation of black women, but also because they were excluded from the growing number of women's clubs. In 1903, the National American Women's Suffrage Association agreed to let individual states determine their own policies on women's suffrage, thus guaranteeing that African American women in the South would be denied the vote.

If the Bible has been an indispensable tool for different perspectives in America's great debates leading up to, during, and ever since the Civil War, that most acute of national crises also marks a shift in the Bible's position in collective discussions of political and social affairs. During the sixty years following the Civil War, not only did Americans draw on Scripture to defend conflicting ideas but also vigorously debated the status of the Bible itself.

Affected by the unique experiences of the political and social experiment they had undertaken and increasingly aware of developing methods of scientific and historical investigation, many Americans began to wonder aloud in what ways Scripture was true. By the 1820s, new approaches to the study of the Bible began to make their way from Europe into the halls of American theology. Often linked to the legacy of the great German theologian Friedrich Schleiermacher (1768–1834), these new methods came to be identified as "the German theories," "the historical-critical methods," or, most famously, "Higher Criticism."

By the 1880s, the historical-critical methods had taken hold in the United States and generated fierce debates among biblical scholars about the accuracy of the Bible. As seen in the selections below, questions and claims about the nature of biblical truth generated dramatic shifts, both personal and collective. Religious leaders had to rethink their previous conceptions of the Bible and were forced to defend them or to adopt profoundly different perspectives. Within religious institutions, factions formed. Denominations split. Previously established authorities were censured and kicked out. Some leaders – and, with them, the Bible itself – were put on trial. Still, the foundations of non-literalist interpretation had taken root, and historical criticism emerged as a hallmark of biblical scholarship and of so-called "Modernism."

By the beginning of the twentieth century, the tensions among scholars and religious authorities over the truth-status of the Bible continued to ripple far and wide through the public sphere. By 1910, some California gentlemen – flush with money from the burgeoning oil trade – considered the Modernist assault on the Bible so serious that they put up a chunk of their fortune to enlist some of the world's most recognized biblical scholars in a global campaign to defend and to restore Scripture to what they considered its rightful place. The multi-volume paperbacks, *The Fundamentals*, resulted from these efforts by the Stewart brothers, and in producing the books those two American entrepreneurs, brothers in life and in the Christian cause, helped give shape – and a name – to a broad, anti-"Modernism" counter-movement that gained popular recognition by the 1920s as "Fundamentalism."

While the controversies surrounding the Bible's truth-status morphed from scholarly debates in the late 1800s about the validity of "Higher Criticism" to the face-off in the 1920s between "Modernism" and "Fundamentalism," one issue in particular remained a primary battleground throughout: the theory of evolution. After all, Darwin's explanation of the development of humankind, beginning with his discussions of common descent and natural selection in *The Origin of Species* (1859), undermined literalist views of Genesis. By positing that humans and all other species evolved through a process of natural selection, Darwin appeared to contradict the account of the origins of life that unfolds in the Bible's first chapters and on which all other scriptural claims ostensibly build. Thus, in the minds of opponents and proponents alike, historical-critical approaches to the Bible connected directly with evolutionary theory. Attacking or defending Higher Criticism was attacking or defending the theory of evolution. Nevertheless, most defenders of the critical/evolutionary approaches refused to concede that acceptance of the new historical perspectives amounted to an abandonment of the Bible as repository of fundamental truth. Instead, the historical critics/evolutionists – those marked by opponents as unrepentant "Modernists" – insisted on a more figurative, rather than literal, accuracy in Scripture. In fact, as the included selections suggest, many (if not most) of the participants in the debates over evolution and scriptural authority occupied common ground by virtue of a shared insistence that history did (and would) bear out the Bible's most profound claims.

By the third decade of the twentieth century, the most acute question became, "What, and how, should our children learn about evolution and about the Bible?" What began in the mid-nineteenth century primarily as debates among specialists, by the early 1920s reached a crisis where participants cast the future of civilization itself as at stake. The teaching of evolution was metonymy for the inculcation in children of ideas about the truth (or untruth) of the Bible. This context produced the Scopes Trial, one of the most famous courtroom dramas in American history. The debates over evolution, its relation to the truth-status of the Bible, and the place of evolution and the Bible in public education continued after that famous July 1925 showdown – described by the historian Willard B. Gatewood as "Modernists and Fundamentalists at Armageddon" – but the public discourse passed into another phase.

Other issues claimed the attention of Bible-reading Americans. After the Civil War, the Industrial Revolution and the expansion of commerce and industry created a "gilded age," a luxurious lifestyle for the wealthy few. But workers in factories, shipyards, and other places of manual labor crowded into unhealthy slums. The city became a symbol of exploitation, political corruption, and suffering. Religiously motivated groups responded with a series of reforms: support for labor unions, laws against child labor, free public education, temperance, soup kitchens, and more. The "social gospel" rejected an other-worldly orientation and sought to create the "kingdom of God" on earth. Emulating Jesus' example, it taught his followers to feed the hungry, clothe the naked, to indict wealth gained by exploiting the poor and working classes. These thinkers, including Walter Rauschenbusch and Josiah Strong, were less concerned with questions of biblical inerrancy than with human experience as the only grounding for biblical faith. Consumption of alcohol also was seen by many as a moral threat, destructive to families and individuals. Organizations like the Women's Christian Temperance Union rarely concerned themselves solely with the evils of liquor, but promoted a larger program of social reform. Frances Willard, the president of WCTU, could hardly argue that the Bible forbade all alcohol, but employed creative exegesis to promote temperance, women's equality and a "do-everything" policy of creating a better society.

The Civil Rights movement arose in the black churches of the South. While in 1903 W.E.B. Dubois predicted race would be the main problem of the twentieth century, he considered the Bible a mixed blessing for African Americans, since it could be used to promote passive submission to injustice as well as liberation. By the middle of the century, however, it seemed the Civil Rights movement had taken sole possession of the Bible. While the occasional segregationist tried to invoke biblical themes, they were not taken seriously by many. Opponents to equality turned more often to the Constitution, particularly the laws protecting states' rights. Preachers like Fannie Lou Hamer and Martin Luther King Jr, on the other hand, wove together biblical stories of God's liberation of the slaves of the Exodus, rescue of Daniel, the example of Jesus, Paul, the Good Samaritan, and statements of the equality of all people like Acts 17:26 with their own experiences fighting for freedom. Hamer is famous for the song "This Little Light of Mine," which is based on Matt 5:14–16.

The understanding of the Exodus story as the liberation brought by God to the oppressed forms the basis of black liberation theology. James Cone, who grew up an African American in the segregated South, was trained in the traditions of white Protestant theology. He developed a theology that formally acknowledged the understanding of black experience in light of God's actions as liberator in the Bible.

Contemporary movements continue to draw strength from the Bible. Painful public breaches over gay marriage and the ordination of gay/lesbian clergy have regularly invoked the Bible. From the placard at a gay rights rally, "Don't talk to me about Leviticus unless you've sacrificed a goat today," to more intricate discussions of the meanings of Greek words for different kinds of homosexual activity, Scripture is used in the same ways as in earlier controversies. The "Manhattan Declaration: A Call of Christian Conscience," released in November, 2009, signed by prominent evangelicals, Catholics, and Orthodox leaders, called for public acknowledgment of religion, and affirmed positions on marriage, abortion, assisted suicide, homosexuality, poverty relief, and more. In rejecting gay marriage, it invoked the Creation story (Gen 2:23–24) and the earliest church (Eph 5:32–33), employing a familiar argument of return to origins. Environmentalism, while not primarily a religious movement, contains within it Jews and Christians who argue from a religious perspective of God's created world as sacred. International sex trafficking, a modern form of slavery, is the target of several religious groups, particularly evangelicals. The drives to eliminate war, hunger, and poverty contain some groups that argue from a biblical perspective. The Bible remains a vital resource as Americans continue to engage in social and political debate.

SLAVERY AND ABOLITIONISM: PRO-SLAVERY ARGUMENTS

THE SIN OF HAM

> An anonymous pamphlet from 1860, *African Servitude*, presents a popular argument that the slavery of the African peoples emanated from the curse against Canaan, the son of Ham, in retaliation for the sin of Ham's dishonoring his father Noah. The sin and the curse appear in a somewhat ambiguous passage (Genesis 9:18–29). Yet slavery advocates present it as a permanent curse, endorsed by God.
>
> Source: *African Servitude* (New York: Davies and Kent, 1860), 5, 8–9. From *Sabin Americana Digital Collection*. © Gale, a part of Cengage Learning, Inc. Reproduced by permission.

… Noah became a husbandman, planted a vineyard, and, partaking too freely of the fruit of the vine, exposed himself to shame. The Scriptures do not state that he was guilty of anything more than an act of imprudence. In his exposed state he was discovered by his younger son, probably his grandson Canaan, who informed his father Ham, and one or both of them, so far from seeking or expressing grief for the dishonor of their parent, exultingly informed others of it, glorying in his shame, despising his power and authority, and his office as ruler and priest of God to them and the rest of their father's family, lightly esteeming also his parental blessing, as well as the blessing of God.

A true spirit of filial regard, love, honor, and obedience moved Shem and Japheth to protect their father just the reverse of that which influenced their brother Ham to dishonor him. On the part of the former, it was an act of faith; of the latter, unbelief. The sin of Ham was not only great, but aggravated. He was probably more than six-score years old; for Canaan, his fourth son, all born after the flood, must have been old enough to discern between right and wrong, to have received the curse that fell upon him …

… That there might not in after-ages be any mistake or doubt upon whom the curse was laid, it would seem that the Almighty put upon the descendants of Ham, not only the black mark of disobedience and condemnation to service, but also prepared and adapted both mind and body for the service required of them.

The fall, or defection of Ham, considered in all its results, is one of the most, if not the most, important event to the human race that has transpired since the flood; save, always, the advent and death of the Saviour, the great event of the universe.

Before this important event (the fall of Ham) it might be truly said that "all men were born free and equal" in rights and privileges, but after the curse, who shall say, in opposition to God's Word, that there is an equality in conditions, rights, and privileges of all the inhabitants of the earth?

To assert that *all* men are born free and equal in rights, privileges, and conditions, is to say what every man of common sense knows to be untrue. To assert that *all* men ought to be, is to call in question the wisdom and goodness of God. To say that *all* men will be, is to declare that which has not yet been revealed.

Let us take the history of the world as we find it recorded in the Bible and other approved books, and we shall find that this condition or dispensation of servitude resting upon the children of Ham, as far back as we have any authentic history of the race after the flood.

Those old patriarchs, Abraham, Isaac, and Jacob, had their servants, or bond men and women, in great numbers. A system of servitude had already, at that time, become a known and established condition in society.

We find, in times past, the prophetic declarations of the Patriarch Noah have been fulfilled, and that the curse and the blessing extend to our day, and are still in process of fulfillment according to God's sure Word.

The venerable Dr. Mede says: "There never has been a son of Ham who has shaken a scepter over the head of Japheth. Shem has subdued Japheth, and Japheth has subdued Shem, but Ham never subdued either."

That inspired servant of God and prototype of our Saviour, by the command of God, gave to the children of Israel the following permission, direction, and command, as found in Leviticus xxv.44–46; "Both thy bondmen, and thy bondmaids, which thou shalt have, shall be of the heathen that are round about you; of them shall ye buy, and of their families that are with you, which they begat in your land: and they shall be your possession. And ye shall take them as an inheritance for your children after you, to inherit them for a possession; they shall be your bondmen forever: but over your brethren the children of Israel, ye shall not rule one over another with rigor."

Here the Israelites have full permission from the Almighty to buy, hold, and use forever the services of the heathen, or Canaanites, about them, who were descendants of Ham ...

SLAVERY AND THE NEW TESTAMENT

If the Hebrew Bible could be mined to support slavery, repairing to the New Testament would prove equally useful. Literalists observe that Jesus never condemns slavery, and assumes its existence in some of the parables (e.g. Luke 12:42–47). Paul seems to endorse it. A widely circulated pro-slavery tract by the Virginia minister Thornton Stringfellow, published in 1856, invokes Jesus, Paul, and strangely, the Golden Rule.

Source: Thornton Stringfellow, *Scriptural and Statistical Views in Favor of Slavery* (1856), electronic edition, *Documenting the American South*, University Library, University of North Carolina at Chapel Hill: http://docsouth.unc.edu.

Having shown from the Scriptures that slavery existed with Abraham and the patriarchs, with divine approbation, and having shown from the Scriptures that the Almighty incorporated it in the law, as an institution among Abraham's seed, until the coming of Christ, our precise object now is to ascertain if *Jesus Christ has abolished it, or recognized it as a lawful relation*, existing among men, and prescribed duties which belong to it, as he has other relations such as those between husband and wife, parent and child, magistrate and subject.

And first, I may take it for granted, without proof, that he has not abolished it by commandment, for none pretend to this. This, by the way, is a singular circumstance, that Jesus Christ should put a system of measures into operation, which have for their object the subjugation of all men to him as a law-giver – kings, legislators, and private citizens in all nations; at a time, too, when hereditary slavery existed in all; and after it had been incorporated for fifteen hundred years into the Jewish constitution, immediately given by God himself, I say, it is passing strange, that under such circumstances, Jesus should fail to prohibit its further existence, if it was his intention to abolish it. Such an omission or oversight cannot be charged upon any other legislator the world has ever seen. But, says the Abolitionist, he has introduced new moral principles, which will extinguish it as unavoidable consequence, without a direct prohibitory command. What are they? "Do unto others as you would they should do to you." Taking these words of Christ to be a body inclosing a moral soul in them, what soul, I ask, is it?

The same embodied in these words of Moses, Lev 19:18, "thou shalt love thy neighbor as thyself;" or is it another? It cannot be another, but it must be the very same, because Jesus says, there are but two principles in being in God's moral government, one including all that is *due to God,* the *other all that is due to men.*

If, therefore, doing unto others as we would they should do to us, means precisely what loving our neighbor as ourself means, then Jesus has added no new moral principle above those in the law of Moses, to prohibit slavery for in his law is found this principle, and slavery also.

The very God that said to them, they should love him supremely, and their neighbors as themselves said to then also, "of the heathen that are round about you, thou shalt buy bond-men and bond-women, and they shall be your possession, and ye shall take them as an inheritance for your children after you to inherit them as a possession; they shall be your bond-men forever." Now, to suppose that Jesus Christ left his disciples to find out, without a revelation, that slavery must be abolished, as a natural consequence from the fact that when God established the relation of master and servant under the law, he said to the master and servant, each of you must love the other as yourself, is, to say the least, making Jesus to presume largely upon the intensity of their intellect, that they would be able to spy out a discrepancy in the law of Moses, which God himself never saw …

… Now for the proof: To the church planted at Ephesus, the capital of lesser Asia, Paul ordains by letter subordination in the fear of God – first between wife and husband; second, child and parent; third, servant and master; all as statutes or conditions, existing among the members.

The relative duties of each state are pointed out; those between the servant and master in these words; "Servants be obedient to them who are your masters according to the flesh, with fear and trembling, in singleness of your heart as unto Christ; not with eye service as men pleasers, but as the servants of Christ, doing the will of God from the heart, with good will, doing service, as to the Lord and not to men, knowing that whatsoever good thing any man doeth, the same shall he receive of the Lord, whether he be bond or free. And ye masters do the same things to them, forebearing threatening, knowing that your master is also in heaven, neither is there respect of persons with him."

To the church at Colosse, a city of Phrygia, in the lesser Asia, – Paul in his letter to them, recognizes the three relations of wives and husbands, parents and children, servants and masters, as relations existing among the members; (here the Roman law was the same;) and to the servants and masters he thus writes, "Servants obey in all things your masters, according to the flesh: not with eye service, as men pleasers, but in singleness of heart, fearing God: and whatsoever you do, do it heartily, as to the Lord and not into men; knowing that of the lord Ye shall receive the reward of the inheritance, for ye serve the Lord Christ. But he that doeth wrong shall receive for the wrong he has done; and there is no respect of persons with God. Masters give unto you servants that which is just and equal, knowing that you also have a master in heaven."

SLAVE OWNERS' PUBLICATIONS

A curious set of voices within the institution of slavery comes from the agricultural journals of the antebellum South. Planters wrote articles proffering advice on "slave management." A highly paternalistic picture emerges, with masters claiming to love their slaves, appreciate them as "immortal beings," and arguing that a certain amount of religion is beneficial. Yet the power of literacy and the Bible's potentially subversive themes is not lost on slave-holders. An uneasiness about the possibilities of slaves hearing preaching or reading the Bible for themselves echoes through these texts. The following excerpts from the editor of a Mississippi farm publication (1843) and a Louisiana planter illustrate a set of mixed attitudes.

Source: James Breeden, *Advice among Masters. Slave Management in the Old South*, 225–7, 232. Copyright © 1980 by Greenwood Press. Reproduced with permission of ABC-CLIO, LLC.

The fanatics of the North and of foreign countries have no idea of the deep anxiety entertained by our planters upon the subject announced at the head of this article [the moral culture of slaves]. The slaves on our large plantations are not regarded by us as so many beasts of burden or dumb brutes, as is often falsely stated; but they are regarded by the owner, provided he be an intelligent and upright man, as moral beings whose welfare, both mental and bodily, are entrusted to his charge by an all-wise Providence. To him they look up, not only for food and clothing – but for such instruction, by precept and example, as will give a stamp, either for good or evil, to their characters. Principles, either salutary or pernicious, are at the foundation of all conduct – and even slaves may be taught to do right on principle. Let no one sneer at this – for it is among the colored race – to say whether we utter anything absurd – nay, whether we tell not that which is as clear as a sunbeam – that a negro can, by proper instruction, be taught to act right, *from principle*.

This being premised – which, we have no doubt, will be admitted by all our readers – a question arises which, of course, will be solved in many different ways – that is – how shall the minds of slaves be operated upon so as to instill into them correct principles of action?

On this principle we have reflected much, and we have inquired much of those who have had the best opportunities of judging, and the result is that we are confirmed more strongly than ever in the opinion we have long entertained that the best way to operate upon their minds is *through religious truth*. The reasons of our opinion it is hardly necessary to give, we presume, for we think that the most of our readers are men who believe and acknowledge the divine origin of the scripture.

The great duty, then, to be performed is – not to convince the Mississippi[ans] of the importance of instructing their slaves in the principles of religion – but to point out the best methods. Here, happily, we are not left in the dark to grope our way with untried theories – for many planters, both in this state and Louisiana, have long been pursuing a systematic plan in this matter, and as we are happy to learn, with the most pleasing results. Indeed, so far back as 1835, when the lamentable excitement took place in this country in consequence of the mad schemes of the negro's worst enemy, Abolitionism, measures were in extensive progress upon many of our plantations, which bade fair to produce highly beneficial effects upon our black population. But the benevolent schemes of our planters were nipped in the bud, and the melioration of the moral condition of their servants was set back at least ten years.

To instruct our negroes in the truths of the Bible, it is not necessary to teach them to read. By mere oral instruction, they have, in many instances, become well versed in the doctrinal, perceptive, and especially in the historical parts of the sacred writings – also in the catechisms – while, in the committing of hymns to memory, in learning sacred music, and in other devotional exercises, their quickness is proverbial. We well recollect hearing a negro preacher, a slave, many years ago, who went through all the usual clerical exercises with considerable cleverness – giving out his hymns, line by line – announcing his text, and directing his audience to chapter and verse – all this, too, without using any book, and without being able to read if he had had one.

To us, it would be most gratifying to travel around for a while from plantation to plantation in those sections where a systematic course of religious instruction is pursued, for we believe that a publication of the facts which might thus be obtained would be one of the most acceptable, because most profitable, services we could perform to the agricultural community. Such a tour, however, is impracticable – and we must therefore appeal to others, who are conversant with facts to correspond with us and furnish us, for publication, with such information and such suggestions in regard to this subject, as may benefit the public ...

In indulging a lively wish for the religious instruction of our servants – in the desire to see a solemn *duty* performed – it is gratifying to know, at the same time, that we are only urging a measure of *interest* – the interest of the owners and the community at large. And we earnestly hope that self-interest, if no other consideration, will open the way for ministers to enter more generally, and more frequently, and with more devotedness, upon this interesting field of labor.

... No negro preachers but my own will be permitted to preach or remain on any of my places.

The regularly appointed minister for my places must preach on Sundays during daylight, or quit.

The negroes must not be suffered to continue their night meetings beyond ten o'clock.

A SLAVE CATECHISM

Instruction of the slaves sometimes took the form of teaching them from slave catechisms, whose short question and answer form was tailored to oral instruction and memorization.

Source: *Frederick Douglass' Paper*, June 2, 1854, from the *Southern Episcopalian*, Charleston, SC, April, 1854. Reprinted in Leslie Fishel and Benjamin Quarles, eds, *The Black American: A Documentary History* (New York: William Morrow [Scott Foresman] 1970), 114.

Q   Who keeps the snakes and all bad things from hurting you?
A   God does.
Q   Who gave you a master and a mistress?
A   God gave them to me.
Q   Who says that you must obey them?
A   God says that I must.
Q   What book tells you these things?
A   The Bible.
Q   How does God do all his work?
A   He always does it right.
Q   Does God love to work?
A   Yes, God is always at work.
Q   Do the angels work?
A   Yes, they do what God tells them.
Q   Do they love to work?
A   Yes, they love to please God.
Q   What does God say about your work?
A   He that will not work shall not eat.
Q   Did Adam and Eve have to work?
A   Yes, they had to keep the garden.
Q   Was it hard to keep that garden?
A   No, it was very easy.
Q   What makes the crops so hard to grow now?
A   Sin makes it.

Q   What makes you lazy?
A   My wicked heart.
Q   How do you know your heart is wicked?
A   I feel it every day.
Q   Who teaches you so many wicked things?
A   The Devil.
Q   Must you let the Devil teach you?
A   No, I must not.

AFTER EMANCIPATION

Polygenesis, the idea that Africans and other races descended not from Adam, but from another pre-human ancestor, appears in a number of writers, despite its outright contradiction of the curse of Canaan theory. A dubious science of ethnology arose in the mid-nineteenth century, which investigated racial differences and origins, ranking the value of the races. This material and the attendant controversy continued after the Civil War and Emancipation, into the twentieth century. It displays a measure of horror at the idea of miscegenation, or mixing of the races. In this example, by A. Hoyle Lester published in 1875, the potent mix of racism, sexuality, and fear is evident in the identification of the black seducer with the serpent in the Garden of Eden.

Source: A. Hoyle Lester, *The Pre-Adamite, or Who Tempted Eve?* (Philadelphia, PA: Lippincott, 1874), 20–1, 23–4, 33, 46.

The Pre-Adamite, or Who Tempted Eve?

"Say first of God above, or man below,
Of man what see we but his station here,
From which to reason or to which refer."

It is highly probable that there may have existed a dozen or more distinct races of the genus homo, and they may be in existence now! Still, it answers our purpose to recognize only five races, as this subdivision has already been made, and is sanctioned by ethnologists of our age. They have, however, almost universally been traced back to the same ancestor, under a belief of the unity of the races, which theory attaches itself like an incubus to the fair Caucasian, and brings a blush to the cheek of intelligent beauty. I would wipe this stain from our escutcheon, and set at right the inquiring mind, as regards the error in question ...

... He was named Adam because he was red, of a ruddy countenance. He was the father of the blushing race. Created He him in his own image and likeness. The only immortal soul beneath the wide-expanded canopy of heaven to whose cheeks gushed the crimson blood to manifest the intense shame of conscious guilt! and if the darker races blush, with whom we claim no kindred blood, then like the wild-flower in its native wilderness, it blushes unseen and wastes its virtue on the desert air. The side of Adam gave birth to Eve, the mother of all living; and she, the fairest queen that ever graced the courts of the earth, made her debut on the arena of life in the romantic shades of Eden ... Imagine her surprise; innocent and unsuspecting, she meets a stranger, the serpent who had beheld her beauty (for Eve, at this unlucky hour, was not arrayed in the habiliments of modern style). She felt lonely, and was surprised to meet this handsome stranger amidst the solitudes of Eden's bower. Knowing little of this world save her own innocence, and unaware of the great gulf that lay between God and the fallen races that preceded her, she listened with attentive ear to the enchanting conversation of this son of perdition. He belonged most assuredly to the highest order of the inferior races, around whom our heavenly Father had thrown the benign influences of his exalted nature, and had offered time and again to make them sons and priests unto God, and they rejected the proffered mercy ...

Who was this serpent that beguiled our first parents? In our language it could not be the snake, or the viper, that besets our pathway and strikes into our flesh the fangs that bring death by the venom infused into the system. By no means! Does the adder speak, or does the boa-constrictor give utterance to language? Preposterous thought! The fall of man as revealed to us in Genesis is no metaphor. Consider, kind reader, a venomous reptile approaching a lovely maiden, do hold gentle converse in the silent wood: would she take the accursed reptile to her bosom and associate with him day after day and week after week? Never! even though his hissing voice had the melody of the enchanting siren. His shape and his demeanor in aping a deceiver would carry with it the nause-ating venom, at which the native modesty and timidity of the first Caucasian damsel would have revolted, and she like the affrighted hare before its pursuers, would have fled from its presence, and sought refuge under the protecting aegis of her Lord. then tell us not that the devil approached our first mother in the form of a snake, as seen in the so-called sacred pictures of the passing age.

But he did present himself to Eve in the form and likeness of a man, one of Mongolia's comeliest sons. He came possessed of all the attributes of the evil genius of perdition, clothed from head to heel with the accumulated curses of an avenging God. ... Eve, poor woman, yielded to the evil machinations of this seductive deceiver. She rose from the mossy couch a wiser but fallen crea-ture, and returned to the presence of her lawful companion disrobed of virtue, that precious jewel, the brightest ornament of her sex ... From this intercourse or intimacy that subsisted between this son of perdition and the fair consort of Adam arose the mongrel offspring who bears in the Bible the name of Cain, the vile monster who watered the earth with the blood of his brother Abel. View him as the descendant of the Asiatic nomad or pre-Adamite, and we are not surprised that his offering was rejected by the Lord, or that the inherent instincts of his nature should find vent in the life-blood of so near a relative; and, in consequence of this deed, the vengeance of high heaven was visited on this fratricide.

... "There were giants in the earth in those days; and also after that, when the sons of God came in unto the daughters of men, and they bare children to them, the same became mighty men which were of old, men of renown (Gen 6:4)." There were giants in the earth in those days prior to the intermarriage of the sons of God and the daughters of men; and if so, from whom did they descend? Their progenitors certainly must have been of an earlier stock and different from our first parents ... [The Flood story follows.] It is forcibly presented why God would destroy this people, because of the amalgamation of the races ...

... The most striking difference found to exist among the various types of the human family is observed in the facial angle of the skull; and by measurement it is established that the facial angle of the Caucasian is larger than the corresponding angle in either of the lower tribes of our species, which illustrates the never-to-be forgotten fact that larger space for brain is allotted to the Adamic race, for purposes of intellectuality and the practice of virtue, and less for the brutal passions and native instincts of our nature, than is developed even in the highest type of the Mongolian ... and in the peculiar formation of the skull of the inferior tribes of Africa, the least space is allotted for the development of brain, for the exhibition of intellect, the basis of moral worth, goodness, and excellence.

SLAVERY AND ABOLITIONISM: ANTI-SLAVERY ARGUMENTS

THE BARNES HYPOTHESIS

Presbyterian minister Albert Barnes wrote a detailed refutation of pro-slavery uses of the Bible which was published in 1856. His contextualizing of slavery in the time of the patriarchs would anticipate historical criticism, which emerged a few decades later. He claimed that the word "slave" carried varied and different meanings in the time of the Old, and especially New, Testaments. Thus Onesimus, whom Paul sends back to his master, is not a slave, and Paul never condoned slavery. This distancing of biblical references to slavery from American slavery was dubbed "the Barnes Hypothesis."

Source: Albert Barnes, *An Inquiry into the Scriptural Views of Slavery* (Philadelphia, PA: Perkins and Purvis, 1846), 64–7, 181–2, 243, 323, 368–70, 381.

In order now adequately to understand what was the real character of the servitude which existed among the patriarchs, on which so much reliance is placed by those who attempt to sustain the system by an appeal to the Bible, it is of the utmost importance to understand what is the exact sense of the word used to designate this relation in the Scriptures. If the word rendered *servant* in the Old Testament necessarily means *slave* in the modern sense of the term, it will do something to settle the question whether slavery as it now exists is in accordance with the will of God. It must be *assumed* by those who bring the example of the patriarchs in support of slavery, that the word had the same signification then which it has now; for if the word, as used in their times, meant an essentially different thing from what it does now, it is obvious that its use furnishes no argument in support of slavery ...

... that δοῦλος – *doulos* might be a slave, and that the word is most commonly applied to slaves in the classic writers, and frequently in the New Testament, no one can doubt; but its mere use in any case does not of necessity denote the relation sustained, or make it proper to infer that he to whom it is applied was bought with money, or held as property, or even in any way regarded as a *slave*. It might be true also that the various terms *doulos, dmōs, andrapodon, oiketes,* and possibly *hypekoos,* might all be applied to persons who had been obtained in the same way – either by purchase, or by being made prisoners of war; but these terms, except those of *andrapodon and dmōs,* would not designate the *origin* of the relation, or the nature of the *tenure* by which the servant was bound. The words used in our language, *servant, slave, waiter, hired man,* though not marking the relations with quite as much accuracy as the Greek words, will indicate somewhat the nature of the distinction ...

... The Hebrews made no such minute distinctions as the Greeks did. Their language was less cultivated, and much less adapted to express nice discriminations of thought. They used but one word, עֶבֶד, *ēbĕdh,* to express *all* the relations of servitude – somewhat as the word *servant* is used in the slave-holding states of our own country ...

... the word, in various forms, is used to denote the following kinds of service: (1) To work for another (Gen 29:29; 27:40; 29:15; 30:26; 1 Sam 4:9. (2) To serve or be servants of a king, 2 Sam 16:19; Gen 40:20; 41:10, 37, 38; l. 7, Ex 5:21, 7:10, 10:7. (3) To serve as a soldier, 2 Sam 2:12, 13, 15, 30, 31, iii. 22, viii 7, *et saepe.* (4) To serve as an ambassador, 2 Sam 10:2–4. (5) To serve as a people: that is, when one people were subject to another, or tributary to another. Gen 14:4; 15:13, 14; 25:23; Isa 19:23; Gen 9:26, 27; 27:37. (6) To serve God or idols, Ex 3:12; 9:1, 13; Deut 4:19; 8:19. Under this head the word is often used in the sense of "the *servant* of JEHOVAH," applied (a) to a *worshipper* of the true God, Neh 1:10 Ezra 5:11, Dan 6:21, *et saepe*; (b) a *minister,* or ambassador of God, Isa 49:6; Jer 25:9; 27:6; 43:10; Deut 34:5; Josh 1:1; Psalms 105:26; Isa 20:3. (7) The word is often employed to denote a servant, whether hired, bought, or inherited – one who was involuntarily held to service to another ... It is a very material circumstance also that *there is not the slightest evidence that either Abraham, Isaac, or Jacob ever* SOLD *a slave, or offered one for sale, or regarded them as liable to be sold* ...

... the sum of the matter is this: the slave is held as the property of his master [in America], as much as the horse is, and to all that he earns his master has a legal title, as much as he has to the earnings of his horse. How different this from the mild Mosaic statutes! *Can* it be believed that God ever meant to sanction this enormous system of wrong? There is a very material contrast between the Mosaic institutions and those in our country in regard to the religious privileges allowed by law to the slaves. In examining the Mosaic institutions in regard to servants, we found (a) that they were received into covenant with God, and as members of the family were recognized as in that covenant by the customary rites of religion. (b) They were guests at the national and family festivals. (c) They were statedly instructed in the duties of morality and religion. (d) They might become proselytes and be admitted to the full privileges of religion. (e) In securing to them the Sabbath, and the Sabbatical year, and the time for attending on the great festivals, there was ample *time* secured to them *by law* for the performance of all their religious duties. Between these arrangements and those existing in our own country, we shall now see there is the strongest possible contrast. On illustration of this we may remark, (1) that the benefits of education are withheld from the slave. This is so well known that it is scarcely necessary to prove the existence of *the fact* ... (2) The means for moral and religious instruction are not granted to the slave ... (3) That all night-meetings are prohibited. (4) That the law ordains that the slave shall not be taught to read, and of course the oral instruction which he can receive will be of comparatively little benefit to him. (5) That slaves can never have a church of their own, or a pastor of their own, and can never feel that they are in any way a free congregation. (6) That they are a mere appendage, in most circumstances, to a white congregation, with less advantageous seats and privileges. (7) That in most states it is made a penal offence to teach them to read the Bible: and (8) that in regard to a preacher, they are altogether dependent on the will of their masters, who have the power of "*presentation*," and "the right of *patronage*," in the most absolute and odious form in which it has ever existed on earth ...

[Regarding Jesus' apparent silence on slavery] There is no conclusive evidence that he ever came into contact with slavery at all. The only instance that is ever referred to of the kind, and the only one that can be, is the case of the Roman centurion who had a servant sick at Capernaum. Matt 8:5, seq. But this case does not prove the point for which it is adduced; for the terms which are used as descriptive of the case, do not prove it. The centurion himself applies to the sick servant at home the term *pais*, (Matt 8:5) which is a word much too general to demonstrate that he was a slave. It was rarely applied to a slave at all, and when it was, it was only as the term *boy* now is in the slaveholding states of this Union.

[Regarding Paul's sending Onesimus back to his owner Philemon] There is no positive or certain evidence that Onesimus was a slave at all ... *all* the proof that there can be on that point must be derived from ver. 16, and *all* the evidence in that verse is in the fact that he is there called "*a servant*" – δοῦλος ... The word denotes servant of any kind, and it should never be assumed that those to whom it was applied were slaves ... There is not the least evidence that Paul used any force, or even persuasion, to induce Onesimus to return to Philemon.

[Even if slavery did exist the spirit of Christianity opposed it and would lead to its demise] ... (a) The attention of Christianity was early turned to the subject of slavery, and to the evils of the system ...

(b) Freedom, under the influence of Christianity, was regarded as a great blessing, and the desire to promote it led to great sacrifices on the part of the early Christians ...

(c) Emancipation became a very common thing in the early Christian church, and was attended with such ceremonies as to show that it was regarded as a matter of great importance, and that an invaluable privilege was thus conferred on the slave …

(d) Under the influence of Christianity, the laws were greatly modified, and many of the former oppressive and harsh treatments came to an end …

(e) It is admitted that the tendency of things under the Roman empire, in the early ages of Christianity was to bring slavery to an end; and that, in fact, it brought it almost to a termination …

The result of this investigation in regard to Roman slavery is, therefore, in entire accordance with the statement in the Princeton Repertory, *that the fair application of the Christian religion would ultimately bring the institution to an end.*

THEODORE DWIGHT WELD (1803–95)

Theodore Dwight Weld, a leading abolitionist, was influenced by revivalist Charles Finney, and dismissed from Lane Theological Seminary in Cincinnati for his part in organizing a famous public debate over slavery in 1834. He married Angelina Grimké, who, with her sister Sarah, worked actively in the cause of abolition. In his tract *The Bible Against Slavery*, Weld confronts directly some of the classic arguments for slavery.

Source: T. D. Weld, *The Bible Against Slavery: An Inquiry into the Patriarchal and Mosaic Systems on the Subject of Human Rights*, 4th edn, enl. (New York: American Anti-Slavery Society, 1838). From *Sabin Americana Digital Collection*. © Gale, a part of Cengage Learning, Inc. Reproduced by permission.

… Two of those [ten] commandments deal death to slavery. "THOU SHALT NOT STEAL," or, "Thou shalt not take from another what *belongs* to him." All a man's powers are God's gift to HIM. Each of them is a part of himself, and all of them together constitute himself. All else that belongs to man is acquired by the *use* of these powers. The interest belongs to him, because the principal does; the product is his, because he is the producer. Ownership of anything is ownership of its *use*. The right to use according to will is *itself* ownership. The eighth commandment presupposes the right of every man to his powers, and their product. Slavery robs of both. A man's right to himself, is the only right absolutely original and intrinsic – his right to anything else is merely *relative* to this, is derived from it, and held only by virtue of it. SELF-RIGHT is the *foundation right* – the *post in the middle*, to which all other rights are fastened. Slaveholders, when talking about their RIGHT to their slaves, always assume their own right to themselves. What slaveholder ever undertook to prove his right to himself? He knows it to be a self-evident proposition, that *a man belongs to himself* – that that right is intrinsic and absolute. In making out his own title, he makes out the title of every human being. As the fact of being a *man* is itself the title, the whole human family have one common title deed. If one man's title is valid, all are valid. If one is worthless, all are. To deny the validity of the *slave's title* is to deny the validity of *his own*; and yet in making a man a slave, the slaveholder *asserts* the validity of his own title, while he seizes him as his property who has the *same* title. Further, in making him a slave, he does not merely disfranchise [sic] of humanity *one* individual, but UNIVERSAL MAN. He destroys the foundations. He annihilates *all rights*. He attacks not only the human race, but *universal being*, and rushes upon JEHOVAH. For rights are rights; God's are no more – man's are no less …

… The eighth commandment forbids the taking away, and the tenth adds, "Thou shalt not covet anything that is thy neighbor's;" thus guarding every man's right to himself and property by making not only the actual taking away a sin, but even that state of mind which would *tempt* to it. Who ever made human beings slaves, without *coveting* them?

… OBJECTION 1 "Cursed be Canaan, a servant of servants shall he be unto his brethren." Gen 9:25.

This prophecy of Noah is the *vade mecum* of slaveholders, and they never venture abroad without it; it is a pocket-piece for sudden occasion, a keepsake to dote over, a charm to spell-bind opposition, and a magnet to draw to their standard "whatsoever worketh abomination or maketh a lie." But "cursed be Canaan" is a poor drug to ease a throbbing conscience – a mocking lullaby to unquiet tossings. Those who justify negro slavery by the curse on Canaan *assume*, as usual, all the points in debate. 1. That *slavery* was prophesied, rather than mere *service* to others, and *individual* bondage rather than *national* subjection and tribute. 2. That the *prediction* of crime justifies it; or, at least, absolves those whose crimes fulfill it. How piously the Pharaohs might have quoted the prophecy, *"Thy seed shall be a stranger in a land that is not theirs, and they shall afflict them four hundred years!"* And then what saints were those that crucified the Lord of glory! 3. That the Africans are descended from Canaan. Africa was peopled from Egypt and Ethiopia, which countries were settled by Mizraim and Cush. For the location and boundaries of Canaan's posterity, see Gen. 10:15–19. So a prophecy of evil to one people, is quoted to justify its infliction upon another. Perhaps it may be argued that Canaan includes all Ham's posterity. If so, the prophecy is yet unfulfilled. The other sons of Ham settled Egypt and Assyria, and conjointly with Shem, Persia, and to some extent, the Grecian and Roman empires. The history of these nations gives no verification of the prophecy …

THE SPIRIT OF THE SCRIPTURES

Some anti-slavery advocates like George Cheever appealed to the broad themes of liberation that undergird the Exodus story, the Hebrew Bible's command to take in the runaway slave, and its commandment to love one's neighbor. Jesus' teaching could only expand upon the law of love, thus a Christian slave-holder is a contradiction. In his pamphlet *The Guilt of Slavery*, published in 1860, he argues a liberationist ethic at the heart of both testaments.

Source: George Cheever, *The Guilt of Slavery and the Crime of Slaveholding Demonstrated from the Hebrew and Greek Scriptures* (Boston: John Jewett, 1860). Making of America Books, University of Michigan: http://quod.lib.umich.edu.

The whole spirit of the Bible, from beginning to end, is against it [slavery]. The first legislation in regard to domestic servitude was for freedom, not slavery; it was to guard against slavery, and prevent the possibility of it coming in from abroad.

God himself referred to that great fact in the announcement of his last vengeance on the kingdom and people for their attempt to set up slavery instead of liberty for that was just the essence of their crime. I made a covenant of liberty *in the day that I brought your fathers out of Egypt,* out of the house of bondage, liberty every man to his neighbor. The covenant so made, so established, and so referred to, was of freedom *against* slavery, not in toleration or regulation of it. The nation was about to enter on a series of conquests, and to be brought in contact with other nations, where slavery might be found prevailing, and where temptations would arise to practice and establish the iniquity themselves, and under those circumstances, in preparation for future junctures, such admirable laws were passed, as rendered slavery and the slave traffic, either domestic or foreign, either of Hebrews or heathen, impossible. If those laws were obeyed, then, under God's old covenant, as well as new, such a crime as that of holding men as property, or maintaining the claim of property in man, was impossible …

… Under the Old Testament dispensation the right of servants to escape from bondage was admitted, and men were forbidden to return them into bondage when so escaped, but were commanded to aid and to shelter them, and not to oppress them. It would be oppressing them in the highest degree to return them into bondage; and the law of God that they should not be so returned proved that no creature had any right of ownership in them, but that they themselves had the most perfect right of ownership in themselves and the right to take themselves away, to assert and take their own freedom. To take this right away from them, and deliver them up into slavery, would be again the crime of stealing them.

Under the new dispensation it is asserted by the apologists for slavery under the gospel, that slaves must not escape from their masters, that they have no right to their freedom, that if they do escape they must be captured and sent back into slavery, especially if their owners were members of the Christian church, It is asserted that both they, as slaves, and their masters as their owners, were together members of Christian churches, and being such, having been admitted as such, the law of Christianity sanctions slavery as right, and forbids the slave from escaping and the Christian from sheltering him if he escapes.

The amount of this is, that while, under Moses, under the law of God as given by Moses, oppression was forbidden as sinful, under Christ oppression is baptized and sanctioned as a Christian grace. Under Moses the worst kind of oppression, that of slavery and the MAN-STEALING, by which slavery is created and maintained, was branded as a crime to be punished by death. Under Christ and the gospel the injunction against it is removed, and it is not only consecrated by the Christian sacraments, the seal of the church's sanction being put upon it, but it becomes sinful for Christian men to speak against it as a sin. The gospel of Christ becomes, in fact, a deliverance to do those very abominations which the law of God punished with death; a license of selfishness and cruelty, a freedom to sin, and to violate the law of love …

… It is averred that Christ's own silence on the subject of this sin gives consent to it. Christ was silent in regard to the sin of sodomy, in regard to infanticide, in regard to idolatry; and by this method of reasoning, not only is the law of God against these crimes abolished, and the crimes themselves made innocent by such silence, but he that speaks against them, when Christ did not, is himself guilty of a presumptuous sin, and may think himself happy if he is not struck with some divine judgment.

Now, dreadful as the blasphemy against the divine inspiration of the Old Testament has been, in asserting that slavery was sanctioned of God there, the blasphemy against Christ is worse, in asserting that the cast off vices under God's reprobation in the laws of Moses and the prophets have been taken up, endorsed, patronized and received to Christian communion and credit, in the teachings of Christ and the apostles …

To maintain that Christ and his apostles would set up as a Christian institution, what Moses and the prophets had forbidden on pain of death, what they had put in the same category of sin with the worship of Moloch, of Baal, of Dagon, what they had classified with sodomy and matricide, is to introduce into divine revelation a profaneness and confusion worse than that which is denounced of God in the 18th of Leviticus and the 27th of Deuteronomy …

… They who support such a [slaveholding] Christianity are the infidels; and they who deny it are the believers, they who deny and reject with scorn and hatred such a libel against God, such a monstrous perversion of His Word, and cleave to the letter and spirit of the law and gospel.

BIBLICAL TYPOLOGY

> James D. Liggett, who spoke from his pulpit in Leavenworth on September 7, 1862, cites the Bible typologically. Not unlike Lincoln, who saw the death of young soldiers as atonement for the sin of slavery, Liggett explains the Union's recent losses as a result of their moral failure to make the end of slavery their prime goal. Cleverly, he cites the war between brothers in Judges 20, where the other tribes go out against the tribe of Benjamin.
>
> Source: James D. Liggett, "Our National Reverses," reprinted in David B. Chesebrough, "*God Ordained This War*": *Sermons on the Sectional Crisis* (Columbia: University of South Carolina Press, 1991), 95–7. Reprinted by permission.

Shall we say then that God was, even temporarily, on the side of wicked men and wrongdoers, and gave them the victory? Certainly not. But we must say that his power was exerted as to result ultimately on the greatest good to Israel, whom he really did favor; and the greatest evil to Benjamin, whom it was his will and purpose to punish with a most signal punishment. The facts will make this interpretation clear.

(a) Israel did not consult God, their king and leader, as was his duty to do before making that war; but a mass meeting of the people was called, and a

Congress of the chief men of the tribes deliberated and determined for them-selves the question of duty.

(b) They were evidently actuated by a wrong spirit; that of revenge rather than an humble and conscientious desire to vindicate the cause of justice in the fear of God.

(c) In the heat and haste of passion, they evidently sought to glorify them-selves rather than God.

(d) They evidently trusted in their own superiority of strength for an easy victory, and forgot their dependence on the God of battles …

… Israel had one Bull Run disaster, and had passionately resolved to avenge it, and wipe out the disgrace at all hazards and their feelings of pride and unholy ambition, alike dishonoring to God and degrading to themselves, made another such disaster necessary. Again they are defeated and massa-cred in heaps on the same bloody and fatal field. Their second defeat brought them to a proper sense of their own weakness and error. While in their vain glory and zeal, they undertook the correction of other transgressors, they found themselves corrected. This time they go to God with fastings, tears and confessions … This, then, makes this seemingly dark chapter of the Divine Providence luminous and instructive. God is always consistent with himself, and works for righteous ends. If his hand is for a time against even his own people, it is not in anger, not without a just reason, and for a glorious purpose. If he uses his enemies to scourge his own people, and to correct them, it is in mercy, and it does not follow that his favor is even temporarily with his enemies, and against his own people, but the contrary.

This history and its lessons of instruction are old, but today they seem to us new and profitable.

EXPERIENCES OF AFRICAN AMERICANS

RESISTANCE AND REVOLT IN CHARLESTON

> Free black Denmark Vesey and others in the African Methodist Episcopal Church planned a slave revolt to take place in 1822. According to the trial records and oral traditions, Vesey drew the justification for his uprising and confidence in its success from Scripture, and "ransacked the text the Bible for apposite and terrible texts" (12), finding Zechariah 14:1–3 and Joshua 4:21 especially apt. The plot was uncovered and Vesey and his co-conspirators hanged. A few years later, David Walker, also active in Charleston's AME church, published his radical call for action, *Appeal to the Coloured Citizens of the World* (1829), which also drew on biblical motifs, especially America as the new Egypt.

> Source: David Walker, *Appeal to the Coloured Citizens of the World*, rev. edn (1830); elec-tronic edn, 3, 9–13, 44–5. *Documenting the American South*, University Library, University of North Carolina at Chapel Hill: http://docsouth.unc.edu.

My dearly beloved Brethren and Fellow Citizens.

Having travelled over a considerable portion of these United States, and having, in the course of my travels, taken the most accurate observations of things as they exist – the result of my observations has warranted the full and unshaken conviction, that we, (coloured people of these United States) are the most degraded, wretched, and abject set of beings that ever lived since the world began; and I pray God that none like us ever may live again until time shall be no more. They tell us of the Israelites in Egypt, the Helots in Sparta, and of the Roman Slaves, which last were made up from almost every nation under heaven, whose sufferings under those ancient and heathen nations, were, in comparison with ours, under this enlightened and Christian nation, no more than a cypher – or, in other words, those heathen nations of antiquity, had but little more among them than the name and form of slavery while wretchedness and endless miseries were reserved, apparently in a phial, to be poured out upon our fathers, ourselves, and our children, by *Christian* Americans!

… These affirmations are so well confirmed in the minds of all unprejudiced men, who have taken the trouble to read histories, that they need no elucidation from me. But to put them beyond all doubt, I refer you in the first place to the children of Jacob, or of Israel in Egypt under Pharoah and his people. Some of my brethren do not know who Pharoah and the Egyptians were – I know it to be a fact some of them take the Egyptians to have been a gang of *devils*, not knowing any better, and that they (Egyptians) having got possession of the Lord's people, treated them *nearly* as cruel as *Christian Americans* do us, at the present day. For the information of such, I would only mention that the Egyptians, were Africans, or coloured people, such as we are – some of them yellow and others dark – a mixture of Ethiopians and the natives of Egypt – about the same as you see the coloured people of the United States at the present day – I say, I call your attention then, to the children of Jacob, while I point out particularly to you his son Joseph, among the rest, in Egypt.

"And Pharoah, said unto Joseph, thou shalt be over my house, and according unto thy word shall all my people be ruled only in the throne will I be greater than thou." [See Genesis, chap. xli.]

"And Pharaoh said unto Joseph, see, I have set thee over all the land of Egypt." [xli. 42.]

"And Pharoah said unto Joseph, I am Pharoah, and without thee shall no man lift up his hand or foot in all the land of Egypt." [xli. 44.]

Now I appeal to heaven and to earth, and particularly to the American people themselves, who cease not to declare that our condition is not *hard*, and that we are comparatively satisfied to rest in wretchedness and misery, under them and their children. Not, indeed, to show me a coloured President, a Governor, a Legislator, a Senator, a Mayor, or an Attorney at the Bar – But to show me a man of colour, who holds the low office of a Constable, or one who sits in a Juror Box, even on a case of one of his wretched brethren, throughout this great Republic!! – But let us pass Joseph the son of Israel a little farther in review, as he existed with that heathen nation.

"And Pharoah called Joseph's name Zaphnath-paaneah; and he gave him to wife Asenath the daughter of Potipherah priest of On. And Joseph went out over all the land of Egypt." [xli, 45.]

Compare the above, with the American institutions. Do they not institute laws to prohibit us from marrying among the whites? I would wish, candidly, however, before the Lord, to be understood, that I would not give a *pinch of snuff* to be married to any white person I ever saw in all the days of my life. And I so say it, that the black man, or man of colour who will leave his own colour (provided he can get one, who is good for any thing) and marry a white woman, to be a double slave to her, just because she is *white*, ought to be treated by her as he surely will be, viz; as a NIGER!!!! It is not, indeed, what I care about inter-marriages with the whites, which induced me to pass the subject in review; for the Lord knows, that there is a day coming when they will be glad enough to get into the company of the blacks, notwithstanding, we are, in this generation, levelled them, almost on a level with the brute creation; and some of us they treat even worse than the brutes that perish. I only made this extract to show how much lower we are held, and how much more cruel we are treated by the American, than were the children of Jacob, by the Egyptians. – We will notice the sufferings of Israel some further, under *heathen Pharoah*, compared with ours under the *enlightened Christians of America*.

... Show me a page of history, either sacred or profane, on which a verse can be found, which maintains, that the Egyptians heaped the *insupportable insult* upon the children of Israel, by telling them that they were not of the *human family*. Can the whites deny this charge? Have they not, after having reduced us to the deplorable condition of slaves under their feet, held us up as descending originally from the tribes of *Monkeys* or *Orang-Outangs?* O! my God! I appeal to every man of feeling – is not this insupportable? Is it not heaping the most gross insult upon our miseries, because they have got us under their feet and we cannot help ourselves? Oh! pity us we pray thee, Lord Jesus, Master. – Has Mr. Jefferson declared to the world, that we are inferior to the whites, both in the endowments of our bodies and of minds? It is indeed surprising, that a man of such great learning, combined with such excellent natural parts should speak so of a set of men in chains. I do not know what to compare it to, unless, like putting one wild deer in an iron cage, where it will be secured, and hold another by the side of the same, then let it go, and expect the one in the cage to run as fast as the one at liberty. So far, my brethren, were the Egyptians from heaping these insults upon their slaves, that Pharoah's daughter took Moses, a son of Israel for her own, as will appear by the following.

"And Pharoah's daughter said unto her, [Moses' mother] take this child away, and nurse it for me, and I will pay thee thy wages. And the woman took the child [Moses] and nursed it." [See Exodus, chap. ii. 9, 10.]

... I remember a Camp Meeting in South Carolina, for which I embarked in a Steam Boat at Charleston, and having been five or six hours on the water, we at last arrived at the place of hearing, where was a very great concourse of people, who were no doubt, collected together to hear the word of God, (that some had collected barely as spectators to the scene, I will not here pretend to doubt, however, that is left to themselves and their God). Myself and boat companions, having been there a little while, we were all called up to hear; I among the rest went up and took my seat – being seated, I fixed myself in a complete position to hear the word of my Saviour and to receive such as I thought was authenticated by the Holy Scriptures; but to my no ordinary astonishment, our Reverend gentleman got up and told us (coloured people) that slaves must be obedient to their masters – must do their duty to their masters or be whipped – the whip was made for the backs of fools. &c. Here I pause for a moment, to give the world time to consider what was my surprise, to hear such preaching from a minister of My Master, whose very gospel is that of peace and not of blood and whips, as this pretended preacher tried to make us believe. What the American preachers can think of us, I aver this day before my God, I have never been able to define. They have newspapers and monthly periodicals, which they receive in continual succession, but on the pages of which, you will scarcely ever find a paragraph respecting slavery, which is ten thousand times more injurious to this country than all the others put together; and which will be the final overthrow of its government, unless something is very speedily done; for their cup is nearly full. – Perhaps they will laugh or make light of this; but I tell you Americans! that unless you speedily alter your course, *you and your Country are gone!!!!!!* For God Almighty will tear up the very face of the earth!!! Will not that very remarkable passage of Scripture be fulfilled on Christian Americans? Hear it Americans!! "He that is unjust, let him be unjust still: and he which is filthy, let him be filthy still: and he that is righteous, let him be righteous still: and he that is holy, let him be holy still ... " [See Revelation, chap. xxii. 11.]

FREDERICK DOUGLASS

For slaves and former slaves, the Exodus narrative of liberation, themes of wandering, exile and journey to the Promised Land were symbols of their own experience (see more extensive material in other chapters on music, literature, the Civil Rights movement, and African American interpretation). Literacy was a powerful tool of self-determination, so was often forbidden to the slaves. Its power was amplified when slaves were taught, as was often the case, to read the Bible. Frederick Douglass (1818–95) describes the liberating quality of biblical themes, fulfilling his master's prediction that his mistress teaching him to read would make him unfit to be a slave. Douglass distinguished true Christianity from oppression in its name. He escaped to the North and gained his own freedom in 1838. In *My Bondage and My Freedom*, published in 1855, he addresses the British public as part of his abolition campaign.

Source: *My Bondage and My Freedom, The Frederick Douglass Papers Series 2*, ed. J. W. Blassingame, J. R. McKivigan, and P. P. Hinks, vol. 2 (New Haven, CT: Yale University Press, 1999–), 242–5. © Yale University Press. Reproduced by permission.

Whips, chains, gags, and thumb-screws have all lain under the droppings of the sanctuary, and instead of rusting from off the limbs of the bondman, those droppings have served to preserve them in all their strength. Instead of preaching the gospel against this tyranny, rebuke, and wrong, ministers of religion have sought, by all and every means, to throw into the background whatever in the Bible could be construed into opposition to slavery, and to bring forward that which they could torture into its support. This I conceive to be the darkest feature of slavery, and the most difficult to attack, because it is identified with religion, and exposes those who denounce it to the charge of infidelity. Yes, those with whom I have been laboring, namely, the old organization anti-slavery society of America, have been again and again stigmatized as infidels, and for what reason? Why solely in consequence of the faithfulness of their attacks upon the slaveholding of the southern states, and the northern religion that sympathizes with it. I have found it difficult to speak on this matter without people coming forward and saying, "Douglass, are you not afraid of injuring the cause of Christ? You do not desire to do so, we know; but are you not undermining religion?" This has been said to me time and again, even since I came to this country, but I cannot be induced to leave off these exposures. I love the religion of our blessed Savior. I love that religion that comes from above, in the "wisdom of God which is first pure, then peaceable, gentle, and easy to be entreated, full of mercy and good fruits, without partiality and without hypocrisy." I love that religion that sends its votaries to bind up the wounds of him that has fallen among thieves. I love that religion that makes it the duty of its disciples to visit the fatherless and the widow in their affliction. I love that religion that is based on the glorious principle, of love to God and love to man; which makes its followers do unto others as they themselves would be done by. If you demand liberty to yourself, it says, grant it to your neighbors. If you claim a right to think for yourself, it says, allow your neighbors the same right. If you claim to act for yourself, it says, allow your neighbors the same right. It is because I love this religion that I hate the slaveholding, the woman-whipping, the mind-darkening, the soul-destroying religion that exists in the southern states of America. It is because I regard the one as good, and pure, and holy, that I cannot but regard the other as bad, corrupt, and wicked. Loving the one I must hate the other; holding to the one I must reject the other.

WOMEN'S PUBLIC ROLE AND THE VOTE

SARAH GRIMKÉ

Two Quaker women active in abolitionism were Sarah Grimké (1792–1873) and her younger sister Angelina. While Angelina's primary concern remained the abolition of slavery, Sarah's became the extension of equal rights to women. Her *Letters on the Equality of the Sexes*, written to Mary Parker, the president of the Boston Female Anti-Slavery Society in 1837, is the first sustained analysis by an American of women's rights that stems from biblical and theological argument. She anticipated later scholarship in separating the essential meaning of the Bible from its transmission and interpretation by a male-dominated culture. In the first selection, Genesis presents an egalitarian creation story, she argues, both Adam and Eve precipitated the Fall, and the curse of women's subjection in Genesis 3 is a sorry prediction, not a God-given ideal. In the second selection, biblical women of status appear in the Old and New Testament as forerunners of the women preachers of Grimké's own day. Jesus and Paul are champions of women's equality. To explain Paul's order of women's silence in the churches, she resorts to an anti-Jewish interpretation common to nineteenth-century (and later) interpreters.

Source: Elizabeth Ann Bartlett, ed., *Sarah Grimké: Letters on the Equality of the Sexes and Other Essays* (New Haven, CT: Yale University Press, 1988), Letter 1.31–4; Letter 14.85–94. © Yale University Press. Reproduced by permission.

1

… In examining this important subject, I shall depend solely on the Bible to designate the sphere of woman, because I believe almost everything that has been written on this subject, has been the result of a misconception of the simple truths revealed in the Scriptures, in consequence of the false translation of many passages of Holy Writ. My mind is entirely delivered from the superstitious reverence which is attached to the English version of the Bible. King James's translators certainly were not inspired. I therefore claim the original as my standard, *believing that to have been inspired,* and I also claim to judge for myself what is the meaning of the inspired writers, because I believe it to be the solemn duty of every individual to search the Scriptures for themselves, with the aid of the Holy Spirit, and not be governed by the views of any man, or set of men

We must first view woman at the period of her creation. "And God said, Let us make man in our own image, after our likeness, and let them have dominion over the fish of the sea, and over the fowl of the air, and over the cattle, and over all the earth and over every creeping thing that creepeth upon the earth. So God created man in his own image, in the image of God created he him, male and female, created he them." [Gen 1:26–27]. In all this sublime description of the creation of man, (which is a generic term including man and woman), there is not one particle of difference intimated as existing between them. They were both made in the image of God; dominion was given to both over every other creature, but not over each other. Created in perfect equality, they were expected to exercise the viceregence intrusted to them by their Maker, in harmony and love.

Let us pass on now to the recapitulation of the creation of man – "The Lord God formed man of the dust of the ground, and breathed into his nostrils the breath of life; and man became a living soul." And the Lord God said, "it is not good that man should be alone, I will make him an help meet for him" [Gen 2:7–18]. All creation swarmed with animated beings capable of natural affection, as we know they still are; it was not, therefore, merely to give man a creature susceptible of loving, obeying, and looking up to him, for all that the animals could do and did do. It was to give him a companion, *in all respects* his equal; one who was like himself a *free agent*, gifted with intellect and endowed with immortality; not a partaker merely of his animal gratifications, but able to enter into all his feelings as a moral and responsible being. If this had not been the case, how could she have been an help meet for him? I understand this as applying not only to the parties entering into the marriage contract, but to all men and women, because I believe God designed woman to be an help meet for man in every good and perfect work. She was a part of himself, as if Jehovah designed to make the oneness and identity of man and woman perfect and complete; and when the glorious work of the creation was finished, "the morning stars sang together, and all the sons of God shouted for joy" [Job 38:7].

The blissful condition was not long enjoyed by our first parents. Eve, it would seem from the history, was wandering alone amid the bowers of Paradise, when the serpent met with her. From her reply to Satan, it is evident that the command not to eat "of the tree that is in the midst of the garden," was given to both, although the term man was used when the prohibition was issued by God. "And the woman said unto the serpent, WE may eat of the fruit of the trees of the garden, but of the fruit of the tree which is in the midst of the garden, God hath said, YE shall not eat of it, neither shall YE touch it, lest YE die" [Gen 3:3]. Here the woman was exposed to temptation from a being with whom she was unacquainted. She had been accustomed to associate with her beloved partner, and to hold communion with God and with angels; but of satanic intelligence, she was in all probability entirely ignorant. Through the subtlety of the serpent, she was beguiled. And "when she saw that the tree was good for food, and that it was pleasant to the eyes, and a tree to be desired to make one wise, she took of the fruit thereof and did eat" [Gen 3:6].

We next find Adam involved in the same sin, not through the instrumentality of a supernatural agent, but through that of his equal, a being whom he must have known was liable to transgress the divine command, because he must have felt that he was himself a free agent, and that he was restrained from disobedience only by the exercise of faith and love towards his Creator. Had Adam tenderly reproved his wife, and endeavored to lead her to repentance instead of sharing in her guilt, I should be much more ready to accord to man that superiority which he claims; but as the facts stand disclosed by the sacred historian, it appears to me that to say the least, there was as much weakness exhibited by Adam as by Eve. They both fell from innocence, and consequently from happiness, *but not from equality* …

… And the Lord God said unto the woman, "Thou wilt be subject unto thy husband, and he will rule over thee" [Gen 3:16]. That this did not allude to the subjection of woman to man is manifest, because the same mode of expression is used in speaking to Cain of Abel [Gen. 4:10–12]. The truth is that the curse, as it is termed, which was pronounced by Jehovah upon woman, is a simple prophecy. The Hebrew, like the French language, uses the same word to express shall and will. Our translators having been accustomed to exercise lordship over their wives, and seeing only though the medium of a perverted judgment, very naturally, though I think not very learnedly or very kindly, translated it *shall* instead of *will*, and thus converted a prediction to Eve into a command to Adam; for observe, it is addressed to the woman and not to the man. The consequence of the fall was an immediate struggle for dominion, and Jehovah foretold which would gain the ascendancy ...

2

That women were called to the prophetic office, I believe is universally admitted. Miriam, Deborah, and Huldah were prophetesses. The judgments of the Lord are denounced by Ezekiel on false prophetesses, as well as false prophets [Ezek. 13:17–18]. And if Christian ministers are, as I apprehend, successors of the prophets, and not of the priests, then of course, women are now called to that office, as well as men, because God has nowhere withdrawn from them the privilege of doing what is the great business of preachers, viz. to point the penitent sinner to the Redeemer. "Behold the Lamb of God, which taketh away the sins of the world" [John 1:29]. ... I will mention Anna, the (last) prophetess under the Jewish dispensation. "She departed not from the temple, but served God with fasting and prayers night and day." And coming into the temple, while Simeon was yet speaking to Mary, with the infant Savior in his arms, "spake of Christ to all them that looked for redemption in Jerusalem." Blackwall, a learned English critic, in his work entitled, "Sacred Classics," says, in reference to this passage, Luke 2:37 – "According to the *original* reading, the sense will be, that the devout Anna, who attended in the temple, both night and day, spoke of the Messiah to all the inhabitants of that city, who constantly worshipped there, and who prepared themselves for the worthy reception of that divine person, whom they expected at this time. And 'tis certain, that other devout Jews, not inhabitants of Jerusalem, frequently repaired to the temple-worship, and might, at this remarkable time, and several others, hear this admirable woman discourse upon the blessed advent of the Redeemer. A various reading has Israel instead of Jerusalem, which expresses that religious Jews, from distant places, came thither to divine offices, and would with high pleasure, hear the discourses of this great prophetess, so famed for her extraordinary piety and valuable talents, upon the most important and desirable subject."

I shall now examine the testimony of the Bible on this point, after the ascension of our Lord, beginning with the glorious effusion of the Holy Spirit on the day of Pentecost. I presume it will not be denied, that women, as well as men, were at that time filled with the Holy Ghost, because it is expressly stated, that women were among those who continued in prayer and supplication, waiting for the fulfillment of the promise, that they should be imbued with power from on high [All of the following passages are from Acts 2]. "When the day of Pentecost was fully come, they were ALL with one accord in one place. And there appeared unto them cloven tongues like as of fire, and it sat upon each of them; and they were all filled with the Holy Ghost, and began to speak with other tongues as the Spirit gave them utterance." Peter says, in reference to this miracle, "this is that which was spoken by the prophet Joel. And it will come to pass in the last days, said God, I will pour out my Spirit upon all flesh; and your sons and your daughters shall prophesy – and on my servants and on my hand-maidens, I will pour out in those days of my Spirit, and they shall prophesy." There is not the least intimation that this was a spasmodic influence which was soon to cease. The men and the women are classed together; and if the power to preach the gospel was a supernatural and short-lived impulse in women, then it was equally so in men. But we are told, those were the days of miracles. I grant it; but the men, equally with the women, were the subjects of this marvelous fulfillment of prophecy, and of course, if women have lost the gift of prophesying, so have men. We are also gravely told, that if a woman pretends to inspiration, and thereupon grounds the right to plead the cause of a crucified Redeemer in public, she will be believed when she shows credentials from heaven, i.e. when she works a miracle. I reply, if this be necessary to prove her right to preach the gospel, then I demand of my brethren to show me their credentials; else I cannot receive their ministry, by their own showing. John Newton has justly said, that no power but that which created a world, can make a minister of the gospel; and man may task his ingenuity to the utmost to prove that this power is not exercised on women as well as men, He cannot do it until he has first disclaimed that simple, but all comprehensive truth, "in Christ Jesus there is neither male nor female" [Gal 3:28].

... Let us now examine whether women actually exercised the office of minister, under the gospel dispensation. Philip had four daughters, who prophesied or preached. Paul called Priscilla, as well as Aquila, his helpers; or, as in the Greek, his fellow laborers in Christ Jesus. Diverse other passages might be adduced to prove that women continued to be preachers, and that *many* of them filled this dignified station.

The principal support of the dogma of woman's inferiority, and consequent submission to her husband, is found in some passages of Paul's epistles ... I have no particular reverence for them, *merely* because they have been regarded with veneration from generation to generation ... notwithstanding my full belief that the apostle Paul's testimony, respecting himself, is true ... yet I believe his mind was under the influence of Jewish prejudices respecting women, just as Peter's and the apostles were about the uncleanness of the Gentiles ... I do not conceive that I derogate in the least from his character as an inspired apostle, to suppose that he may have been imbued with the prevalent prejudices against women ...

... But there are certain passages in the Epistles of St. Paul, which seem to be of doubtful interpretation; at which we cannot much marvel, seeing that as his brother Peter says, there are some things in there hard to be understood. Most commentators, having their minds preoccupied with the prejudices of education, afford little aid; they rather tend to darken the text by the multitude of words. One of these passages occurs in 1 Cor. 14. I have already remarked, that this chapter, with several of the preceding, was evidently designed to correct abuses which had crept into the assemblies of Christians in Corinth. Hence we find that the men were commanded to be silent, as well as the women, when they were guilty of anything which deserved reprehension. The apostle says, "If there be no interpreter, let him keep silence in the church" [1 Cor. 14:28]. The men were doubtless in the practice of speaking in unknown tongues, when there was no interpreter present; and Paul reproves them, because this kind of preaching conveyed no instruction to the people. Again he says, "If anything be revealed to another that sitteth by, let the first hold his peace" [1 Cor. 14:30]. We may infer from this that two men sometimes attempted to speak at the same time, and the apostle rebukes them, and adds, "ye may ALL prophesy one by one, for God is not the author of confusion, but of peace" [1 Cor. 14:31–33]. He then proceeds to notice the disorderly conduct of the women, who were guilty of other improprieties. They were probably in the habit of asking questions, on any points of doctrine which they wished more thoroughly explained. This custom was common among the men in the Jewish synagogues, after the pattern of which, the meetings of the early Christians were in all probability conducted. And the Christian women, presuming upon the liberty which they enjoyed under the new religion, interrupted the assembly, by asking questions. The apostle disapproved of this, because it disturbed the solemnity of the meeting: he therefore admonished the women to keep silence in the churches. That the apostle did not allude to preaching is manifest, because he tells them, "If they will *learn* any thing, let them ask their husbands at home" [1 Cor. 14:34]. Now a person endowed with a gift in the ministry, does not ask questions in the public exercise of that gift, for the purpose of gaining information: she is instructing others. Moreover, the apostle, in closing his remarks on this subject, says, "Wherefore, brethren (a generic term, applying equally to men and women) covet to prophesy, and forbid not to speak with tongues. Let all things be done decently and in order" [1 Cor. 14:39].

Clark [a commentator] on the passage, "Let women keep silence in the churches" [1 Cor. 14:34] says;

> This was a Jewish ordinance. Women were not permitted to teach in the assemblies, or even to ask questions. The rabbis taught that a woman should know nothing but the use of her distaff; and the saying of Rabbi Eliezer is worthy of remark and execration: "Let the words of the law be burned, rather than that they should be delivered by women."

SOJOURNER TRUTH

African American women could not separate the struggle against slavery and racism from the struggle for women's rights because they suffered discrimination because of both their race and sex. Sojourner Truth (c.1797–1883) grew up as a slave and was freed in Kingston, NY in 1827 at the approximate age of 30. One of the most charismatic speakers of her day, she relied on her knowledge of the Bible from memory and the experience of hearing it read to her. She preferred children to read the Bible to her, since they would not add their own explanations. Intuition, reason, and fidelity to her own experience guided her, causing her to reject a literalist reading of the creation story. In her *Narrative*, she, like Grimké, attributed the appearance of women's subordination in the Bible to the imprint of culture on its editors and interpreters. In her famous "Ar'n't I a Woman?" speech before the Women's Rights Convention in Akron, Ohio in 1851, Truth cleverly turns back on itself the argument about Eve as the author of the Fall, and emphasizes heroines of the New Testament, including Jesus' mother and associates. According to editor Margaret Washington, the version of Truth's speech in the *Anti-Slavery Bugle*, our second excerpt, is more accurate although less well-known.

Sources: Margaret Washington, ed., *The Narrative of Sojourner Truth* (New York: Random House, 1993), 86–7; *The Anti-Slavery Bugle*, June 21, 1851, reprinted in Washington's edition.

1

As soon as Isabella [Sojourner Truth] saw God as an all-powerful, all-pervading spirit, she became desirous of hearing all that had been written of him, and listened to the account of the creation of the world and its first inhabitants, as contained in the first chapters of Genesis, with peculiar interest. For some time she received it all literally, though it appeared strange to her that "God worked by the day, got tired, and stopped to rest," etc. But after a little time, she began to reason upon it, thus – "Why, if God works by the day, and one day's work tires him, and if he is obliged to rest, either from weariness or on account of darkness, or if he waited for the 'cool of the day to walk in the garden,' because he was inconvenienced by the heat of the sun, why then it seems that God cannot do as much as *I* can; for I can bear the sun at noon and work several days and nights in succession without being much tired. Or if he rested nights because of the darkness, it is very queer that he should make the night so dark that he could not see himself. If *I* had been God, I would have made the night light enough for my own convenience, surely." But the moment she placed this idea of God by the side of the impression she had once so suddenly received of his inconceivable greatness and entire spirituality, that moment she exclaimed mentally, "No, God does not stop to rest, for he is a spirit, and cannot tire; he cannot want for light, for he hath all light in himself. And if 'God is all in all,' and 'worketh all in all,' as I have heard them read, then it is impossible he should rest at all; for if he did, every other thing would stop and rest too; the waters would not flow, and the fishes could not swim; and all motion must cease. God could have no pauses in his work, and he needed no Sabbaths of rest. Man might need them and he should take them when he needed them, whenever he required rest. As it regarded the worship of God, he was to be worshipped at all times and in all places and one portion of time never seemed to her more holy than another." … She wished to compare the teachings of the Bible with the witness within her; and she came to the conclusion, that the spirit of truth spoke in those records, but that the recorders of those truths had intermingled with them ideas and suppositions of their own.

2

One of the most unique and interesting speeches of the convention was made by Sojourner Truth, an emancipated slave. It is impossible to transfer it to paper, or convey any adequate idea of the effect it produced upon the audience. … She came forward to the platform and addressing the President said with great simplicity: "May I say a few words?" Receiving an affirmative answer, she proceeded: I want to say a few words about this matter. I am a woman's rights. I have as much muscle as any man, and can do as much work as any man. I have plowed and reaped and husked and chopped and mowed, and can any man do more than that? I have heard much about the sexes being equal. I can carry as much as any man, and can eat as much too, if I can get it. I am as strong as any man that is now. As for intellect, all I can say is, if woman have a pint, and man a quart – why can't she have her little pint full? You need not be afraid to give us our rights for fear we will take too much, – for we can't take more than our pint'll hold. The poor men seem to be all in confusion, and don't know what to do. Why children, if you have woman's rights, give it to her and you will feel better. You will have your own rights, and they won't be so much trouble. I can't read, but I can hear. I have heard the Bible and have learned that Eve caused man to sin. Well, if woman upset the world, do give her a chance to set it right side up again. The Lady has spoken about Jesus, how he never spurned woman from him, and she was right. When Lazarus died, Mary and Martha came to him with faith and love and besought him to raise their brother. And Jesus wept and Lazarus came forth. And how came Jesus into the world? Through God who created him and a woman who bore him. Man, where is your part? But the women are coming up blessed be God and a few of the men are coming up with them. But man is in a tight place, the poor slave is on him, woman is coming on him, he is surely between a hawk and a buzzard.

PREACHING THE BIBLE AND WOMEN'S EQUALITY

Virginia Broughton (c.1856–1934), the daughter of freed slaves, graduated from Fisk University in 1875. After attending a revivalist meeting in Memphis, she and others organized "a Bible Band," for women to study the Bible daily. After a near-death experience, she felt called to be a missionary and traveled throughout Tennessee preaching and organizing. In her reflections and autobiography, she organizes the biblical texts that promote women's public role and religious authority.

Source: *Twenty Years' Experience of a Missionary* (Chicago: Pony Press, 1907), electronic edition, 130–1, 137–9. The Digital Schomburg, New York Public Library: http://digilib.nypl.

Bible authority for women's work. Text, Gen. 2:18.

(1) Woman's creation.

    (a)   Made of refined material.
    (b)   Man's helpmeet.
    (c)   Man incomplete without woman.

(2) Marriage ordained of God.

    (a)   Woman, mother of all being.
    (b)   Hope of man's restoration. Gen 3:15.
    (c)   Woman's help indispensable in the home, as man's comforter and the trainer of children.

(3) Woman as helpmeet in business. Illustrations: Deborah, Esther, Ruth, Lydia.

(4) Woman as helpmeet in church.

    (a)   As teacher. 2 Kings 22:14. Acts 18:26.
    (b)   As hostess to care for God's servants. II Kings 4:10. I Kings 17:15.
    (c)   As missionaries. Acts 9:39. Rom 16:1.

(5) Called of God to service. Eph. 2:1–10.

    (a)   All believers one in Christ. Gal. 3:28.
    (b)   All required to work according to respective gifts. I Cor. 12:7. Matt. 25:14, 15.

[…]

(1) Paul's opportunity.

    (a)   To preach to Gentiles. Acts 14:27.
    (b)   He entered heartily upon his work.
    (c)   Opposition met and overcome. Acts 14:19, 26.

(2) Applied to Negro women.

    (a)   Opportunities or open doors to serve great. Race to uplift. Beginning in the home.
    (b)   Professions and schools of all kinds open to women.
    (c)   Responsibilities in proportion to opportunities.
    (d)   Woman's Christian organizations great means of development.

(3) Appeal to use given opportunities.

    (a)   Present results spurs to greater effort.
    (b)   Some results mentioned. Rescue homes, orphanages, homes for the aged, reforms in home life, kindergartens, temperance societies, and charitable organizations of all kinds have begun to be established

and fostered since women have begun to enter the doors of usefulness open to them.

(c)   The gospel is being encouraged and sent to the ends of the earth
through the generous support of good women.

(d)   Negro women have evidently come to the kingdom for such a time
as this. Esther 4:14. Negro men's hearts are failing before the ruth-
less hand of oppression and persecution of all kinds and if our nation
is encouraged and saved from the fiery furnace through which it now
passes Negro women like Esther of old must take the case to the King
of kings and by her prayers and tears plead for their deliverance.

(e)   In the encouragement given these sisters in black by their more
favored white Christian sisters the light begins to dawn and we are
nerved for the fray.

(f)   Enter the open doors for the judge of all the earth will do right.

Praise. Text. Ps. 150:6 ...

ANNA JULIA COOPER

Anna Julia Cooper (1858–1964) was born to a slave mother in North
Carolina. She never knew her biological father's identity, but assumed
it to be her mother's white master. She graduated from Oberlin College
in 1884 with a classical education that included knowledge of the biblical
languages Greek and Latin. In 1925 she earned her doctorate from the
University of Paris (the Sorbonne) and became president of a university,
along the way raising another woman's five children after their mother's
early death. Like Grimké and Sojourner Truth, she saw Christianity in its
ideal form as congenial to women's equality. Celibacy and hypocrisy in
the church had diminished the image of women, but Jesus' teaching was
all good news for women. She expresses the idea of the "seed growing
secretly," which abolitionists also used. If Jesus did not explicitly preach
against slavery or for women's equality, he sowed the seeds of liberation
by his teaching. It would take millennia for these seeds to come to fruition and be fully recognized. For example, his positive relationships with
women like Mary and Martha of Bethany, his mother, and the woman
caught in adultery, pointed to the dignity of women. Cooper argues that
wives and mothers are a fundamental source of morality and should therefore need equal access to education. In her extended work, *A Voice from the
South*, she laments that racism from without and sexism from within the
community impede women's progress and influence.

Source: Anna Julia Cooper, *A Voice from the South* (1892), electronic edition, 14, 16–18,
28–9, 44–45. *Documenting the American South*, reprinted by permission, University
Library, University of North Carolina at Chapel Hill: http://docsouth.unc.edu.

1

The idea of the radical amelioration of womankind, reverence for woman as woman regardless of rank, wealth, or culture, was to come from that rich and bounteous fountain from which flow all our liberal and universal ideas – the gospel of Jesus Christ.

2

… Christ gave us ideals, not formulae. The Gospel is a germ requiring millennia for its growth and ripening. It needs and at the same time helps to form around itself a soil enriched in civilization, and perfected in culture and insight without which the embryo can neither be unfolded or comprehended. With all the strides our civilization has made from the first to the nineteenth century, we can boast not an idea, not a principle of action, not a progressive social force but was already mutely foreshadowed, or directly enjoined in that simple tale of a meek and lowly life. The quiet face of the Nazarene is ever seen a little way ahead, never too far to come down to and touch the life of the lowest in days the darkest, yet ever leading onward, still onward, the tottering childish feet of our strangely boastful civilization.

By laying down for woman the same code of morality, the same standard of purity, as for man; by refusing to countenance the shameless and equally monsters who were gloating over her fall, – graciously stooping in all the majesty of his own spotlessness to wipe away the filth and grime of her guilty past and bid her go in peace and sin no more; and again in the moments of his own careworn and footsore dejection, turning trustfully and lovingly, away from the heartless snubbing and sneers, away from the cruel malignity of mobs and prelates in the dusty marts of Jerusalem to the ready sympathy, loving appreciation and unfaltering friendship of that quiet home at Bethany; and even at the last, by his dying bequest to the disciple whom he loved, signifying the protection and tender regard to be extended to that sorrowing mother and ever afterward to the sex she represented; – throughout his life and in his death he has given to men a rule and guide for the estima-tion of woman as an equal, as a helper, as a friend, and as a sacred charge to be sheltered and cared for with a brother's love and sympathy, lessons which nineteen centuries' gigantic strides in knowledge, arts, and sciences, in social and ethical principles have not been able to probe to their depth or to exhaust in practice.

3

… Now the fundamental agency under God in the regeneration, the re-training of the race, as well as the ground work and starting point of its progress upward, must be the *black woman* … A race cannot be purified from without. Preachers and teachers are helps, and stimulants and conditions as necessary as the gracious rain and sunshine are to plant growth. But what are rain and dew and sunshine and cloud if there be no life in the plant germ? We must go to the root and see that it is sound and healthy and vigorous; and not deceive ourselves with waxen flowers and painted leaves of mock chlorophyll ... A stream cannot rise higher than its source. The atmosphere of homes is no rarer and purer and sweeter than are the mothers in those homes. A race is but a total of families. The nation is the aggregate of its homes. As the whole is sum of all its parts, so the character of the parts will determine the characteristics of the whole. These are all axioms and so evident that it seems gratuitous to remark it.

4

... The institution of the Church in the South to which she mainly looks for the training of her colored clergy and for the help of the "Black Woman" and "Colored Girl" of the South, has graduated since the year 1868, when the school was founded, *five young women*; and while yearly numerous young men have been kept and trained for the ministry by the charities of the Church, the number of indigent females who have been supported, sheltered and trained, is phenomenally small. Indeed, to my mind, the attitude of the Church toward this feature of her work is as if the solution of the problem of Negro Missions depended solely on sending a quota of deacons and priests into the field, girls being a sort of *tertium quid* whose development may be promoted if they can pay their way and fall in with the plans mapped out for the training of the other sex. Now I would ask in all earnestness, does not this force potential deserve by education and stimulus to be made dynamic? Is it not a solemn duty incumbent on all colored churchmen to make it so? Will not the aid of the Church be given to prepare our girls in head, heart, and hand for the duties and responsibilities that the intelligent wife, the Christian mother, the earnest, virtuous, helpful woman, at once both the lever and the fulcrum for uplifting the race?

WOMEN AND SOCIAL REFORM

Ideas about the crucial social role of mothers also fueled women's reform movements of the late nineteenth century, most famous among them the Women's Christian Temperance Union. Their aim was not primarily suffrage itself, but in promoting social reform, they moved women out of the domestic sphere and onto the public stage. Frances Willard (1839–98), president of the WCTU, argued that the Bible gave women the right to preach and to be ordained as ministers in *Woman in the Pulpit* (1889). She encouraged women to study Hebrew and Greek to make their case from the original text, suggesting women's interpretation would add "a pinch of common sense." She cites the usual heroines of the Old Testament. Temperance was a form of "home protection" that would elevate the woman and safeguard the home. In *Woman and Temperance* (1883), she asserts that the steady progress of the temperance movement would lead to women's full participation in civic life and by extension, to women's right to vote.

Sources: Frances Willard, *Woman in the Pulpit* (Boston: D. Lothrop, 1888), 21, 23–4, 29–30, 33–4; *Woman and Temperance* (Hartford, CT: Park Publishing, 1883), 44.

1

In the presence of these multiplied instances, and many others that might be named, what must a plain Bible-reading member of the laity conclude? For my own part, I long ago found in these two conflicting methods of exegesis, one of which strenuously insisted on a literal view, and the other played fast and loose with God's word according to personal predilection, a pointed illustration of the divine declaration that "it is not good for man to be alone." We need women commentators to bring out the women's side of the book. We need the stereoscopic view of truth in general, which can only be had when woman's eye and man's together shall discern the perspective of the Bible's full-orbed revelation …

From all of which considerations the plain wayfaring woman cannot help concluding that exegesis, thus conducted, is one of the most time-serving and man-made of the sciences, and one of the most misleading of all arts. It has broken Christendom into sects that confuse and astound the heathen world, and to-day imposes the heaviest yoke now worn by woman upon that most faithful follower of Him who is her emancipator no less than humanity's Saviour. But as the world becomes more deeply permeated by the principles of Christ's Gospel, methods of exegesis are revised. The old texts stand there, just as before, but we interpret them less narrowly. Universal liberty of person and of opinion are now conceded to be Bible-precept principles; Onesimus and Canaan are no longer quoted as the slave-holders' main-stay; the theory of unfermented wine as well as bread is accepted by our temperance people generally;

The great Russian writer, Count Tolstoi, stands as the representative of a school that accepts the precepts of Christ's Sermon on the Mount with perfect literalness, and theologians, not a few, find in the Bible no warrant whatever for the subjection of woman in anything …

And yet, be it noted, the same theologians who would outlaw as unorthodox any one who did not believe Christ an equal member of that Trinity of which the Supreme Creator of the world is one (declaring Him to be "very God of very God," etc.) do not only preach but practice the heresy that woman is in subjection to man, when Paul distinctly declares that her relation to man is the same as that of Christ to God [I Cor 11:3].

Take the description of men's babbling, tumult, and confusion, as given in the fourteenth chapter of 1 Cor., and imagine that a woman's meeting had been therein described; would not the ages have rung with an exegesis harrowing to the soul of woman? But who ever heard this unseemly behavior of men referred to as the basis of the doctrine for man's subjection to woman, or as the basis of a binding rule of church discipline in reference to the conduct of the men in public worship?

"How great a difference here we see,
'Twixt Tweedle-dum and Tweedle-dee!"

Reasoning from the present customs of oriental countries, we must conclude that places of worship, in the age of the Apostles, were not built as they are with us, but that the women had a corner of their own, railed off by a close fence reaching above their heads. It was thus made difficult for them to hear, and in their eager, untutored state, wholly unaccustomed to public audiences, they "chattered" and asked questions. Upon this light foundation behold a doctrine built that would subject and silence two-thirds of Christ's disciples in the free and intelligent English-speaking world!

... Time would fail me to tell of Miriam, the first prophetess, and Deborah, the first judge; of Hannah, whose answered prayer brought Samuel to be the hope and stay of a dejected nation; of Esther, the deliverer of her people; of Judith, their avenger; of the gracious group of Marys that clustered around her who was blessed among women; of Elizabeth, and Anna; of Martha, and those "daughters of Jerusalem who lamented while men crucified the world's Redeemer"; of Lois and Eunice, who trained Timothy for the ministerial office; of "Tryphena and Tryphosa and the beloved Persis." Suffice it to say that these all stand forth the equal stewards with their brethren of God's manifold grace.

There are thirty or forty passages in favor of woman's public work for Christ, and only two against it, and these not really so when rightly understood. But in the face of all these embodied arguments, it is objected that Paul specifies (in 2 Tim. ii.2) men only as his successors; "And the things that thou hast heard of me, the same commit thou to faithful *men*, who shall be able to teach others also." But the word translated "men" is the same as that in the text, "God now commandeth *men* everywhere to repent," and event the literalists will admit that women are, of all people, "commanded to repent"! But here comes in again the "fast and loose" method of interpretation; for preachers almost never refer to the women of their audiences, but tell about "men," and what "a man" was and is and is to be.

2

Having thus come to the heart of the drinking man in the plenitude of his redeeming power, Christ entered the next wider circle, in which two human hearts unite to form a home, and here, by the revelation of her place in His kingdom, He lifted to an equal level with her husband the gentle companion who had supposed herself happy in being the favorite vassal of her liege lord. "There is neither male nor female in Christ Jesus;" this was the "open sesame," a declaration utterly opposed to all custom and tradition, but so steadily the light has shone, and so kindly has it made the heart of man, that without strife of tongues, or edict of sovereigns, it is coming now to pass that in proportion as any home is really Christian, the husband and the wife are peers in dignity and power. There are no homes on earth where woman is "revered, beloved," and individualized in character and work, so thoroughly as the fifty thousand in America where "her children arise up and call her blessed, her husband also and he praiseth her" because of her part in the work of our W.C.T.U.

THE WOMAN'S BIBLE

Elizabeth Cady Stanton (1815–1902) did not hesitate to critique the Bible, and Christianity itself, as one of the chief causes of women's subordination. She brought together a committee of 20 women from the USA and UK to examine and comment upon all the passages that refer to women or where "women are made prominent by exclusion." The project was not particularly popular in its own time. NAWSA (the National American Woman Suffrage Association), the coalition of Stanton's NWSA and the more conservative AWSA, issued a disclaimer to the project at its convention in January, 1896. Like other feminist interpreters, Stanton looks to the Creation story of Genesis 1 as egalitarian, but goes beyond them in asserting a feminine aspect to God. Genesis 2 is mere editorial bias (one interpreter says it "was manipulated by some Jew"), and the story of Eve's provocation of the Fall contradicts Darwin. The commentary fails to note some of the potential feminist heroines of the Hebrew Bible. Mary Magdalene's part in Matthew, Mark, and Luke is minimized, but her role in John is trumpeted. So too are the roles of the Canaanite woman in Matt 15, Jesus' mother, and the women co-workers of Paul. The work does not include a separate discussion of Gal 3:28, a verse cited frequently in the commentary. Paul's command for women to keep silent in the churches is dismissed as a remnant of Jewish practices and influences on Paul. Stanton finally sums up her views in her response to the letters of reaction to the commentary. It was a view too radical for some, and not radical enough for others.

Source: Elizabeth Cady Stanton, *The Woman's Bible* (New York: European Publishing, 1895, 1898), I.14–20, I.26–7, II.121, II.143–4, II.214.

1

Here [Gen 1:26–28] is the sacred historian's first account of the advent of woman; a simultaneous creation of both sexes, in the image of God. It is evident from the language that there was consultation in the Godhead, and that the masculine and feminine elements were equally represented. Scott, in his commentaries says, "this consultation of the Gods is the origin of the doctrine of the trinity." But instead of three male personages, as generally represented, a Heavenly Father, Mother, and Son would seem more rational.

The first step in the elevation of woman to her true position as an equal factor in human progress, is the cultivation of the religious sentiment in regard to her dignity and equality, the recognition by the rising generation of an ideal

Heavenly Mother, to whom their prayers should be addressed, as well as to a Father.

If language has any meaning, we have in these texts a plain declaration of the existence of the feminine element in the Godhead, equal in power and glory with the masculine. The Heavenly Mother and Father! "God created man in his *own image, male and female.*" Thus Scripture, as well as science and philosophy, declares the eternity and equality of sex ...

As to woman's subjection, on which both the canon and the civil law delight to dwell, it is important to note that equal dominion is given to woman over every living thing, but not one word is said giving man dominion over woman.

... Now it is manifest that both of these stories cannot be true; intelligent women, who feel bound to give the preference to either may decide according to their own judgment of which is more worthy of an intelligent woman's acceptance ... My own opinion is that the second story was manipulated by some Jew, in an endeavor to give "heavenly authority" for requiring a woman to obey the man she married. In a work which I am now completing, I give some facts concerning ancient Israelitish History, which will be of peculiar interest to those who wish to understand the origin of woman's subjection ...

... Accepting the view that man was prior in the creation, some Scriptural writers say that ... Why should there be two contradictory accounts in the same book, of the same event? It is fair to infer that the second version, which is found in some form in the different religions of all nations, is a mere allegory, symbolizing some mysterious conception of a highly imaginative editor.

2

... Reading this narrative carefully, it is amazing that any set of men ever claimed that the dogma of the inferiority of woman is here set forth ...

Then the woman fearless of death if she can gain wisdom takes of the fruit; and all this time Adam standing beside her interposes no word of objection. "Her husband with her" are the words of v. 6. Had he been the representative of the divinely appointed head in married life, he assuredly would have taken upon himself the burden of the discussion with the serpent, but no, he is silent in this crisis of their fate. Having had the command from God himself he interposes no word of warning or remonstrance, but takes the fruit from the hand of his wife without a protest. It takes six verses to describe the "fall" of woman, the fall of man is contemptuously dismissed in a line and a half.

The subsequent conduct of Adam was to the last degree dastardly. When the awful time of reckoning comes, and the Jehovah God appears to demand why his command has been disobeyed, Adam endeavors to shield himself behind the gentle being he has declared to be so dear. "The woman thou gavest to be with me, she gave me and I did eat," he whines – trying to shield himself at this wife's expense! Again we are amazed that upon such a story men have built up a theory of their superiority!

3

… The woman of Canaan proved herself quite equal in argument with Jesus; and though by her persistency she tired the patience of the disciples, she made her points with Jesus with remarkable clearness. His patience with women was a sore trial to the disciples, who were always disposed to nip their appeals in the bud. It was very ungracious in Jesus to speak of the Jews as dogs, saying, "It is not meet to take the children's food, and to cast it to dogs:" Her reply, "Yet the dogs eat of the crumbs which fall from the master's table," was bright and appropriate. Jesus appreciated her tact and her perseverance, and granted her request, and her daughter, the text says, was healed.

4

… Is it not astonishing that so little is in the New Testament concerning the mother of Christ? My own opinion is that she was an excellent woman, and the wife of Joseph, and that Joseph was the actual father of Christ. I think there can be no reasonable doubt that such was the opinion of the authors of the original Gospels. Upon any other hypothesis it is impossible to account for their having given the geneaology of Joseph to prove that Christ was of the blood of David. The idea that he was the Son of God, or in any way miraculously produced, was an afterthought, and is hardly entitled now to serious consideration. The Gospels were written so long after the death of Christ that very little was known of him, and substantially nothing of his parents …

The best thing about the Catholic Church is the deification of Mary, and yet this is denounced by Protestantism as idolatry. There is something in the human heart that prompts man to tell his faults more freely to the mother than to the father. The cruelty of Jehovah is softened by the mercy of Mary.

… Mary Magdalene is, in many respects, the tenderest and most loving character in the New Testament. According to the account her love for Christ knew no abatement, no change – true even in the hopeless shadow of the cross. Neither did it die with his death. She waited at the sepulcher, she hastened in the early morning to this tomb; and yet the only comfort Christ gave to this true and loving soul lies in these strangely cold and heartless words "Touch me not."

5

… The real difficulty in woman's case is that the whole foundation of the Christian religion rests on her temptation and man's fall, hence the necessity of a Redeemer and a plan of salvation. As the chief cause of this dire calamity, woman's degradation and subordination were made a necessity. If, however, we accept the Darwinian theory, that the race has been a gradual growth from the lower to a higher form of life, and that the story of the fall is a myth, we can exonerate the snake, emancipate the woman, and reconstruct a more rational religion for the nineteenth century, and thus escape all the perplexities of the Jewish mythology as of no more importance than those of the Greek, Persian and Egyptian.

ANTI-SUFFRAGE ARGUMENTS AND SCRIPTURE

Horace Bushnell

Several groups opposed women's suffrage because it threatened their own business or political interests. The liquor industry, big business, and party bosses feared women in the electorate would be more difficult to predict and control, so some secretly gave money to the anti-suffragette groups. Those who opposed women's suffrage did not use the Bible for their primary argument. They argued from Nature, and invoked Divine design as laid out in the Bible, but did not engage in close exegesis. Some invoked Victorian ideas of the home and the moral superiority and influence of mothers, but these ideas already had been invoked by the pro-suffrage ranks. Horace Bushnell, a prominent Congregationalist clergyman and theologian, invoked Nature to argue against the vote for women. Scripture was a secondary support, which merely reiterated Nature's argument.

Source: Horace Bushnell, *Women's Suffrage: The Reform against Nature* (New York: Charles Scribner, 1869), 73–7.

Happily, we are not obliged to hang our opinions in this matter of women's suffrage on the moral expositions and dictations of Scripture; for the two points now made in respect to the natural subordination, or subject state, of women and to the secondary, complementary office they hold in filling out the manhood of men, when merged politically in their protectorship, need no scriptural authority to support them ... they seem to merely reiterate, and put in stronger emphasis, just what we learn by the sight of our eyes – that and nothing more ...

Coming then to the Word, what saith the Word? ... the representation is, in any case, that the woman is created, not to be the man's re-duplication, or a second man, but to be the meet-helper of the man. She is to be a subsidiary nature, filling out the complete humanity of the man, and this fact is figured in a way of representation that makes her nature derivative from his, and so far of a quality at once cognate and complementary. "And Adam said, this is now bone of my bone and flesh of my flesh; she shall be called woman, because she was taken out of man. Therefore shall a man leave his father and mother, and cleave unto his wife, and they shall be one flesh."

... [Of Paul's commands that women keep silent in church and cover their heads, Bushnell is critical. He argues that if Paul had been married,] I think he would have learned some things about women which, in fact, he never did learn, and would have been as much more courteous and tenderly gracious in his words. And if he had lived in this particular age, I am not quite sure that he would have had as much to say of the obedience of women; ...

... And yet he is perfectly right in every positive utterance and moral pronouncement he makes. So far he indorses and sanctions the grand first truth of the sexly nature seen by us all; the superior headship of man, and the subordinated, complementary life of woman.

JAMES CARDINAL GIBBONS

One of the most vocal opponents of women's suffrage was James Cardinal Gibbons (1834–1921), of Baltimore. Over decades, in sermons and commencement speeches, he argued that women were already elevated as wives and mothers. Their moral influence upon their husbands and sons translates into suffrage by proxy. Direct involvement in politics would only degrade women.

Source: *The New York Times*, April 30, 1913.

When I deprecate female suffrage I am pleading for the dignity of woman. I am contending for her honor. I am striving to perpetuate those peerless prerogatives inherent in her sex, those charms and graces which exalt womankind and make her the ornament and the coveted companion of man. We must remember that, though woman does not personally vote, she exercises the right of suffrage by proxy. So powerful is the influence which a sensible matron exerts over her husband and sons that they will rarely fail to follow her counsel which comes from inspired rather than labored reasoning.

DEBATING THE BIBLE'S AUTHORITY: THE HIGHER CRITICISM CONTROVERSY

WILLIAM NEWTON CLARKE

Perhaps no one was more representative of, or more central to, shifting American perspectives on the Bible in the late nineteenth century than William Newton Clarke (1841–1912). By Clarke's own account, he grew up committed to the notion of biblical inerrancy. The son of a Baptist minister, Clarke followed in his father's footsteps and entered ministry after his graduation from Hamilton Theological Seminary (New York) in 1863. When Clarke encountered new perspectives among colleagues in Newton, Massachusetts, and Toronto during the 1870s and the 1880s, his own understanding of biblical truth began to change. By 1890, he had left the pastorate to assume a faculty position in theology at Colgate Theological Seminary, where he remained for the rest of his life. During that time, he wrote *An Outline of Christian Theology* (1898), a groundbreaking and widely used textbook, as well as numerous other critical studies. The following selection comes from Clarke's well-known intellectual memoir, *Sixty Years with the Bible* (1909).

Source: William Newton Clarke, *Sixty Years with the Bible* (New York: Charles Scribner's Sons, 1912 [1909]), 3, 6–7, 173–81, 192.

Not for the sake of telling the story, but for the sake of what the story may tell, do I sit down to write these notes of memory. With respect to the Bible, I am one of the men who have lived through the crisis of the Nineteenth Century, and experienced the change which that century has wrought. I began, as a child must begin, with viewing the Bible in the manner of my father's day, but am ending with a view that was never possible until the large work of the Nineteenth Century upon the Bible had been done. Thus I am entering into the heritage of my generation, which I consider it both my privilege and my duty to accept ...

What if a man who has made the change without losing his faith were to recount the stages of his journey? What if he were to show by what steps he had come, and offer his comrades opportunity to judge whether his processes had been legitimate, valid, spiritual, worthy of a child of God? I can well believe that such a revelation of experience might be an enlightening and encouraging thing to many a perplexed and anxious soul. More than once it has occurred to me that if I were to tell the story of my own life in the single character of a student, lover, and user of the Bible, exhibiting the mental processes through which the change in my own attitude toward the Bible has come to pass, I might be offering to many a veritable helping hand. For I know that in my case the change has been an honest one, and am equally sure that it has been a legitimate one, which I could not have refused to make without being false to the true light. It sprang out of the very necessities of my life and thought, and resulted directly from my worthiest work. It has followed sound processes, and stands as a genuine element in Christian experience. It was necessary, it was Christian, it was beneficent. Knowing well these facts about it, I am inclined to place my experience with the Bible at the disposal of any whom it may help ...

[During the 1880s, when I had entered my forties,] I returned to the pastorate [in Hamilton, New York after years of teaching]. It was at this time that the higher criticism began to influence my thinking about the Bible. Of course many questions of the higher criticism had long been familiar, and entirely free. With such light as I had, I had unreservedly discussed questions of authorship, date, historical setting, and literary character. But thus far these questions had practically been separate from one another, pertaining to one book at a time, or to some one group. Inquiry as to the authorship of the Epistle to the Hebrews, for example, was absolutely free, and decidedly interesting, and quite indispensable to our studies, but it had not yet presented itself to my mind as a sample of a method that was to be applied with equal freedom to the entire Bible. Now, however, I became aware of a new situation of great interest and importance. The method that I had used as a matter of course in fragmentary fashion was now organized into a system, and was used in examination of all that the Bible contained. It now presented itself as the coming method, destined to be characteristic of a period in the history of biblical science. Its advent marked a new era. I had been brought up in a period of exegesis, in which attention was, directed to the contents of the sacred books, sentence by sentence and word by word; a period therefore of textual criticism also, verifying the very words as far as possible. But now was ushered in a period in which attention was to be turned less upon the contents of the books for interpretation, and more upon the books themselves, their origin, their general character, and their external history. On general principles it might seem that this class of questions would be considered first, when once the scientific study of the Bible had begun. It would seem right to search out the quality and history of the books before sitting down to read them word by word. But the esteem in which the Bible was held determined the order of the studies, and it was quite inevitable that the first scientific work upon it should be devoted to ascertaining what the Bible says. But it was equally inevitable that after a generation of students had bent itself to this task, another generation should set itself to inquire with equal diligence what the Bible is. This was the inquiry of the higher criticism.

    ... I well remember how the conviction was borne in upon me that the higher criticism was a thoroughly revolutionary thing. I plainly saw that the Bible would not come out of this crucible as it went in. From the generally accepted views there would certainly be great changes. No one could tell beforehand what they would be, but it was not to be supposed for a moment that the popular conceptions of the Bible, inherited from the Jews and from uncritical Christian ages, would all stand the test of critical investigation. Many of them would have to yield to new conceptions. The coming of great changes was as certain as the coming of the future, if this work went on.

    What should I think of all this? And what should I do? There was no room for doubt. The inquiry that was undertaken by the higher criticism was perfectly legitimate, and I had no right to resist it or to wish it away. It was as legitimate, and as important in its place, as laboratory work in chemistry or investigation of the causes of disease. Moreover, though I should never be an expert in the practice of criticism, I was pledged to approval of the enterprise by all my history as a student of the Bible. I had sought to be a sound interpreter of the sacred writings; but sound interpretation is quite impossible without just such examination of time, place, history, and literary character as the higher criticism proposes. This I had always assumed, for long before I ever heard the name of it I had undertaken elementary work of higher criticism, as something indispensable to the understanding of a book. However imperfectly I had lived up to it, my rule had always been to let the Bible mean whatever it does mean. But if I am to let it mean whatever it does mean, I must consent to let it be whatever it is. I must not dictate its character, any more than its utterance: I must leave these to be determined for me by the facts, and must do my utmost to ascertain the facts. If they prove to be other than I thought, it is I, not they, that must change, and to make the needful change must be my first desire. And if by tradition or by reverence I were tempted to exempt the Bible from critical judgment as to its origins and character, my experience in interpretation should recall me to a braver and more reasonable mind. I had not found it to be an infallible book in its counsel to a reader, for it contained old forms of truth that were long ago superseded by truth in higher forms, and the Bible itself contains the record of that superseding. It was not inerrant, for I had found its writers often irreconcilable in details, and sometimes demonstrably in error. The Bible was commended to me by its spiritual character as exceeding precious, but it was not marked by qualities that should set it apart from examination – if indeed any qualities could do that. Least of all did I find the Bible claiming any such exemption. It claimed neither inerrancy nor perfection of any kind. It was simply itself, and asked for no privileges.

Thus by all my studies I was pledged to this new form of study which they called the higher criticism. How it has been misunderstood! Well I remember the solemnity with which a minister said in my hearing, "The higher criticism is not higher, morally." No one ever said it was. But it is legitimate morally, and necessary to the understanding of the Bible. And so it has been my duty to accept the general conclusions of the higher criticism. I must be patient in doing so, and must allow time for a good degree of certainty to be reached, for I do not wish to accept new views prematurely. Yet even on this point I must not be too cautious. It is just as undesirable to retain an erroneous idea as it is to accept one. It is a popular charge against the higher criticism that its conclusions keep changing; there is no finality; if we adopt something now we may have to change again by and by. This aspect of the matter is often alleged as a sufficient reason for doing nothing at all about it. "When the higher critics have got their final conclusions," it is said, "we will begin to think of dropping our old ideas." But students do not talk in that way about chemistry, or physics, or astronomy, or any other science, or even about the geography of the North Pole. All genuine study assumes that knowledge is a growing thing, and as changes have come already, so they must come again. No one waits for the end of a movement in thought to be reached, before beginning to go along with it. All students of science are glad to let old ideas give place to new, with the perfect understanding that final conclusions may still be far away. All sciences, indeed, are revolutionized as often as new facts can revolutionize them. In like manner, if my old notions of the Bible are untenable, I must leave them behind and join those who are seeking for true ideas to take their place …

I commend this experience of mine to the many Christians who have been led to suppose that the higher criticism can be nothing else than a weapon of unbelief. For me it has made the Bible to be far more consistently a Christian book than it had ever been before, and has placed it in my hands more ready for all Christian use. In my progress toward the restful attitude concerning the Bible which I now hold, I thankfully recognize the higher criticism as one of the most valuable of helps.

INSPIRATION: THE "PRINCETON DOCTRINE"

Archibald A. Hodge (1823–86) and Benjamin B. Warfield (1851–1921) were two prominent conservative critics of William Newton Clarke (see previous selection) and other proponents of "liberal" theology. Hodge was the principal of Princeton Seminary (New Jersey) from 1878 to 1886 and his young colleague Warfield followed in that capacity from 1887 to 1921. In 1881, under Hodge's leadership, the two respected Presbyterian theologians presented "Inspiration," their now-classic defense of biblical inerrancy. The article has come to represent the defining statement of "Princeton Doctrine."

Source: A. A Hodge and B. B. Warfield, "Inspiration," *The Presbyterian Review* 2/6 (1881), 225–6, 228–32.

Inspiration

It is important that distinguishable ideas should be connoted by distinct terms, and that the terms themselves should be fixed in a definite sense. Thus we have come to distinguish sharply between Revelation, which is the frequent, and Inspiration, which is the constant attribute of all the thoughts and statements of Scripture, and between the problem of the genesis of Scripture on the one hand, which includes historic processes and the concurrence of natural and supernatural forces, and must account for all the phenomena of Scripture; and the mere fact of Inspiration on the other hand, or the superintendence by God of the writers in the entire process of their writing, which accounts for nothing whatever but the absolute infallibility of the record in which the revelation, once generated, appears in the original autograph ...

The importance of limiting the word "Inspiration" to a definite and never varying sense, and one which is shown, by the facts of the case, to be applicable equally to every part of Scripture, is self-evident, and is emphasized by the embarrassment which is continually recurring in the discussions of this subject, arising sometimes from the wide, and sometimes from the various, senses in which this term is used by different parties ...

The genesis of Scripture

We allude here to this wide, and as yet imperfectly explored subject, only for the purpose of distinctly setting apart the various problems it presents, and isolating the specific point of Inspiration, with which we, as well as the Church in general are more particularly interested. All parties of believers admit that this genesis of Holy Scripture was the result of the co-operation, in various ways, of the agency of men and of the agency of God.

The human agency, both in the histories out of which the Scriptures sprang, and in their immediate composition and inscription, is everywhere apparent, and gives substance and form to the entire collection of writings. It is not merely in the matter of verbal expression or literary composition that the personal idiosyncrasies of each author are freely manifested by the untrammeled play of all his faculties, but the very substance of what they write is evidently for the most part the product of their own mental and spiritual activities. This is true except in that comparatively small element of the whole body of sacred writing, in which the human authors simply report the word of God objectively communicated, or as in some of the prophecies they wrote by Divine dictation. As the general characteristic of all their work, each writer was put to that special part of the general work for which he alone was adapted by his original endowments, education, special information, and providential position. Each drew from the stores of his own original information, from the contributions of other men, and from all other natural sources. Each sought knowledge, like all other authors, from the use of his own natural faculties of thought and feeling, of intuition, and of logical inference, of memory, and imagination, and of religious experience. Each gave evidence of his own special limitations of knowledge and mental power and of his personal defects, as well as of his powers. Each wrote upon a definite occasion, under special historically grouped circumstances, from his own standpoint in the progressively unfolded plan of redemption, and each made his own special contribution to the fabric of God's Word.

The divine agency, although originating in a different source, yet emerges into the effect very much through the same channels. The Scriptures have been generated, as the Plan of Redemption has been evolved, through an historic process. From the beginning, God has dealt with man in the concrete, by self-manifestation and transactions. The revelation proceeds from facts to ideas, and has been gradually unfolded, as the preparation for the execution of the work of redemption has advanced through its successive stages. The general Providence unfolding this plan has always been divine, yet has also been largely natural in its method while specially directed to its ends, and at the same time surcharged along portions of its line, especially at the beginning and at great crises with the supernatural, as a cloud is surcharged with electricity. There were divine voices, appearances, covenants, supernatural communications and interventions; the introduction of new institutions, and their growth under special providential conditions. The prophet of God was sent with special revelations and authority at particular junctures to gather and interpret the lessons of the past, and to add to them lessons springing out of the providential conditions of the present. The Scriptures were generated through sixteen centuries of this divinely regulated concurrence of God and man, of the natural and the supernatural, of reason and revelation, of providence and grace. It is an organism consisting of many parts, each adjusted to all the rest, as the "many members" to the "one body." Each sacred writer was by God specially formed, endowed, educated, providentially conditioned, and then supplied with knowledge naturally, supernaturally, or spiritually conveyed, so that he, and he alone could, and freely would, produce his allotted part. Thus God predetermined all the matter and form of the several books largely by the formation and training of the several authors, as an organist determines the character of his music as much when he builds his organ and when he tunes his pipes, as when he plays his keys. Each writer also is put providentially at the very point of view in the general process of revelation to which his part assigns him. He inherits all the contributions of the past. He is brought into place and set to work at definite providential junctures, the occasion affording him object and motive, giving form to the writing God appoints him to execute.

The Bible, moreover, being a work of the Spirit for spiritual ends, each writer was prepared precisely for his part in the work by the personal dealings of the Holy Spirit with his soul. Spiritual illumination is very different from either revelation or inspiration, and yet it had under the providence of God a large share in the genesis of Scripture, contributing to it a portion of that divine element which makes it the Word of God. The Psalms are divinely inspired records of the religious experience of their writers, and are by God himself authoritatively set forth as typical and exemplary for all men forever. Paul and John and Peter largely drew upon the resources, and followed the lines of their own personal religious experience in the intuitional or the logical development of their doctrine, and their experience had, of course, been previously divinely determined for that very purpose. And in determining their religious experience, God so far forth determined their contributions to Scripture. And He furnished each of the sacred writers, in addition to that which came to him through natural channels, all the knowledge needed for his appointed task, either by vision, suggestion, dictation, or elevation of faculty, or otherwise, according to His will. The natural knowledge came from all sources, as traditions, documents, testimonies, personal observations, and recollections; by means also of intuitions, logical processes of thought, feeling, experience, etc., and yet all were alike under the general direction of God's providence. The supernatural knowledge became confluent with the natural in a manner which violated no law of reason or of freedom. And throughout the whole of his work the Holy Spirit was present, causing His energies to flow into the spontaneous exercises of the writer's faculties, elevating and directing where need be, and everywhere securing the errorless expression in language of the thought designed by God. This last element is what we call Inspiration.

In all this process, except in a small element of prophecy, it is evident that as the sacred writers were free and active in their thinking and in the expression of their thought, so they were conscious of what they were doing, of what their words meant, and of the design of their utterance. Yet, even then, it is no less evident that they all, like other free instruments of Providence, "builded better than they knew." The meanings of their words, the bearing of the principles they taught, of the facts they narrated, and the relation of their own part to the great organism of divine revelation, while luminous to their own consciousness, yet reached out into infinitely wider horizons than those penetrated by any thought of theirs.

THE BRIGGS CASE

Charles A. Briggs (1842–1912), a member of the faculty at the Union Theological Seminary in New York City, stood out as another of the well-known theologians who participated forcefully in the debates among scholars about the truth-status of the Bible. In fact, Hodge and Warfield's 1881 article "Inspiration" (excerpted in the preceding selection) served as a direct response to Briggs. The essay appeared in *The Presbyterian Review* as one part of a widely read exchange among the theologians. But, for Briggs, the disagreement became by the early 1890s much more than an academic debate. Briggs was brought to trial before the official Presbyterian judicial body on charges of deviation from Church orthodoxy. The selection below, published in 1893, includes part of Briggs' response to the accusation that his teachings undermined the Presbyterian Church's assertion of "the inerrancy of Holy Scripture." Briggs continued his work at Union, but the council found him guilty and stripped him of his standing within the Presbyterian Church.

Source: Charles A. Briggs, *The Defence of Professor Briggs Before the Presbytery of New York* (New York: Charles Scribner's Sons, 1893), 84–5, 88–90.

"The Presbyterian Church in the United States of America charges the Rev. Charles A. Briggs, D.D., being a Minister of the said Church and a member of the Presbytery of New York, with teaching that errors may have existed in the original text of the Holy Scripture, as it came from its authors, which is contrary to the essential doctrine taught in the Holy Scriptures and in the Standards of the said Church, that the Holy Scripture is the Word of God written, immediately inspired, and the rule of faith and practice" ...

(1) The Charge alleges three offences. It alleges that the doctrine taught by me is contrary to these three essential doctrines – (a) that the Holy Scripture is the Word of God, written; (b) that Holy Scripture is immediately inspired; and (c) that Holy Scripture is the rule of faith and practice.

(2) It is alleged that I teach "that errors may have existed in the original text of the Holy Scripture, as it came from its authors." This statement of my doctrine I can admit is fairly accurate. But ... you have no right to vote me guilty on the ground of any other objection to my words than that stated in the Charge. This is all the more important in view of the irrelevant passages of Scripture cited to sustain the Charge, which may be interpreted by you in a sense different from the true sense. You have no right to vote me guilty on the basis of these passages. You can consider nothing but my doctrine as stated in the Charge and determine whether that is contrary or not contrary to the essential doctrines named in the Charge.

(3) The only question which need concern us, therefore, is whether my doctrine is contrary to any one, or any two, or all three of the essential doctrines of the Confession stated in the Charge. Doubtless the prosecution thinks that there is contradiction here; and it may be that a majority of this Presbytery think so ...

I agree to the doctrines (1) that "Holy Scripture is the Word of God written;" (2) "immediately inspired;" and (3) "the rule of faith and practice."

Do these statements necessarily involve the doctrine that there are no errors in Holy Scripture? (a) The doctrine that "the Holy Scriptures are the rule in matters other than faith and practice." If I find fallibility in Holy Scripture in matters of faith and practice, I am inconsistent with the Confession. But ... the only errors I have found or ever recognized in Holy Scripture have been beyond the range of faith and practice, and therefore they do not impair the infallibility of Holy Scripture as a rule of faith and practice.

But it is claimed that if I recognize errors in matters beyond the range of faith and practice, I excite suspicion as to the infallibility of Holy Scripture within the range of faith and practice. You are entitled to that opinion for yourselves, but you have no right to force your opinion upon me. The Confession does not say "rule of all things," but "the rule of faith and practice." You must judge by the Confession, not by your fears, or your impressions, or by the conclusions you have made. But is it true that fallibility in the Bible in matters beyond the scope of the divine revelation impairs the infallibility in matters within the scope of divine revelation? We claim that it does not. The sacred writings were not composed in heaven by the Holy Spirit, they were sent down from heaven by angel hands, they were not committed to the care of perfect men, they were not kept by a succession of perfect priests from that moment until the present time. If these had been the facts in the case, we might have had a Bible infallible in every particular. But none of these things are true. God gave His Holy Word to men in an entirely different way. He used the human reason and all the faculties of imperfect human nature. He used the voice and hands of imperfect men. He allowed the sacred writings to be edited and re-edited, arranged and rearranged and rearranged again by imperfect scribes. It is improbable that such imperfect instrumentalities should attain perfect results. It was improbable that fallible men should produce a series of writings infallible in every respect. It was sufficient that divine inspiration and the guidance of the Holy Spirit should make their writings an infallible rule of faith and practice, and that the divine energy should push the human and the fallible into the external forms, into the unessential and unnecessary matters, in the human setting of the divine ideals. As the river of life flowing forth from the throne of God, according to Ezekiel's Vision, entering into the Dead Sea quickens its waters and fills them with new life, so that "everything shall live whithersoever the river cometh" … "But the miry places thereof and the marshes thereof shall not be healed" (Ez. Xlvii, 9–11); so may it be with that divine influence which we call inspiration, when it flows into a man. It quickens and enriches his whole nature, his experience, his utterance, his expressions, with truth and life divine, and yet leaves some human infirmities unhealed in order the revelation may be essentially divine and infallible and yet bear traces of the human and fallible into the midst of which it came.

DEBATING THE BIBLE'S AUTHORITY: THE MODERNIST/FUNDAMENTALIST SHOWDOWN

THE FUNDAMENTALS

With an increasing sense of embattlement over traditional meanings of the Bible, Lyman Stewart (1840–1923), an oil tycoon from southern California, proposed the idea of a series of paperback volumes scripted by "the best and most loyal Bible teachers in the world." Stewart and his brother, Milton, contracted a team of prominent conservative American and European scholars, editors, and popular writers, and then the Stewarts put up most of the money to distribute free of charge around three million individual volumes across all economic and professional sectors of the

English-speaking world. Released in twelve volumes between 1910 and 1915, *The Fundamentals* elicited positive response from thousands but less public momentum than the publishers expected. However, in retrospect the project assumed critical importance among conservative Christians and historians alike. *The Fundamentals* catalyzed the general movement that by the 1920s the public knew as "Fundamentalism." The following excerpt from James Orr's "Holy Scripture and Modern Negations" appeared in 1910 in the first volume of *The Fundamentals*. Orr, a well-known Scottish professor of theology who contributed multiple essays throughout the course of the project, concludes his argument about the unique nature and structure of the Bible with the insistence that the entire biblical enterprise depends upon "whole-hearted acceptance" of God's miraculous intervention in worldly affairs.

Source: James Orr, "Holy Scripture and Modern Negations," in R. A. Torrey and A. C. Dixon, eds, *The Fundamentals: A Testimony to the Truth*, vol. 1 (Grand Rapids, MI: Baker Books, 1917), chapter V.

Is there today in the midst of criticism and unsettlement a tenable doctrine of Holy Scripture for the Christian Church and for the world; and if there is, what is that doctrine? That is unquestionably a very pressing question at the present time. "Is there a book which we can regard as the repository of a true revelation of God and an infallible guide in the way of life, and as to our duties to God and man?" is a question of immense importance to us all. Fifty years ago, perhaps less than that, the question hardly needed to be asked among Christian people. It was universally conceded, taken for granted, that there is such a book, the book which we call the Bible. Here, it was believed, is a volume which is an inspired record of the whole will of God for man's salvation; accept as true and inspired the teaching of that book, follow its guidance, and you cannot stumble, you cannot err in attaining the supreme end of existence, in finding salvation, in grasping the prize of a glorious immortality.

Now, a change has come. There is no disguising the fact that we live in an age when, even within the Church, there is much uneasy and distrustful feeling about the Holy Scriptures – a hesitancy to lean upon them as an authority and to use them as the weapons of precision they once were; with a corresponding anxiety to find some surer basis in external Church authority, or with others, in Christ Himself, or again in a Christian consciousness, as it is named, – a surer basis for Christian belief and life.

We often hear in these days reference to the substitution, in Protestantism, of an "INFALLIBLE BIBLE FOR AN INFALLIBLE CHURCH," and the implication is that the one idea is just as baseless as the other. Sometimes the idea is taken up, quite commonly perhaps, that the thought of an authority external to ourselves – to our own reason or conscience or spiritual nature – must be wholly given up; that only that can be accepted which carries its authority within itself by the appeal it makes to reason or to our spiritual being, and therein lies the judge for us of what is true and what is false.

That proposition has an element of truth in it; it may be true or may be false according as we interpret it. However, as it is frequently interpreted it leaves the Scriptures – but more than that, it leaves Jesus Christ Himself – without any authority for us save that with which our own minds see fit to clothe Him. But in regard to the INFALLIBLE BIBLE AND THE INFALLIBLE CHURCH, it is proper to point out that there is a considerable difference between these two things – between the idea of an authoritative Scripture and the idea of an infallible Church or an infallible Pope, in the Roman sense of that word. It may be a clever antithesis to say that Protestantism substituted the idea of an infallible Book for the older Romish dogma of an infallible Church; but the antithesis, the contrast, unfortunately has one fatal inaccuracy about it. The idea of the authority of Scripture is not younger, but older than Romanism. It is not a late invention of Protestantism. It is not something that Protestants invented and substituted for the Roman conception of the infallible Church; but it is the original conception that lies in the Scriptures themselves. There is a great difference there. It is a belief – this belief in the Holy Scripture – which was accepted and acted upon by the Church of Christ from the first. The Bible itself claims to be an authoritative Book, and an infallible guide to the true knowledge of God and of the way of salvation …

It has now become fashionable among a class of religious teachers to speak disparagingly of or belittle the Holy Scriptures as an authoritative rule of faith for the Church. The leading cause of this has undoubtedly been the trend which the criticism of the Holy Scriptures has assumed during the last half century or more. By all means, let criticism have its rights. Let purely literary questions about the Bible receive full and fair discussion. Let the structure of books be impartially examined. If a reverent science has light to throw on the composition or authority or age of these books, let its voice be heard. If this thing is of God we cannot overthrow it; if it be of man, or so far as it is of man, or so far as it comes in conflict with the reality of things in the Bible, it will come to naught – as in my opinion a great deal of it is fast coming today through its own excesses. No fright, therefore, need be taken at the mere word, "Criticism." On the other hand, we are not bound to accept every wild critical theory that any critic may choose to put forward and assert, as the final word on this matter. We are entitled, nay, we are bound, to look at the presuppositions on which each criticism proceeds, and to ask, How far is the criticism controlled by those presuppositions? We are bound to look at the evidence by which the theory is supported, and to ask, Is it really borne out by that evidence? And when theories are put forward with every confidence as fixed results, and we find them, as we observe them, still in constant process of evolution and change, constantly becoming more complicated, more extreme, more fanciful, we are entitled to inquire, Is this the certainty that it was alleged to be? Now that is my complaint against much of the current criticism of the Bible – not that it is criticism, but that it starts from the wrong basis, that it proceeds by arbitrary methods, and that it arrives at results which I think are demonstrably false results …

I do not speak especially of those whose philosophical standpoint compels them to take up an attitude of negation to supernatural revelation, or to books which profess to convey such a revelation. Criticism of this kind, criticism that starts from the basis of the denial of the supernatural, has of course, to be reckoned with. In its hands everything is engineered from that basis. There is the denial to begin with, that God ever has entered into human history, in word and deed, in any supernatural way. The necessary result is that whatever in the Bible affirms or flows from such interposition of God is expounded or explained away ...

Leaving, however, such futile, rationalistic criticism out of account – because that is not the kind of criticism with which we as Christian people have chiefly to deal in our own circles – there is certainly an immense change of attitude on the part of many who still sincerely hold faith in the supernatural revelation of God. [...] The process of thought in regard to Scripture is easily traced. First, there is an ostentatious throwing overboard, joined with some expression of contempt, of what is called the verbal inspiration of Scripture – a very much abused term. Jesus is still spoken of as the highest revealer, and it is allowed that His words, if only we could get at them – and on the whole it is thought we can – furnish the highest rule of guidance for time and for eternity. But even criticism, we are told, must have its rights. Even in the New Testament the Gospels go into the crucible, and in the name of synoptical criticism, historical criticism; they are subject to wonderful processes, in the course of which much of the history gets melted out or is peeled off as Christian characteristics. Jesus, we are reminded, was still a man of His generation, liable to error in His human knowledge, and allowance must be made for the limitations in His conceptions and judgments. Paul is alleged to be still largely dominated by his inheritance of Rabbinical and Pharisaic ideas. He had been brought up a Pharisee, brought up with the rabbis, and when he became a Christian, he carried a great deal of that into his Christian thought, and we have to strip off that thought when we come to the study of his Epistles. He is therefore a teacher not to be followed further than our own judgment of Christian truth leads us. That gets rid of a great deal that is inconvenient about Paul's teaching ...

The structure of the Bible

First as to the structure of the Bible, there is needed a more positive idea of that structure than is at present prevalent. You take much of the criticism and you find the Bible being disintegrated in many ways, and everything like structure falling away from it. You are told, for example, that these books – say the Books of Moses are made up of many documents, which are very late in origin and cannot claim historical value ... Thus you have the history of the Bible turned pretty much upside down, and things take on a new aspect altogether. Must I then, in deference to criticism, accept these theories, and give up the structure which the Bible presents? Taking the Bible as it stands, I find and you will find if you look there also, without any particular critical learning you will find it – what seems to be evidence of a very definite internal structure, part fitting into part and leading on to part, making up a unity of the whole in that Bible. The Bible has undeniably a structure as it stands. It is distinguished from all other books of the kind, from all sacred books in the world, from Koran and Buddhist scriptures and Indian scriptures and every other kind of religious books. It is distinguished just by this fact, that it is the embodiment of a great plan or scheme or purpose of Divine grace extending from the beginning of time through successive ages and dispensations down to its culmination in Jesus Christ and the Pentecostal outpourings of the Spirit. The history of the Bible is the history of that development of God's redemptive purpose. The promises of the Bible mark the stages of its progress and its hope. The covenants of the Bible stand before us in the order of its unfolding. You begin with Genesis. Genesis lays the foundation and leads up to the Book of Exodus; and the Book of Exodus, with its introduction of the law-giving, leads up to what follows. Deuteronomy looks back upon the history of the rebellions and the laws given to the people, and leads up to the conquest. I need not follow the later developments, coming away down through the monarchy and the prophecy and the rest, but you find it all gathered up and fulfilled in the New Testament. The Bible, as we have it, closes in Gospel and Epistle and Apocalypse, fulfilling all the ideas of the Old Testament. There the circle completes itself with the new heaven and the new earth wherein dwelleth righteousness. Here is a structure; here is the fact; here is a structure, a connected story, a unity of purpose extending through this Book and binding all its parts together. Is that structure an illusion? Do we only, and many with us, dream that it is there? Do our eyes deceive us when we think we see it? Or has somebody of a later date invented it, and put it all, inwrought it all, in these earlier records, legends and stories, or whatever you like to call it – skillfully woven into the story until it presents there the appearance of naturalness and truth? I would like to find the mind capable of inventing it, and then the mind capable of putting it in and working it into a history once they got the idea itself …

A supernatural revelation

I think it is an essential element in a tenable doctrine of Scripture, in fact the core of the matter, that it contains a record of a true supernatural revelation; and that is what the Bible claims to be – not a development of man's thoughts about God, and not what this man and that one came to think about God, how they came to have the ideas of a Jehovah or Yahveh, who was originally the storm-god of Sinai, and how they manufactured out of this the great universal God of the prophets – but a supernatural revelation of what God revealed Himself in word and deed to men in history. And if that claim to a supernatural revelation from God falls, the Bible falls, because it is bound up with it from beginning to end. Now, it is just here that a great deal of our modern thought parts company with the Bible. I am quite well aware that many of our friends who accept these newer critical theories, claim to be just as firm believers in Divine revelation as I am myself, and in Jesus Christ and all that concerns Him. I rejoice in the fact, and I believe that they are warranted in saying that there is that in the religion of Israel which you cannot expunge, or explain on any other hypothesis but Divine revelation.

But what I maintain is that this theory of the religion of the Bible which has been evolved, which has peculiarly come to be known as the critical view, had a very different origin in men who did not believe in the supernatural revelation of God in the Bible. This school as a whole, as a wide-spread school, holds the fundamental position – the position which its adherents call that of the modern mind, that miracles did not happen and cannot happen ... But the question is, Has this natural working not its limits? Is there not something that nature and natural workings cannot reach, cannot do for men, that we need to have done for us? And are we so to bind God that He cannot enter into communion with man in a supernatural economy of grace, an economy of revelation, an economy of salvation? Are we to deny that He has done so? That is really the dividing line both in Old Testament and New between the different theories. Revelation, surely, all must admit if man is to attain the clear knowledge of God that is needed; and the question is one of fact, Has God so revealed Himself? And I believe that it is an essential part of the answer, the true doctrine of Scripture, to say, "Yes, God has so revealed Himself, and the Bible is the record of that revelation, and that revelation shines in its light from the beginning to the end of it." And unless there is a whole-hearted acceptance of the fact that God has entered, in word and deed, into human history for man's salvation, for man's renovation, for the deliverance of this world, a revelation culminating in the great Revealer Himself – unless we accept that, we do not get the foundation for the true doctrine of Holy Scripture.

CURTIS LEE LAWS

In the face-off that developed in the 1910s and 1920s between self-identified "progressive" and "traditional" Christians, Curtis Lee Laws (1868–1946) played a significant role. As the editor of the conservative Baptist *Watchman-Examiner*, Laws leveraged the power of the press in the war of opinions. In so doing, he reflects the shift of debate from the intellectual confines of theology and biblical scholarship to a broader sphere of public discourse. In that arena, Laws made a definite impact. His paper consistently garnered attention among and beyond American Protestants. And in a singularly decisive set of writings from 1920, Laws instituted the term "fundamentalist" to describe a faction of anti-modernists with whom he sympathized – those prepared "to do battle royal for the Fundamentals" – within the Northern Baptist Convention. The following selection exhibits Laws' characteristic crusading spirit. He draws sharp distinctions between "the old and new theologies" by seizing from his opponents their rhetorical high-ground: the claim to "assured results of scientific study of the Bible."

Source: Curtis Lee Laws, "The Old and New Theologies: The Bible and Authority," *The Watchman-Examiner* 5/5 (February 1, 1917), 133–4.

There is much vagueness and confusion in the minds of many as to the real issue between the old and the new theologies touching the place of the Bible in the Christian life. The word "authority" is in bad repute with some. They say we have transcended or outgrown the idea of authority. It has been passed as a way station on the main line of human thought. Since Schleiermacher the Christian consciousness has been alleged by the advocates of the new theology to be the seat of authority. There is no truth for the Christian except what he can assimilate. God's message written in our own moral constitution is his decisive and final message. Only such truth as we can appreciate or assimilate is truth for us. We judge the Scriptures, not the Scriptures us.

In order to strengthen the subjective basis of authority the attack on the old view has taken a number of extreme forms. Some of these oppose not what is in essentials the older view, but a caricature of it. It is charged that the Bible is made a sort of fetish to which believers are required to bow down. Its authority, so it is alleged, is based on a verbal-mechanical or dictation theory of inspiration. Its authoritativeness is also identified with the old outgrown 'proof-text' method of interpretation, according to which it is simply a storehouse of weapons for our spiritual warfare, rather than a record of religious experience. Especially it is urged as the supreme and fatal objection to the older view that is Roman Catholic and not Protestant in principle; that it makes of the Bible a sort of pope, which Christians are bound to obey. And finally it is alleged that if the Bible possesses any kind of infallibility it must be faultless in every particular.

Now, without denying the existence of extreme forms of the older view, illogical developments which it has undergone, and untenable claims which its advocates have sometimes made, we assert that none of the charges named has any bearing on the true conception of an authoritative Bible. When that conception is clearly grasped it is seen to depend on no mere theory of inspiration, nor is it identified with any of the abuses mentioned. Moreover it is entirely consonant with the most approved methods of historical science and exegesis.

In brief, the older view in its fundamental expression is as follows: The Bible is the record of a progressive revelation made by God to man through the religious experience of his people. The unity of the revelation covering many centuries is one of its most marked characteristics. That revelation reached its climax in Jesus Christ who is the final word of God to men as a divine self-disclosure for our salvation. The revelation of God through Christ became a revelation to men only as men were redeemed by its power. The revelation to men is essentially bound up with the redemption of men. Truth experienced is truth understood. Christ failed as Revealer and Teacher unless the first group of apostles and disciples understood his message. Hence the New Testament records of Christian experience complete those of the old. Their authoritativeness is grounded in part in their direct historical relation to Christ, a relation which no later literature can possess; and, in part, in the fact that in them God was, through his Spirit, speaking to his people. The New Testament then becomes the final form of God's progressive revelation and is sufficient for the purposes of our religious life. Technicalities have been avoided in order to make the main point clear in the preceding statement.

Now the point at issue between the older and the newer school is clear. The older takes the New Testament as a whole; the new rejects what the Christian consciousness does not approve.

Consider now some points in detail. The old view holds with the new that we assimilate spiritual truth in order to possess it. But the old emphasizes spiritual as well as mental assimilation. The new is concerned first with mental needs in a scientific age; the old with the religious needs of the soul in all ages. Evangelical Christians have assimilated all the great New Testament truths for nearly two thousand years. The mature Christian consciousness is in harmony with all revealed truth. But the "Christian" consciousness may be partly Christian and partly fleshly and unchristian. When the Christian consciousness is most mature it is most conscious of its limitations and defects. It is most nearly perfect when it has a sense of its own imperfection. At least it was so with Paul as we see from Philippians 3:15. The last thing the adult Christian consciousness desires to attempt is the adjudication of ultimate questions by its own wisdom. The Christian consciousness that is youthful and unripe is also over-confident as to its judgments. When it grows it becomes spiritually docile and tractable. Humility is an organ of knowledge. To imagine that we know all is deadly to growth in knowledge.

The view that makes the Christian consciousness the seat of authority is pantheistic in its main implications, as was the whole system of Schleiermacher from which it is derived. Pantheism makes all forms of consciousness equally valid since there is no personal God or standard of truth objective to man. Men are like flowers or trees. Each is perfect after its kind, since each is a manifestation of the eternal substance. There can be no contradiction except in appearance. The attributes of "true" and "good" are irrelevant to our states of consciousness because there exists no ground for the assertion that there is anything "untrue" or "bad." If we admit degrees of "trueness" and "badness" we at once assume an external standard that is regulative. To attempt to save the day by calling the authoritative consciousness "Christian" fails of its purpose because this implies Christ as regulative of consciousness. He is historical. His career was an outward event. His teachings are external to us. If we depend on Christ for truth we swing at once to the old view. The only "consciousness" that can be authoritative is unchristian and pantheistic. And this gives us as many systems as there are consciousnesses.

The Bible according to the older view is authoritative for Christians, not because an early council decreed it or a pope ordained it; nor because any abstract theory of inspiration compels it; nor because any sublimated conception of infallibility demands it. It is our authority because it does for us what our souls need. It claims to be God's word to us and proves its claim by its deed. Our experience echoes the experience recorded in the New Testament. We are related to the same redemptive forces, and find the same salvation. The infallibility of the Bible is the infallibility of common sense, and of the experimental triumph in us. We do not ask it about chemistry or astronomy or the constitution of matter, or the expansive power of gases, just as we do not ask a compass to tell us the time of the day, or a watch to predict the weather. The living power of the Bible is due to its living function in man's religious life.

The old view of an authoritative Bible welcomes all scientific study and all assured results of scientific study of the Bible. It does not accept guesses or devour eagerly the green apples of premature criticism. It has too much respect for its digestive apparatus ...

The old view in its vital essence is totally opposed to the Catholic conception of authority, as unreasoning obedience to external commands. In the Catholic view the spirit is passive; under our view it is active. In the latter the whole spiritual nature is aroused. It discerns, discriminates, appreciates and estimates the contents of the Gospel and approves it as the New Testament presents it. It knows itself dependent on the New Testament for knowledge of Christ in his historic life. It is dependent on it for knowledge of that life when it became revelation to men through redemptive power. We know Christ thus, and we know him as organic in the humanity he came to redeem, through this New Testament record. Our own experience vindicates and confirms the early experience. We accept the Newtonian law of gravitation as normative and regulative in astronomy, and do not feel humiliated because we are not the original discoverer of the law. So also we accept the New Testament as regulative in our religious life. It antedates us. It anticipates our needs. It was thus external to us. But it came to us. It "found" us most deeply. It awakened us and showed the creative forces of the soul's life to which the soul responded and found emancipation and victory and self-realization. So we came to accept the New Testament as final for our religious needs and the Old as the completely trustworthy preliminary revelation. And this means an authoritative Bible. It is incompatible with exclusively subjective criterion. Yet it is a spiritual, not an ecclesiastical merely dogmatic form of authority. Our ascending thought meets and owns God's descending truth. Our spiritual yearnings find themselves satisfied by these revealed facts. The Bible thus works redemption in us, and by a universal law takes place as the authoritative source of redemptive truth for mankind.

HARRY EMERSON FOSDICK

Harry Emerson Fosdick (1878–1969), a popular Baptist minister and respected professor at Union Theological Seminary in New York, stands out as one of the most forceful defenders of liberal theology. His May 21, 1922 sermon "Shall the Fundamentalists Win?" – the source of the following selection – immediately became a rallying point for self-identifying "modernists" as well as for counterattacks by conservative critics. The now-famous sermon encapsulates Fosdick's own theologically grounded polemic. He appeals to the Bible itself to justify new historical-critical approaches to scripture. In his subsequent scholarly work, including an influential series of lectures from 1924 on "The Modern Use of the

Bible," Fosdick further developed the contrast between "mature," scientific perspectives and Fundamentalists' "immature" biblical literalism.

Source: Harry Emerson Fosdick, "Shall the Fundamentalists Win?" *Christian Work* 102 (June 10, 1922), 716–22.

This morning we are to think of the fundamentalist controversy which threatens to divide the American churches as though already they were not sufficiently split and riven. A scene, suggestive for our thought, is depicted in the fifth chapter of the Book of the Acts, where the Jewish leaders hale before them Peter and other of the apostles because they had been preaching Jesus as the Messiah. Moreover, the Jewish leaders propose to slay them, when in opposition Gamaliel speaks "Refrain from these men, and let them alone; for if this counsel or this work be of men, it will be overthrown; but if it is of God ye will not be able to overthrow them; lest haply ye be found even to be fighting against God" ...

Already all of us must have heard about the people who call themselves the Fundamentalists. Their apparent intention is to drive out of the evangelical churches men and women of liberal opinions ... All Fundamentalists are conservatives, but not all conservatives are Fundamentalists. The best conservatives can often give lessons to the liberals in true liberality of spirit, but the Fundamentalist program is essentially illiberal and intolerant.

The Fundamentalists see, and they see truly, that in this last generation there have been strange new movements in Christian thought. A great mass of new knowledge has come into man's possession – new knowledge about the physical universe, its origin, its forces, its laws; new knowledge about human history and in particular about the ways in which the ancient peoples used to think in matters of religion and the methods by which they phrased and explained their spiritual experiences; and new knowledge, also, about other religions and the strangely similar ways in which men's faiths and religious practices have developed everywhere ...

Now, there are multitudes of reverent Christians who have been unable to keep this new knowledge in one compartment of their minds and the Christian faith in another. They have been sure that all truth comes from the one God and is His revelation. Not, therefore, from irreverence or caprice or destructive zeal but for the sake of intellectual and spiritual integrity, that they might really love the Lord their God, not only with all their heart and soul and strength but with all their mind, they have been trying to see this new knowledge in terms of the Christian faith and to see the Christian faith in terms of this new knowledge ...

The new knowledge and the old faith cannot be left antagonistic or even disparate, as though a man on Saturday could use one set of regulative ideas for his life and on Sunday could change gear to another altogether. We must be able to think our modern life clear through in Christian terms, and to do that we also must be able to think our Christian faith clear through in modern terms.

There is nothing new about the situation. It has happened again and again in history, as, for example, when the stationary earth suddenly began to move and the universe that had been centered in this planet was centered in the sun around which the planets whirled. Whenever such a situation has arisen, there has been only one way out – the new knowledge and the old faith had to be blended in a new combination. Now, the people in this generation who are trying to do this are the liberals, and the Fundamentalists are out on a campaign to shut against them the doors of the Christian fellowship. Shall they be allowed to succeed?

It is interesting to note where the Fundamentalists are driving in their stakes to mark out the deadline of doctrine around the church, across which no one is to pass except on terms of agreement. They insist that we must all believe in the historicity of certain special miracles, preeminently the virgin birth of our Lord; that we must believe in a special theory of inspiration – that the original documents of the Scripture, which of course we no longer possess, were inerrantly dictated to men a good deal as a man might dictate to a stenographer; that we must believe in a special theory of the Atonement – that the blood of our Lord, shed in a substitutionary death, placates an alienated Deity and makes possible welcome for the returning sinner; and that we must believe in the second coming of our Lord upon the clouds of heaven to set up a millennium here, as the only way in which God can bring history to a worthy denouement. Such are some of the stakes which are being driven to mark a deadline of doctrine around the church ...

The question is – Has anybody a right to deny the Christian name to those who differ with him on such points and to shut against them the doors of the Christian fellowship? The Fundamentalists say that this must be done. In this country and on the foreign field they are trying to do it. They have actually endeavored to put on the statute books of a whole state binding laws against teaching modern biology. If they had their way, within the church, they would set up in Protestantism a doctrinal tribunal more rigid than the pope's ...

Consider [a] matter on which there is a sincere difference of opinion between evangelical Christians: the inspiration of the Bible. One point of view is that the original documents of the Scripture were inerrantly dictated by God to men. Whether we deal with the story of creation or the list of the dukes of Edom or the narratives of Solomon's reign or the Sermon on the Mount or the thirteenth chapter of First Corinthians, they all came in the same way, and they all came as no other book ever came. They were inerrantly dictated; everything there – scientific opinions, medical theories, historical judgments, as well as spiritual insight – is infallible. That is one idea of the Bible's inspiration. But side by side with those who hold it, lovers of the Book as much as they, are multitudes of people who never think about the Bible so. Indeed, that static and mechanical theory of inspiration seems to them a positive peril to the spiritual life ... Finality in the Bible is ahead. We have not reached it. We cannot yet compass all of it. God is leading us out toward it. There are multitudes of Christians, then, who think, and rejoice as they think, of the Bible as the record of the progressive unfolding of the character of God to his people from early primitive days until the great unveiling in Christ; to them the Book is more inspired and more inspiring than ever it was before. To go back to a mechanical and static theory of inspiration would mean to them the loss of some of the most vital elements in their spiritual experience and in their appreciation of the Book …

Consider another matter upon which there is a serious and sincere difference of opinion between evangelical Christians: the second coming of our Lord. The second coming was the early Christian phrasing of hope. No one in the ancient world had ever thought, as we do, of development, progress, gradual change as God's way of working out His will in human life and institutions. They thought of human history as a series of ages succeeding one another with abrupt suddenness …

In the evangelical churches today there are differing views of this matter. One view is that Christ is literally coming, externally, on the clouds of heaven, to set up His kingdom here. I never heard that teaching in my youth at all. It has always had a new resurrection when desperate circumstances came and man's only hope seemed to lie in divine intervention. It is not strange, then, that during these chaotic, catastrophic years there has been a fresh rebirth of this old phrasing of expectancy. "Christ is coming!" seems to many Christians the central message of the Gospel. In the strength of it some of them are doing great service for the world. But, unhappily, many so overemphasize it that they outdo anything the ancient Hebrews or the ancient Christians ever did. They sit still and do nothing and expect the world to grow worse and worse until He comes.

Side by side with these to whom the second coming is a literal expectation, another group exists in the evangelical churches. They, too, say, "Christ is coming!" They say it with all their hearts; but they are not thinking of an external arrival on the clouds. They have assimilated as part of the divine revelation the exhilarating insight which these recent generations have given to us, that development is God's way of working out His will … These two groups exist in the Christian churches and the question raised by the Fundamentalists is – Shall one of them drive the other out? Will that get us anywhere? …

I do not believe for one moment that the Fundamentalists are going to succeed. Nobody's intolerance can contribute anything to the solution of the situation which we have described. If, then, the Fundamentalists have no solution of the problem, where may we expect to find it? In two concluding comments let us consider our reply to that inquiry.

The first element that is necessary is a spirit of tolerance and Christian liberty. When will the world learn that intolerance solves no problems? This is not a lesson which the Fundamentalists alone need to learn; the liberals also need to learn it … It was a wise liberal, the most adventurous man of his day – Paul the Apostle – who said, "Knowledge puffeth up, but love buildeth up" …

As I plead thus for an intellectually hospitable, tolerant, liberty-loving church, I am, of course, thinking primarily about this new generation. We have boys and girls growing up in our homes and schools, and because we love them we may well wonder about the church which will be waiting to receive them …

My friends, nothing in all the world is so much worth thinking of as God, Christ, the Bible, sin and salvation, the divine purposes for humankind, life everlasting. But you cannot challenge the dedicated thinking of this generation to these sublime themes upon any such terms as are laid down by an intolerant church.

The second element which is needed if we are to reach a happy solution of this problem is a clear insight into the main issues of modern Christianity and a sense of penitent shame that the Christian Church should be quarreling over little matters when the world is dying of great needs. If, during the war, when the nations were wrestling upon the very brink of hell and at times all seemed lost, you chanced to hear two men in an altercation about some minor matter of sectarian denominationalism, could you restrain your indignation? You said, "What can you do with folks like this who, in the face of colossal issues, play with the tiddledywinks and peccadillos of religion?" ...

The present world situation smells to heaven! And now, in the presence of colossal problems, which must be solved in Christ's name and for Christ's sake, the Fundamentalists propose to drive out from the Christian churches all the consecrated souls who do not agree with their theory of inspiration. What immeasurable folly!

Well, they are not going to do it; certainly not in this vicinity. I do not even know in this congregation whether anybody has been tempted to be a Fundamentalist. Never in this church have I caught one accent of intolerance. God keep us always so and ever increasing areas of the Christian fellowship; intellectually hospitable, open-minded, liberty-loving, fair, tolerant, not with the tolerance of indifference, as though we did not care about the faith, but because always our major emphasis is upon the weightier matters of the law.

DEBATING THE BIBLE'S AUTHORITY: EVOLUTION AND CREATIONISM

T. DeWitt Talmage

Although in many ways a unique figure on the nineteenth-century American religious landscape, T. DeWitt Talmage (1832–1902) also voiced some of the most common sentiments of the day with his fierce condemnation of contemporary science in general and of evolution in particular. Much of his teaching – popularly known as "Talmagic" – unfolded from the pulpit at the Free Tabernacle in Brooklyn, which bucked tradition and drew crowds by waiving fees to sit in the pews. Although a Calvinist by training and by conviction, Talmage insisted on freedom from denominational obligations. His fiery sermons circulated widely. In "The Missing Link," an 1885 sermon from which the following selection derives, Talmage emphasizes how dim the ideas of evolution appear next to the eternal illumination of biblical truths.

Source: T. DeWitt Talmage, "The Missing Link," in *Live Coals* (New York: Wilbur B. Ketcham, 1885), 271–5.

Evolution is one great mystery. It hatches out fifty mysteries, and the fifty hatch out a thousand, and the thousand hatch out a million. Why, my brother, not admit the one great mystery of God, and have that settle all the other mysteries? I can more easily appreciate the fact that God, by one stroke, of His omnipotence could make man, than I could realize how, out of five million ages, He could have evolved one, putting on a little here and a little there. It would have been just as great a miracle for God to have turned an orang-outang into a man as to make a man out and out – the one job just as big as the other.

It seems to me we had better let God have a little place in our world some-where. It seems to me if we cannot have Him make all creatures, we had better have Him make two or three. There ought to be some place where He could stay without interfering with the evolutionists. "No," says Darwin, and so for years he is trying to raise fan-tailed pigeons, and to turn these fan-tail pigeons into some other kind of pigeon, or to have them go into something that is not a pigeon – turning them into quail, or barnyard fowl, or brown thresher. But pigeon it is. And others have tried with the ox and the dog and the horse, but they stayed in their species. If they attempt to cross over it is a hybrid, and a hybrid is always sterile and goes into extinction. There has been one successful attempt to pass over from speechless animal to the articulation of man, and that was the attempt which Baalam witnessed in the beast that he rode; but an angel of the Lord, with drawn sword, soon stopped that long-eared evolu-tionist ...

As near as I can tell, these evolutionists seem to think that God at the start had not made up His mind as to exactly what He would make, and having made up His mind partially, He has been changing it all through the ages. I believe that God made the world as He wanted to have it, and that the happi-ness of all the species will depend upon their staying in the species where they were created.

But, my friends, evolution is not only infidel and atheistic and absurd; *it is brutalizing in its tendencies* ... Born of a beast, to die like a beast; for the evolu-tionists have no idea of a future world. They say the mind is only a superior part of the body. They say our thoughts are only molecular formation. They say when a body dies, the whole nature dies. The slab of the sepulcher is not a milestone on a journey upward, but a wall shutting us into eternal nothing-ness. We all die alike – the cow, the horse, the sheep, the man, the reptile. Annihilation is the heaven of the evolutionist.

From such a stenchful and damnable doctrine turn away. Compare that idea of your origin – an idea filled with the chatter of apes, and the hiss of serpents, and the croak of frogs – to an idea in one or two stanzas which I shall read to you from an old book of more than Demosthenic, or Homeric, or Dantesque power: "What is man, that thou art mindful of him? And the son of man, that thou visitest him? Thou hast made him a little lower than the angels, and hast crowned him with glory and honor. Thou madest him to have dominion over the works of thy hand; thou hast put all things under his feet. All sheep and oxen, yea, and the beasts of the field; the fowl of the air, and the fish of the sea, and whatsoever passeth through the paths of the seas. Oh, Lord, our Lord, how excellent is Thy name in all the earth."

How do you like that origin? The lion the monarch of the field, the eagle the monarch of the air, behemoth the monarch of the deep, but man monarch of all. Ah! My friends, I have to say to you that I am not so anxious to know what was my origin as to know what will be my destiny. I do not care so much where I came from as where I am going to. I am not so interested in who was my ancestry ten million years ago as I am to know where I will be ten million years from now. I am not so much interested in the preface to my cradle as I am interested in the appendix to my grave. I do not care so much about protoplasm as I do about eternasm. The "was" is overwhelmed with the "to be." And here comes in the evolution I believe in: not nature evolution, but gracious and divine and heavenly evolution – evolution out of sin into holiness, out of grief into gladness, out of mortality into immortality, out of earth into heaven! That is the evolution I believe in.

HENRY WARD BEECHER (1885)

> Henry Ward Beecher (1813–87), the well-known pastor at Plymouth Congregational Church in Brooklyn, played a critical role as the controversies over the relation of religion and science swelled in the latter half of the nineteenth century. In every way, Beecher acted as mediator: he carried the issues from academic contexts to the pews and, in doing so, staked out the middle ground. He presented a position of Christian faith in which biblical and scientific claims were fundamentally consistent. In the last years of his life, Beecher offered a series of sermons on "evolution and religion." The selection below comes from the sixth of those seven talks delivered – like the Talmage selection above – from a Brooklyn pulpit in 1885.
>
> Source: Henry Ward Beecher, "Divine Providence and Design," in De Witte Holland, ed., *Sermons in American History* (Nashville, TN: Abingdon, 1970), 271–81.

"To whom will ye liken me, and make me equal, and compare me, that we may be like?" Isaiah XLVI: 5.

There is no attempt in the Hebrew Scriptures to give definite form to God, nor strict analysis, nor any comprehensive theory; as we formulate in modern times "the philosophy of things," there is no philosophy of God made known in the Bible, – any more than there is science in nature. Science is the recognition by men of things pre-existing in the world of matter; and theologies are the consciousness and the intellectual views of men respecting the facts that are set forth in the Bible. It was expressly forbidden, indeed, that there should be any form given to God in carved statues. They were not to be allowed to make images, and the spirit of the command is equally strong against pictures and against fashioning in the imagination any definite conception of form. It degrades God in the mind and imagination of men to limit him by forms of matter. There is, to be sure, addressed not to the senses but to the imagination, some form given to God by descriptions – Isaiah, Daniel, John, the Apocalyptic writer; yet even then there was but sublime indefiniteness. There was the declaration of will, the quality of disposition, the attributes of power and of glory; but they were all diffused through time and space, and with no definite outlines. The "word-pictures" in Isaiah and Daniel and the Revelation of John, though descriptions, are symbols and figures playing on the imagination; ... Any formulation of the divine nature, which becomes definite, crystalline, philosophic, is a perpetual affront to the method of God's revelation, whether in Scripture or in science ... It will be my design this morning, therefore, to discuss ... the question of Design in creation and the question of a general and a special Providence, as they stand related, not to the Scriptural testimony alone, but to what we now know of the course of natural law in this world ...

The law of cause and effect is fundamental to the very existence of science, and, I had almost said, to the very operation of the human mind. So, then, we gain nothing by excluding divine intelligence, and to include it smoothes the way to investigation, and is agreeable to the nature of the human mind. It is easier to conceive of the personal divine being with intelligence, will and power, than it is to conceive of a world of such vast and varied substance as this, performing all the functions of intelligence and will and power. That would be giving to miscellaneous matter the attributes which we denied to a personal God.

The doctrine of Evolution, at first sight, seems to destroy the theory of intelligent design in creation, and in its earlier stages left those who investigated it very doubtful whether there was anything in creation but matter, or whether there was a knowable God.

So sprang up the Agnostic school, which includes in it some of the noblest spirits of our day. "God may exist, but we do not know it." That is what the Bible says from beginning to end; that is what philosophy is now beginning to explain. We cannot understand the divine nature, so exalted above everything that has yet been developed in human consciousness, except it dawns upon us when we are ourselves unfolding, and rising to such a higher operation of our own minds as does not belong to the great mass of the human race. God is to be seen only by those faculties that verge upon the divine nature, and to them only when they are in a state of exaltation. Moral intuitions are not absolute revelations, but they are as sure of higher truths as the physical senses are of material truths.

But the question of design in creation, which has been a stable argument for the proof of the existence of God and his attributes, seems to have been shaken from its former basis. It is being restored in a larger and grander way, which only places the fact upon a wider space, and makes the outcome more wonderful ...

[Still,] the theory of Evolution is as much a theory of destruction and degradation as of development and building up. As the carpenter has number-less shavings, and a vast amount of wastage of every log which he would shape to some use, so creation has been an enormous waste, such as seems like squandering, on the scale of human life, but not to Him that dwells in Eternity ... Vast waste and the perishing of things is one of the most striking facts in the existence of this world; for while life is the consummation, death seems to be the instrument by which life itself is supplied with improvement and advancement. Death prepares the way for life. Things are adapted thus to their condition, to their climate, to their food; or by their power of escape from their adversaries, or their power of establishing themselves and of defending their position, they make it secure. The vast universe, looked at largely, is moving onward and upward in determinate lines and directions, while on the way the weak are perishing. Yet, there is an unfolding process that is carrying creation up to higher planes and upon higher lines, reaching more complicated conditions in structure, in function, in adaptation, with systematic and harmonious results, so that the whole physical creation is organizing itself for a sublime march toward perfectness.

If single acts would evince design, how much more a vast universe, that by inherent laws gradually builded itself, and then created its own plants and animals, a universe so adjusted that it left by the way the poorest things, and steadily wrought toward more complex, ingenious, and beautiful results! Who designed this mighty machine, created matter, gave to it its laws, and impressed upon it that tendency which has brought forth the almost infinite results on the glove, and wrought them into a perfect system? Design by wholesale is grander than design by retail ... It may be safely said, then, that Evolution, instead of obliterating the evidence of divine Design, has lifted it to a higher plane, and made it more sublime than it ever was contemplated to be under the old reasonings.

Next, it has been thought that science, by introducing the doctrine of the universality and invariableness of law, and giving it a larger and a more definite field of operation, destroys all possibility of a special Providence of God over men and events. It has been said that everything that we know anything about in this world has happened by the force of law, and that it is not likely that God will turn law aside or change law and interject his immediate creative will for the sake of any favorites that he had in this world. I need hardly say to you, after the reading of the passage (Matt. vi: 19–34) this morning in our opening services, that no doctrine is taught more explicitly by the Lord Jesus Christ than this doctrine of the personal watch and care of God over men and things, – that nothing happens without his inspection. The theist admits that there may be a general Providence supervising the machinery of the universe. But the Christian doctrine of special Providence, the adaptation of all the forms of nature to the welfare of particular individuals, races and nations, if this doctrine of Providence were to be overthrown by science, I need not say that it would make a very great breach in our faith, in the New Testament and as to the divinity of Christ himself ...

But is there any *reason* in the doctrine of a Natural Law which controls all things, and no God who controls law itself? ... All the talk about the inevitableness of natural laws and their being utterly irresistible is inconsiderate and unfounded. [God] can use these laws without violating them, just as men use them. He can exert, directly or indirectly, upon the consciousness of men, an influence which shall make them enactors of his decree. Theists recognize a general Providence, by which the world and all its laws and apparatus are preserved and, kept in working order. But Jesus taught more than this; he taught that God uses the machinery of the world for his own special ends. It does not follow that God overrides stated forces; he can, with superior skill, direct the great powers of Nature to special results. God's will, or mind, may be supposed to act upon the human mind, either through ordinary laws, or directly, without any intermediate instruments.

In the case of direct influence the effect may be supposed to be an exaltation of the whole mind or of special parts of it. The result would be not merely a quickening of faculties, but an exaltation of the mind to a higher plane, on or around which play new energies or forces; and to this superior condition of mind there would be easily opened new vision, new powers – especially the power to more wisely adapt, direct, and use natural laws, even those which pertain to the higher planes.

In this direction, it may be, we shall find a philosophy of miracle, of the powers of faith, of prophecy, of a human control of matter which allies exalted manhood to the creative power of God. Such an augmented power of the human soul was unquestionably taught by Jesus. As science is teaching us that hitherto men have known but little of the infinite truths of the material world, so we are beginning to find out that there are infinite possibilities in the human soul which have never been included in our philosophies … When men are hampered and find themselves in such emergencies, if they are right-minded, if they can lift themselves higher than flesh and blood, higher than the lower forms of material law, into the communion of God, they have a right to believe that there is a divine influence, an atmospheric one, shall I call it? – like sunlight to the leaves and flowers; that which will lift them up and compel such laws to serve them; and, what is better, will direct them in such a way that they shall come under the influence of those laws which should give them relief.

There is one other view, however, that may supplement this, namely, that we are to take into consideration the location of this life and its relation to the life to come. As in autumn the leaves fall gently from the trees without harming the tree, externally stripped and apparently dead, whose life is yet in it, and which waits the snowy season through for resurrection which is to come, so is it with human life. Our seeking is often folly, and our regrets often more foolish. We lose to gain, and gain to lose. Providence is wiser than man's judgment of his own needs. We are to bear in mind that this life is a mere planting-time. We are started here; we await transplantation through resurrection, and what may seem the neglect of God and a want of providence will reveal itself a step beyond, as being an illustrious Providence, watchful, tender, careful.

So, brethren, be not in haste to cast away, on the instruction or the misinterpretation of science, yet crude in many of its parts, that faith of childhood, that faith of your fathers, that faith which is the joy and should be the courage of every right-minded man, the faith that God's eye is on you, and that he cares, he guides, he defends, and will bring you safely from earth to life eternal.

JOHN ZAHM

Like Beecher (see previous selection), Father John Zahm (1851–1921) sought to reconcile Darwin's theory with Christian teaching. As a priest as well as a professor of physics at Notre Dame, Zahm insisted on the viability of "theistic evolutionism." Numerous people, including many of Zahm's fellow Catholics agreed, but many did not. His 1896 book, *Evolution and Dogma* from which the selection below is taken, landed a couple of years later on the Index of Prohibited Books.

Source: John Augustine Zahm, *Evolution and Dogma* (Chicago: D. H. McBride & Co., 1896), 428–30, 435–8.

Can a Catholic, can a Christian of any denomination, consistently with the faith he holds dear, be an evolutionist; or is there something in the theory that is so antagonistic to faith and Scripture as to render its acceptance tantamount to the denial of the fundamental tenets of religious belief? …

Whatever may be the outcome of the controversy, whatever may be the results of future research and discovery, there is absolutely no room for apprehension respecting the claims and authority of Scripture and Catholic Dogma. Science will never be able to contradict aught that God has revealed; for it is not possible that the Divine works and the Divine words should ever be in any relation to each other but one of the most perfect harmony. Doubts and difficulties may obtain for a time; the forces of error may for a while appear triumphant; the testimonies of the Lord may be tried to the uttermost; but in the long run it will always be found, as has so often been the case in the past, that the Bible and faith, like truth, will come forth unharmed and intact from any ordeal, however severe, to which they may be subjected. For error is impotent against truth; the pride of man's intellect is of no avail against the wisdom of the Almighty … The fictions of opinions are ephemeral, but the testimonies of the Lord are everlasting …

It is because Evolution contains so large an element of truth, because it explains countless facts and phenomena which are explicable on no other theory, that it has met with such universal favor, and that it has proved such a powerful agency in the dissemination of error and in giving verisimilitude to the most damnable of doctrines. Such being the case, ours is the duty to withdraw the truth from its enforced and unnatural alliance, and to show that there is a sense in which Evolution can be understood – in which it must be understood, if it repose on a rational basis – in which, far from contributing to the propagation of false views of nature and God, it is calculated to render invaluable aid in the cause of both science and religion …

In proportion as Evolution shall be placed on a solider foundation, and the objections which are now urged against it shall disappear, so also will it be evinced, that far from being an enemy of religion, it is, on the contrary, its strongest and most natural ally. Even those who have no sympathy with the traditional forms of belief, who are, in principle, if not personally, opposed to the Church and her dogmas, perceive that there is no necessary antagonism between Evolution and faith, between the conclusions of science and the declarations of revelation. Indeed, so avowed an opponent of Church and Dogma as Huxley informs us that: "The doctrine of Evolution does not even come into contact with Theism, considered as a philosophical doctrine. That with which it does collide, and with which it is absolutely inconsistent, is the conception of creation which theological speculators have based upon the history narrated in the opening book of Genesis."

In other words, Evolution is not opposed to revelation, but to certain interpretations of what some have imagined to be revealed truths. It is not opposed to the dogmas of the Church, but to the opinions of certain individual exponents of Dogma, who would have us believe that their views of the Inspired Records are the veritable expressions of Divine truth ...

To say that Evolution is agnostic or atheistic in tendency, if not in fact, is to betray a lamentable ignorance of what it actually teaches, and to display a singular incapacity for comprehending the relation of a scientific induction to a philosophical – or, more truthfully, an anti-philosophical – system ... Rather should it be affirmed that Evolution, in so far as it is true, makes for religion and Dogma; because it must needs be that a true theory of the origin and development of things must, when properly understood and applied, both strengthen and illustrate the teachings of faith ...

Evolution does, indeed, to employ the words of Carlyle, destroy the conception of "an absentee God, sitting idle, ever since the first Sabbath, as the outside of His universe and seeing it go." But it compels us to recognize that "this fair universe, were it in the meanest province thereof, is, in very deed, the star-domed city of God; that through every star, through every grass-blade, and most, through every living soul, the glory of a present God still beams ..."

But the derivation of man from the ape, we are told, degrades man. Not at all. It would be truer to say that such derivation ennobles the ape. Sentiment aside, it is quite unimportant to the Christian "whether he is to trace back to his pedigree directly or indirectly to the dust." St. Francis of Assisi, as we learn from his life, "called the birds his brothers." Whether he was correct, either theologically or zoologically, he was plainly free from the fear of being mistaken for an ape which haunts so many in these modern times. Perfectly sure that he, himself, was a spiritual being, he thought it at least possible that birds might be spiritual beings, likewise incarnate like himself in mortal flesh; and saw no degradation to the dignity of human nature in claiming kindred lovingly with creatures so beautiful, so wonderful, who, as he fancied, "praised God in the forest, even as angels did in heaven."

Many, it may here be observed, look to the theory of Evolution with suspicion, because they fail to understand its true significance. They seem to think that it is an attempt to account for the origin of things when, in reality, it deals only with their historical development ... Evolution, then, postulates creation as an intellectual necessity, for if there had not been a creation there would have been nothing to evolve, and Evolution would, therefore, have been an impossibility. And for the same reason, Evolution postulates and must postulate, a Creator, the sovereign Lord of all things, the Cause of causes ...

But this is not all, In order to have an intelligible theory of Evolution, a theory that can meet the exacting demands of a sound philosophy as well as of a true theology, still another postulate is necessary. We must hold not only that there was an actual creation in matter in the beginning, that there was potential creation which rendered matter capable of Evolution, in accordance with the laws impressed by God on matter, but we must also believe that creative action and influence still persist, that they have always persisted from the dawn of creation, that they, and they alone, have been efficient in all the countless stages of evolutionary progress from atoms to monads, from monads to man.

This ever-present action of the Deity, this immanence of Him in the work of His hands, this continuing existence and developing of creatures He has made, is what St. Thomas calls the "Divine administration," and what is ordinarily known as Providence. It connotes the active and constant cooperation of the Creator with the creature, and implies that if the multitudinous forms of terrestrial life have been evolved from the potentiality of matter, they have been so evolved because matter was in the first instance proximately disposed for Evolution by God Himself, and has even remained so disposed ... Evolution, therefore, is neither a "philosophy of mud," nor "a gospel of dirt," as it has been denominated. So far, indeed, is this from being the case that, when properly understood, it is found to be a strong and useful ally of Catholic Dogma. For if Evolution be true, the existence of God and an original creation follow as necessary inferences.

WILLIAM JENNINGS BRYAN

William Jennings Bryan (1860–1925) – the Democratic Party nominee for President in 1896, 1900, and 1908 and, more generally, among the nation's most recognized public figures – in the last years of his life became a *de facto* spokesman for fundamentalism. And like many other self-identified "fundamentalists," Bryan identified the issue of evolution as the springboard for far-reaching considerations about the state of contemporary culture. While Bryan had long opposed Darwin's theory, in early 1921 he took up an explicit crusade against dissemination of evolutionary thought on the premise that such ideas finally presented an imminent danger to humankind by undermining faith in biblical inerrancy. In the following selection – excerpted from "God and Evolution," a speech reprinted on February 26, 1922 in the *New York Times* – Bryan follows precisely that line of thought: His discussion begins with the fundamentals of evolution and its contradiction of the Bible and arrives at the "harmful" consequences of that "insidious enemy."

Source: William Jennings Bryan, "God and Evolution," in De Witte Holland, ed., *Sermons in American History* (Nashville, TN: Abingdon, 1970), 262–70.

I appreciate your invitation to present the objections to Darwinism, or evolution, applied to man, and beg to submit to your readers the following:

The only part of evolution in which any considerable interest is felt is evolution applied to man. A hypothesis in regard to the rocks and plant life does not affect the philosophy upon which one's life is built. Evolution applied to fish, birds and beasts would not materially affect man's view of his own responsibilities except as the acceptance of an unsupported hypothesis as to these would be used to support a similar hypothesis as to man. The evolution that is harmful – distinctly so – is the evolution that destroys man's family tree as taught by the Bible and makes him a descendant of the lower forms of life. This, as I shall try to show, is a very vital matter.

I deal with Darwinism because it is a definite hypothesis. In his "Descent of Man" and "Origin of Species" Darwin has presumed to outline a family tree that begins, according to his estimate, about two hundred million years ago with marine animals. He attempts to trace man's line of descent from this obscure beginning up through fish, reptile, bird and animal to man. He has us descend from European, rather than American, apes and locates our first ancestors in Africa. Then he says, "But why speculate?" – a very significant phrase because it applies to everything that he says. His entire discussion is speculation.

Darwin's "laws"

Darwin set forth two (so-called) laws by which he attempts to explain the changes which he thought had taken place in the development of life from the earlier forms to man. One of these is called "natural selection" or "survival of the fittest," his argument being that a form of life which had any characteristic that was beneficial had a better chance of survival than a form of life that lacked that characteristic. The second law that he assumed to declare was called "sexual selection," by which he attempted to account for every change that was not accounted for by natural selection. Sexual selection has been laughed out of the class room … But many evolutionists adhere to Darwin's conclusions while discarding his explanations. In other words, they accept the line of descent which he suggested without any explanation whatever to support it …

The first objection to Darwinism is that it is only a guess and was never anything more. It is called a "hypothesis," but the word "hypothesis," though euphonious, dignified and high-sounding, is merely a scientific synonym for the old-fashioned word "guess." If Darwin had advanced his views as a guess they would not have survived for a year, but they have floated for a half a century, buoyed up by the inflated word "hypothesis." When it is understood that "hypothesis" means "guess," people will inspect it more carefully before accepting it.

No support in the Bible

The second objection to Darwin's guess is that it has not one syllable in the Bible to support it. This ought to make Christians cautious about accepting it without thorough investigation. The Bible not only describes man's creation, but gives a reason for it; man is a part of God's plan and is placed on earth for a purpose. Both the Old and New Testament deal with man and with man only. They tell of God's creation of him, of God's dealings with him and of God's plans for him. Is it not strange that a Christian will accept Darwinism as a substitute for the Bible when the Bible not only does not support Darwin's hypothesis but directly and expressly contradicts it?

Third – Neither Darwin nor his supporters have been able to find a fact in the universe to support their hypothesis. With millions of species, the investigators have not been able to find one single instance in which one species has changed into another, although, according to the hypothesis, all species have developed from one or a few germs of life, the development being through the action of "resident forces" and without outside aid. Wherever a form of life, found in the rocks, is found among living organisms, there is no material change from the earliest form in which it is found. With millions of examples, nothing imperfect is found – nothing in the process of change. This statement may surprise those who have accepted evolution without investigation, as most of those who call themselves evolutionists have done … [Evolutionists] fall back on faith. They have not yet found the origin of species, and yet how can evolution explain life unless it can account for change in species? Is it not more rational to believe in creation of man by separate act of God than to believe in evolution without a particle of evidence?

Fourth – Darwinism is not only without foundation, but it compels its believers to resort to explanations that are more absurd than anything found in the "Arabian Nights." Darwin explains that man's mind became superior to woman's because, among our brute ancestors, the males fought for their females and thus strengthened their minds. If he had lived until now, he would not have felt it necessary to make so ridiculous an explanation, because woman's mind is not now believed to be inferior to man's …

Guessing is not science

Guesses are not science. Science is classified knowledge, and a scientist ought to be the last person to insist upon a guess being accepted until proof removes it from the field of hypothesis into the field of demonstrated truth. Christianity has nothing to fear from any *truth*; no *fact* disturbs the Christian religion or the Christian. It is the unsupported *guess* that is substituted for science to which opposition is made, and I think the objection is a valid one.

But, it may be asked, why should one object to Darwinism even though it is not true? This is a proper question and deserves a candid answer. There are many guesses which are perfectly groundless and at the same time entirely harmless; and it is not worth while to worry about a guess or to disturb the guesser so long as his guess does not harm others.

The objection to Darwinism is that it is harmful, as well as groundless. It entirely changes one's view of life and undermines faith in the Bible. Evolution has no place for the miracle or the supernatural. It flatters the egotist to be told that there is nothing that his mind cannot understand. Evolution proposes to bring all the processes of nature within the comprehension of man by making it the explanation of everything that is known. Creation implies a Creator, and the finite mind cannot comprehend the infinite. We can understand some things, but we run across mystery at every point. Evolution attempts to solve the mystery of life by suggesting a process of development commencing "in the dawn of time" and continuing uninterrupted up until now. Evolution does not explain creation: it simply diverts attention from it by hiding it behind eons of time. If a man accepts Darwinism, or evolution applied to man, and is consistent, he rejects the miracle and the supernatural as impossible. He commences with the first chapter of Genesis and blots out the Bible story of man's creation, not because the evidence is insufficient, but because the miracle is inconsistent with evolution. If he is consistent, he will go through the Old Testament step, by step and cut out all the miracles and all the supernatural. He will then take up the New Testament and cut out all the supernatural – the virgin birth of Christ, His miracles and His resurrection, leaving the Bible a story book without binding authority upon the conscience of man. Of course, not all evolutionists are consistent; some fail to apply their hypothesis to the end just as some Christians fail to apply their Christianity to life.

Religion waning among children

… Evolution naturally leads to agnosticism. Those who teach Darwinism are undermining the faith of Christians; they are raising questions about the Bible as an authoritative source of truth; they are teaching materialistic views that rob the life of the young of spiritual values. Christians do not object to freedom of speech; they believe that Biblical truth can hold its own in a fair field. They concede the right of ministers to pass from belief to agnosticism or atheism, but they contend that they should be honest enough to separate themselves from the ministry and not attempt to debase the religion which they profess.

And so in the matter of education, Christians do not dispute the right of any teacher to be agnostic or atheistic, but Christians do deny the right of agnostics and atheists to use the public school as a forum for the teaching of their doctrines. The Bible has in many places been excluded from the schools on the ground that religion should not be taught by those paid by public taxation. If this doctrine is sound, what right have the enemies of religion to teach irreligion in the public schools? If the Bible cannot be taught, why should Christian taxpayers permit the teaching of guesses that make the Bible a lie? A teacher might just as well write over the door of his room, "Leave Christianity behind you, all ye who enter here," as to ask his students to accept a hypothesis directly and irreconcilably antagonistic to the Bible. Our opponents are not fair …

We stamp upon our coins "In God We Trust;" we administer to witnesses an oath in which God's name appears, our President takes his oath of office upon the Bible. Is it fanatical to suggest that public taxes should not be employed for the purpose of undermining the nation's God? When we defend the Mosaic account of man's creation and contend that man has no brute blood in him, but was made in God's image by separate act and placed on earth to carry out a divine decree, we are defending the God of the Jews as well as the God of the Gentiles, the God of the Catholics as well as the God of the Protestants. We believe that faith in a Supreme Being is essential to civilization as well as to religion and that abandonment of God means ruin to the world and chaos to society ... As religion is the only basis of morals, it is time for Christians to protect religion from its most insidious enemy.

THE SCOPES TRIAL

In mid-July of 1925, the world trained its eyes on Dayton, Tennessee. The small town became the focus of international attention for a trial that, legally speaking, was a rather minor affair. John Thomas Scopes, a young substitute high school teacher, was charged with violating the state's recently enacted anti-evolution Butler Act for teaching about Darwin's theory in a science class. Culturally speaking, the now-famous "monkey trial" was anything but minor. Although Scopes admitted he was unsure whether he had even taught evolution, some prominent figures in town persuaded him to stand as the defendant in a legal test of the constitutionality of the Butler Act. Thus, Scopes became the namesake for a purported showdown over evolutionary theory in public schools and its relation to biblical understanding, morality, and the general state of "civilization." The famous William Jennings Bryan (see preceding selection) took on the role of principal prosecutor, arguing the case against evolution and for Fundamentalism. The leading trial lawyer of the day, Clarence Darrow, assumed Scopes's defense, and all sides called well-known and high-powered expert witnesses to Dayton to testify. The following selection is taken from a journalist's transcription of Darrow's famous cross-examination of Bryan on the seventh day (July 20) of the trial. In the exchange – the basis for one of the climatic scenes in *Inherit the Wind*, the award-winning 1955 play and 1960 movie inspired by the trial – Darrow questions Bryan on the idea of biblical inerrancy. Following the episode, Darrow cut the trial short – and pushed the case toward federal appeal – by submitting a guilty plea on Scopes's behalf. Bryan died the following week while still in Dayton. Then and now, Bryan's passing seemed to mark the waning of an era of public debate about biblical inerrancy.

Source: John Thomas Scopes, and William Jennings Bryan. *The World's Most Famous Court Trial, State of Tennessee v. John Thomas Scopes. Complete Stenographic Report of the Court Test of the Tennessee Anti-Evolution Act at Dayton, July 10 to 21, 1925* (New York: Da Capo Press, 1971); *Famous Trials in American History,* "Tennessee vs. John Scopes. The Monkey Trial": www.law.umkc.edu.

Day 7: "Read Your Bible" banner removed from courthouse

DARROW – Your honor, before you send for the jury, I think it my duty to make this motion. Off to the left of where the jury sits a little bit and about ten feet in front of them is a large sign about ten feet long reading, "Read Your Bible," and a hand pointing to it … I move that it be removed. … This sign is not here for any purpose, and it can have no effect but to influence this case, and I read the Bible myself – more or less – and it is pretty good reading in places. But this case has been made a case where it is to be the Bible or evolution … We have been informed that a Tennessee jury who are not especially educated are better judges of the Bible than all the scholars in the world, and when they see that sign, it means to them their construction of the Bible. It is pretty obvious, it is not fair, your honor, and we object to it …

THE COURT – The issues in this case, as they have been finally determined by this court is whether or not it is unlawful to teach that man descended from a lower order of animals. I do not understand that issue involved the Bible. If the Bible is involved, I believe in it and am always on its side, but it is not for me to decide in this case …

(The sign was thereupon removed from the courthouse wall.)

HAYS – The defense desires to call Mr. Bryan as a witness … We recognize what Mr. Bryan says as a witness would not be very valuable. We think there are other questions involved, and we should want to take Mr. Bryan's testimony for the purpose of our record, even if your honor thinks it is not admissible in general, so we wish to call him now …

THE COURT – Mr. Bryan, you are not objecting to going on the stand?

BRYAN – Not at all …

Examination of W.J. BRYAN by CLARENCE DARROW, of counsel for the defense:

Q   You have given considerable study to the Bible, haven't you, Mr. Bryan?
    …
A   Yes, I have; I have studied the Bible for about fifty years, or sometime more than that, but, of course, I have studied it more as I have become older than when I was but a boy.

Q   You claim that everything in the Bible should be literally interpreted?

A   I believe everything in the Bible should be accepted as it is given there: some of the Bible is given illustratively. For instance: "Ye are the salt of the earth." I would not insist that man was actually salt, or that he had flesh of salt, but it is used in the sense of salt as saving God's people.

Q   But when you read that Jonah swallowed the whale – or that the whale swallowed Jonah – excuse me please – how do you literally interpret that?

A   When I read that a big fish swallowed Jonah – it does not say whale … That is my recollection of it. A big fish, and I believe it, and I believe in a God who can make a whale and can make a man and make both what He pleases.

Q   Now, you say, the big fish swallowed Jonah, and he there remained how long – three days – and then he spewed him upon the land. You believe that the big fish was made to swallow Jonah?

A   I am not prepared to say that; the Bible merely says it was done.

Q   You don't know whether it was the ordinary run of fish, or made for that purpose?

A   You may guess; you evolutionists guess …

Q   You are not prepared to say whether that fish was made especially to swallow a man or not?

A   The Bible doesn't say, so I am not prepared to say.

Q   But do you believe He made them – that He made such a fish and that it was big enough to swallow Jonah?

A   Yes, sir. Let me add: One miracle is just as easy to believe as another

Q   Just as hard?

A   It is hard to believe for you, but easy for me. A miracle is a thing performed beyond what man can perform. When you get within the realm of miracles; and it is just as easy to believe the miracle of Jonah as any other miracle in the Bible.

Q   Perfectly easy to believe that Jonah swallowed the whale?

A   If the Bible said so; the Bible doesn't make as extreme statements as evolutionists do …

Q   You believe the story of the flood to be a literal interpretation?

A   Yes, sir.

Q   When was that Flood?

A   I would not attempt to fix the date. The date is fixed, as suggested this morning.

Q   About 4004 B.C.? …

A   I never made a calculation …

Q   What do you think?

A   I do not think about things I don't think about.

Q   Do you think about things you do think about?

A   Well, sometimes …

    (Laughter in the courtyard.) […]

THE COURT – Are you about through, Mr. Darrow?

DARROW – I want to ask a few more questions about the creation …

BRYAN – Your honor, they have not asked a question legally and the only reason they have asked any question is for the purpose, as the question about Jonah was asked, for a chance to give this agnostic an opportunity to criticize a believer in the world of God; and I answered the question in order to shut his mouth so that he cannot go out and tell his atheistic friends that I would not answer his questions. That is the only reason, no more reason in the world …

Q   Does the statement, "The morning and the evening were the first day," and "The morning and the evening were the second day," mean anything to you?

A   I do not think it necessarily means a twenty-four-hour day.

Q   You do not?

A   No.

Q   What do you consider it to be?

A   I have not attempted to explain it. If you will take the second chapter –
let me have the book. (Examining Bible.) The fourth verse of the second
chapter says: "These are the generations of the heavens and of the earth,
when they were created in the day that the Lord God made the earth
and the heavens," the word "day" there in the very next chapter is used
to describe a period. I do not see that there is any necessity for construing
the words, "the evening and the morning," as meaning necessarily a
twenty-four-hour day, "in the day when the Lord made the heaven and
the earth."

Q   Then, when the Bible said, for instance, "and God called the firmament
heaven. And the evening and the morning were the second day," that
does not necessarily mean twenty-four hours?

A   I do not think it necessarily does.

Q   Do you think it does or does not?

A   I know a great many think so.

Q   What do you think?

A   I do not think it does.

Q   You think those were not literal days?

A   I do not think they were twenty-four-hour days.

Q   What do you think about it?

A   That is my opinion – I do not know that my opinion is better on that
subject than those who think it does.

Q   You do not think that?

A   No. But I think it would be just as easy for the kind of God we believe in
to make the earth in six days as in six years or in 6,000,000 years or in
600,000,000 years. I do not think it important whether we believe one or
the other.

Q   Do you think those were literal days?

A   My impression is they were periods, but I would not attempt to argue as
against anybody who wanted to believe in literal days.

Q   I will read it to you from the Bible: …

A   Read it.

Q   All right, Mr. Bryan, I will read it for you.

BRYAN – Your Honor, I think I can shorten this testimony. The only purpose
Mr. Darrow has is to slur at the Bible, but I will answer his question. I
will answer it all at once, and I have no objection in the world, I want the
world to know that this man, who does not believe in a God, is trying to
use a court in Tennessee –

DARROW – I object to that.

BRYAN – (Continuing) to slur at it, and while it will require time, I am willing
to take it.

DARROW – I object to your statement. I am exempting you on your fool ideas
that no intelligent Christian on earth believes.

THE COURT – Court is adjourned until 9 o'clock tomorrow morning.

REFORMING SOCIETY

THE SOCIAL GOSPEL

After the Civil War, the United States experienced rapid growth in industry, railroads, and commerce, and a rush to possess the country's natural resources. The "gilded age," as Mark Twain satirically called it, provided great wealth to the few, while the poor and working classes suffered under harsh conditions and lived in overcrowded slums. A series of thinkers in the late nineteenth century formulated a new theology that reacted against individualistic religion that concentrated on reward after death. They focused on the social principles of Jesus, the goodness of humanity, and the possibility of creating a just society in this world. Walter Rauschenbusch, the best-known of this group, drew his principles of social responsibility from Jesus' teaching of the coming Kingdom, which could be brought forth on earth.

Source: Walter Rauschenbusch, *Christianity and the Social Crisis* (New York: Macmillan, 1907), 339–40, 380–1.

The gospel, to have full power over an age, must be the highest expression of the moral and religious truths held by that age. If it lags behind and deals in outgrown conceptions of life and duty, it will lose power over the ablest minds and the young men first, and gradually over all. In our thought today the social problems irresistibly take the lead. If the Church has no live and bold thought on this dominant question of modern life, its teaching authority on all other questions will dwindle and be despised. It cannot afford to have young men sniff the air as in a stuffy room when they enter the sphere of religious thought. When the world is in travail with a higher ideal of justice, the Church dare not ignore it if it would retain its moral leadership. On the other hand, if the Church does incorporate the new social terms in its synthesis of truth, they are certain to throw new light on all the older elements of its teaching. The conception of race sin and race salvation become comprehensible once more to those who have made the idea of social solidarity in good and evil a part of their thought. The law of sacrifice loses its arbitrary and mechanical aspect when we understand the vital union of all humanity. Individualistic Christianity has almost lost sight of the great idea of the kingdom of God, which was the inspiration and centre of the thought of Jesus. Social Christianity would once more enable us to understand, the purpose and thought of Jesus and take the veil from our eyes when we read the synoptic gospels ...

Jesus in his teachings alluded with surprising frequency to the use and abuse of intrusted wealth and power. In the parable of the talents and pounds [Matt 25:14–30; Luke 19:11–27] he evidently meant to define all human ability and opportunity as a trust. His description of the head servant who is made confident by the continued absence of his master, tyrannizes over his subordinates, and fattens his paunch on his master's property [Matt 25:45–51], is meant to show the temptation which besets all in authority to forget the responsibility that goes with power. His portrayal of the tricky steward who is to be dismissed for dishonesty, but manages to make one more grand coup before his authority ends, not only shows the keen insight of Jesus into the ways of the grafter, but also shows that he regarded all men of wealth as stewards of the property they hold.

THE CITY AS MENACE

The offshoot of the Industrial Revolution, the modern city, was viewed by some as a threat to morality. Social Gospel thinker Josiah Strong (1847–1916) argued that urban materialism and political corruption hurt wealthy and poor alike. The crowded slums breed hopelessness, crime, and disease. The church, like the Hebrew prophets, has a mission to lift up the poor and call the wealthy to service of their brothers and sisters.

Source: Josiah Strong, *The Challenge of the City* (New York: Presbyterian Home Missions, 1907), 199, 203–5.

Shelley said: "Hell is a city much like London"; but the Revelator used a redeemed city to symbolize heaven – heaven come down to earth – the kingdom fully come.

Even if no solution of the problem of the city had yet been found, every one who believes that the prophetic prayer of our Lord, "thy kingdom come," is to receive its fulfilling answer must have confidence that the problem is soluble …

Certain fundamental Christian principles embodied in the example and teachings of Jesus

… 2. Closely connected with the preceding principle [of the incarnation] is that of *personal contact*. It has been demonstrated in every department of philanthropic and charitable work that personal, vital touch is the most essential thing; and this is the great power in all redemptive work. Says Jeremy Taylor, "When God would save a man he does it by way of a man." Christ in the flesh personally touched the sick, the maimed, the leprous. The Church, which is Christ's body in the world, has lost this personal touch with the multitude of the downtown city, and needs to be brought into actual contact with its miseries.

3. Another Christian principle is *the inherent worth of humanity*. Jesus taught that the whole world would not compensate for the loss of a single soul (life). So great is the value even of the ruined and depraved that the return of one such to a righteous life is celebrated in heaven. Jesus has been called the discoverer of the individual. He died for every man. It is because he recognized the value of human nature, apart from position or possession, that Lowell speaks of him as "the first true democrat that ever breathed."

Let us not imagine that we can do much either to Americanize or to Christianize the mixed multitude of the downtown city so long as we can

speak of any human being as "sheeny," or "dago," or "coon." Such charac-
terizations are an insult to our common human nature, and degrade those
who are guilty of using them. "I should not call any man common or unclean"
[Acts 10:28].

LABOR UNIONS

Roman Catholics and Jews were the prime movers of the organization of
labor unions, buoyed by a spirit of reform around the turn of the twentieth century. Yet the Protestant Social Gospel provided the religious
rationale, linking the struggle for a living wage and better working conditions to Jesus' teaching. Charles Stelzle (1869–1941) – a champion of labor
unions, a Progressive Party activist, and founder of the first Protestant
social service agency – makes the case that Jesus and Paul were working
men.

Source: Charles Stelzle, *Christianity's Storm Centre* (New York: Fleming Revell, 1907),
66–7.

The increase in wages, the shortening of his hours of work, the multiplication of his comforts, his new educational advantages, his superior position
as a citizen and a man – all these have made the average workingman a
progressive, right-thinking individual. Viewed in the light of history, all this
must appear revolutionary. Out of Christ's teaching have sprung the great
world movements which have ushered in the larger liberty and the fuller life
which He came to proclaim. The message which the angels sang on the first
Christmas morning is being taught more widely than ever before.

It was among the members of the labor guilds of the apostolic days that
the Gospel had its freest course. In those days practically every workingman
belonged to the guild composed of the men and women of his craft. It is
not unlikely that some of the apostles themselves were identified with these
organizations. This may have been especially true of Paul, who still worked
at his trade as a tent-maker, usually seeking out those who were of the same
craft when visiting a strange city. As he was dependent upon his trade for a
living, and as he constantly traveled from place to place, it seems reasonable
to suppose that Paul identified himself with an organization which would give
him greater opportunities for gaining his support. If, in connection with this
benefit, there might come an opportunity for doing a larger service among
a great class of toilers, it may be that Paul again "became all things to all
men, that by all means he might win some," following out the principle of his
approach to men.

This we know without dispute – it was among the guilds of the large cities
which Paul visited that he established the churches whose name are given us in
the inspired record. And these very guilds of working people became centres
for the proclamation of the Gospel.

Always have there been organizations of working people, born of a desire
to better their social and economic conditions, sometimes developed in secret

on account of the oppression of the government, or the opposition of the employing class, and having its periods of depression as well as its times of exaltation, organized labor has gone steadily forward until today, throughout the world, it is eight million strong.

TEMPERANCE

The movement for temperance, or complete abstention from alcohol, started in America in 1810. Hundreds of pamphlets and speeches warned of the dangers of drinking, encouraging people to take the pledge of abstinence. These pledges were often pasted into family Bibles. The argument against alcohol invoked general Christian values, health, the family, and the good of society. The Bible presented a problem, as alcohol is presented in a positive light in many places (Psalm 104:15; Ecc 9:7), and is central to the Last Supper. This excerpt, from an address to a Temperance Society at Harvard University in 1834, attempts to answer this problem.

Source: "An Address delivered before the Temperance Society of Harvard University, November 20, 1834," published by Request of the Society (Cambridge, MA: Cambridge Press: Metcalf, Torry, and Ballou, 1834), 31–3.

It is quite amusing to some, and equally grievous to others, to observe the unprofitable pains, which the lovers of wine have taken to justify its use, from holy writ. A few passages are selected, and paraded forth, with about as much wisdom, as the fellow, in the jest book of Hierocles exhibited, who had a house for sale, and ran about with a brick, as a sample. It is truly a subject of regret, that such persons, will not search the Scriptures, for some worthier purpose, than to raise, from its distorted parts, an untenantable shelter for the wine-drinker's defence. How absurd is the inference, because, in the days of the apostles, the days of necessities and distresses, one of the disciples recommended to a valetudinarian brother to take a *little* wine, for his *stomach's sake and often infirmities*; that every modern apostle, who has neither stomach's sake nor often infirmities to plead, should drink as much wine, during the parochial visitations of a single day, as would have sufficed the whole twelve apostles for a month. Let us imagine our blessed Redeemer upon earth, contemplating this glorious work, in which we are engaged, in all its bearings and connections; the grievous stumbling block, which ministers of the Gospel and others cast in its path, by refusing to serve any longer, in the army of the revolution, without their daily allowance of strong drink, in some form or other; – the pernicious effects of wine, as a *conductor generalis* to every other species of tippling, either where wine cannot be had, or when the vitiated appetite seeks a more active stimulant, or the debilitated stomach turns for a restorative to brandy; what would be the language of him, who made every sacrifice for mankind, to those who are unwilling to crucify their unnatural appetites in the cause of God and man! What would be the burthen of his terrible rebuke to those, who quote his example and his words, in justification of their luxurious habits, but who refuse to bear the cross of their Lord and Master!

The whole text and context of the holy volume is full of admonition, exhortation, and reproof, in relation to the use of wine and the danger of employing it. The very first allusion to this beverage, in holy writ, is in connection with the drunkenness of Noah, and the paternal curse, which fell upon Canaan. Under its brutalizing influence, Lot committed incest with his daughters; Belshazzar and his inebriated nobles flung insult in the face of Almighty God; and, when the earlier Christians assembled to commemorate the death of their Lord and Master, we have it, upon the testimony of an indignant apostle, that *"one was hungry and another was drunken!"* What then is the measure of our own security, in our ordinary convivial assemblies!

THE WOMEN'S CHRISTIAN TEMPERANCE UNION

The most powerful organization promoting abstinence from alcohol, the WCTU promoted temperance as a form of "home protection," stressing the ill effects of drunkenness on families. The motto of the organization, attached to the temperance pledge cards, was "For God and Home and Native Land." The head of the WCTU for many years, Frances Willard (1839–98), promoted a policy of general societal reform that included equal rights for women. In 1919, Congress enacted the Eighteenth amendment, prohibiting the manufacture, sale, transportation, import, and export of "intoxicating liquors," beginning the phase in American life called Prohibition.

Source: Frances Willard, *Woman and Temperance* (Hartford, CT: Park Publishing, 1883), 42–6.

The W.C.T.U. stands as the exponent, not alone of that return to physical sanity which will follow the downfall of the drink habit, but of the reign of a religion of the body which for the first time in history shall correlate with Christ's wholesome, practical, yet blessedly spiritual religion of the soul. "The kingdom of heaven is within you" – shall have a new meaning to the clear-eyed, steady-limbed Christians of the future, from whose brain and blood the taint of alcohol and nicotine has been eliminated by ages of pure habits, and noble heredity. "The body is the temple of the Holy Ghost," will not then seem so mystical a statement, nor one indicative of a temple so insalubrious as now. "He that destroyeth this temple, him shall God destroy," will be seen to involve no element of vengeance, but instead to be the declaration of such boundless love and pity for our race, as would not suffer its deterioration to reach the point of absolute failure and irremediable loss …

But to help forward the coming of Christ into all departments of life, is in its last analysis, the purpose and aim of the W.C.T.U. For we believe this correlation of New Testament religion with philanthropy, and of the church with civilization, is the perpetual miracle which furnishes the only sufficient antidote to current skepticism. Higher toward the zenith climbs the Sun of Righteousness, making circle after circle of human endeavor and achievement warm and radiant with the healing of its beams. First of all, in our gospel temperance work, this heavenly light penetrated the gloom of the individual, tempted heart (that smallest circle, in which all others are involved), illumined its darkness, melted its hardness, made it a sweet and sunny place – a temple filled with the Holy Ghost.

Having thus come to the heart of the drinking man in the plenitude of his redeeming power, Christ entered the next wider circle, in which two human hearts unite to form a home, and here, by the revelation of her place in His kingdom, He lifted to an equal level with her husband the gentle companion who had supposed herself happy in being the favorite vassal of her liege lord. "There is neither male nor female in Christ Jesus;" this was the "open sesame," a declaration utterly opposed to all custom and tradition, but so steadily the light has shone, and so kindly has it made the heart of man, that without strife of tongues, or edict of sovereigns, it is coming now to pass that in proportion as any home is really Christian, the husband and the wife are peers in dignity and power. There are no homes on earth where women is "revered, beloved," and individualized in character and work, so thoroughly as the fifty thousand in America where "her children arise up and call her blessed, her husband also, and he praiseth her" because of her part in the work of our W.C.T.U ...

But the modern temperance movement, born of Christ's gospel and cradled at His altars, is rapidly filling one more circle of influence, wide as the widest zone of earthly weal or woe, and that is government. "The government shall be upon his shoulder." "Unto us a king is given." "He shall reign whose right it is." "He shall not fail, nor be discouraged until he hath set judgment in the earth." "For at the name of Jesus every knee shall bow, and every tongue confess that Christ is Lord to the glory of God the Father." "Thy kingdom come, thy will be done, *on earth*." Christ shall reign, not visibly, but invisibly; not in form, but in fact; not in substance, but in essence, and the day draws nigh; Then surely the traffic in intoxicating liquors as a drink will no longer be protected by the statute book, the lawyer's plea, the affirmation of the witness, and decision of the judge ... Upon those who in largest numbers love Him who has filled their hearts with peace and their homes with blessing, slowly dawns the conscious-ness that they may – nay, better still, *they ought* to – ask for power to help forward the coming of their Lord in government – to throw the safeguard of their prohi-bition ballots around those who have left the shelter of their arms only to be entrapped by the saloons that bad men legalize and set along the streets.

THE STRUGGLE FOR CIVIL RIGHTS

ANTICIPATING THE MOVEMENT

W. E. B. Dubois (1868–1963) published *The Souls of Black Folk* in 1903, midway between the abolition of slavery and the modern Civil Rights movement. He predicted "the problem of the Twentieth Century is the problem of the color-line." He describes living as a black as living in a world "within the veil," utterly different from the world of fellow white citizens. "Negro religion" went through several phases, he says, with Christianity sometimes promoting passive acceptance of suffering, and at other times promoting liberation.

Source: W. E. B. Dubois, *The Souls of Black Folk*, 7th edn (Chicago: A. C. McClurg, 1907), 197–201.

The second fact noted, that the Negro church antedates the Negro home, leads to an explanation of much that is paradoxical in this communistic institution and in the morals of its members … Let us turn, then, from the outer physical development of the church to the more important inner ethical life of the people who compose it. The Negro has already been pointed out many times as a religious animal, – a being of that deep emotional nature which turns instinctively toward the supernatural. Endowed with a rich tropical imagination and a keen, delicate appreciation of Nature, the transplanted African lived in a world animate with gods and devils, elves and witches; full of strange influences, – of Good to be implored, of Evil to be propitiated. Slavery, then, was to him the dark triumph of Evil over him.

In spite, however, of such success as that of the fierce Maroons, the Danish blacks, and others, the spirit of revolt gradually died away under the untiring energy and superior strength of the slave masters. By the middle of the eighteenth century the black slave had sunk, with hushed murmurs, to his place at the bottom of a new economic system, and was unconsciously ripe for a new philosophy of life. Nothing suited his condition then better than the doctrines of passive submission embodied in the newly learned Christianity. Slave masters early realized this, and cheerfully aided religious propaganda within certain bounds. The long system of repression and degradation of the Negro tended to emphasize the elements in his character which made him a valuable chattel: courtesy became humility, moral strength degenerated into submission, and the exquisite native appreciation of the beautiful became an infinite capacity for dumb suffering. The Negro, losing the joy of this world, eagerly seized upon the offered conceptions of the next; the avenging Spirit of Lord enjoining patience in this world, under sorrow and tribulation until the Great Day when He should lead His dark children home, – this became his comforting dream. His preacher repeated the prophecy, and his bards sang, –

> "Children, we all shall be free
> When the Lord shall appear!"

This deep religious fatalism, painted so beautifully in "Uncle Tom," came soon to breed, as all fatalistic faiths will, the sensualist side by side with the martyr. Under the lax moral life of the plantation, where marriage was a farce, laziness a virtue, and property a theft, a religion of resignation and submission degenerated easily, in less strenuous minds, into a philosophy of indulgence and crime …

With the beginning of the abolition movement and the gradual growth of a class of free Negroes came a change. We often neglect the influence of the freedman before the war, because of the paucity of his numbers and the small weight he had in the history of the nation. But we must not forget that his chief influence was internal, – was exerted on the black world; and that there he was the ethical and social leader. Huddled as he was in a few centres like Philadelphia, New York, and New Orleans, the masses of the freedmen sank into poverty and listlessness; but not all of them. The free Negro leader early arose and his chief characteristic was intense earnestness and deep feeling on the slavery question. Freedom became to him a real thing and not a dream. His religion became darker and more intense, and into his ethics crept a note of revenge, into his songs a day of reckoning close at hand. The "Coming of the Lord" swept this side of Death, and came to be a thing to be hoped for in this day. Through fugitive slaves and irrepressible discussion this desire for freedom seized the black millions still in bondage, and became their one ideal of life. The black bards caught new notes, and sometimes even dared to sing, –

> "Oh Freedom, O Freedom, O Freedom over me!
> Before I'll be a slave
> I'll be buried in my grave,
> And go home to my Lord
> And be free."

For fifty years Negro religion thus transformed itself and identified itself with the dream of Abolition, until that which was a radical fad in the white North and an anarchistic plot in the white South had become a religion to the black world. Thus, when Emancipation finally came, it seemed to the freedman a literal Coming of the Lord.

... Today the two groups of Negroes, the one in the North, the other in the South, represent these divergent ethical tendencies, the first tending toward radicalism, the other toward hypocritical compromise ... But back of this still broods silently the deep religious feeling of the real Negro heart, the stirring, unguided might of powerful human souls who have lost the guiding star of the past and are seeking in the great night a new religious ideal. Some day the Awakening will come, when the pent-up vigor of ten million souls shall sweep irresistibly toward the Goal, out of the Valley of the Shadow of Death, where all that makes life worth living – Liberty, Justice, and Right – is marked "For White People Only."

SUPPORT FOR SEGREGATION

Most who opposed integration did not argue from the Bible, but rather from the Constitution, citing the argument for states' rights. An exception is Dr. H. L. Lyon who lived in Montgomery, Alabama, site of a year-long bus boycott by African Americans in 1955–56. He addressed a group of segregationist Baptist laymen in 1958.

Source: H. L. Lyon, "Is Racial Segregation Christian?" *The Alabama Bible Society Quarterly* 14 (1958), 21–3.

... with unbowed head I proclaim the truth about racial integration. I am not a trouble-maker. I am a humble minister of the Gospel of Christ. Separation of the races is not only Christian, but good and morally right for humanity in every respect. I call your attention to Acts 17:26–27, "And hath made of one blood all nations of men for to dwell on all the face of the earth, and hath determined the times before appointed, and the bounds of their habitation; that they should seek the Lord, if haply they might feel after him, and find him, though he be not far from every one of us." This scripture reveals to us that man exists on the earth due to the creative act of God; that God is the creator of all the peoples on the earth; that God moved from "one" to "every nation or race of men"; that God has determined the "bounds of their habitation." God separated the races in creation. Separation of the races is God's method of carrying out his eternal purpose of each of the races that inhabit the earth. This is the law of God. The entire seventh chapter of Deuteronomy reveals God's separation law for Israel. The eleventh chapter of 1 Kings tells how Solomon lost the kingdom during the reign of his son because he failed to obey this law of separation. The ninth chapter of Ezra pictures Israel suffering because they rebelled against the same law. In the New Testament we do not find Jesus Christ voiding this divine law – separation of the races. Jesus gave the Golden Rule to guide us in our dealings with all men of all races, "Therefore all things whatsoever ye would that men should do to you, do ye even so to them: for this is the law and the prophets." (Matthew 7:12). Under the "Golden Rule" there is no room for racial abuse. The dignity of every individual is to be recognized. The "Golden Rule" did not void God's law of racial separation. There is not one single passage of scripture in the entire Holy Bible supporting racial integration.

Now let us apply these scriptural truths to our present racial problem. I believe that God has made some men white. His will is for them to remain white. Racially, the glory of the white man is in his white face. I believe that God has made some men black. His will is for them to remain black. Racially, the glory of the black man is in his black face. No white or black man has reason to be ashamed of the color of his face. Both races please God as they cooperate in keeping intact the separation of the races. History proves that integration of the races produces ultimately and inevitably amalgamation. This is why the children of America should not be integrated in our public school system.

Martin Luther King, Jr

> The leading figure of the Civil Rights movement, Martin Luther King, Jr (1929–68) grew up in his father's church, Ebenezer Baptist Church, in Atlanta. He was ordained a minister, and earned a doctorate in systematic theology. His theory of non-violent resistance drew from many sources, including the teachings of Jesus and Gandhi. Biblical images and words are woven into his speeches. This is his last speech, given in Memphis on April 3, 1968 to support the sanitation workers' strike. He was shot to

death on a hotel balcony the next day. King invokes the image of Moses looking over to the Promised Land before his own death. The speech is printed in its entirety to show King's skillful interweaving of the Bible, the Constitution, and history.

Thank you very kindly, my friends. As I listened to Ralph Abernathy in his eloquent and generous introduction and then thought about myself, I wondered who he was talking about. It's always good to have your closest friend and associate say something good about you. And Ralph is the best friend that I have in the world.

I'm delighted to see each of you here tonight in spite of a storm warning. You reveal that you are determined to go on anyhow. Something is happening in Memphis, something is happening in our world.

As you know, if I were standing at the beginning of time, with the possibility of general and panoramic view of the whole human history up to now, and the Almighty said to me, "Martin Luther King, which age would you like to live in" – I would take my mental flight by Egypt through, or rather across the Red Sea, through the wilderness on toward the promised land. And in spite of its magnificence, I wouldn't stop there. I would move on by Greece, and take my mind to Mount Olympus. And I would see Plato, Aristotle, Socrates, Euripides and Aristophanes assembled around the Parthenon as they discussed the great and eternal issues of reality.

But I wouldn't stop there. I would go on, even to the great heyday of the Roman Empire, And I would see developments around there, through various emperors and leaders. But I wouldn't stop there. I would even come up to the day of the Renaissance, and get a quick picture of all that the Renaissance did for the cultural and esthetic life of man. But I wouldn't stop there. I would even go by the way that the man for whom I'm named had his habitat. And I would watch Martin Luther as he tacked his ninety-five theses on the door at the church in Wittenberg.

But I wouldn't stop there. I would come on up even to 1863, and watch a vacillating president by the name of Abraham Lincoln finally come to the conclusion that he had to sign the Emancipation Proclamation. But I wouldn't stop there. I would even come up to the early thirties, and see a man grappling with the problems of the bankruptcy of his nation. And come with an eloquent cry that we have nothing to fear but fear itself.

But I wouldn't stop there. Strangely enough, I would turn to the Almighty, and say, "If you allow me to live just a few years in the second half of the twentieth century, I will be happy." Now that's a strange statement. But I know, somehow, that only when it is dark enough, can you see the stars. And I see God working in this period of the twentieth century in a way that men, in some strange way, are responding – something is happening in our world. The masses of people are rising up. And wherever they are assembled today, whether they are in Johannesburg, South Africa; Nairobi, Kenya; Accra, Ghana; New York City; Atlanta, Georgia; Jackson, Mississippi; or Memphis, Tennessee – the cry is always the same – "We want to be free."

And another reason that I'm happy to live in this period is that we have been forced to a point where we're going to have to grapple with the problems that men have been trying to grapple with through history, but the demands didn't force them to do it. Survival demands that we grapple with them. Men, for years now, have been talking about war and peace. But now, no longer can they just talk about it. It is no longer a choice between violence and nonviolence in this world; it's nonviolence or nonexistence.

That is where we are today. And also in the human rights revolution, if something isn't done, and in a hurry, to bring the colored peoples of the world out of their long years of poverty, their long years of hurt and neglect, the whole world is doomed. Now, I'm just happy that God has allowed me to live in this period, to see what is unfolding. And I'm happy that he's allowed me to be in Memphis.

I can remember, I can remember when Negroes were just going around as Ralph has said, so often, scratching where they didn't itch, and laughing when they were not tickled. But that day is all over. We mean business now, and we are determined to gain our rightful place in God's world.

And that's all this whole thing is about. We aren't engaged in any negative protest and in any negative arguments with anybody. We are saying that we are determined to be men. We are determined to be people. We are saying that we are God's children. And that we don't have to live like we are forced to live.

Now, what does all of this mean in this great period of history? It means that we've got to stay together. We've got to stay together and maintain unity. You know, whenever Pharoah wanted to prolong the period of slavery in Egypt, he had a favorite, favorite formula for doing it. What was that? He kept the slaves fighting among themselves. But whenever the slaves get together, something happens in Pharoah's court, and he cannot hold the slaves in slavery. When the slaves get together, that's the beginning of getting out of slavery. Now let us maintain unity.

Secondly, let us keep the issues where they are. The issue is injustice. The issue is the refusal of Memphis to be fair and honest in its dealings with its public servants, who happen to be sanitation workers. Now, we've got to keep attention on that. That's always the problem with a little violence. You know what happened the other day, and the press dealt only with the window-breaking. I read the articles. They seldom got around to mentioning the fact that one thousand, three hundred sanitation workers were on strike, and that Memphis is not being fair to them, and that Mayor Loeb is in dire need of a doctor. They didn't get around to that.

Now we're going to march again, and we've got to march again, in order to put the issue where it is supposed to be. And force everybody to see that there are thirteen hundred of God's children here suffering, sometimes going hungry, going through dark and dreary nights wondering how this thing is going to come out. That's the issue. And we've got to say to the nation: we know it's coming out. For when people get caught up with that which is right and they are willing to sacrifice for it, there is no stopping point short of victory.

We aren't going to let any mace stop us. We are masters in our nonviolent movement in disarming police forces; they don't know what to do. I've seen them so often. I remember in Birmingham, Alabama, when we were in that majestic struggle there we would move out of the 16th Street Baptist Church day after day; by the hundreds we would move out. And Bull Connor would tell them to send the dogs forth and they did come; but we just went before the dogs singing, "Ain't gonna let nobody turn me round." Bull Connor next would say, "Turn the fire hoses on." And as I said to you the other night, Bull Connor didn't know history. He knew a kind of physics that somehow didn't relate to the transphysics that we knew about. And that was the fact that there was a certain kind of fire that no water could put out. And we went before the fire hoses; we had known water. If we were Baptist or some other denomination, we had been immersed. If we were Methodist, and some others, we had been sprinkled, but we knew water.

That couldn't stop us. And we just went on before the dogs and we would look at them; and we'd go on before the water hoses and we would look at it, and we'd just go on singing "Over my head I see freedom in the air." And then we would be thrown in the paddy wagons, and sometimes we were stacked in there like sardines in a can. And they would throw us in, and old Bull would say, "Take them off," and they did; and we would just go in the paddy wagon singing, "We Shall Overcome," And every now and then we'd get in the jail, and we'd see the jailers looking through the windows being moved by our prayers, and being moved by our words and our songs. And there was a power there which Bull Connor couldn't adjust to; and so we ended up transforming Bull into a steer, and we won our struggle in Birmingham.

Now we've got to go on to Memphis just like that. I call upon you to be with us Monday. Now about injunctions: We have an injunction and we're going into court tomorrow morning to fight this illegal, unconstitutional injunction. All we say to America is, "Be true to what you said on paper." If I lived in China or even Russia, or any totalitarian country, maybe I could understand the denial of certain basic First Amendment privileges, because they hadn't committed themselves to that over there. But somewhere I read of the freedom of assembly. Somewhere I read of the freedom of speech. Somewhere I read of the freedom of the press. Somewhere I read that the greatness of America is the right to protest for right. And so just as I say, we aren't going to let any injunction turn us around. We are going on.

We need all of you. And you know what's beautiful to me, is to see all of these ministers of the Gospel. It's a marvelous picture. Who is it that is supposed to articulate the longings and aspirations of the people more than the preacher? Somehow the preacher must be an Amos, and say, "Let justice roll down like waters and righteousness like a mighty stream." Somehow, the preacher must say with Jesus, "The spirit of the Lord is upon me, because he hath anointed me to deal with the problems of the poor."

And I want to commend the preachers, under the leadership of these noble men: James Lawson, one who has been in this struggle for many years; he's been to jail for struggling; but he's still going on, fighting for the rights of his people. Rev. Ralph Jackson, Billy Kyles; I could just go right on down the list, but time will not permit. But I want to thank them all. And I want you to thank them, because so often, preachers aren't concerned about anything but themselves. And I'm always happy to see a relevant ministry.

It's alright to talk about "long white robes over yonder," in all of its symbolism. But ultimately people want some suits and dresses and shoes to wear down here. It's alright to talk about "streets flowing with milk and honey," but God has commanded us to be concerned about the slums down here, and his children who can't eat three square meals a day. It's alright to talk about the new Jerusalem, but one day, God's preacher must talk about the New York, the new Atlanta, the new Philadelphia, the new Los Angeles, the new Memphis, Tennessee. This is what we have to do.

Now the other thing we'll have to do is this: Always anchor our external direct action with the power of economic withdrawal. Now, we are poor people individually, we are poor when you compare us with white society in America. We are poor. Never stop and forget that collectively, that means all of us together, collectively we are richer than all the nations in the world, with the exception of nine. Did you ever think about that? After you leave the United States, Soviet Russia, Great Britain, West Germany, France, and I could name the others, the Negro collectively is richer than most nations of the world. We have an annual income of more than thirty billion dollars a year, which is more than all of the exports of the United States, and more than the national budget of Canada. Did you know that: That's power right there, if we know how to pool it.

We don't have to argue with anybody. We don't have to curse and go around acting bad with our words. We don't need any bricks and bottles, we don't need any Molotov cocktails, we just need to go around to these stores, and to these massive industries in our country, and say, "God sent us by here, to say to you that you're not treating his children right. And we've come by here to ask you to make the first item on your agenda – fair treatment, where God's children are concerned. Now, if you are not prepared to do that, we do have an agenda that we must follow. And our agenda calls for withdrawing economic support from you."

And so, as a result of this, we are asking you tonight, to go out and tell your neighbors not to buy Coca-Cola in Memphis. Go by and tell them not to buy Sealtest milk. Tell them not to buy – what is the other bread? Wonder Bread. And what is the other bread company, Jesse? Tell them not to buy Hart's bread. As Jesse Jackson has said, up to now, only the garbage men have been feeling pain; now we must kind of redistribute the pain. We are choosing these companies because they haven't been fair in their hiring policies; and we are choosing them because they can begin the process of saying, they are going to support the needs and the rights of these men who are on strike. And then they can move on downtown and tell Mayor Loeb to do what is right.

But not only that, we've got to strengthen black institutions. I call upon you to take your money out of the banks downtown and deposit your money in Tri-State Bank – we want a 'bank-in" movement in Memphis. So go by the savings and loan association. I'm not asking you something that we don't do ourselves at SCLC. Judge [Benjamin] Hooks and others will tell you that we have an account here in the savings and loan association from the Southern Christian Leadership Conference. We're just telling you to follow what we're doing. Put your money there. You have six or seven Black insurance companies in Memphis. Take out your insurance there. We want to have an "insurance-in."

Now these are some practical things we can do. We begin the process of building a greater economic base. And at the same time, we are putting pressure where it really hurts. I ask you to follow through here.

Now, let me say as I move to my conclusion that we've got to give ourselves to this struggle until the end. Nothing would be more tragic than to stop at this point, in Memphis. We've got to see it through. And when we have our march, you need to be there. Be concerned about your brother. You may not be on strike. But either we go up together or we go down together.

Let us develop a kind of dangerous unselfishness. One day a man came to Jesus; and he wanted to raise some questions about some vital matters in life. At points, he wanted to trick Jesus, and show him that he knew a little more than Jesus knew, and through this, throw him off base. Now that question could have easily ended up in a philosophical and theological debate. But Jesus immediately pulled that question from mid-air, and placed it on a dangerous curve between Jerusalem and Jericho. And he talked about a certain man, who fell among thieves. You remember that a Levite and a priest passed by on the other side. They didn't stop to help him. And finally a man of another race came by. He got down from his beast, decided not to be compassionate by proxy. But with him, administered first aid, and helped the man in need. Jesus ended up saying, this was the good man, this was the great man, because he had the capacity to project the "I" into the "thou," and to be concerned about his brother. Now you know, we use our imagination a great deal to try to determine why the priest and the Levite didn't stop. At times we say that they were busy going to church meetings – an ecclesiastical gathering – and they had to get on down to Jerusalem so they wouldn't be late for their meeting. At other times we would speculate that there was a religious law that "One who was engaged in religious ceremonials was not to touch a human body twenty-four hours before the ceremony." And every now and then we begin to wonder whether maybe they were not going down to Jerusalem, or down to Jericho, rather to organize a "Jericho Road Improvement Association." That's a possibility. Maybe they felt that it was better to deal with the problem from the causal root, rather than to get bogged down with an individual effort.

But, I'm going to tell you what my imagination tells me. It's possible that these men were afraid. You see, the Jericho road is a dangerous road. I remember when Mrs. King and I were first in Jerusalem. We rented a car and drove from Jerusalem down to Jericho. And as soon as we got on that road,

I said to my wife, "I can see why Jesus used this as a setting for his parable." It's a winding, meandering road. It's really conducive for ambush. You start out in Jerusalem, which is about 1200 miles, or rather 1200 feet above sea level. And by the time you get down to Jericho, fifteen or twenty minutes later, you're about 2200 feet below sea level. That's a dangerous road. In the days of Jesus it came to be known as the "Bloody Pass." And you know, it's possible that the priest and the Levite looked over the man on the ground and wondered if the robbers were still around. Or it's possible that they felt that the man on the ground was merely faking. And he was acting like he had been robbed and hurt, in order to seize them over there, lure them there for quick and easy seizure. And so the first question that the Levite asked was, "If I stop to help this man, what will happen to me?" But then the Good Samaritan came by. And he reversed the question: "If I do not stop to help this man, what will happen to him?"

That's the question before you tonight. Not, "If I stop to help the sanitation workers, what will happen to all of the hours that I usually spend in my office every day and every week as a pastor?" The question is not, "If I stop to help this man in need, what will happen to me?" "If I do not stop to help the sanitation workers, what will happen to them?" That's the question.

Let us rise up tonight with greater readiness. Let us stand with a greater determination. And let us move on in these powerful days, these days of challenge to make America what it ought to be. We have an opportunity to make America a better nation. And I want to thank God, once more, for allowing me to be here with you.

You know, several years ago, I was in New York City autographing the first book that I had written. And while sitting there autographing books, a demented black woman came up. The only question I heard from her was, "Are you Martin Luther King?"

And I was looking down writing, and I said yes. And the next minute I felt something beating on my chest. Before I knew it I had been stabbed by this demented woman. I was rushed to Harlem Hospital. It was a dark Saturday afternoon. And that blade had gone through, and the X-rays revealed that the tip of the blade was on the edge of my aorta, the main artery. And once that's punctured, you drown in your own blood – that's the end of you.

It came out in the *New York Times* the next morning, that if I had sneezed, I would have died. Well, about four days later, they allowed me, after the operation, after my chest had been opened, and the blade had been taken out, to move around in the wheelchair in the hospital. They allowed me to read some of the mail that came in, and from all over the states, and the world, kind letters came in. I read a few, but one of them I will never forget. I had received one from the President and the Vice-President. I've forgotten what those telegrams said. I'd received a visit and a letter from the Governor of New York, but I've forgotten what the letter said. But there was another letter that came from a little girl, a young girl who was a student at the White Plains High School. And I looked at that letter, and I'll never forget it. It said simply, "Dear Dr. King; I am a ninth-grade student at the White Plains High School."

She said, "While it should not matter, I would like to mention that I am a white girl. I read in the paper of your misfortune, and of your suffering. And I read that if you had sneezed, you would have died. And I'm simply writing you to say that I'm so happy that you didn't sneeze."

And I want to say tonight, I want to say that I am happy that I didn't sneeze. Because if I had sneezed, I wouldn't have been around here in 1960, when students all over the South started sitting in at lunch counters. And I knew that as they were sitting in, they were really standing up for the best in the American dream. And taking the whole nation back to those great walls of democracy which were dug deep by the Founding Fathers in the Declaration of Independence and the Constitution. If I had sneezed, I wouldn't have been around in 1962, when Negroes in Albany, Georgia, decided to straighten their backs up. And whenever men and women straighten their backs up, they are going somewhere, because a man can't ride your back unless it is bent. If I had sneezed, I wouldn't have been here in 1963, when the black people of Birmingham, Alabama, aroused the conscience of this nation, and brought into being the Civil Rights Bill. If I had sneezed, I wouldn't have had a chance later that year, in August, to try to tell America about a dream that I had had. If I had sneezed, I wouldn't have been down in Selma, Alabama, to see the great movement there. If I had sneezed, I wouldn't have been in Memphis to see a community rally around those brother and sisters who are suffering. I'm so happy that I didn't sneeze.

And they were telling me, now it doesn't matter now. It really doesn't matter what happens now. I left Atlanta this morning, and as we got started on the plane, there were six of us, the pilot said over the public address system, "We are sorry for the delay, but we have Dr. Martin Luther King on the plane. And to be sure that all of the bags were checked, and to be sure that nothing would be wrong with the plane, we had to check out everything carefully. And we've had the plane protected and guarded all night."

And then I got into Memphis. And some began to say the threats, or talk about the threats that were out. What would happen to me from some of our sick white brothers?

Well, I don't know what will happen now. We've got some difficult days ahead. But it doesn't matter with me now. Because I've been to the mountaintop. And I don't mind. Like anybody, I would like to live a long life. Longevity has its place. But I'm not concerned about that now. I just want to do God's will. And He's allowed me to go up to the mountain. And I've looked over. And I've seen the promised land. I may not get there with you. But I want you to know tonight, that we, as a people will get to the promised land. And I'm happy, tonight. I'm not worried about anything. I'm not fearing any man. Mine eyes have seen the glory of the coming of the Lord.

FANNIE LOU HAMER

> Unlike Martin Luther King, Mrs. Hamer had little formal education. The daughter of sharecroppers, she began picking cotton at the age of six. She was a powerful, gifted speaker and singer, leading the mass meetings in

songs like "This Little Light of Mine," which refers to Matthew 5:15–16. Here she relates how she was arrested and beaten badly in jail for trying to register to vote. This excerpt, from a mass meeting in Greenwood, Mississippi in 1963, shows how she identifies the biblical struggle against injustice with the civil rights struggle of her own time.

Source: Fannie Lou Hamer, Moses Moon Papers, Archives Center, National Museum of American History, Smithsonian Institution.

From the fourth chapter of St. Luke, beginning at the eighteenth verse: "The Spirit of the Lord is upon me, because he has anointed me to preach the gospel to the poor. He has sent me to heal the broken-hearted, to preach deliverance to the captive, and recovering the sight to the blind, to set at liberty to them who are bruised, to preach the acceptable year of the Lord."

Now the time have come that was Christ's purpose on earth, and we only been getting by, by paying our way to hell. But the time is out. When Simon Cyrene was helping Christ to bear his cross up the hill, he said; "Must Jesus bear this cross alone and all the world go free?" He said, "No, there's a cross for everyone and there's a cross for me. This consecrated cross I'll bear, till death shall set me free. And then go home a crown to wear, for there's a crown for me." ["Must Jesus Bear This Cross Alone?" Thomas Shepherd, George Allen, *The Oberlin Social and Sabbath Hymn Book*, 1844.]

And it's no easy way out. We just got to wake up and face it, folks. And if I can face the issue, you can too. You see the thing that was so pitiful now about it – the men been wanting to be the boss all of these years, and the ones that ain't up under the house is under the bed. But you see it's poison – it's poison for us not to speak what we know is right. As Christ said from the seventeenth chapter of Acts, in the twenty-sixth verse says, "has made of one blood all nations for to dwell on the face of the earth," then it's no different. We just have different colors. And brother you can believe this or not – I been sick of this system as long as I can remember. I heard some people speak of Depression – in the thirties. In the twenties it was 'pression with me – depression. I've been as hungry – It's a funny thing, since I started working for Christ. It's kind of like in the twenty-third of the psalms, when he said, "Thou preparest a table before me in the presence of my enemies. Thou anointeth my head with oil and my cup runneth over." And I have walked through the shadows of death, because it was on the tenth of September in '62 when they shot sixteen times in the house, and it wasn't a foot over the bed where my head was. But that night I wasn't there. Don't you see what God can do?

Quit running around trying to dodge-step because this book says, "he that seeketh to save his life is going to lose it anyhow." So as long as you know you going for something, you put up a light. That it can be like Paul, saying "I've fought a good fight, and I've kept the faith." You know it's been a long time, people. I have worked, I have worked as hard as anybody, I have been picking cotton and would be so hungry and wanted to pardon things about it, wondering what I was going to cook that night … But you see, all of them things was wrong, you see.

And I have asked God, I said "Now, Lord," and you have too [inaudible] and said, "Open a way for us." Say, "please make a way for us, Jesus," say where I can stand up and speak for my race, and speak for these hungry children. And he opened a way, and all of them mostly back out. You see he made it so plain for us. He sent a man in Mississippi, with the same man that Moses had to go to Egypt, and tell him to go down in Mississippi and tell Ross Barnett to "Let my people go."

And you know, I feel good, I feel good. I never know today what's going to happen to me tonight. But I do know, as I walk along, I walk with my hand in God's hand. And you see, you know the ballot is good. If it wasn't good, how come he trying to keep you from it, and he's still using it? Don't be foolish, folks. They going in now by the droves and droves and they had [inaudible] to keep us out of there the other day. And dogs. Now if that's good enough for them, I want some of it, too.

You see, as I said, it was on the tenth of September when they shot in the house for me sixteen times, but I didn't stop. Now some of the time since then I got hungry but I got consolation because I had got hungry before I got in it. Wasn't going to mean any more for me to be hungry now than it was then.

Then on the ninth of June this year, I was beaten in a jail house, until I was hard as metal. And I told the policeman, I said "It's going to be miserable when you have to face God" I said, because one day you going to pay up for the things you have done. I said, because, as the Scripture says, "has made of one blood all nations." He said, "It's a damn lie. Abraham Lincoln said that." So that's pitiful. I'm telling you the truth, but it's pitiful, you see, that people can have so much hate, that it make them beat a person and don't know they're doing wrong. But open your New Testament when you get home and read from the twenty-sixth chapter of Proverbs in the twenty-seventh verse "Whoso diggeth a pit shall fall down in it." Pits have been dug for us for ages, but they didn't know, when they was digging pits for us, they had some pits dug for themselves. And the Bible, it said, "Before one jot of my word will fail, heaven and earth will pass away." Be not deceived, for God is not mocked. "For whatsoever a man sow, that shall he also reap."

All we got to do – That's why I love the song "This Little Light of Mine," from the fifth chapter of Matthew, he said, "a city that set on a hill cannot be hid." And I don't mind my light shining. I don't hide that I'm fighting for freedom. Because Christ died to set us free. And he stayed here till he got 33 years old, letting us know how we would have to walk. And we can come to this church, and we can shout, till we look foolish because that's what we do. And we can come out here and live a life, and act a life and we going just as straight to hell if we don't do something, because we got a charge to keep too. Until we can sing this song of Dr. Watts, "Should earth against my soul engage and fiery darts be hurled. But when I can smile at Satan's rage and face a frowning world" ["When I Can Read My Title Clear," by Isaac Watts.] Thank you.

BLACK LIBERATION THEOLOGY

> The continued reality of racism in America challenged mainstream theology. James Cone grew up in the South in the time of the Jim Crow laws that maintained segregation. Trained in the tradition of white Protestant theology, his experience as an African American inspired him to formulate a theology of black liberation that made sense of biblical Christianity in the light of African American experience. This excerpt is from *A Black Theology of Liberation*, published in 1970. Cone went on to develop his theology, particularly in response to critiques from womanist and other theologians.
>
> Source: James Cone, *A Black Theology of Liberation* (Maryknoll, NY: Orbis, 1990), 46–8. Reproduced by permission.

… God's revelation has nothing to do with white suburban ministers admonishing their people to be nice to black persons. It has nothing to do with voting for open occupancy or holding a memorial service for Martin Luther King, Jr. God's revelation means a radical encounter with the structures of power which King fought against to his death. It is what happens in a black ghetto when the ghettoized decide to strike against their enemies. In a word, God's revelation means *liberation*, nothing more and nothing less …

The emphasis that black theology puts on liberation as an indispensable ingredient of revelation is inherently biblical. The biblical emphasis on liberation may be approached through an analysis of the relationship of revelation, faith and history … the God of the Bible is a God who makes his will and purpose known through his participation in human history. That is why Christianity has been described as a historical religion … It is important to note the history in which God chose to grant a self-disclosure. It was granted to an oppressed people, and the nature of his revelatory deed was synonymous with the emancipation of that people. The exodus of Israel from Egypt was a revelation-liberation. In this revelatory event, Israel came to know God as the liberator of the oppressed, and also realized that its being as a people was inseparable from divine concomitance. Thus Yahweh was known primarily for the deed done for Israel when other political powers threatened its existence as a community. The biblical writers expressed Israel's view of God's revelation by describing Yahweh as a warrior.

> I will sing to the Lord, for he has triumphed gloriously;
> the horse and his rider he has thrown into the sea.
> The Lord is my strength and my song,
> and he has become my salvation;
> this is my God, and I will praise him,
> my father's God, and I will exalt him.
> The Lord is a man of war;
> the Lord is his name. (Exodus 15:1b–3)

In this passage God's revelation means political emancipation, which involves his destruction of the enemy. In view of God overwhelming defeat of the Egyptians, a covenant is made with Israel. The covenant is an expression of God's identification with Israel and his will to be its God and of Israel's will to be God's people. The entire history of Israel is a history of what God has done, is doing, and will do in moments of oppression ...

... It is not difficult to make a contemporary application of this view to the plight of black Americans today. Indeed it is difficult to ignore. How could we speak about God's revelation in the exodus, the conquest of Palestine, the role of the judges of Israel without seeing parallels in black history? In Israel the judge was a charismatic leader, endowed with the spirit of Yahweh; he led his people in battle against the enemy. Is it really hard for us to believe that black examples of this would be Nat Turner, Denmark Vesey, and Malcolm X? These men represent the "soul" of blackness, and what black people mean by black liberation. They are the black judges endowed with the spirit of Yahweh for the sole purpose of creating the spirit of freedom among their people.

INCLUSION OF GAY/LESBIAN/BISEXUAL/ TRANSEXUAL PERSONS

PAUL'S STATEMENTS IN ROMANS 1

Discussions of homoerotic acts, gay marriage, and the ordination of gays/ lesbians as clergy, when they invoke the Bible, tend to focus on a small group of biblical texts: (1) the creation story in Gen 1–2; (2) the Sodom story in Gen 19 (sometimes in tandem with Judges 19); (3) Leviticus 18:22 and 20:13, which identifies a man lying with a man as with a woman as an "abomination"; (4) 1 Cor 6:9 and 1 Tim 1:10, which are lists of prohibited vices; and (5) Romans 1:26–27, where Paul condemns the giving up of "natural intercourse." Marion Lloyd Soards, a professor at Louisville Presbyterian seminary, examines these verses, and contextualizes them, and does not see a mandate against homosexuality in the first four. The Romans reference proves more serious. While Soards, coming from his understanding of biblical teaching and the Presbyterian church's rootedness in the authority of Scripture, cannot condone homosexual activity or the ordination of gays and lesbians, he argues for their belonging in the church.

Source: Reproduced from *Scripture and Homosexuality* by Marion L. Soards © 1995 Westminster John Knox, 20–4, 75–6. Used by permission of Westminster John Knox Press.

1

The case is different when we come to Romans. Paul's explicit statements concerning both male and female homosexuality in Rom. 1:26–27 are made in the course of serious and significant theological reflection. Paul states his major theme in Rom 1:16–17, "For I am not ashamed of the gospel; it is the power of God for salvation to everyone who has faith, to the Jew first and also to the Greek. For in it the righteousness of God is revealed through faith for faith, as it is written, 'The one who is righteous will live by faith.'" Then in Rom. 1:18–3:20 Paul carefully crafts an argument designed to make the point stated in 3:9. "All, both Jews and Greeks, are under the power of sin." The point is reiterated in 3:23, "All have sinned and fall short of the glory of God."

… As Paul discusses the Gentile sin of idolatry, he refers to their homosexual behavior as the clear symptom of their sinfulness. Note well: homosexuality is not the Gentiles' problem, it is a *symptom* of their problem. They are under the power of sin, and they are isolated from God. Writing on this passage, Richard Hays remarks,

> Paul singles out homosexual intercourse for special attention because he regards it as providing a particularly graphic image of the way in which human fallenness distorts God's created order. God the creator made man and woman for each other, to cleave together, to be fruitful and multiply. When human beings engage in homosexual activity, they enact an outward and visible sign of an inward and spiritual reality: the rejection of the Creator's design. They *embody* the spiritual condition of those who have "exchanged the truth about God for a lie" (*Sojourners* 20 [July 1991]: 19).

Listen to Paul in vv. 25–27: "Because they exchanged the truth about God for a lie and worshiped and served the creature rather than the Creator, … for this reason God gave them up to degrading passions … [they] received in their own persons the due penalty for their error."

According to Paul, homosexuality is not a sin that provokes God's wrath; rather the wrath of God comes on humans who are under the power of sin. A sign of both God's wrath and human sin is that humans engage in homosexual acts.

One approach to this passage that tries to tone down the negative assessment of homosexuality suggests that Paul is not denouncing those who are truly homosexual. Rather, it is argued that Paul is referring to licentious heterosexual persons who have engaged in homosexual acts. The text says that "their women exchanged natural intercourse for unnatural" and that the men gave up "natural intercourse with women" and "were consumed with passion for one another." Paul however, is not concerned with individual decisions. He is discussing the sinful guilt of all humans; moreover, neither Paul nor any other ancient person had a concept of "sexual orientation." For Paul and the Jewish thinkers such as Philo and Josephus, as well as first century Greco-Roman moralists such as Seneca, Plutarch, and Dio Chrysostom, homosexual acts were willful actions of unbridled lust.

… As Paul discerned and declared God's relationship to humans, homosexual acts were outside the boundaries of God's intentions for humanity. Homosexuality was one vivid indication of the real problem of sin, and Paul states bluntly that all humans are sinners. On the matter of homosexuality, we should see clearly that the biblical understanding of homosexual behavior is univocal (although this issue is at most a minor concern). Homosexual activity is not consistent with the will of God; it is not merely a sin but evidence of sin, and there is no way to read the Bible as condoning homosexual acts.

2

The doors of the church stand open to all who confess their allegiance to Jesus Christ. Many of the arguments from experience for the approval of homosexuality cite the clear, real evidences of God's grace in the lives of homosexuals. While such arguments do not prove the appropriateness of homosexual behavior, they do testify to the reality of grace in particular human lives. One heterosexual Christian has said, "When I confessed Jesus Christ as Lord and Savior, I began to find him at work in my life saving me from things I didn't know were sinful and from which I didn't know I needed saving." Perfection is not a prerequisite for a genuine confession of faith in Christ.

While the church cannot offer approval of homosexual activity, the church can also not deny the validity of faith in less-than-perfect humans. If approval of one's homosexual behavior becomes a condition for one's joining the church, then the church faces an insurmountable problem; for Christians seeking to recognize and to honor the authority of the Bible will insist that no such approval is possible. If there is no demand for approval of homosexual activity, there is no reason to deny church membership to the homosexual who takes her or his place along with other forgiven sinners in the corporate body of Christ.

ANOTHER INTERPRETATION OF ROMANS 1

> Like Marion Soards, Jack Rogers is a Presbyterian and a seminary professor (emeritus). He notes that the biblical references pertaining to homosexuality are, at most, eight texts, about twelve pages in all, a very small "canon within a canon." He understands Paul's statements in Romans as referring to idolatry, not homosexuality. Both writers share several assumptions about sin, grace, and the authority of the Bible and both suggest that sexuality was not a central focus of Paul's theology. Rogers, unlike Soards, does not understand homosexual activity as inherently sinful. He grew up as a conservative evangelical, but changed his views on some matters. His book draws analogies between current biblical arguments against the full participation of LGBT persons and earlier biblical arguments that justified slavery and the subordination of women.
>
> Source: Reproduced from *Jesus, the Bible, and Homosexuality* by Jack Rogers © 2009 Westminster John Knox Press, 72–6. Used by permission Westminster John Knox.

The conflict over the meaning of biblical texts becomes acute when we look at Romans 1. Some conservative scholars who dismiss the relevance of the seven previously discussed texts to the issue of homosexuality argue that Romans 1 is a theological statement that has direct application for our time. I believe, however, that a close and careful look at the text, using the best methods of biblical interpretation, will reveal that Paul is making a statement about idolatry, not sexuality per se, and that Paul's writings also reflect many of the cultural assumptions of his time ...

In Romans 1:18–32, Paul is writing about idolatry, that is, worshiping, giving our ultimate allegiance to anything in the creation instead of God, the Creator. Paul is writing from Corinth, a bustling seaport town that was "notorious for vice of all kinds."

... Paul makes this point again in Romans 2:1. We are without excuse, especially when we judge others. Why? Because in God's sight we are all given to idolatry. Paul is driving home the point that is at the heart of Reformation theology: no one is righteous before God. Paul has been criticizing those idolatrous Corinthian Gentiles. Now he is saying to his Jewish colleagues, and to us. No one is righteous. We are all sinners. That is Paul's point in Romans 1.

Cultural norms, not a theology of Creation

What does Paul mean by "natural" and "unnatural" in Romans 1:26–27? In the original Greek, the words are *physis*, "nature," and *para physis*, "against nature."

For Paul, "unnatural" is a synonym for "unconventional." It means something surprisingly out of the ordinary. The most significant evidence that "natural" meant "conventional" is that God acted "contrary to nature" (Rom. 11:13–24). That is, God did something very unusual in pruning the Gentiles from a wild olive tree, where they grew in their natural state, and grafting them into the cultivated olive tree of God's people (Rom. 11:24). Since it cannot be that God sinned, to say that God did what was "contrary to nature" or "against nature" (v. 24) means that God did something surprising or out of the ordinary.

Paul is not talking in Romans 1:26–27 about a violation of the order of creation. In Paul's vocabulary, *physis* (nature) is not a synonym for *ktisis* (creation). In speaking about what is "natural," Paul is merely accepting the conventional view of people and how they ought to behave in first-century Hellenistic-Jewish culture ...

Those who are opposed to equal rights for Christian gay and lesbian people make several serious errors in interpreting Romans 1: (1) they lose sight of the fact that this passage is primarily about idolatry, (2) they overlook Paul's point that we are all sinners, (3) they miss the cultural subtext, and (4) they apply Paul's condemnation of immoral sexual activity to faithful gay and lesbian Christians who are not idolaters, who love God, and who seek to live in faithful obedience to God.

Heterosexual sex can be either moral or immoral, depending on its context. The same is true of homosexual sex. If Paul walked into a party at the Playboy mansion today or observed college students "hooking up" at a fraternity party, he would be appalled and rightly condemn the activities going on there. But no one would conclude from that observation that Paul had ruled out all heterosexual sex as immoral. Everyone would understand that Paul was not talking about married Christian heterosexual couples who love God and seek to follow Jesus.

Paul's condemnation of immoral sexual behavior is not appropriately applied to contemporary gay or lesbian Christians who are not idolaters, who love God, and who seek to live in thankful obedience to God. I think Jeffrey Siker, professor of New Testament at Loyola Marymount University, says it best: "We know of gay and lesbian Christians who truly worship and serve the one true God and yet still affirm in positive ways their identity as gay and lesbian people. Paul apparently knew of no homosexual Christians. We do." (Siker 1996: 143).

SUGGESTIONS FOR FURTHER RESEARCH

Breeden, James O. 1980. *Advice among Masters: The Ideal in Slave Management in the Old South.* Westport, CT: Greenwood Press.

Callahan, Allen Dwight. 2006. *The Talking Book: African Americans and the Bible.* New Haven, CT: Yale University Press.

Chesebrough, David B. 1991. *"God Ordained This War": Sermons on the Sectional Crisis, 1830–1865.* Columbia, SC: University of South Carolina Press.

Douglass, Frederick. 2003. *My Bondage and My Freedom. The Frederick Douglass Papers Series 2,* ed. J. W. Blassingame, J. R. McKivigan and P. P. Hink, vol. 2. New Haven, CT: Yale University Press.

Edwards, George R. 1984. *Gay/Lesbian Liberation: A Biblical Perspective.* New York: Pilgrim Press.

Fredrickson, George M. 1971. *The Black Image in the White Mind: The Debate on Afro-American Character and Destiny, 1817–1914.* New York: Harper & Row.

Gagnon, Robert A. J. 2001. *The Bible and Homosexual Practice: Texts and Hermeneutics.* Nashville, TN: Abingdon Press.

Harrill, J. Albert. 2000. "The Use of the New Testament in the American Slave Controversy: A Case History in the Hermeneutical Tension between Biblical Criticism and Christian Moral Debate." *Religion and American Culture* 10: 149–86.

Kern, Kathi. 2001. *Mrs. Stanton's Bible.* Ithaca, NY: Cornell University Press.

Killens, John Oliver. 1970. *The Trial Record of Denmark Vesey.* Boston: Beacon.

Kling, David William. 2004. *The Bible in History: How the Texts have Shaped the Times.* New York: Oxford University Press.

Manhattan Declaration: A Call of Christian Conscience. Available from www.manhattandeclaration.org.

Mathews, Donald G. 1977. *Religion in the Old South.* Chicago: University of Chicago Press.

Noll, Mark A. 2002. *America's God: From Jonathan Edwards to Abraham Lincoln.* New York: Oxford University Press.

Raboteau, Albert J. 1978. *Slave Religion: The "Invisible Institution" in the Antebellum South.* New York: Oxford University Press.

—— 1999. *Canaan Land: A Religious History of African Americans.* New York: Oxford University Press.

Rogers, Jack Bartlett. 2009. *Jesus, the Bible, and Homosexuality: Explode the Myths, Heal the Church.* Rev. and exp. edition. Louisville, KY: Westminster John Knox Press.

Saillant, John. 2000. "Origins of African American Biblical Hermeneutics in Eighteenth Century Opposition to the Slave Trade and Slavery." In V. L. Wimbush, ed., *African Americans and the Bible: Sacred Texts and Social Textures.* New York: Continuum.

Siker, Jeffrey S., ed. 1994. *Homosexuality in the Church: Both Sides of the Debate.* Louisville, KY: Westminster/John Knox Press.

—— 1996. "Gentile Wheat and Homosexual Christians: New Testament Directions for the Heterosexual Church." In R. L. Brawley, ed., *Biblical Ethics & Homosexuality: Listening to Scripture.* Louisville, KY: Westminster John Knox Press.

—— ed. 2007. *Homosexuality and Religion: An Encyclopedia.* Westport, CT: Greenwood Press.

Smith, John David. 1985. *An Old Creed for the New South: Proslavery Ideology and Historiography, 1865–1918.* Westport, CT: Greenwood Press.

—— 1993. *The Biblical and "Scientific" Defense of Slavery.* New York: Garland.

Soards, Marion L. 1995. *Scripture and Homosexuality: Biblical Authority and the Church Today.* Louisville, KY: Westminster John Knox Press.

Stuckey, Sterling. 2000. "'My Burden Lightened': Frederick Douglass, the Bible, and Slave Culture." In V. L. Wimbush, ed., *African Americans and the Bible: Sacred Texts and Social Textures.* New York: Continuum.

Wimbush, Vincent L., ed. 2000. *African Americans and the Bible: Sacred Texts and Social Textures.* New York: Continuum.

Wood, Forrest G. 1990. *The Arrogance of Faith: Christianity and Race in America from the Colonial Era to the Twentieth Century.* New York: Knopf.

4   Reading in the margins

The Bible was central to many social movements, as the material in Chapter 3 on America's great debates shows. Progressives and conservatives alike brought its words to bear to debate slavery, women's rights, civil rights, and evolution. Yet these groups did not tinker with the Bible itself. They assumed its authority, trading on it to support their causes.

Others had a more complex relationship to the Bible. In this chapter we look at people who feel that in some way things had gone badly wrong in the way the Bible was understood. They seek to *restore* an aspect of the Bible that has been forgotten, lost, misunderstood, or deliberately covered up. Their touchstone is their own lived experience and their interpretations are often at odds with mainstream, institutionalized understandings. They see themselves as training a light on realities or figures that have been in the shadows, amplifying truths that mainstream religious institutions have forgotten or deliberately obscured.

These sources do not fit neatly together. The reader may wonder what gay theology has to do with Pentecostalism, or contemporary feminist critique with the Shakers. Yet all these sources contain a thread of restorationism, a supplying of a lack, or correcting a misunderstanding. As Richard Hughes and C. Leonard Allen explain in their book, *Illusions of Innocence* (1988), a common theme in the American story is the recovery of an earlier, more perfect epoch or community, like the return to Eden, the Exodus and Promised Land, or the first generation of the early church. A corollary to the idea of the idyllic past is that a small group of the Saved will survive the coming conflagration predicted in the book of Revelation. Hughes and Allen suggest that the identification with "the purity of first times" assumes identification with transcendent norms that are beyond particular cultures and histories (xiii). While many of the selections in this group do not indulge in such naivety (some do), they share a desire to rid the text of what they see as false cultural accretions, getting back to "what the text really means."

Three kinds of material appear in this section. A first grouping involves people who may, as individuals, be well-situated in society – well-educated, professional, comfortably middle-class. But they experience a deep discomfort with traditional interpretations. Something has been missed, or turned around, in the way the Bible is taught. Fortunately the Bible contains the seeds of its own regeneration in its own egalitarian elements. Rosemary Radford Ruether calls it the "prophetic corrective," the strand of biblical thought that professes God's care for the marginalized. Richard Cleaver presents an understanding of the Good Samaritan story in Luke that places the gay person in the same position of vulnerability as the marginalized Samaritan. Both he and Gary Comstock reorient their relationship to the Bible. Comstock treats it not as absolute, but as an intimate friend, beloved but imperfect. He confronts it with honesty and compassion, as he would confront a friend. Another theologian whose own experience is the measure by which she reads the Bible is Jacquelyn Grant. As an African American woman, she feels an affinity to Jesus as a fellow-suffering, marginalized human. This Jesus contrasts with institutional religion's more sanitized figure, who she calls "white women's Christ."

Hewing closer to the text, Phyllis Trible amplifies literary elements in the text that promote equality. In this section, she works with the Creation story itself, historically used to preach women's subordination. Approaching the text historically, Elisabeth Schüssler Fiorenza uncovers traditions of women's discipleship, nearly obscured by the gospels themselves, and ignored by the church, that suggest the early circle of people around Jesus was an egalitarian "discipleship of equals."

The second grouping of sources is of individuals or groups who experience a direct sense of the Spirit. This experience is the source of their authority to preach and lead. Some, like Jarena Lee, Phoebe Palmer, and the Catholic charismatics, are not separatist, but operate within existing churches. Yet their extra-institutional activities are an implicit critique of what their churches have to offer. Their experience is for them a restoration of the same experience of the Spirit that visited the apostles in Acts 2. Their authority comes from a combination of their personal experience and a distinctive reading of the Bible. Palmer's Holiness movement gave rise to currents of practice and belief that fed the Pentecostal movement, including the influential Azusa Street movement. Taking their practice from the experience of the visitation of the gift of tongues on the apostles, they developed the practice of speaking in tongues, or glossolalia. Pentecostal, or more broadly, charismatic Christianity, begins as a Protestant phenomenon. It becomes part of the Catholic Church in 1967, at a weekend retreat of a group of Duquesne University students and faculty. The value of charismatic faith and practice within the church is affirmed by Pope Paul VI and John Paul II.

The third section includes materials in which the process of re-reading the Bible holds even more profound consequences. In these cases, critique is cast far and wide as the writers connect shortcomings in biblical interpretation with irrevocable flaws in the contemporary world. The authors see the recovery of obscured or lost religious truths as the path to profound remaking of society itself, such that each of these writers initiated or participated in a community that separated itself in some way from mainstream society in hopes of participating in – or even creating – a radical alternative.

In each of the examples included here, the writers find particular inspiration in the biblical prophecies – especially as laid out in the New Testament book of Revelation – of God's clearing of a contemporary world of sin to make way for the Kingdom Come: the new, earthly paradise signaled by the arrival, once again, of a divinely "anointed one" ("messiah" in Hebrew; "Christ" in Greek). Fittingly, the Shaker elder F. W. Evans equates his group with "the Millennium" in the opening of the first selection of this section. With these words, Evans directly invokes the thousand-year period (millennium) of peace figured in the Book of Revelation that, along with the new messianic appearance, offers a clear sign of the impending end of the existing world and approaching arrival of the earthly paradise, of a "new" Jerusalem" to surpass the former glory of the city that serves as the Bible's political and spiritual center.

The expectations tied up with these biblical images have earned those who hold out for the fulfillment of the Millennium's promise a now familiar label: "millennialists." Despite their diverse origins, intentions, and perspectives, the sources here – taken as a whole – offer a vivid reminder of the enduring power in American culture of millennial expectation. Catherine Albanese argues that "millennialism" serves as the "creed" of an overarching, Protestant-inflected, American "religion." However, Albanese insists that the power and persistence of millennialism, as with the Bible itself, stems from its breadth and flexibility. Millennialism carries a standard narrative structure – a flawed world in time will be superseded by a new, better one – but each part of the story, and the tale as a whole, gets imagined in different ways.

From that perspective, all of the sources here offer glimpses of American millennialism. Each of these writers – and the groups to which they are linked – took the biblically foretold promise of a new and better society literally to some degree. Yet, just as significantly, the authors differ greatly in their understanding of when and how the prophecies come to fruition, as well as the Bible's particular vision of the future. For instance, even as the writers agree on the importance of the Americas in the unfolding of a universal historical drama, they understand the continent's role in various ways. Is America "Babylon," the embodiment of the sinful society in the Bible? Is it the site of the coming kingdom? Or, as in many cases, does the continent represent both the dying old and emergent new worlds? Similarly, the sources provide different responses to other questions inspired by the biblical texts. Who is the "Christ" who heralds the new age? Is it Jesus or someone else? Has he – or she! – already arrived? Are we supposed to wait for God to install the new kingdom, or do we have the mandate to try to bring the earthly paradise to fruition?

This last question generates particularly interesting and significant relations among the sources in this section. As already noted, the first selection reveals F. W. Evans' and the Shakers' understanding of themselves *as* "the Millennium" and, therefore, authorized by God to build the perfect society. Among the groups represented here, the Mormons as well as John Humphrey Hoyes and the Oneida Perfectionists exhibit a similar sense of divine mandate, even if they do so at different times, in distinct places, and with divergent motivations. In contrast, William Miller establishes another tone. Through his careful studies of the Bible in the first part of the eighteenth century, Miller suggests that we can gain a sense of and prepare for the arrival of the Kingdom Come but that, in the end, it will spring to life by God's will alone. We really only can prepare by holding steadfast faith. Among other sources, Miller's influence on Ellen White and the Seventh-Day Adventists, Charles Taze Russell and the Jehovah's Witnesses, and David Koresh and the Branch Davidians surfaces clearly. His position also seems to resonate with the activities of Mary Baker Eddy and the Christian Scientists, Jim Jones and the People's Temple, as well as with Elijah Muhammad and the Nation of Islam.

Readers should feel encouraged to look for other resonances and dissonances across the sources in this chapter that, even in their diversity, convey a persistent, biblically informed conviction about the eventual redemption of society's present shortcomings.

IDENTITY AND TEXTUAL INTERPRETATION

JARENA LEE

Jarena Lee (1783–c.1850), an African American, was born free in New Jersey. After conversion to Christianity, she learned of the Methodist doctrine of sanctification, a second stage of spiritual development, and adopted Methodism. Feeling the call to preach, she challenged the limitations to women's leadership in the Methodist Church by citing the examples of the male disciples and Mary Magdalene. Rev. Richard Allen (1760–1831), founder of the African Methodist Episcopal (AME) Church, initially discouraged her but endorsed her preaching years later. She became a very successful itinerant evangelist. In 1836 she published this spiritual autobiography in a pamphlet, "The Life and Experience of Jarena Lee."

Source: Jarena Lee, *The Life and Experience of Jarena Lee*. In William L. Andrews, ed., *Sisters of the Spirit* (Bloomington: Indiana University Press, 1986), 35–7. Reproduced by permission of Indiana University Press.

Between four and five years after my sanctification, on a certain time, an impressive silence fell upon me, and I stood as if some one was about to speak to me, yet I had no such thought in my heart. But to my utter surprise there seemed to sound a voice which I thought I distinctly heard, and most certainly understood, which said to me, "Go preach the Gospel!" I immediately replied aloud, "No one will believe me." Again I listened, and again the same voice seemed to say, "Preach the Gospel; I will put words in your mouth, and will turn your enemies to become your friends."

At first I supposed that Satan had spoken to me, for I had read that he could transform himself into an angel of light, for the purpose of deception. Immediately I went into a secret place, and called upon the Lord to know if he had called me to preach, and whether I was deceived or not; when there appeared to my view the form and figure of a pulpit, with a Bible lying thereon, the back of which was presented to me as plainly as if it had been a literal fact ...

Two days after. I went to see the preacher in charge of the African society, who was the Rev. Richard Allen, the same before named in these pages, to tell him that I felt it my duty to preach the gospel ...

I now told him, that the Lord had revealed it to me, that I must preach the gospel. He replied by asking, in what sphere I wished to move in? I said, among the Methodists. He then replied that a Mrs. Cook, a Methodist lady, had also some time before requested the same privilege; who it was believed, had done much good in the way of exhortation, and holding prayer meetings; and who had been permitted to do so by the verbal license of the preacher in charge at the time. But as to women preaching, he said that our Discipline knew nothing at all about it – that it did not call for women preachers. This I was glad to hear, because it removed the fear of the cross – but not no sooner did this feeling cross my mind, than I found that a love of souls had in a measure departed from me; that holy energy which burned within me, as a fire, began to be smothered. This I soon perceived.

O how careful ought we to be, lest through our by-laws of church govern-ment and discipline, we bring into disrepute even the word of life. For as unseemly as it may appear now-a-days for a woman to preach, it should be remembered that nothing is impossible with God. And why should it be thought impossible, heterodox, or improper, for a woman to preach? seeing the Saviour died for the woman as well as the man.

If a man may preach, because the Saviour died for him, why not the woman? seeing he died for her also. Is he not a whole Saviour, instead of a half one? as those who hold it wrong for a woman to preach would seem to make it appear.

Did not Mary *first* preach the risen Saviour, and is not the doctrine of the resurrection the very climax of Christianity – hangs not all our hope on this, as argued by St. Paul? Then did not Mary, a woman, preach the gospel? for she preached the resurrection of the crucified Son of God.

But some will say, that Mary did not expound the Scripture, therefore, she did not preach, in the proper sense of the term. To this I reply, it may be that the term *preach*, in those primitive times, did not mean exactly what it is now *made* to mean; perhaps it was a great deal more simple then, than it is now: if it were not, the unlearned fishermen could not have preached the gospel at all, as they had no learning.

To this it may be replied, by those who are determined not to believe that it is right for a woman to preach, that the disciples, though they were fish-ermen, and ignorant of letters too, were inspired so to do ... If then, to preach the gospel, by the gift of heaven, comes by inspiration solely, is God straitened; must he take the man exclusively? May he not, did he not, and can he not inspire a female to preach the simple story of the birth, life, death, and resur-rection of our Lord, and accompany it too, with power to the sinner's heart. As for me, I am fully persuaded that the Lord called me to labour according to what I have received, in his vineyard. If he has not, how could he consistently bear testimony in favour of my poor labours, in awakening and converting sinners?

THE BIBLE AS PATRIARCHAL

Matilda Joslyn Gage (1826–98), an important figure in the battle for women's suffrage, argued that Bible and Christianity were obstacles to women's equality. Earlier forms of religion elevated women, and understood God as male and female. With the advent of the Hebrew Bible, and its offshoot, Christianity, these views were suppressed. These excerpts are from *Woman, Church and State*, first published in 1893.

Source: Matilda Joslyn Gage, *Woman, Church, and State* (New York: Truth Seeker Co., 1893), 11, 13, 22, 43, 46.

Woman is told that her present position in society is entirely due to Christianity; that it is superior to that of her sex at any prior age of the world, Church and State both maintaining that she has ever been inferior and dependent, man superior and ruler. These assertions are made the basis of opposition to her demands for exact equality with man in all the relations of life, although they are not true either of the family, the church, or the state. Such assertions are due to non-acquaintance with the existing phase of historical knowledge, whose records the majority of mankind have neither time nor opportunity of investigating.

Christianity tended somewhat from its foundation to restrict the liberty woman enjoyed under the old civilizations ... A form of society existed at an early age known as the Matriarchate or Mother-rule. Under the Matriarchate, except as son and inferior, man was not recognized in either of these great institutions, family, state or church. A father and husband as such, had no place either in the social, political or religious scheme; woman was ruler in each. The primal priest on earth, she was also supreme as goddess in heaven. The earliest resemblance of the family is traceable to the relationship of mother and child alone. Here the primal idea of the family had birth ...

The Supreme Being has a Form, and yet has no Form; he can be likened to nothing; we cannot define him and say that he is this or that; he is neither Man or Woman; neither Heaven or Earth, and yet he is all; subject to no corruption, no mortality and with neither sleep nor rest, he is Almighty and Omnipotent without Beginning and without End ...

The Patriarchate under which Biblical history and Judaism commence, was a rule of men whose lives and religion were based upon passions of the grossest kind, showing but few indications of softness or refinement. Monogamous family life, did not exist, but a polygamy whose primal object was the formation of a clan possessing hereditary chiefs ruling aristocratically. To this end the dominion of man over woman and the birth of many children was requisite. To this end polygamy was instituted, becoming as marked a feature of the Patriarchate as monogamy was of the Matriarchate. Not until the Patriarchate were wives regarded as property, the sale of daughters as a legitimate means of family income, or their destruction at birth looked upon as a justifiable act. Under the Patriarchate society became morally revolutionized, the family, the state, the form of religion entirely changed. The theory of a male supreme God in the interests of force and authority, wars, family discord, the sacrifice of children to appease the wrath of an offended (male) deity are all due to the Patriarchate. These were practices entirely out of consonance with woman's thought and life …

The Holy Spirit, symbolized by a dove, is a distinctively feminine principle – the Comforter – and yet has ever been treated by the Christian Church as masculine, alike in dogmas propounded from the pulpit, and in translations of the Scriptures.

African American women's experience

Womanist theology saw much of white feminist theology as inadequate to represent the needs and legacy of black women's experiences. Jacquelyn Grant shows how black women identified with Jesus as a co-sufferer. She draws on the legacy of black women preachers like Jarena Lee and Sojourner Truth.

Source: Jacquelyn Grant, *White Women's Christ and Black Women's Jesus: Feminist Christology and Womanist Response* (New York: Oxford University Press, 2000), 211–13, 220. Reproduced by permission of Oxford University Press.

Theological investigation into the experiences of Christian Black women reveals that Black women considered the Bible to be a major source for religious validation in their lives. Though Black women's relationship with God preceded their introduction to the Bible, this Bible gave some content to their God-consciousness. The source for Black women's understanding of God has been twofold: first, God's revelation directly to them, and secondly, God's revelation as witnessed in the Bible and as read and heard in the context of their experience. The understanding of God as creator, sustainer, comforter, and liberator took on life as they agonized over their pain, and celebrated the hope that as God delivered the Israelites, they would be delivered as well. The God of the Old and New Testament became real in the consciousness of oppressed Black women. Though they were politically impotent, they were able to appropriate certain themes of the Bible which spoke to their reality. For example, Jarena Lee, a nineteenth-century Black woman preacher in the African Methodist Episcopal Church, constantly emphasized the theme "Life and Liberty" in her sermons, which were always biblically based …

In the experiences of Black people, Jesus was "all things." Chief among these, however, was the belief in Jesus as the divine co-sufferer, who empowers them in situations of oppression. For Christian Black women in the past, Jesus was their central frame of reference. They identified with Jesus because they believed that Jesus identified with them. As Jesus was persecuted and made to suffer undeservedly, so were they. His suffering culminated in the crucifixion.

Their crucifixion included rape, and babies being sold. But Jesus' suffering was not the suffering of a mere human, for Jesus was understood to be God incarnate … Black women's affirmation of Jesus as God meant that White people were not God …

I would argue, as suggested by both Lee and Sojourner, that the significance of Christ is not his maleness, but his humanity. The most significant events of Jesus Christ were the life and ministry, the crucifixion, and the resurrection. The significance of these events, in one sense is that in them the absolute becomes concrete. God becomes concrete not only in the man Jesus, for he was crucified, but in the lives of those who will accept the challenges of the risen Saviour the Christ. For Lee, this meant that women could preach; for Sojourner, it meant that women could possibly save the world; for me, it means today, this Christ, found in the experience of Black women, is a Black woman. The commitment to struggle, not only with symptoms (church structures, structures of society), as Black women have done, but with the causes (those beliefs which produce and re-inforce structures) yields deeper theological and Christological questions having to do with images and symbolism. Christ challenges us to ask new questions demanded by the context on which we find ourselves.

THE TEXT INTERPRETS ITSELF

> Phyllis Trible broke new ground with her work, *God and the Rhetoric of Sexuality* (1978). Using clues from within the text, she shows how the Bible offers multiple interpretations of itself. She notes that the elements of the traditional understanding of "the Fall" and Eve's curse are not implied by the text. Here she interrogates the language and syntax of the Hebrew text to indicate humanity's oneness with the earth and mutuality of the sexes.
>
> Source: Phyllis Trible, *God and the Rhetoric of Sexuality*, 75–7; 89–90. © 1986 Fortress Press. Reproduced by permission of Augsburg Fortress Publishers.

This overview of subject, structure, and worlds prepares us to enter the story. And yet a compound-complex sentence, which prefaces the narrative, delays its beginning:

> When Yahweh God made earth and heavens –
> when no plant of the field was in the earth
> and no grain of the field had yet sprouted,
> because Yahweh God had not let it rain upon the earth,
> and [because] no earth creature was there to serve the earth –
> then a subterranean stream went up from the earth
> and watered the whole face of the earth;
> and then Yahweh God formed the earth creature,
> dust from the earth,
> and breathed into its nostrils the breath of life,
> and the earth creature became a living *nephesh*.
>
> (2:4b–7)

This tedious sentence struggles both to present and to limit a cosmic perspective, since it does not introduce a story about the universe but rather uses cosmic creation as a prelude to the advent and fulfillment of human life on earth …

Immediately following the making of earth and heavens, a clause interrupts to report the barrenness of the earth:

> when no plant of the field was in the **earth** [*'eretz*]
> and no grain of the field had yet sprouted.
>
> (2:5ab)

Since it interjects death in the presence of creation, a barren field requires explanation. Hence, this subordinate clause stretches beyond syntactical propriety to cite two reasons, one from the divine world and the other from the human:

> because [*kî*] Yahweh God had not let it rain upon the **earth** [*'eretz*]
> and [because] no **earth creature** [*'ādām*] was there
> to serve **the earth** [*hā-' ªdāmâ*].
>
> (2:5cd)

By repeating the subject and one of the objects that occurred at the very beginning of the sentence, the first reason increases tension between Creator and creation: "When Yahweh God made earth … because Yahweh God had not let it rain upon the earth." The deity who has not let it rain upon the earth made the earth. Thus the negative of barrenness recalls the positive of creation, to return the form and content of this first reason to the beginning of the sentence with a countermeaning.

But the second reason moves the sentence forward. It enlarges the vocabulary of the earth (*hā-' ªdāmâ*) and it plays with this new language to introduce an earth creature (*ādām*). Although God and an earth creature are the subjects of the verbs in the two parallel clauses, the parallelism itself is skewed. By a negative act of withholding rain, Yahweh God *causes* the barrenness of the earth. Strikingly, however, the passive absence of an earth creature *occasions* this barrenness. In other words, this second reason is attributed proleptically to the human world. But the account refrains from explaining that Yahweh God had not yet made a creature to serve the earth – even though such a statement would be an exact parallel to the first reason, would accord with the facts of the case, and would unequivocally assign cause to Yahweh God for the barrenness of the earth. Thus, the relationship between these two subjects, divine and human, awaits clarification.

Nevertheless, a play on words already establishes relationship between earth creature (*ādām*) and the earth (*hā-' ªdāmâ*). This pun is accessible to sight and sound. While uniting creature and soil, it also separates them. *ādām* is not yet; *hā-' ªdāmâ* already is. Furthermore, this *ādām* is described as potentially acting upon the *ªdāmâ* (2:5d): "no earth creature [*ādām*] was there to serve the earth [*hā-' ªdāmâ*] … "

... The divine evaluation "it is not good for the earth creature to be alone" contrasts wholeness with isolation. This contrast highlights distinctions that have appeared in the story from the first moment that Yahweh God formed the earth creature out of the earth. Although this original distinction indicated rapport between the creature and the soil, it also set the creature apart from the earth. Moreover, in the second episode it set the creature over the earth with the assignment to till and keep the garden. Further, although the earth creature shares common ground with the plants that grow from the earth, the creature is set over the trees with the freedom to eat them and the restriction not to eat one of them. In episodes one and two, then, the creature's relationship to the rest of creation is ambiguous; a part of and yet apart from; of common ground but with power over; joined yet separated. Since the creature is not only of the earth, but also other than the earth, it needs fulfillment from that which is other than in the earth. This need Yahweh God recognizes: "I will make a companion corresponding to it." The Hebrew word *'ēzer*, rendered here as "companion," has been traditionally translated "helper" – a translation that is totally misleading because the English word *helper* suggests an assistant, a subordinate, indeed, an inferior, while the Hebrew word *'ēzer* carries no such connotation. To the contrary, in the Hebrew scriptures this word often describes God as the superior who creates and saves Israel.

THE PROPHETIC CORRECTIVE

Rosemary Radford Ruether identified the sins of sexism and anti-Semitism within Christian biblical interpretation and theology. Yet the Bible contains its own corrective in its prophetic call to social justice and advocacy for the downtrodden. In her influential *Sexism and God-talk* (1983), Ruether cites these liberationist ideas as starting points for feminist critique.

Source: Rosemary Radford Ruether, *Sexism and God-talk*, 23–5. Copyright © 1983, 1993 by Rosemary Radford Ruether. Reprinted by permission of Beacon Press, Boston.

There is no question that patriarchy is the social context for both the Old and New Testament and that this social context has been incorporated into religious ideology on many levels. Nevertheless both Testaments contain resources for the critique of patriarchy and of the religious sanctification of patriarchy. We make it clear from the start that feminism must not use the critical prophetic principles in Biblical religion to apologize for or cover up patriarchal ideology. Rather, the prophetic-liberating traditions can be appropriated by feminism only as normative principles of Biblical faith which, in turn, criticize and reject patriarchal ideology. Patriarchal ideology thus loses its normative character. It is to be denounced, not cleaned up or explained away.

Feminism appropriates the prophetic principles in ways the Biblical writers for the most part do not appropriate them, namely, to criticize this unexamined patriarchal framework ...

Feminism, in claiming the prophetic-liberating tradition of Biblical faith as a norm through which to criticize the Bible, does not choose an arbitrary or marginal idea in the Bible. It chooses a tradition that can be fairly claimed, on the basis of generally accepted Biblical scholarship, to be the central tradition, the tradition by which Biblical faith constantly criticizes and renews itself and its own vision. Again, what is innovative in feminist hermeneutics is not the prophetic norm but rather feminism's appropriation of this norm *for women*. Feminism claims that *women too* are among those oppressed whom God comes to vindicate and liberate. By including women in the prophetic norm, feminism sees what male prophetic thought generally had not seen: that once the prophetic norm is asserted to be central to Biblical faith, then patriarchy can no longer be maintained as authoritative.

Four themes are essential to the prophetic-liberating tradition of Biblical faith: (1) God's defense and vindication of the oppressed; (2) the critique of the dominant systems of power and their powerholders; (3) the vision of a new age to come in which the present system of injustice is overcome and God's intended reign of peace and justice is installed in history; and (4) finally, the critique of ideology, or of religion, since ideology in this context is primarily religious. Prophetic faith denounces religious ideologies and systems that function to justify and sanctify the dominant, unjust social order. These traditions are central to the Prophets and to the mission of Jesus. Hence the critical-liberating tradition of the axis around which the prophetic-messianic line of Biblical faith revolves as a foundation for Christianity. These themes can be illustrated briefly by the texts of the Prophets and the Synoptic gospels ...

The God of Amos denounces the exploitative economic practices of the times and, because of them, declares that he will send a famine upon the land, not a famine of food but a famine "of hearing the words of the Lord" (Amos 8:11):

> Hear this, you who trample upon the needy and bring the poor of the land to an end, saying, "When will the new moon be over, that we may sell the grain? And the Sabbath, that we may offer wheat for sale, that we may make the ephah small and the shekel great and deal deceitfully with false balances, that we may buy the poor for silver and the needy for a pair of sandals and sell the refuse of the wheat?" (Amos 8:4–6)

In this context God is seen not as the one who represents the powerful, but one who comes to vindicate the oppressed. God's intervention in history is to judge those who grind the faces of the poor, those who deprive the widow and the orphan. Divine advocacy of the oppressed is also a key to Jesus' preaching in the synoptic tradition. Jesus frames the announcement of his prophetic mission in his hometown synagogue in Nazareth in the language of Isaiah 61:1–2:

> The Spirit of the Lord is upon me, because he has anointed me to preach the good news to the poor. He has sent me to proclaim release to the captives, the recovering of sight to the blind; to set at liberty those who are oppressed. (Luke 4:18–19)

Luke pointedly frames the beatitudes of Jesus both to stress their social content and to underline their judgmental side for those who are rich and powerful. Luke also transforms the traditional image of Israel as wife and servant of God. As maid-servant, the New Israel or the Church represents the oppressed, who will be exalted in God's messianic revolution in history

A "HERMENEUTICS OF SUSPICION"

Elisabeth Schüssler Fiorenza inaugurated the discipline of feminist New Testament criticism with her provocative book, *In Memory of Her* (1983). She combined traditional historical-critical methods with feminist-liberation theology to create a "hermeneutics of suspicion." The New Testament texts show an androcentric perspective that must be identified. Schüssler Fiorenza argues that Jesus preached a concern for the marginalized that included women, and the people around him represented a "discipleship of equals."

Source: Elisabeth Schüssler Fiorenza, *In Memory of Her* (New York: Crossroad, 1983), xii, 140–1. Reproduced by permission of Crossroad Press.

In the passion account of Mark's Gospel three disciples figure prominently: on the one hand, two of the twelve – Judas who betrays Jesus and Peter who betrays him – and on the other, the unnamed woman who anoints Jesus. But while the stories of Judas and Peter are engraved in the memory of Christians, the story of the woman is virtually forgotten. Although Jesus pronounces in Mark: "And truly I say to you, wherever the gospel is preached in the whole world, what she has done will be told in memory of her" (14:9), the woman's prophetic sign-action did not become a part of the gospel knowledge of Christians. Even her name is lost to us. Wherever the gospel is proclaimed and the eucharist celebrated another story is told: the story of the apostle who betrayed Jesus. The name of the betrayer is remembered, but the name of the faithful disciple is forgotten because she is a woman.

Although the story of the anointing is told in all four Gospels, it is obvious that the redactional retelling of the story seeks to make the story more palatable to a patriarchal Greco-Roman audience. Whereas the Fourth Gospel identifies the woman as Mary of Bethany who as faithful friend of Jesus shows her love by anointing him, Luke shifts the focus of the story from woman as disciple to woman as sinner. Whether Luke used Mark's text or transmits a different tradition is disputed. But this exegetical dispute does not matter much since we are used to reading the Markan story in the light of Luke. In the process the woman becomes a great sinner who is forgiven by Jesus.

... Previously I attempted to show that the early Christian movement was inclusive of women's leadership and can therefore be called "egalitarian." As a conflict movement with Palestine, Syria, Greece, Asia Minor, and Rome, it challenged and opposed the dominant patriarchal ethos through the praxis of equal discipleship ...

... The assertion [by other scholars] that liberation from patriarchal structures was not of primary concern to Jesus and his movement overlooks not only the androcentric tendencies that can be detected in the tradition and redaction of the Jesus materials, but also the "intrusion" of Jesus and this movement into the dominant religious ethos of the people. The prescription of the Holiness Code, as well as the scribal regulations, controlled women's lives even more than men's lives, and more stringently determined their access to God's presence in Temple and Torah. Jesus and his movement offered an alternative interpretation of the Torah that opened up access to God for everyone who was a member of the elect people of Israel, and especially for those who, because of their societal situation, had little chance to experience God's power in Temple and Torah.

A GAY THEOLOGY OF LIBERATION

Writer and activist Richard Cleaver employs the insights of Latin American liberation theology to construct a theology that speaks to the experience of gay men and lesbians. Drawing from the fundamental tenets of the Bible, he critiques how some have used it to marginalize others. Here he re-reads the story of the Good Samaritan relative to violence and oppression of gay people. The example is particularly apt, since three years after this work was published, on the night of October 6–7, 1998, Matthew Shepard, a gay college student, was targeted as a gay man, pistol-whipped, and left to die by the side of a deserted Wyoming road. At his funeral, members of an anti-gay Kansas church carried signs, "God hates fags," and "Matthew Shepard rots in hell." His death sparked several plays, including the well-known "The Laramie Project." In 2007, the House and Senate passed the Matthew Shepard Act, expanding the definition of hate crimes to include crimes against people because of their sexual orientation, gender, gender identity, or disability. It was signed into law on October 28, 2009 as the Shepard-Byrd Act, in honor of Shepard and James Byrd Jr, an African American who was dragged to death by white supremacists in 1998.

Source: Reproduced from *Know My Name: A Gay Liberation Theology* © 1995 Richard Cleaver, I, 3–6. Used by permission of Westminster John Knox Press: www.wjkbooks. com.

I have a beautiful Japanese bowl. It is mended where it once broke. I once saw some new pieces of the same ware in a shop, and they were not so beautiful. The glaze seemed too shiny. My first reaction was to denounce the debasement of a fine old craft. On consideration, I realized what was different was not how the bowls were made. My bowl has been used, and that has given it the rich glow that the new bowls lacked. Even being broken has not harmed either its beauty or its usefulness. Japanese traditionally have treasured priceless old tea things that have been broken and repaired with gold; the place where they were broken now gleams proudly, and the utensil is even more valuable. This is the spirit in which Christians should approach scripture. Its beauty and value come from being used, even broken. In the liturgy of the

Mass, we balance the breaking of the Word with the breaking of the bread. Unless we live with Scripture, even risk breaking it again, as I do with my broken bowl, it will have no meaning for us.

Jesus' plan of salvation, to use the language of tract writers, is even more subversive in the other story associated with this question [Who is good?] (Luke 10:25–37). Jesus told this parable in answer to a lawyer who Luke (the only evangelist to use this tale) tells us was moved not by genuine concern but by a desire to trap Jesus and cause a scandal. If this was the lawyer's intention, then Jesus walked deliberately into the trap, because the parable is a scandalous one: the parable of the good Samaritan.

We are so used to this story that we have fallen into the Sunday school habit of thinking of it as the story of the *good* (Samaritan) as opposed to the story of the (good) *Samaritan*. But goodness as such is never talked about in the story. Jesus told it to answer a more concrete question: Who is my neighbor? in other words, Toward whom do I have social responsibilities?

Many illustrations could have been given in reply to this fairly conventional question. Indeed, the scripture expert (the meaning of "lawyer" in this context) may have posed it to locate Jesus among the various schools of Jewish interpretation then in flower. But Jesus answers by turning the whole question upside down. His parable directs our attention not to the man who was robbed, the object of our neighborliness (although that is the use to which the parable is put nowadays: to remind us to be good to the needy). Instead, Jesus points to the identity of the person who saw the man as neighbor.

Therein lies the scandal, which our familiarity with the story has bleached out. The model held up to us for imitation is a Samaritan, that is, a rejecter of religious truth, and practice; worse, a willful one. To recover the scandalousness of the parable, we might retell it by replacing the Samaritan with a gay man ...

... A traveler was going from Jerusalem to Jericho when some muggers attacked him. They not only took his money, they took his dignity too; they beat him up and stole his clothes, then ran away, leaving him half-dead in the gutter.

Soon a bishop came by. He was on his way home after going to Jerusalem to pick up a car given to him by a Cadillac dealer there, who was one of the biggest financial supporters of the diocese. The car rode beautifully, and the bishop particularly appreciated the cream-colored glove-leather upholstery. A little luxurious, perhaps, but after all (the bishop was thinking as he took the curve just beyond Bethany), good quality was better than shoddy goods. In the long run, what looks like luxury is prudence.

Just beyond the curve, where the road descends to the Jordan Valley, he noticed something piled beside the road. "Litterbugs" was his first thought, but when he got closer, he could see it was a body. He slowed to see more, wondering if he should stop, and noticed that whoever it was had been beaten and was bleeding. He didn't really want blood all over the interior of his new car, but somehow that seemed like a petty reason not to stop. Then he realized that the person was naked. That settled it; it would never do for a bishop to be seen with a naked person in his car. Think of the scandal! Preserving the good name of the church was more important than any passing act of charity, espe-cially in times when the institution was under attack from wild, semi-educated preachers from the backwoods – and trying to keep the goodwill of the colo-nial administration, too. Anyway, this was a job for the social service profes-sionals. Their agencies got a lot of funding from the diocese. It wasn't as if the bishop weren't helping, indirectly. He drove on.

Fortunately, this being a main route for travelers, it wasn't more than a quarter hour before another car came along. It was driven by a promi-nent layman, active in the local church and in an organization devoted to restoring religious values to a community that needed them desperately during a period of moral decay and spiritual uncertainty. Noticing what looked like a body beside the road, he too slowed down to find out more. The body, which was bloody and naked, wasn't moving – for by now the mugged traveler had fainted.

The layman, like the bishop, wondered if he should stop and do some-thing. After all, he was someone concerned about his community, not just a person caught up in his own well-being. This might prove an opening to evangelize this poor soul, who, judging from his naked condition, undoubt-edly knew not the Lord. But when the person still didn't move, the layman began to have second thoughts. What if the man was already dead? The police would involve him in all kinds of legal red tape. He didn't have time for that; he had more important work. And what if the man lived but sued the layman afterward, claiming he was liable for something or other that happened on the way to the hospital? You couldn't be too careful. Besides, why wasn't the man wearing anything? Robbers don't steal people's clothes. This guy must have done something to provoke the beating. Probably made some kind of disgusting proposition to the wrong person, a healthy if hotheaded young foot-ball player perhaps, who did what any man would do in response to a filthy suggestion. Overreacted, of course, but boys will be boys. This guy must have deserved what he got. A God-fearing layman like himself couldn't be going around with low-life scum; it would drag the reputation of his lay ministry through the mud.

The promoter of religious values drove on, too. This time it was only a few minutes before the next person happened by.

A certain gay man was returning home after having been summoned to his head office in Jerusalem. He had been fired because of a rumor that he was gay. As he drove he wondered if he should have denied the rumor. No, he decided, it wouldn't have done any good. The truth would have come out anyway, when he went into court to testify against the gay-basher who had beaten his lover to death last month. Unconsciously he rubbed the dent in his own skull left by a similar incident he had suffered three years previously.

Suddenly he noticed what looked like a body beside the road. Stopping the car, he jumped out and rushed to look. A naked man, covered with blood and bruises. They looked a lot like the ones he had seen on Adam's body when he had found him in the alley outside their building. Obviously, this man too had been mugged, and judging from the fact that the muggers took all his clothes, the gay may figured it couldn't have been a simple robbery. He felt for a pulse; the man was still alive. Adam had not been; there had been nothing left to do for him. He was being given a chance to make up now for his helplessness then.

He rushed back to his car, returned with the first-aid kit, and did what was needed to transport the man safely. Then he drove him to the nearest emergency room. Because the man had no clothes and there was no way the admissions clerk could tell whether he had insurance, the gay man wrote a blank check to the hospital and promised to come back the next day to clear up whatever else might need to be taken care of.

Later the newspapers got hold of the story and came to interview him. The bishop read the story and called a press conference, at which he announced that the diocese was giving its Good Samaritan Award to the man who had helped the mugging victim he himself had driven past.

At the award banquet, held at the Episcopal palace, the bishop stood with his arm around the Good Samaritan and gave a little homily about showing mercy to our neighbor in distress. This act, he concluded, showed a true Christian spirit. He turned to the man and shook his hand, adding, "God will bless you abundantly for this."

"Oh, I didn't do it for religious reasons. It just seemed like the human thing to do. I haven't been to church since my priest refused me absolution when I confessed that I was in love with the redheaded guy who was captain of the wrestling team." The gay man smiled at the cameras.

The bishop was trying to figure out how to deal with the question he knew was coming next.

Could this parable, far from being a conventional tale about the importance of loving our neighbor, be telling us instead that it is to the oppressed, the heretic, the bugger that we must go for teaching, rather than resting in the conventional pieties dispensed by the usual professionals? Can Jesus be saying that suffering oppression brings an understanding that the religiously "good," who are revered in society and thus immune from the reality of hatred and violence, can never share?

THE BIBLE AS INTIMATE FRIEND

Gary Comstock, a scholar, minister, and college chaplain, also constructs a gay theology. In his *Gay Theology Without Apology* (1993), he explains that his relation to the Bible undergoes transformation. Once he viewed it as similar to a parent, authoritative, a source of both approval and censure. In engaging it as a friend, he sees it more clearly, and is able to both love and criticize it for its failings.

Source: Gary Comstock, *Gay Theology Without Apology* (Cleveland, OH: Pilgrim, 1993), 11–12. Reproduced by permission of Pilgrim Press.

… As part of a lingering desire to regard the Bible as a parental authority from which I wanted and needed approval and permission, I have tended to compromise it and myself. I have been more willing to apologize for it than to criticize it; and I have been slow to admit or accept the Bible's bias against homosexuality. I have, in turn, come to terms with that bias by consciously changing my relationship with the Bible and that change has meant a more intimate reading of and relationship with it.

Instead of making the Bible into a parental authority, I have begun to engage it as I would a friend – as one to whom I have made a commitment and in whom I have invested dearly, but with whom I insist on a mutual exchange of critique, encouragement, support, and challenge. Such investment and commitment hinge on deeply felt and shared experience, meaning, and outlook – a cooperative project to live fully that both changes and remains steady through joys and sorrow. The connection I have shared with some friends and family members has been so vital and meaningful that troubled times, disagreements, and shortcoming have been tolerated, invited, and worked through precisely so that the relationship would not only endure, but continue to grow, change, and become richer. Some of those disagreements have been over homophobia. It has been important for me not to let my friends and family members get away with attitudes, thinking, and behaviors that oppress and diminish lesbians and gay men. Perhaps James Baldwin best captures my meaning when he says, "If I love you, I have to make you conscious of the things you do not see." I worked through those problems because I valued my relationship with these people and because their homophobia was a contradiction to that combination of experience, meaning, outlook, and project that we otherwise shared.

The Exodus and Jesus events represent a similar combination of experience, meaning, outlook, and project that I share, commit to, invest in, and because of which I grow, change, and struggle. As with my friends, I cannot take the relationship lightly, nor will I give it up quickly; and as with my friends, I criticize and call it to account for its homophobia. Although its homophobic statements sting and condemn me, I counter that those statements are themselves condemned by its own Exodus and Jesus events. Just as I have said to my friends, "How can you express love and be a justice-seeking person and not work to overcome the oppression of lesbian and gay men?" in my dialogue with the Bible I ask, "How can you be based on two events that are about transforming pain, suffering, and death into life, liberation, and healing, and yet call for the misery and death of lesbians and gay men?"

EXPERIENCE AND THE AUTHORITY OF SPIRIT

THE HOLINESS MOVEMENT

> Phoebe Palmer (1807–74) preached in the USA, Canada, and the United Kingdom, published her teachings, and held weekly meetings in her New York home, "Tuesday Meetings for the Promotion of Holiness." These meetings, which included Bible study, prayer, and spontaneous testimony to the activity of the Spirit, modeled the revival meetings of the

nineteenth century. Palmer's teaching is rooted in Methodism, especially John Wesley's teaching of a second experience of purification and being enlivened by the Spirit that occurs separate from the first experience of conversion. This experience, called "perfection", or "sanctification," recalls the experience of the first apostles at Pentecost (Acts 2). Palmer elaborated on the life of holiness, teaching the altar covenant, the offering of one's entire self to God, and holiness as a state one can experience in this world. The Holiness movement gave birth to many movements, including multiple forms of Pentecostalism and charismatic religion. A lay woman preacher and abolitionist, Palmer also belongs in the stories of American movements for women's rights and abolition of slavery. Her teaching on holiness, she insists, is not about a sect, but about the Bible, "if you are not a *holy* Christian, you are not a *Bible* Christian" (Palmer 1998: 186).

Source: Phoebe Palmer, *The Way of Holiness* (New York: Piercy and Reed, 1843), 7–8, 11–12, 59–60, 62–3.

1

… And here, dear child of Jesus, permit the writer to tell you just how that sister found "the shorter way" [to sanctification]. On looking at the requirements of the word of God, she beheld the command, "Be ye holy." She then began to say in her heart, "Whatever my former deficiencies may have been, God requires that I should *now* be holy. Whether *convicted*, or otherwise, *duty is plain*. God requires *present* holiness." On coming to this point, she at once apprehended a simple truth before unthought of, i.e., *Knowledge is conviction*. She well knew that, for a long time, she had been assured that God required holiness. But she had never deemed this knowledge a sufficient plea to take to God – and because of present need, to ask a present bestowment of the gift.

Convinced that in this respect she had mistaken the path, she now, with renewed energy, began to make use of the knowledge already received, and to discern a "shorter way."

Another difficulty by which her course had been delayed she found to be here. She had been accustomed to look at the blessing of holiness as such a high attainment, that her general habit of soul inclined her to think it almost beyond her reach. This erroneous impression rather influenced her to rest the matter thus: – "I will let every high state of grace, in name, alone, and seek only to be *fully conformed to the will of God, as recorded in his written word*. My chief endeavors shall be centred in the aim to be an humble *Bible Christian*. By the grace of God, all my energies shall be directed to this one point …"

2

"We by his Spirit prove,
        and know the things of God,
The things which freely of his love
        He hath on us bestow'd."

After having thus resolved on devoting the entire service of her heart and life to God, the following questions occasioned much serious solicitude: – How shall I know *when* I have consecrated all to God? And how ascertain whether God *accepts* the sacrifice – and how know the manner of its acceptance? Here again the blessed Bible, which she had now taken as her counselor, said to her heart, "We have received not the spirit of the world, but the Spirit which is of God, that we might know the things freely given to us of God."

... It was thus she became assured that it was her privilege to *know when she* had consecrated all to God, and also to know that the sacrifice was *accepted*, and the resolve was solemnly made that the subject should not cease to be absorbing, until this knowledge was obtained.

3

... By the resolve to be a "Bible Christian," this traveler in the "way of holiness" placed herself in the way to receive the direct teachings of the Spirit, and in the *one* and the only *way* for the attainment of the salvation promised in the gospel of Christ, inasmuch as it is written, "He became the author of eternal salvation to all them that *obey him*."

And by the determination to consecrate all upon the altar of sacrifice to God, with the resolve to "enter into the bonds of an everlasting covenant to be wholly the Lord's for time and eternity," and then acting in conformity with this decision, *actually laying all upon the altar*, by the most unequivocal Scripture testimony, she laid herself under the most solemn obligation to *believe that the sacrifice became the Lord's property; and by virtue of the altar upon which the offering was laid, became "holy" and "acceptable."*

4

It was thus, by "laying all upon this altar," she, by the most unequivocal Scripture testimony, laid herself under the most sacred obligation to *believe* that the sacrifice became "holy and acceptable," and virtually the *Lord's property*, even by virtue of the sanctity of the *altar* upon which it was laid, and continued "holy and acceptable," so long as kept inviolably upon this hallowed altar. At an early stage of her experience in the "way of holiness," the Holy Spirit powerfully opened to her understanding the following passage, as corroborative of this view of the subject: Rom. xii, 1, "I beseech you therefore, brethren, by the mercies of God, that ye present your bodies a living sacrifice, holy, acceptable unto God, which is your reasonable service."

From these important considerations she perceived that it was indeed by the Spirit's teachings she had been led to "enter into the bonds of an everlasting covenant to be wholly the Lord's," inasmuch as by the removal of this offering from off this *hallowing* altar, she should *cease to be holy*, as it is "the altar that sanctifieth the gift." In this light she also saw why it is, that *all* is so imperatively required, inasmuch as it is the Redeemer who makes the demand for the "living sacrifice," having purchased *all* body, soul, and spirit, unto himself.

THE AZUSA STREET REVIVAL

The quest for immediate experience of the Spirit was seen as restorationist, bringing the church back to its origins in the outpouring of the Spirit at the first Pentecost. Pentecostalism developed from the Holiness movement, emphasizing baptism of the Spirit and speaking in tongues. While Pentecostalism had several early expressions, a formative event occurred in Los Angeles on April 14, 1906, when William Seymour founded the Azusa Street Mission in Los Angeles. Seymour, the son of former slaves, drew so many hearers to his powerful message of sanctification and a coming judgment that he was forced to move from his pulpit at the home of a fellow preacher. Renting a former stable and warehouse in the black section of town, he created a popular movement that brought in black, white, Asian, and Mexican worshippers. As an urban phenomenon that drew especially from the less privileged, his Pentecostal vision saw a new age at hand, one that included interracial harmony. When the Great San Francisco earthquake hit only four days after the church was founded, it only added to the sense that the hour of divine judgment was at hand. The following is an excerpt from Seymour's newspaper, *The Apostolic Faith*.

Source: *The Apostolic Faith*, 1.1 (September, 1906), 1: available at http://312Azusa. dunamai.com.

LETTER FROM BRO. PARHAM

Bro. Chas. Parham, who is God's leader in the Apostolic Faith movement, writes from Tongazoxie, Kansas, that he expects (D. V.) to be in Los Angeles Sept. 15. Hearing that Pentecost had come to Los Angeles, he writes, "I rejoice in God over you all, my children, but wait on the Lord and praise Him, and they commenced speaking in tongues, as they did at Pentecost, and the Spirit sang songs through them."

The meeting was then transferred to Azusa Street, and since then multitudes have been coming. The meetings begin about ten o'clock in the morning and can hardly stop before ten or twelve at night, and sometimes two or three in the morning, because so many are seeking, and some are slain under the power of God. People are seeking three times a day at the altar and row after row of seats have to be emptied and filled with seekers. We cannot tell how many people have been saved, and sanctified, and baptized with the Holy Ghost, and healed of all manner of sicknesses. Many are speaking in new tongues, and some are on their way to the foreign fields, with the gift of the language. We are going on to get more of the power of God.

Many have laid aside their glasses and had their eyesight perfectly restored. The deaf have had their hearing restored.

A man was healed of asthma of twenty years standing. Many have been healed of heart trouble and lung trouble.

Many are saying that God has given the message that He is going to shake Los Angeles with an earthquake. First, there will be a revival to give all an opportunity to be saved. The revival is now in progress.

SPEAKING IN TONGUES

> Scholar Harvey Cox, not a Pentecostal himself, describes a gathering where Christians engage in glossolalia, or speaking in tongues. Pentecostals, though equated with fundamentalists in the popular mind, differ from them in their stress on experience of the Spirit over adherence to literalist biblical interpretation. Cox also stressed Pentecostalism as a mainly urban movement, characterized by "primal speech, primal piety, and primal hope" (82).
>
> Source: Harvey Cox, *Fire from Heaven: The Rise of Pentecostal Spirituality and the Reshaping of Religion in the Twenty-first Century* (New York: Da Capo, 2001), 84–6. Reprinted by permission of Perseus Books.

At that point the speaker invited those who had already received the Spirit to help "pray through" those who were seeking. I was not in a seeking mood that evening, nor was my friend. So when a stout young man in a rumpled sportcoat asked us if we would like to kneel at our seats and seek the baptism, we politely declined. He seemed to understand and did not press us. But then, as we watched over the balcony railing, an amazing scene opened below us. Hundred of seekers did kneel at their seats, with others – their guides and helpers – kneeling beside them, hugging them, usually with one arm, while the other arm was extended upward. People cried out, called, moaned, and wept. Blacks and whites and men and women knelt together in an unintentional reenactment of what must have both thrilled and upset those astonished visitors at Azusa Street. Then, individuals would stand, extend both arms to the heavens and cry out in phrases that sounded to me a little like Jesus's last words on the cross, "Eli, Eli, lama sabachtani," but in a different order and with many other syllables mixed in.

The "praying through" and speaking in tongues went on for about half an hour. I watched transfixed. Then one of the song leaders tried to lead a hymn, but despite the efforts of the electric organist and his own energetic arm waving, only a few people joined in. The rest continued the praying through, welcoming the newly sanctified with laughter and hugs. Then someone gave a benediction, hardly audible over the clamor. As the leaders left the stage and others began moving toward the exits my friend and I glanced at each other. Then we also left. We walked to his trolley stop without saying anything, and as he climbed on board I just said, "Really something, eh Bill?"

"Yeah," he answered, still staring straight ahead as the trolley pulled away. I could sense that although we had both come mainly out of curiosity, maybe even to be entertained, we had found ourselves in the presence of something that was more than we had expected. It didn't seem right, somehow, to talk about it just then.

Since that night in Philadelphia many years ago I have visited dozens of churches and congregations in which tongue speaking of one sort or another took place. Sometimes virtually the entire congregation does it all at once, and the sound is like small waves of murmurs and gentle sighs, mounting into billows of muffled vowels and muted consonants. Sometimes it begins as a tiny trickle, grows into a roaring cascade, then wanes again into a rustle. Sometimes it is a single person who stands and for thirty seconds or so, rarely more speaks clearly discernible but incomprehensible syllables. Sometimes this is followed by an interpretation by another person, sometimes not. Sometimes it happens with music, a polyphony of tones and vocables but with no recognizable words. Sometimes the speakers sound anxious or urgent. More often they sound joyful, thankful, or serene.

CATHOLIC CHARISMATIC RENEWAL

The experience of receiving the Holy Spirit in a new Pentecost and speaking in tongues did not confine itself to Pentecostals. Episcopalians, Presbyterians, Lutherans, and Catholics also formed prayer groups to experience the gifts (charisms) of the Spirit. The Catholic Charismatic movement began in February, 1967, at a weekend retreat by some Duquesne University students and professors. Like Pentecostalism, Catholic Charismatic Christianity began in the United States, but has become a world-wide movement. Patti Gallagher Mansfield, one of the students at the Duquesne retreat, describes her life-changing experience.

Source: Patti Gallagher Mansfield, *As By a New Pentecost* (1992), 39–40: available from her website at www.ccrno.org.

Because the birthday party never really got started, I decided to go to various parts of the retreat house and call all the students to gather downstairs for the celebration. Even though I was a newcomer to *Chi Rho*, I had experience in leading groups and organizing activities. I thought that if we all assembled in the same place, the party might happen. It was at this point that I wandered up to the chapel. I wasn't going in to pray … just to tell any students there to come down to the party. When I entered the chapel I saw a few people sitting on the floor praying. I knelt down too in the presence of Jesus in the Blessed Sacrament. Then something happened I wasn't expecting.

I'd always believed by the gift of faith that Jesus is really present in the Blessed Sacrament, but I had never experienced his glory before. As I knelt there that night, my body literally trembled before His majesty and holiness. I was filled with awe in His presence. He was there … the King of Kings, the Lord of Lords, the Great God of the Universe! I felt really frightened and I said to myself, "Get out of here quick, because something is going to happen to you if you stay in the presence of God." And yet, overriding this fear, was the desire to remain before the Lord.

Then Bill Deigan, the president of *Chi Rho*, came into the chapel and knelt next to me. I described to him what I was experiencing. He said, "I was just talking to a few other people. Something's going on here; something we didn't plan. Just stay and pray until you feel you should leave."

As I knelt there before the Lord Jesus Christ in the Blessed Sacrament, for the first time in my life, I prayed what I would call "*a prayer of unconditional surrender.*" I prayed in the quiet of my heart, "*Father, I give my life to you, and whatever You want of me, that's what I choose. If it means suffering, then I accept that. Just teach me to follow Your Son, Jesus, and to learn to love the way he loves.*"

When I prayed that prayer, I was kneeling before the altar. The next moment I found myself prostrate, flat on my face, stretched out before the tabernacle. No one had laid hands on me. I had never seen such a thing happen before. I don't know exactly how it took place, but in the process, my shoes came off my feet. Later I realized that, like Moses before the burning bush, I was indeed on holy ground. As I lay there, I was flooded from my fingertips to my toes with a deep sense of God's personal love for me ... His merciful love. I was especially struck by the foolishness of God's love. It is so completely undeserved, so lavishly given. There is nothing that you or I can ever, ever do to earn or merit God's love. It is freely given, generously given, out of the abundance of His mercy. Our God is a God of love. He's created us out of love and destined us for love. We are His people. We belong to Him. His love is *for us* no matter what we've done, no matter who we are.

As I think back over my experience in the chapel that night, the words of St. Augustine so beautifully capture what I felt in those moments; "*You have made us for Yourself, O Lord, and our hearts are restless until they rest in You.*" Within me echoed the fervent plea, "*Stay! Stay! Stay!*" I felt as if I wanted to die right then. That one brief encounter with the Spirit of the Lord taught me more than a lifetime of study could ever have done. I felt myself captivated by the beauty and goodness of the Living God. The mercy and love of Jesus had overwhelmed me.

IMAGINING BABYLON AND THY KINGDOM COME

THE SHAKERS

As reflected in its official name, the United Society of Believers in Christ's Second Appearing took inspiration from the biblical prophecies of the re-emergence of a Christ-figure to usher in a new, earthly Kingdom of God. However, the Society held that, in order to reflect the "dual" nature of life, "Christ's Second Appearing" must of necessity assume female form since the male Jesus served as the first Christ. The Society developed in northern England in the mid-eighteenth century among a group of Quakers caught up in the "Spiritualist" revivals inspired by prophetic predictions of the end of the present, sinful world. As Quakers they felt moved by the presence of God, but the enthusiasm of their singing and dancing earned them the name their familiar name: "Shakers." When one of their early members – a young woman named Ann Lee – began to receive visions in 1770, the Society recognized her as the expected messiah-in-female-form. According to these visions, celibacy was the path to salvation out of fleshly desire – "the root of all evil" – and the Shakers would help establish God's new earthly kingdom in its divinely revealed place: the American continent. Beginning near Albany, New York in 1774, the Shakers put their utopian ideas into practice as they established a series of villages famous – or, to some, infamous – for their separate but equal organization of the sexes and entrepreneurial endeavors in the service of "God's order." The selection below comes from *The Compendium*, a document written in 1859 by one of the Shaker "elders" near the height of the group's expansion. In the document, F. W. Evans documents the Shakers' unique history and practices in order to show how the group fulfills the biblical prophecies.

Source: Frederick W. Evans, *Compendium of the Origin, History, Principles, Rules, and Regulations, Government, and Doctrines of the United Society of Believers in Christ's Second Appearing* (New York: Burt Franklin, 1864), 11–24.

1. Shakerism is claimed, by its advocates, to be the ultimate, or *second Christian, Church* – the *Millennium*.
2. The inquiry naturally arises, What elements produced the Shaker Societies? To meet this, reference must be had to historical facts bearing upon the subject …
4. As the lowest types of humanity are those who seek happiness the most exclusively in the indulgence of the baser and animal propensities, so the saints of all times have moved the farthest in the opposite direction. Abstinence from sexual intercourse, from private property, from war, oaths, and the honors of the world, have ever been the chief characteristics of ascetics, in all ages.
5. The principles and maxims of Jesus, as explained and confirmed by his own teaching and practice, and measurably by that of his first twelve converts and most intimate friends, the Apostles, seem to give countenance to the idea, that some great and important *truths* underlie all these (often) abnormal operations of mind that, from age to age, were struggling for expression and embodiment in human action …
9. Whenever, in [one of the four great cycles of history], the culminating point of Spiritualism has been reached, then the *religious* element has moved thereupon, and finally ultimated itself in a Church, which was emphatically the Church of God of that cycle and period …
13. Spiritual-physical manifestations attended the whole life of John and Jesus, from their conception to their death. The *religious* elements of that cycle were concentrated in Jesus, as an *individual*. At the day of Pentecost,

the same elements concentred, and were organized in the most spiritually endowed body of people, or Church, that any cycle had ever been capable of producing,

14. Jesus and his Apostles continually referred to the next, or *fourth* and *last*, great cycle as the time for *"the restitution of all things,* which God had spoken by the mouth of all his prophets [in all nations and cycles] since the world began." It was at the spiritual acme of this cycle, that the Christ (whom John saw as a dove appear to Jesus) would come *again*, to some other individual. This *second coming*, the Shakers claim, must of necessity have been to a *woman* because the race is *female as well as male*.

15. We will endeavor to show, in its right place, from proper historical data, that the rise of the *Shaker* Church, or order, has been agreeable to the premises above laid down; as has also the formation of all the Shaker communities ...

17. Shaker Societies always originate in the *spiritual* part of a cycle. There is, first, a general agitation of the *spiritual* elements; out of that arises a movement of the *religious* elements in man. This leads to the formation of one or more Shaker Societies, according to the order of the cycle that is revolving. Therefore the Shakers now confidently expect the time has nearly arrived for a further extension of their order.

18. The natural and spiritual worlds are now coming into a state of rapport with each other; and the spiritual faculties in man, which have for a long time been in a state of dormancy, are being aroused and developed very extensively; and soon the religious nature of man will be quickened, and religious revivals will commence on a grander and more effective scale than have ever been witnessed; for they will rest upon the basis of, and spread over the ground prepared by, *Spiritualism*.

19. In the beginning of the eighteenth century, Spiritualism broke out on the continent of Europe, and was followed by most remarkable religious revivals; out of which arose the "French prophets ..."

20. They testified that the end of all things drew nigh; and admonished the people to repent, and amend their lives. They gave warning of the near approach of the kingdom of heaven, the "acceptable year of the Lord;" and, in many prophetic messages, declared to the world, that those numerous Scripture prophecies concerning the new heaven and the new earth, the kingdom of the Messiah, the Marriage of the Lamb, the first resurrection, and the New Jerusalem descending from above, were near at hand, and would shortly be accomplished ...

23. About the year 1747, some members of the Society of Quakers [in England], who had become subjects of the revival, formed themselves into a society ...

25. They boldly testified that the second appearing of Christ was at hand; and that the Church would rise in its full and transcendent glory, and effect the final downfall of *antichrist*. They affirmed that the work of the great day of God was then commencing, and would increase, until every promise of God should be fulfilled.

26. Sometimes, after sitting awhile in silent meditation, they were seized with a mighty trembling, under which they would often express the indignation of God against all sin … These exercises, so strange in the eyes of the beholders, brought upon them the appellation of *Shakers,* which has been their most common name of distinction ever since.

28. They continued to increase in light and power, with occasional additions to their number, till about the year 1770, when, by a special manifestation of Divine light, the present testimony of salvation and eternal life was fully revealed to Ann Lee, and by her to the Society, by whom she, from that time, was acknowledged as *Mother* in Christ, and by them was called *Mother Ann* …

29. Mother Ann said: "I saw in vision the Lord Jesus in his kingdom and glory. He revealed to me the depth of man's loss, what it was, and the way of redemption therefrom. Then I was able to bear an open testimony against the sin that is the root of all evil; and I felt the power of God flow into my soul like a fountain of living water. From that day I have been able to take up a full cross against all the doleful works of the flesh."

30. About the year 1774, Mother Ann received a revelation, directing her to repair to America; also that the second Christian Church would be established in America; that the Colonies would gain their independence; and that liberty of conscience would be secured to all people, whereby they would be able to worship God without hindrance or molestation.

31. This revelation was communicated to the Society, and was confirmed by numerous signs, visions, and extraordinary manifestations, to many of the members; and permission was given for all those of the Society who were able, and who felt any special impressions on their own minds so to do, to accompany her. [Eight members joined her.] … Having settled their affairs and made arrangements for the voyage, they embarked at Liverpool, and set sail on the 19th of May, 1774, and debarked on the 6th of August following, at New York …

33. Arrived in America, they settled in the woods, seven miles from Albany, where is now located the village of Watervliet. Here, surrounded by Dutch settlers, they resided three years and a half, waiting for the fulfillment of Mother Ann's prophecy – the *gathering of persons to the Gospel of Christ's second appearing,* of which she was the Messenger.

"I, NEPHI, …": THE BOOK OF MORMON

In light of the fact that more than twelve million people around the world now identify as Mormons, few documents in American history rival the impact of the Book of Mormon (the opening of which follows below), first released in 1830. In the late twentieth century, an official subtitle – "Another Testament of Jesus Christ" – was added, which reflects the Mormon understanding of the Book of Mormon as a supplement to, and fulfillment of, the "old" and "new" testaments of Christian tradition. The text is based on Joseph Smith's claim that God the Father and Jesus the

Son appeared to him ten years earlier when, as a confused fifteen-year-old, he had gone to the woods alone near his family's farm in Palmyra, New York seeking God's guidance as to which of several competing prophetic claims he should believe. According to Smith, the divine figures informed him of the underlying corruption of all existing religious claims. In the years that followed an angel, Moroni, led him to and enabled the translation of the lost history written on golden tablets buried nearby and through which divine truth could be restored. The Book of Mormon – identified as the fourth-century testimony of Moroni's father, Mormon – recounts the history of the Nephites, a group of Israelites led by God to the Western Hemisphere six hundred years before Jesus' birth. Despite their eventual defeat at the hands of the unrighteous Lamanites, they paved the way for the establishment of God's earthly kingdom in North America in "the latter days." The official "Mormon" organization – the Church of Jesus Christ of Latter-Day Saints – took shape in the decades following the publication of the Book of Mormon.

Source: *The Book of Mormon: An Account Written by the Hand of Mormon Upon Plates Taken From the Plates of Nephi*: text available from www.gutenberg.org.

1. I, NEPHI, having been born of goodly parents, therefore I was taught some-what in all the learning of my father; and having seen many afflictions in the course of my days, nevertheless, having been highly favored of the Lord in all my days; yea, having had a great knowledge of the goodness and the mysteries of God, therefore I make a record of my proceedings in my days.
2   Yea, I make a record in the language of my father, which consists of the learning of the Jews and the language of the Egyptians.
3   And I know that the record which I make is true; and I make it with mine own hand; and I make it according to my knowledge.
4   For it came to pass in the commencement of the first year of the reign of Zedekiah, king of Judah, (my father, Lehi, having dwelt at Jerusalem in all his days); and in that same year there came many prophets, prophesying unto the people that they must repent, or the great city Jerusalem must be destroyed.
5   Wherefore it came to pass that my father, Lehi, as he went forth prayed unto the Lord, yea, even with all his heart, in behalf of his people.
6   And it came to pass as he prayed unto the Lord, there came a pillar of fire and dwelt upon a rock before him; and he saw and heard much; and because of the things which he saw and heard he did quake and tremble exceedingly.
7   And it came to pass that he returned to his own house at Jerusalem; and he cast himself upon his bed, being overcome with the Spirit and the things which he had seen.
8   And being thus overcome with the Spirit, he was carried away in a vision, even that he saw the heavens open, and he thought he saw God sitting upon his throne, surrounded with numberless concourses of angels in the attitude of singing and praising their God.

9   And it came to pass that he saw One descending out of the midst of heaven, and he beheld that his luster was above that of the sun at noon-day.

10 And he also saw twelve others following him, and their brightness did exceed that of the stars in the firmament.

11 And they came down and went forth upon the face of the earth; and the first came and stood before my father, and gave unto him a book, and bade him that he should read.

12 And it came to pass that as he read, he was filled with the Spirit of the Lord.

13 And he read, saying: Wo, wo, unto Jerusalem, for I have seen thine abominations! Yea, and many things did my father read concerning Jerusalem – that it should be destroyed, and the inhabitants thereof; many should perish by the sword, and many should be carried away captive into Babylon.

14 And it came to pass that when my father had read and seen many great and marvelous things, he did exclaim many things unto the Lord; such as: Great and marvelous are thy works, O Lord God Almighty! Thy throne is high in the heavens, and thy power, and goodness, and mercy are over all the inhabitants of the earth; and, because thou art merciful, thou wilt not suffer those who come unto thee that they shall perish!

15 And after this manner was the language of my father in the praising of his God; for his soul did rejoice, and his whole heart was filled, because of the things which he had seen, yea, which the Lord had shown unto him.

16 And now I, Nephi, do not make a full account of the things which my father hath written, for he hath written many things which he saw in visions and in dreams; and he also hath written many things which he prophesied and spake unto his children, of which I shall not make a full account.

17 But I shall make an account of my proceedings in my days. Behold, I make an abridgment of the record of my father, upon plates which I have made with mine own hands; wherefore, after I have abridged the record of my father then will I make an account of mine own life.

18 Therefore, I would that ye should know, that after the Lord had shown so many marvelous things unto my father, Lehi, yea, concerning the destruction of Jerusalem, behold he went forth among the people, and began to prophesy and to declare unto them concerning the things which he had both seen and heard.

19 And it came to pass that the Jews did mock him because of the things which he testified of them; for he truly testified of their wickedness and their abominations; and he testified that the things which he saw and heard, and also the things which he read in the book, manifested plainly of the coming of a Messiah, and also the redemption of the world.

20 And when the Jews heard these things they were angry with him; yea, even as with the prophets of old, whom they had cast out, and stoned, and slain; and they also sought his life, that they might take it away. But behold, I, Nephi, will show unto you that the tender mercies of the Lord are over all those whom he hath chosen, because of their faith, to make them mighty even unto the power of deliverance.

WILLIAM MILLER

William Miller (1782–1849) stands as one of the most influential students of the Bible in American history. Raised as an American Baptist near the Vermont border in upstate New York, Miller embraced deism and Freemasonry during his early adult years, only to turn back to views of a providential God after his seemingly miraculous survival at the Battle of Plattsburgh during the War of 1812. Miller's careful studies of the Bible led him to the conclusion that scriptural prophecy not only was literal but also calculable. Using the biblically recorded visions of Daniel and John, Miller determined the passing of a 2,300-year period before the return of Christ, the restoration of Jerusalem, and the establishment of the new godly kingdom. He identified 1843 as the date of those cataclysmic events. In preaching and writing about these predictions, Miller garnered international attention and gained a widespread following of "Millerites." The following selection, first published in 1836, represents the opening of Miller's famous lectures presenting biblically supported proof of his calculations. In this introductory section, Miller explains and justifies his methods of biblical interpretation.

Source: William Miller, *Evidence from Scripture and History of the Second Coming of Christ about the Year 1843* (Boston: Joshua Himes, 1842), 3–8.

In presenting these Lectures to the public, the writer is only complying with the solicitations of some of his friends, who have requested that his views on the Prophecies of Daniel and John might be made public. The reader is therefore requested to give the subject a careful and candid perusal, and compare every part with the standard of Divine Truth; for if the explanation the writer has given to the scriptures under consideration should prove correct, the reader will readily perceive that it concerns us all, and becomes doubly important to us, because we live on the eve of one of the most important events ever revealed to man by the wisdom of God – the judgment of the great day.

In order that the reader may have an understanding of my manner of studying the Prophecies, by which I have come to the following result, I have thought proper to give some of the rules of interpretation which I have adopted to understand prophecy.

... As prophecy is a language somewhat different from other parts of Scripture, owing to its having been revealed in vision, and that highly figurative, yet God in his wisdom has so interwoven the several prophecies, that the events foretold are not all told by one prophet, and although they lived and prophesied in different ages of the world, yet they tell us the same things; so you take away one, and a link will be wanting. There is a general connection through the whole; like a well-regulated community they all move in unison, speaking the same things, observing the same rules, so that a Bible reader may almost with propriety suppose, let him read in what prophecy he may, that he is reading the same prophet, the same author. This will appear evident to any one who will compare scripture with scripture. For example, see Dan. xii. 1,

Matt. xxiv. 21. Isa. xlvii, 8. Zeph. ii. 15, Rev. xviii. 7. There never was a book written that has a better connection and harmony than the Bible, and yet it has the appearance of a great store-house full of all the precious commodities heart could desire, thrown in promiscuously; therefore, the biblical student must select and bring together every part of the subject he wishes to investigate, from every part of the Bible; then let every word have its own Scripture meaning, every sentence its proper bearing, and have no contradiction, and your theory will and must of necessity be correct. Truth is one undeviating path, that grows brighter and brighter the more it is trodden; it needs no plausible arguments nor pompous dress to make it more bright, for the more naked and simple the fact, the stronger the truth appears.

... There are two important points to which all prophecy seems to centre, like a cluster of grapes upon its stem – the first and second coming of Christ; the first coming to proclaim the gospel, set up his kingdom, suffer for sinners, and bring in an everlasting righteousness. His second coming, to which the ardent faith and pious hope of the tried and tempted child of God centres, is for complete redemption from sin, for the justification and glorification promised to all those who look for his appearing, the destruction of the wicked and mystical Babylon, the abomination of the whole earth.

His first coming was as a man, his human nature being only visible. He comes first, like the "first man of the earth, earthy;" his second coming is "the Lord from heaven." His first coming was literally according to the prophecies. And so we may safely infer will be his second appearance, according to the Scriptures ... [W]hy not suppose that all the prophecies concerning his second coming will be as literally accomplished as the former! Can any man show a single reason why it will not? If this be true, we can obtain much light by reading the Scriptures. We are there informed of the manner of his second coming – "suddenly, in the clouds, in like manner as he ascended;" the majesty of his coming – "on a great white throne, with power and great glory, and all his saints with him;" the object of his coming – "as the Ancient of Days, to send his angels into the four winds of heaven, gather his elect, raise the righteous dead, change the righteous living, chain Satan, destroy anti-Christ, the wicked, and all those who destroy the earth, judge, justify and glorify his people, cleanse his church, present her to his Father, live and reign with her on the new heavens and new earth," the form of the old having passed away.

The time when these things shall take place is also specified, by some of the prophets, unto 2300 days, (meaning years) ... The signs of the times are also given, when we may know, he is near, even at the door ...

If I have erred in my exposition of the prophecies, the time, being so near at hand, will soon expose my folly; but if I have the truth on the subjects treated on in these pages, how important the era in which we live! What vast and important events must soon be realized! and how necessary that every individual be prepared that that day may not come upon them unawares, while they are surfeited with the cares and riches of this life, and the day overtake them as a thief!

... [A]fter fourteen years' study of the prophecies and other parts of the Bible, I have come to the following conclusions, and do now commit myself into the hands of God as my Judge, in giving publicity to the sentiments herein contained, conscientiously desiring that this little book may be the means to incite others to study the Scriptures, and to see whether these things be so, and that some minds may be led to believe in the word of God, and find an interest in the offering and sacrifice of the Lamb of God, that their sins might be forgiven them through the blood of the atonement, "when the refreshing shall come from the presence of the Lord, and from the glory of his power," "when he comes to be admired in all them that believe in that day."

And now, my dear readers, I beg of you to lay aside prejudice; examine this subject candidly and carefully for yourselves ... You may, by your obedience in the faith, secure you an interest in the first resurrection, and a glorious admittance into the New Jerusalem, and an inheritance among the justified in glory, and you may sit down with Abraham, Isaac, and Jacob in the kingdom of God. May this be your lot – is the prayer of your servant, Wm. Miller.

Ellen G. White on "The Book of Books"

Even though William Miller himself never specified an exact day for what came to be known as "the Second Advent" – the biblically envisioned radical transformation of the world – many in the burgeoning "Millerite" movement of the early 1840s came to accept October 22, 1844 as the much-awaited moment. As the day passed with no apparent change, it earned recognition as "the Great Disappointment," that spurred many to abandon their hopes for an imminent Kingdom of God. However, some persisted with that expectation. Ellen G. White (1827–1915) is perhaps the best-known and most influential of these enduring "Adventists." A series of visions beginning in 1844 convinced White and others that the Second Advent was still at hand and that, in line with Miller's predictions, the process had been set in motion in 1844. By the early 1860s White and her husband, James – because of her vision and his editorial activities – stood as central figures in the Adventist movement. The couple played an instrumental role when a group of 3,500 – calling themselves "Seventh-Day Adventists" because of their emphasis on biblically accorded Saturday Sabbath observance – formally established a church during a May 23, 1863 meeting in Battle Creek, Michigan. With her prophetic role and prolific writing, Ellen White was a driving force into the twentieth century – and remains a foundational figure – as the Seventh-Day Adventist [SDA] Church has developed into a global religious institution. The selection below, written in 1888 and excerpted from White's 1893–94 treatise on the establishment of an Adventist educational network, is revealing as White explains the fundamental role of the Bible in proper and effective "Christian education."

Source: Ellen G. White, *Christian Education* (1893–94), in *The Complete Published Ellen G. White Writings* (Silver Spring, MD: The Ellen G. White Estate, 2001), 105–6, 111–12, 114–15.

Chap. 14 – The Book of Books

The study of the Bible will give strength to the intellect. Says the psalmist, "The entrance of thy words giveth light; it giveth understanding unto the simple." [Ps. 119:130.] The question has often been asked me, "Should the Bible become the important book in our schools?" It is a precious book, a wonderful book. It is a treasury containing jewels of precious value. It is a history that opens to us the past centuries. Without the Bible we should have been left to conjectures and fables in regard to the occurrences of past ages. Of all the books that have flooded the world, be they ever so valuable, the Bible is the Book of books, and is most deserving of the closest study and attention. It gives not only the history of the creation of this world, but a description of the world to come. It contains instruction concerning the wonders of the universe, and it reveals to our understanding the Author of the heavens and the earth. It unfolds a simple and complete system of theology and philosophy. Those who are close students of the word of God, and who obey its instructions, and love its plain truths, will improve in mind and manners. It is an endowment of God that should awaken in every heart the most sincere gratitude; for it is the revelation of God to man.

If the truths of the Bible are woven into practical life, they will bring the mind up from its earthliness and debasement. Those who are conversant with the Scriptures, will be found to be men and women who exert an elevating influence. In searching for the heaven-revealed truths, the Spirit of God is brought into close connection with the sincere searcher of the Scriptures. An understanding of the revealed will of God, enlarges the mind, expands, elevates, and endows it with new vigor, by bringing its faculties in contact with stupendous truths. If the study of the Scriptures is made a secondary consideration, great loss is sustained. The Bible was for a time excluded from our schools, and Satan found a rich field, in which he worked with marvelous rapidity, and gathered a harvest to his liking.

... Why is it that our youth, and even those of maturer years, are so easily led into temptation and sin? – It is because the word of God is not studied and meditated upon as it should be. If it were appreciated, there would be an inward rectitude, a strength of spirit, that would resist the temptations of Satan to do evil. A firm, decided will-power is not brought into the life and character, because the sacred instruction of God is not made the study, and the subject of meditation. There is not the effort put forth that there should be to associate the mind with pure, holy thoughts and to divert it from what is impure and untrue. There is not the choosing of the better part, the sitting at the feet of Jesus, as did Mary, to learn the most sacred lessons of the divine Teacher, that they may be laid up in the heart, and practiced in the daily life. Meditation upon holy things will elevate and refine the mind, and will develop Christian ladies and gentlemen.

God will not accept one of us who is belittling his powers in lustful, earthly debasement, by thought, or word, or action. Heaven is a pure and holy place, where none can enter unless they are refined, spiritualized, cleansed, and purified. There is a work for us to do for ourselves, and we shall be capable of doing it only by drawing strength from Jesus. We should make the Bible our study above every other book; we should love it, and obey it as the voice of God. We are to see and to understand his restrictions and requirements, "thou shalt" and "thou shalt not," and realize the true meaning of the word of God.

... The students of our schools should consider that through the contemplation of sin, the sure result has followed, and their God-given faculties have been weakened and unfitted for moral advancement, because they have been misapplied. There are many who admit this as the truth. They have cherished pride and self-conceit, until these evil traits of character have become a ruling power, controlling their desires and inclinations. While they have had a form of godliness, and have performed many acts of self-righteousness, there has been no real heart change. They have not brought their life practices into definite and close measurement with the great standard of righteousness, the law of God. Should they critically compare their life with this standard, they could not but feel that they were deficient, sin-sick, and in need of a physician. They can only understand the depth to which they have fallen, by beholding the infinite sacrifice that has been made by Jesus Christ, to lift them out of their degradation.

... Will the students of our schools study, and endeavor to copy the life and character of Him who came down from heaven to show them what they must be, if they would enter the kingdom of God? I have borne you a message of the near coming of the Son of God in the clouds of heaven with power and great glory. I have not presented before you any definite time, but have repeated to you the injunction of Christ himself, to watch unto prayer, "For in such an hour as ye think not, the Son of man cometh." [Matt. 24:44.] The warning has come echoing down the ages to our time, "Behold, I come quickly; and my reward is with me to give every man according as his work shall be. I am Alpha and Omega, the beginning and the end, the first and the last. Blessed are they that do his commandments, that they may have right to the tree of life, and may enter in through the gates into the city." [Rev. 22:12–14.]

Charles Taze Russell, "Earth's Night of Sin to Terminate in a Morning of Joy"

Like the Seventh-Day Adventists, the Jehovah's Witnesses developed in the nineteenth century out of the Millerite legacy into another of the world's major religious organizations. Beginning in 1870, a group around Charles Taze Russell (1852–1916) – influenced by the Adventist George Storrs and other former Millerites – began an intense process of biblical study that came to a familiar conclusion: in alignment with the Bible's prophecies the contemporary world had entered its last days and a new, earthly Kingdom of God awaited the righteous, who either would be resurrected or survive the upcoming Armageddon. In 1881 in Pittsburgh, Russell's group formally organized as Zion's Watch Tower Tract Society. In July 1931, after decades-long questions of leadership and structure, The Watch Tower Society – under the stewardship of Russell's successor,

Joseph Rutherford – adopted its now familiar designation as "Jehovah's Witnesses" and began to centralize doctrine and organization around the group's Brooklyn headquarters. The selection below was written by Russell in 1886 for the opening "series" of "The Plan of the Ages," the first in a multivolume biblical study titled *Millennial Dawn*. In order to clarify his purpose, in 1904 Russell altered the title of the volume to "The Divine Plan of the Ages" and changed the project's title to *Studies in the Scriptures*. The Witnesses withdrew the *Studies* from circulation as official doctrine concerning the specifics of Christ's return changed over the course of the twentieth century. Still, many Witnesses continue to consult the texts and, as seen below, they provide significant perspective on the foundations of the Witnesses' understanding of and approach to scripture.

Source: Charles Taze Russell, "Earth's Night of Sin to Terminate in a Morning of Joy" (1886) in *Studies in the Scriptures, vol. I: The Divine Plan of the Ages* (New Clawson, MI: Oakland County Bible Students, 2000), 9–12.

The title of this series of Studies, "The Divine Plan of the Ages," suggests a progression in the Divine arrangement, foreknown to our God and orderly. We believe the teachings of Divine revelation can be seen to be both beautiful and harmonious from this standpoint and from no other. The period in which sin is permitted has been a dark night to humanity, never to be forgotten; but the glorious day of righteousness and divine favor, to be ushered in by Messiah, who, as the Sun of Righteousness, shall arise and shine fully and clearly into and upon all, bringing healing and blessing, will more than counterbalance the dreadful night of weeping, sighing, pain, sickness and death, in which the groaning creation has been so long. "Weeping may endure for a night, but joy cometh in the MORNING." Psa. 30:5

... Though in this work we shall endeavor, and we trust with success, to set before the interested and unbiased reader the plan of God as it relates to and explains the past, the present and the future of his dealings, in a way more harmonious, beautiful and reasonable than is generally understood, yet that this is the result of extraordinary wisdom or ability on the part of the writer is positively disclaimed. It is the light from the Sun of Righteousness in this dawning of the Millennial Day that reveals these things as "present truth," now due to be appreciated by the sincere – the pure in heart.

Since skepticism is rife, the very foundation of true religion, and the foundation of truth, is questioned often, even by the sincere. We have endeavored to uncover enough of the foundation upon which all faith should be built – the Word of God – to give confidence and assurance in its testimony, even to the unbeliever. And we have endeavored to do this in a manner that will appeal to and can be accepted by reason as a foundation. Then we have endeavored to build upon that foundation the teachings of Scripture, in such a manner that, so far as possible, purely human judgment may try its squares and angles by the most exacting rules of justice which it can command.

Believing that the Scriptures reveal a consistent and harmonious plan, which, when seen, must commend itself to every sanctified conscience, this work is published in the hope of assisting students of the Word of God, by suggesting lines of thought which harmonize with each other and with the inspired Word. Those who recognize the Bible as the revelation of God's plan – and such we specially address – will doubtless agree that, if inspired of God, its teachings must, when taken as a whole, reveal a plan harmonious and consistent with itself, and with the character of its Divine Author. Our object as truth-seekers should be to obtain the complete, harmonious whole of God's revealed plan; and this, as God's children, we have reason to expect, since it is promised that the spirit of truth shall guide us into all truth. John 16:13

As inquirers, we have two methods open to us. One is to seek among all the views suggested by the various sects of the church, and to take from each that element which we might consider truth – an endless task. A difficulty which we should meet by this method would be, that if our judgment were warped and twisted, or our prejudices bent in any direction – and whose are not? – these difficulties would prevent our correct selection, and we might choose the error and reject the truth. Again, if we should adopt this as our method we should lose much, because the truth is progressive, shining more and more unto the perfect day, to those who search for it and walk in the light of it, while the various creeds of the various sects are fixed and stationary, and were made so centuries ago. And each of them must contain a large proportion of error, since each in some important respects contradicts the others. This method would lead into a labyrinth of bewilderment and confusion. The other method is to divest our minds of all prejudice, and to remember that none can know more about the plans of God than he has revealed in his Word, and that it was given to the meek and lowly of heart; and, as such, earnestly and sincerely seeking its guidance and instruction only, we shall by its great Author be guided to an understanding of it, as it becomes due to be understood, by making use of the various helps divinely provided. See Eph. 4:11–16.

As an aid to this class of students, this work is specially designed. It will be noticed that its references are to Scripture only, except where secular history may be called in to prove the fulfilment of Scripture statements. The testimony of modern theologians has been given no weight, and that of the so-called Early Fathers has been omitted. Many of them have testified in harmony with thoughts herein expressed, but we believe it to be a common failing of the present and all times for men to believe certain doctrines because others did so, in whom they had confidence. This is manifestly a fruitful cause of error, for many good people have believed and taught error in all good conscience. (Acts 26:9) Truth-seekers should empty their vessels of the muddy waters of tradition and fill them at the fountain of truth – God's Word. And no religious teaching should have weight except as it guides the truth-seeker to that fountain.

For even a general and hasty examination of the whole Bible and its teaching, this work is too small; but, recognizing the haste of our day, we have endeavored to be as brief as the importance of the subjects seemed to permit.

MARY BAKER EDDY AND CHRISTIAN SCIENCE

The Church of Christ, Scientist – familiarly known as Christian Scientists – is another of the contemporary world's influential and expansive religious organizations born in the nineteenth-century American context. Christian Science traditionally emphasizes that healing, physical as well as spiritual, comes through comprehension of the basic truths of life: that God set it in motion and continues to direct it according to divine order; that it is fundamentally spiritual and good, such that physicality and evil are fleeting deceptions. These ideas, along with particular methods of healing, were developed most fully by Mary Baker Eddy (1821–1910), who founded the Church of Christ, Scientist in 1866. The most direct statement of and foundational document for Christian Science remains Eddy's 1875 textbook, *Science and Health with a Key to the Scriptures*. The following selection derives from Eddy's prefatory remarks to the text.

Source: Mary Baker Eddy, *Science and Health with a Key to the Scriptures* (Boston: The Christian Science Board of Directors, 1934 [1875]), vii–viii, x–xi.

To those leaning on the sustaining infinite, to-day is big with blessings. The wakeful shepherd beholds the first faint morning beams, ere cometh the full radiance of a risen day. So shone the pale star to the prophet-shepherds; yet it traversed the night, and came where, in cradled obscurity, lay the Bethlehem babe, the human herald of Christ, Truth, who would make plain to benighted understanding the way of salvation through Christ Jesus, till across a night of error should dawn the morning beams and shine the guiding star of being. The Wise-men were led to behold and to follow this daystar of divine Science, lighting the way to eternal harmony.

The time for thinkers has come. Truth, independent of doctrines and time-honored systems, knocks at the portal of humanity. Contentment with the past and the cold conventionality of materialism are crumbling away. Ignorance of God is no longer the stepping-stone to faith. The only guarantee of obedience is a right apprehension of Him whom to know aright is Life eternal. Though empires fall, "the Lord shall reign forever."

A book introduces new thoughts, but it cannot make them speedily understood. It is the task of the sturdy pioneer to hew the tall oak and to cut the rough granite. Future ages must declare what the pioneer has accomplished.

Since the author's discovery of the might of Truth in the treatment of disease as well as of sin, her system has been fully tested and has not been found wanting; but to reach the heights of Christian Science, man must live in obedience to its divine Principle. To develop the full might of this Science, the discords of corporeal sense must yield to the harmony of spiritual sense, even as the science of music corrects false tones and gives sweet concord to sound.

Theology and physics teach that both Spirit and matter are real and good, whereas the fact is that Spirit is good and real, and matter is Spirit's opposite. The question, What is Truth, is answered by demonstration, – by healing both disease and sin; and this demonstration shows that Christian healing confers the most health and makes the best men. On this basis Christian Science will have a fair fight. Sickness has been combated for centuries by doctors using material remedies; but the question arises, Is there less sickness because of these practitioners? A vigorous "No" is the response deducible from two connate facts, – the reputed longevity of the Antediluvians, and the rapid multiplication and increased violence of diseases since the flood.

In the author's work, RETROSPECTION AND INTROSPECTION, may be found a biographical sketch, narrating experiences which led her, in the year 1866, to the discovery of the system that she denominated Christian Science. As early as 1862 she began to write down and give to friends the results of her Scriptural study, for the Bible was her sole teacher ...

The divine Principle of healing is proved in the personal experience of any sincere seeker of Truth. Its purpose is good, and its practice is safer and more potent than that of any other sanitary method. The un-biased Christian thought is soonest touched by Truth, and convinced of it. Only those quarrel with her method who do not understand her meaning, or discerning the truth, come not to the light lest their works be reproved. No intellectual proficiency is requisite in the learner, but sound morals are most desirable. Many imagine that the phenomena of physical healing in Christian Science present only a phase of the action of the human mind, which action in some unexplained way results in the cure of disease. On the contrary, Christian Science rationally explains that all other pathological methods are the fruits of human faith in matter, – faith in the workings, not of Spirit, but of the fleshly mind which must yield to Science.

The physical healing of Christian Science results now, as in Jesus' time, from the operation of divine Principle, before which sin and disease lose their reality in human consciousness and disappear as naturally and as necessarily as darkness gives place to light and sin to reformation. Now, as then, these mighty works are not supernatural, but supremely natural. They are the sign of Immanuel, or "God with us," – a divine influence ever present in human consciousness and repeating itself, coming now as was promised aforetime.

ELIJAH MUHAMMAD, "WHAT IS ISLAM? WHAT IS A MUSLIM?"

The Nation of Islam (originally Allah's Temple of Islam) sprang onto the scene in July 1930 when Wallace D. Fard suddenly appeared in Detroit and proclaimed that he had arrived to resurrect the economic, political, social, and spiritual condition of African Americans through the "original" black religion: Islam. In August 1931, a young man named Elijah Poole joined the Nation and quickly became one of Fard's closest disciples and the organizational head of the Nation. When Fard disappeared from the scene in 1934, Poole, now known as Elijah Muhammad (1897–1975), explained that his assumed name was no accident: like the Prophet Muhammad before him, he was the conduit for Allah's directly revealed truth (in this case brought through Fard as God-incarnate). In the excerpt below, Elijah Muhammad summarizes some of the defining principles of the Nation's unique brand of Islam. Notably, the selection reveals Elijah Muhammad's – and, more generally, the Nation's – ambivalence toward the Bible. Just as he himself was the son of a Georgia preacher, many of the Nation's converts have had intimate familiarity with the Christian Bible. Muhammad's references here show a characteristic view of the Bible as a document of God's active role in history through prophetic revelations that point to a radically different, coming Kingdom, but also as a text corrupted by some diabolical handiwork.

Source: *Muhammad Speaks* newspaper (July 17, 1970): www.muhammadspeaks.com.

Islam is something new to our Black People in America and these two questions are often asked – What is Islam, and What is A Muslim?

The Arab name, Islam, which means entire submission to the will of God in his religion, is what confuses the question. The Arabs call it Islam, Which means, "To submit to the will of God."

Our Black people were brought up by the enemy, white man, who did not want us to ever know anything about Islam, because once the black slave learned Islam, He would never be a slave anymore …

Islam has many significances to it. Islam is wisdom. Islam is guidance of God for Man. Islam is the only way of God. Islam is called a religion, although Islam is not a religion. Islam is referred to as a religion due to the many hundreds of various kinds of religions practiced today …

Islam, as one of the scientists put it, is the sun of law and truth to outshine everything that goes for religion. Islam does not confuse the seeker, nor does Islam confound the believer. Islam is simple. This is why the sign of Islam is representing the Sun, the Moon and the Stars. Islam, the divine duty of man … He has it in the universal order of things.

Islam is righteousness, Islam is Justice. Islam is Equality, Islam is Freedom. Islam is everything the created man needs.

The black people in America are, by nature, born Muslim. The enemy slave-making devil, deprived the Black Man in America of the knowledge of himself. Accordingly they have deprived the Black Man in countries other than America, of the knowledge of self … In America, on the streets and in traffic, you cannot tell the master from the slave. The white master sells the black slave his fine automobiles, if he is able to pay for them. They both look alike with fine clothes. This is to trick other black people, to follow the white man. We must remember that the Jesus foretold the rich and wealthy man and the poor man under the parable of Lazarus and Dives, the rich man. But the end came to both. The end came to the wealth of the rich man and an end came to the poor man's laying down and wishing and grieving for the wealth of his master. Then like a modern Samson, he got angry and he wanted to pull the building down, even if he had to go down with it. He is well angry with the white slave-master when he wakes up and learns that he has been robbed so thoroughly that he does not even know himself … [I]n the Bible, there is a place where it teaches us that God will bring out of the dragon's belly that which he has swallowed. No where in the bible is the white man referred to by a good name. The book begins with the white man symbolized as a snake in Genesis, and it ends with him as a snake, in Revelations. Why style the white man as a snake? He has the characteristics of a snake. By nature, the snake will let you know that he does not like you. When the snake looks at you he begins to stick his tongue out. This is a warning that he does not like you. And the snake has a forked tongue and not a straight tongue. This warns you that he is something that is compared with a human being that also has a forked tongue, who tells lies on one side and the truth on the other side. But he keeps the lie going stronger than the truth. So the forked tongue person is something, which by nature it is not good to take him for a friend. In the nature of the white man, he has a forked tongue. He will talk truth with you and he will talk evil with you. This is what is called tricknollegy. ... It is the God of these white people who is to blame for making such a people, And the white man obeys his God. Everything you see him do he is made to do it. If you Black Man follow the white man, you are to blame for the consequences of your following an open enemy. The white man is not a secret enemy he is an open enemy. Islam is the only thing that can take our Black People into self again, after six thousand (6,000) years away from self. We had four hundred (400) years here in America, as a regular experiment – People, to be experimented on by the devil. ... Also, in the Bible, you have the parable of the bones waking up and uniting together and assembling a frame of bones. Then the lesson teaches you that they all did live. The Holy Qur'an, a later book than the Bible, verifies the Bible parable by teaching you and me that Allah (God) gave life to all. He called them once and they all stood up. The Bible has it symbolically that when the loud trumpet sounded, they all will wake up. Black Brother, Black Sister, you are by nature one of the righteous but you have been robbed of your righteousness and made to live unrighteousness until now you will be whipped into submission, by divine will and power. You will be made to accept yourself. There is no limit to the nation of the Black Man. The Black Man will endure forever. God Himself is with us. Let us submit to Allah (God) and live forever. Peace be with you. The mercy of Allah (God) and his blessings to he that believes and accepts his own ... Islam and the Muslims.

Elijah Muhammad, Messenger of Allah, to you all.

JIM JONES, "THE LETTER KILLETH"

The events at Jonestown (Guyana, South America) on November 18, 1978 are among the most infamous in American history. Nine hundred and nine residents of Jonestown, all members of the Peoples Temple, died in a mass suicide after some were involved in the deaths of US Congressman Leo Ryan, three journalists, and a former Peoples Temple member. Ryan had come to secure custody of some children living at Jonestown. At the center of the controversy and among those who took their lives was Jim Jones (1931–78), the founder and leader of the Peoples Temple, and

Jonestown's namesake. Since late 1978, Jones has been identified most commonly as a charismatic "cult" leader whose brainwashing led followers to their tragic end. Yet from the start of his ministry in the early 1950s, Jones gained attention and recognition for organizing socially and politically progressive activities in his demographically diverse congregations. Around 1955, Jones founded in Indianapolis what became "The Peoples Temple Full Gospel Church," then relocated to northern California in 1965 as their numbers grew. Jones consistently emphasized that the contemporary world had entered an apocalyptic epoch characterized by racial conflict, genocide, and nuclear war and preached that the path to a new state of affairs – often figured as God's biblically revealed Kingdom Come – was through a radical, communist-style reorganization of society. This sense of impending catastrophe and conflict that surrounded Jones and the Peoples Temple as they tried to implement their radical vision led to the group's purchase of and mass emigration to the Guyana site. The selection below comes from an undated, twenty-four page pamphlet written by Jones and later found at Jonestown. In the essay, Jones turns to biblical analysis to explicate some of his most familiar teachings: that "the Christ Principle" was manifested in people's bodies and deeds, not in the abstract "Word," and that he himself exemplified the "living Spirit."

Source: Jim Jones, "The Letter Killeth". California Historical Society, Peoples Temple Records MS 3800.

"The Letter Killeth, but the Spirit Giveth LIFE" (II Cor 3:6)
Let Us Exalt the Name of Jesus, and Not the King James of England!!

Consider this

If you are not a pharmacist, you wouldn't dream of going to a pharmacological bible to attempt to make a drug to help someone; nor would you consider using medical guidebooks to perform surgery to save lives, if you were not a professional surgeon. Thus, no minister should attempt to use the scriptures, unless his life manifests the miraculous gifts of the Holy Spirit (God). Scripture bears this out. "How shall they hear without a preacher (prophet)? and how shall they preach (prophesy), except they be sent?" (Rom 10:14–15).

"Faith cometh by hearing, and hearing by the word of God" (Rom 10:17), not from reading the Bible. The word of God is clearly described as something presently alive. "For the word of God is quick, and powerful, and sharper than any two-edged sword … and is a discerner of the thoughts and intents of the heart" (Heb 4:12). "And the Word was made flesh, and dwelt among us" (John 1:14). Who fulfils this in our day, and clearly has the **word** which is shown by giving the very thoughts of our minds? Who raises the dead, makes the blind to see and the deaf to hear? Who corrects bones? Truth is still in the Bible, but a prophet is needed to make it clear.

"Search the scriptures; for in them ye **think** ye have eternal life: and they are they which testify of me (in the original this means they testify of the Christ annointed [sic] nature), and ye will not come to me that ye might have life" (John 5:39–40).

There is a prophet in our day who unquestioningly proves that he is **sent** from God. He has all the gifts of the spirit as given in the Bible: Word of wisdom, word of knowledge, faith, gifts of healing, working of miracles, prophecy, discerning of spirits, tongues and interpretation of tongues (See I Cor 12:8–10). We must have a prophet who is living the Christ life to direct us in this hour.

Consider the scripture that says "Deceivers are entered into the world, who confess not that Jesus Christ **is** come in the flesh. This is a deceiver and an antichrist" II John 7. "Who shall go up for us to heaven, and bring it unto us … Who shall go over the sea for us, and bring it unto us … But the word is very nigh unto thee" (Deut 30:12–14). This means now. This means today.

"Man shall not live by bread alone (an original Bible writer interprets this as tablets of scripture), but by every word that proceedeth out of the mouth of God" (Matt 4:4).

MESSAGE FROM THE APOSTLE

I have come to make God real in the lives of people. My only desire is to establish the great work of Jesus Christ on our troubled globe. I have taken the true scriptures to heart, where it declares in Philippians 2 for us to "let this mind be in you, which was also in Christ Jesus: Who being in the form of God, thought it not robbery to be **equal with God**" (Phil 2:5–6) (and we are all created in His image and likeness-form). I am crucified with Christ; nevertheless I live; yet not I (my personal ambitions), but Christ liveth in me" (Gal 2:20).

It is written and proven that as a man thinketh in his heart so is he (Prov 23:7). Thus I have decided to be fully and completely the temple of the Holy Ghost, which scripture instructs us all to be (I Cor 6:19). It was *declared* by the savior-teacher, Jesus, in Nazareth consciousness, that there are 30-fold, 60-fold and 100-fold (Mark 4:20). Or to interpret accurately, one can be 30 percent yielded to God or 100 percent. I have settled for nothing less than His fullness dwelling in me.

God and Jesus are as reincarnatable as a child's smile. Matthew 25 says when you feed a hungry person or clothe a naked child you have been doing it directly to Jesus Himself (Matt 25:40). Let me bring to your remembrance that after Jesus left the Body in the Sonship degree, not even those who had lived and worked with him for four years recognized the very same Jesus when he appeared in a different likeness on the road as His followers departed from the tomb. Imagine! they thought they had been speaking with a gardener (John 20:15). Can you not see the mystery? God never appears the same way twice.

God is Love (I John 4:8), therefore whoever reincarnates love more fully should be followed: As Paul the apostle related in yesteryear, "follow me as I follow Christ" (I Cor 11:1). I am causing untold thousands to believe in the Jesus of ancient history by the great miracles of healings, prophecies and discernments I perform in His name! Many have believed God to be dead until I showed them that He is as tangible as the food they eat and the air they breathe. Oh, what a privilege it is to live in this recognition and be able to personify the Mind and Works of God in Christ, therefore enabling the pure in heart to **see** God (Matt 5:8), and know Him aright, which is life eternal.

Jesus asked when they would stone him, For what good works do you stone me? If you cannot receive me for my name sake, receive me for my work sake. I am fulfilling His words that we are gods and sons of the Most High (John 10:33–34), and that these things that He did and greater will ye do because He has gone back to the Father. What I am doing so must ye do, that is become living epistles, read and known of all men, (the only Bible or epistle people really read and believe in nowadays) (II Cor 3:2).

I am letting concerned humanity see my **good works** that they might glorify God, the Father (Matt 5:16).

DAVID KORESH AND THE SEVEN SEALS

In 1919, a Bulgarian-born Illinois man named Victor Houteff joined the Seventh-Day Adventist Church. After joining SDA communities in California in the early 1920s, he earned a reputation as an Adventist Bible teacher for the depth of his scriptural analyses. Because Houteff gave special importance to Isaiah 54–56 and to the cryptic passages on the Seven Seals in Revelation 5–6, his students began to refer to themselves as "Students of the Seven Seals" and "the Seventh-Day Adventist Davidian Branch," or "Branch Davidians." SDA leadership questioned Houteff's teachings, laid out in his 1929 book *The Shepherd's Rod*, and eventually "disfellowshiped" him and his followers. The group bought land outside Waco, Texas and in 1935 established the Mount Carmel Center. More than five decades later – on February 28, 1993 – the Branch Davidians and Mount Carmel sprang suddenly into the international public eye after a raid by the US Bureau of Alcohol, Tobacco, and Firearms (ATF) left four ATF agents and five Davidians dead and many wounded. Among the wounded was David Koresh (1959–93) who, like Houteff, earned recognition among the Davidians as a special emissary of God – a "messiah," in the broadest sense – due to his expansive knowledge and interpretative capacities of the Bible. Born Vernon Howell, he remained unsure of his prophetic status until a vision during a 1985 visit to Israel inspired him to change his name to David Koresh (honoring the celebrated biblical kings David and Cyrus ("Koresh," in Hebrew)), and convinced him he could interpret the Seven Seals. This led the Davidians to the idea that Koresh should father the 24 children who would rule the coming Kingdom of God. Those ideas and practices, and rumors of child abuse led to the deadly ATF raid, which was followed by a stand-off monitored closely around the world. The Davidians promised to come out of Mount Carmel when Koresh finished writing his explanation of the Seven Seals. He released an explanation of the first seal along with an introduction, from which the selection below derives. On April 19 – 51 days after the stand-off began – the FBI decided not to wait for the rest of Koresh's manuscript and tried to force the Davidians out of Mount Carmel. The presence of highly flammable gases caused the complex to erupt into flames, and Koresh and 73 other Davidians perished.

Source: Phillip Arnold and James Tabor, eds. *The David Koresh Manuscript: Exposition of the Seven Seals* (Houston: Reunion Institute, 1994).

Scripture tells us that Pilate was convinced of the truth in Christ, but failing to take heed thereto, he lost his soul, causing the blood of the innocent to be shed. How many of us since the dawning of time have committed such things? Who was this Jesus? Who was this Saviour that nearly a whole religious nation rejected?

... [O]f all the records the most awe inspiring remains to be the most misunderstood, that being the Revelation of Jesus Christ written by the Apostle John to the churches of Asia and left on record that all who follow may ask the question:

"Who is this Christ and what remains to be the mystery of Him?"

In my work to unfold this mystery to you I will not use great techniques of scholarly display nor indepth reasonings of philosophy, no sophisticated, congenial language shall be used, just simple talk and reason.

... First of all, the Revelation of Jesus Christ which God gave unto Him to show unto His servants things which must shortly come to pass are to be seen just as that: a revelation of Jesus to reveal to men His wishes and His desires for those who make up His church. For the kingdom of God being that of heaven, and not of this world, is to be revealed unto this world by the means He has chosen – the foolishness of preaching. John the Apostle while on the Isle of Patmos received the Lord's messenger and in obedience placed in written form all that he saw and all that he heard pertaining to the mysteries of Christ. And in good faith the Apostle stated, "Blessed is he that readeth, and they that hear the words of this prophecy, and keep those things which are written therein for the time is at hand" (Revelation 1:3).

Likewise John was commanded of the angel, "Write the things which thou hast seen, and the things which are, and the things which shall be hereafter" (Revelation 1:19). Simply, John's record contains the past, present, and future events that revolve around the Revelation of Jesus Christ. John in faithfulness sent his writings to the seven churches in Asia and the will of Christ for these churches is plainly revealed from chapter 2 to chapter 4 of Revelation. Therefore on record, all may read and see how Christ has dealt[.]

Our subject of interest will be taken up from chapters 4–22, for these passages entail the events that are to be after John's time.

... Very clearly John tells of a judgment in which only one question is asked, "Who is worthy" to open or to reveal a book found in the right hand of God clearly sealed with seven seals. John states, "No man in heaven nor in earth, neither under the earth was able to open the book neither to look thereon." Then John is pointed to the hope of all men: the Lamb that was slain. Here is a revelation of Christ as our High Priest in heaven. Here His work is revealed: the opening of the mysteries of God. These mysteries of which reveal Christ and His sufficiency to save all whose prayers are directed to God through Him.

... Clearly then, John is showing us of that ... Christ is the mediator of the New Covenant and that New Covenant is contained in the seven seals. If we the church have been so long awaiting that which must be hereafter, why is it that so many of us in Christendom have not even heard of the seven seals? Why is this Revelation of Jesus Christ which God gave to Him such a mystery?

... The servant of God will find as we continue in our searching of the scriptures that every book of the Bible meets and ends in the book of Revelation. Gems of most sacred truth are to be uncovered, golden promises never before seen are to be brought to view, for when has grace ever been needed more than now in the time of which we live?

REFERENCES

Cox, Harvey. 1995. *Fire from Heaven: The Rise of Pentacostal Spirituality and the Reshaping of Religion in the Twenty-first Century.* Reading, MA: Addison-Wesley.

Hughes, Richard T., and Allen, C. Leonard. 1988. *Illusions of Innocence: Protestant Primitivism in America 1630–1875.* Chicago: University of Chicago Press.

Palmer, Phoebe. 1998. "Present to My Christian Friend on Entire Devotion to God," *Phoebe Palmer: Selected Writings,* ed. Thomas Oden. New York: Paulist.

SUGGESTIONS FOR FURTHER RESEARCH

Bloch, Ruth H. 1985. *Visionary Republic: Millennial Themes in American Thought 1756–1800.* Cambridge and New York: Cambridge University Press.

Boyer, Paul S. 1992. *When Time Shall Be No More: Prophecy Belief in Modern American Culture.* Cambridge, MA: Belknap Press of Harvard University Press.

Eskenazi, Tamara Cohn and Weiss, Andrea L, eds. 2008. *The Torah: A Women's Commentary.* New York: URJ Press and Women of Reform Judaism.

Harrison, J. F. C. 1979. *The Second Coming: Popular Millenarianism, 1780–1850.* New Brunswick, NJ: Rutgers University Press.

Hughes, Richard T. 1988. *The American Quest for the Primitive Church.* Urbana: University of Illinois Press.

—— 2009. *Christian America and the Kingdom of God.* Urbana: University of Illinois Press.

Kaplan, Jeffrey. 1997. *Radical Religion in America: Millenarian Movements from the Far Right to the Children of Noah.* 1st edn. Syracuse, NY: Syracuse University Press.

Lefkovitz, Lori Hope. 2010. *In Scripture: The First Stories of Jewish Sexual Identities.* New York: Rowman and Littlefield.

Lesser, Joshua, Schneer, David, Plaskow, Judith and Drinkwater, Gregg. 2009. *Torah Queeries.* New York: New York University Press.

Newsom, Carol, and Ringe, Sharon H. 1998. *The Women's Bible Commentary – Expanded.* Louisville, KY: Westminster John Knox.

Numbers, Ronald L., and Jonathan M. Butler, eds. 1993. *The Disappointed: Millerism and Millenarianism in the Nineteenth Century.* 2nd edn. Knoxville: University of Tennessee Press.

Plaskow, Judith, and Christ, Carol, eds. 1979. *Womanspirit Rising: A Feminist Reader in Religion.* San Francisco: HarperOne.

—— 1989. *Weaving the Visions: New Patterns in Feminist Spirituality.* San Francisco: HarperOne.

Plaskow, Judith. 1991. *Standing Again at Sinai: Judaism from a Feminist Perspective.* San Francisco: HarperOne.

Schüssler Fiorenza, Elisabeth. 1993. *Searching the Scriptures: A Feminist Introduction.* New York: Crossroad.

—— 1997. *Searching the Scriptures*, vol. 2: *A Feminist Commentary.* New York: Crossroad.

Smolinski, Reiner. 1998. *The Kingdom, the Power and the Glory: The Millennial Impulse in Early American Literature.* Dubuque, IO: Kendall/Hunt Pub. Co.

Weber, Timothy P. 1987. *Living in the Shadow of the Second Coming: American Premillennialism, 1875–1982.* Chicago: University of Chicago Press.

Zamora, Lois Parkinson, ed. 1982. *The Apocalyptic Vision in America: Interdisciplinary Essays on Myth and Culture.* Bowling Green, OH: Bowling Green University Popular Press.

5 The Bible and artistic expression

But woe to you, O earth and sea
for the devil has come down to you in great wrath
because he knows that his time is short!
Let him who has understanding
reckon the number of the beast
for it is a human number
its number is six hundred and sixty six.

(Revelation 12:12; 13:18b, RSV, referred to in
"The Number of the Beast")

Today, in the second decade of the twenty-first century, the opening lines of the British heavy-metal band Iron Maiden's 1982 song, "The Number of the Beast," repeatedly blast out of basements and bars across the United States. The verse has become increasingly ubiquitous since 2007, when MTV Games and Harmonix Music Systems released the video game *Rock Band,* which included "The Number of the Beast" along with other songs for players to use. With around four million units sold in the year after *Rock Band*'s introduction, it was not long before players – ages 7, 87, and everything in-between – were slamming along in virtual simulation of Iron Maiden's hard-edged take on the Book of Revelation's cryptic numerology.

The success of *Rock Band* and other music-based simulations like *Guitar Hero* (the pioneer in the field with its 2005 release) has been global. Still, the wild popularity in the United States of songs like "The Number of the Beast" within the games reflects a particular set of trends regarding the place of the Bible in American arts and letters. The *Rock Band* case points to three general patterns in a common dynamic surrounding the Bible in American cultural production. The first pattern entails *diffusion*: biblical elements appear far and wide across almost all fields of creative expression. References cut across all media and domains of creative expression. The allusions remain diverse, ranging from incidental to elaborate and from devotional to iconoclastic.

The second pattern involves *innovation*: the Bible is not merely referenced but rather is taken up in unfamiliar ways toward original ends. In both processes, the Bible's presence remains fundamental but its forms and meanings constantly change. Its elements appear excised and rearranged in new contexts with novel effects. Sometimes the words or images of the text itself become correctives or challenges to other religious or cultural uses of the Bible.

Finally, the Bible is a source of *inspiration*. It may not inspire in a traditional, devotional sense but continues to offer a well-spring of images and to spur creativity. The Bible's legacy and familiarity are invoked to create new works of power, ingenuity, and beauty. However, biblical allusions often remain ambiguous to, or even unrecognized by, the audiences that encounter them. Millions rock along every day to "The Number of the Beast" as virtual band members, most giving no thought to Revelation but instead responding to the gritty image of the Beast.

Diffusion, innovation, and inspiration contribute to what Giles Gunn calls "an enduring antinomian strain" in American creative expression. Building on the title and argument of Herbert Schneidau's essay on American poetry (1983), Gunn notes, "the Bible has simultaneously furnished many of the most stable forms of consciousness in the West while at the same time serving as a chief source of dissatisfaction with them" (Gunn 1983: 2). According to Gunn, this "paradox" is especially pronounced across American history because of the development of a unique cultural perspective. In an early "interpretive turn," exemplified especially by the Puritans, Americans began to see their society not only as informed by the Bible but rather as the fulfillment of biblical prophecies of a Promised Land. Just as readily, however, writers and artists turn the Bible against society, showing the world as worthy of prophetic critique.

The artist's critique, like the theologian's, can take several forms. A poet like Emily Dickinson reacts against the Bible itself, or at least some uses of it, for its limiting of human possibility. Others use the Bible as a model by which to judge society. Robert Lowell, for example, employs biblical images in his poetry to give a bleak diagnosis of his native Boston and, by extension, of mid-century American society, but not without signs of hope. Sometimes the two methods are fused, when parts of the Bible are used to correct other uses of it, a phenomenon we have witnessed at work throughout this book, particularly in the materials from Chapter 4, "Reading in the margins."

Because biblical allusions are so plentiful, and artistic production so rich, we have aimed for a small sample of artistic work rather than attempting to be comprehensive. We present four particular fields of creative expression: art (including several categories), poetry, musical lyric, and the novel. Readers are encouraged to supplement our choices with other works from these fields as well as from media not included here, such as theater, film, television, and video games. We have included suggestions for further exploration in the bibliography.

Even this sampling from the sphere of arts and letters invites reflection on the dynamic between the creative energies of the artist and the creative genius of the Bible. Each artist and writer is simultaneously a creator and interpreter – or, in terms of the three patterns, an inspired agent of diffusion and innovation who translates biblical elements into another medium. We recognize but have not tried to resolve certain tensions inherent in talking about older questions of aesthetics and about newer ones regarding cultural production. We do not, for example, attempt to draw the lines between folk (or vernacular) art and fine art, or between "art" and "craft."

The challenges intensify regarding matters of identity. We have had to think about what makes an artist or an artist's work "American." Benjamin West, born in Pennsylvania, became a famous portrait painter in England in the tradition of Joshua Reynolds. Edmonia Lewis, limited and defined by her race in the United States, settled in Italy. T. S. Eliot, American by birth, moved to England, while British poet W. H. Auden was profoundly shaped by his time in the United States. In all cases, we present artists and writers whose understanding, identity, or artistic influences have been impacted by the American experience.

Finally, we have taken a capacious approach as to what kind of work qualifies as "biblical." In representing the diffusion of the Bible in American creative expression, this chapter includes selections that draw on the Bible as a well-spring of images and ideas rather than interpret it in exclusively "religious" ways. But at what point does using a biblical theme or story become "iconoclastic" or "devotional"? Again, distinctions fall apart. While we have steered away from openly devotional works, we cannot fail to note that Edmonia Lewis and Robert Lowell (for a period) converted to Catholicism, that Tobi Kahn counts his Jewishness as fundamental to his identity, that country musicians like Roy Acuff sprang from and continued to sing at religious revivals, or that Bessie Harvey parallels in her sculptures Voudou and other Afro-Caribbean traditions.

Since these issues arise acutely in the "visual" arts, our chapter opens with examples from that area of creative expression. The only portion of this book that is not based in language, it reveals the unique process of translation into other media – not only into other languages and idioms. Biblical allusion in visual forms produces inevitable frictions and, in turn, unique energies. One traditional religious position has been that the Bible is the enemy of the visual arts. Many, including Puritan colonists, interpreted literally scripture's command against graven images (Ex 20:4; 34:17; Deut 5:8) as forbidding all representational art. Augusta Savage (1892–1962), a sculptor associated with the Harlem Renaissance, reports that her childhood clay figures of animals and people earned her beatings from her father, a strict Methodist minister (Farrington 2005: 100).

Yet, as artist Tobi Kahn notes, the Bible is replete with references to visual beauty, from the descriptive creation stories to the lush descriptions of Israel's tabernacle in the desert, and the frequency of the word and command "to see" (Kahn 2009: 11). Mark Rothko's triptych of murals for Harvard's Holyoke Center ranged from dark to lighter colors, which, Rothko said, symbolized Christ's death and resurrection (Seldes 1996: 51). The art installations of James Turrell, which emphasize light, sky, and space, are not explicitly biblical but stem from a scripturally grounded Quaker principle of finding a spiritual presence in everyday elements.

Vernacular art, also called folk art or self-taught art, is replete with biblical imagery as individuals have attempted to present creatively their particular take on the world. The biblical quilt by Harriet Powers here is but one example, as biblical themes appear in samplers and other textiles, carved wooden figures, sculpted stone images, and many local materials. As a precursor to the contemporary, Quaker-inspired work of Turell, "the Shaking Quakers" – better known as the Shakers – expressed anonymously and communally their convictions about God's material manifestations in simple, beautifully crafted furniture and architecture.

Similarly, poetry's freedom from constraints of narrative enables the isolation and reformulation of particular biblical words and images. As Herbert Schneidau emphasizes, in the American context this relationship among the biblical texts and contemporary verse has produced a tradition of acute ambivalence. American poets continually draw on the Bible while implicitly, and sometimes explicitly, calling into question its continued theological and social relevance. Robert Frost referred to the biblical roots of poetry as "the same old apple tree." Frost, as Schneidau puts it, appears as one "among the many American poets who feel the Bible to be an inescapable heritage, for better, but also for worse" (Schneidau 1983: 11). Schneidau notes too that the earliest Puritan colonists – like Plato more than two thousand years earlier – recognized not only images but also poetry as inherently powerful, and therefore as a latent threat to interpretive cohesion. Accordingly, the preface to the Puritan *Bay Psalm Book* (1640) warned against indulging "poetic tendencies" (15).

The Puritans had good reasons to fear poetry, and a distinct irony resonates in their appeals to biblical adherence. Poetry, including the Song at the Sea in Exodus 15 and the Song of Deborah in Judges 5, comprises some of the oldest and most formative material in the Bible. American poets often sound much like biblical prophets. Since as far back as the Puritan era they have set themselves up as prophetic critics of their culture. Emerson and Whitman both present contemporary society as at odds with the integrity of the self, and both developed that view with attention to the biblical prophets. As Whitman admitted, his innovative forms and "thought rhythms" owe something to his youthful reading of the Bible, Shakespeare, and Homer, among many others (Ellman and O'Clair 1973: 20). Cynthia Griffin Wolff points out that Dickinson's poetry "echoes the Bible more than any other single work or author" (Wolff 1993: 134). Yet a selection from Dickinson in this chapter shows how she can be negative about the Bible as an object and a tool for indoctrination. In one poem, 1545, she calls it "an antique Volume – Written by faded Men" (Johnson 1960: 644). A hundred years later the celebrated Beat poet Allen Ginsberg, on the occasion of his mother's passing, sprinkled biblical allusions throughout the poem "Kaddish," rewriting the traditional Jewish mourning prayer as an extended reflection on life and death in the modern world.

As a form of poetry, song lyrics across American history exhibit many of the same dynamics with the Bible as does written verse. Yet lyrical traditions are distinct from poetry in their role in American cultural life. Songwriters generally construct lyrics as an important thread of a broader sonic fabric, and the creative process differs from the construction of a poem. And, even if lyrics are not originally conceived to accompany music, the reception of them – whether by an audience of one or many – is also inherently different from reading or hearing the words of a poem. Words put to music are retained much longer in the memory than words alone. The direct and visceral performance of songs, whether by a small group live or through a professionally produced, digitally distributed studio recording, typically provides listeners with an experience of lyrics unique among forms of poetry. Finally, when we consider the numbers of people who listen to music or play video games versus the number who read or hear poetry, we can safely say that song lyrics tend to circulate more broadly and travel farther than written verse.

Perhaps more than any other form of creative expression, song lyrics through the years express the varieties of diffusion, innovation, and inspiration in popular American approaches to the Bible. The "antinomian strain" – that mix of simultaneous reliance on and unsettling of scripture – runs deep in American music. An exchange between Robert Hunter, the longtime lyricist for the Grateful Dead, and Bryan Miller, an ardent fan and online commentator, encapsulates this familiar pattern. After Hunter acknowledged his lack of faith in the miraculous, including the miracles recorded in the Bible, Miller inquired why his lyrics were rife with so many biblical references. "My work is influenced by the same culturally predominant stuff anyone of my age living in the USA would have absorbed to some degree," Hunter replied. "The Bible is certainly a rich source of symbol and reference ... Religious content aside, it is a great and enduring work of art" (Miller 2006, n.p.).

Nevertheless, as another highly vernacular art form, American popular music – like visual folk art – also draws heavily on biblical imagery and themes in more devotional terms. A number of selections in the chapter serve as powerful examples of the long, enduring, and diverse traditions of American spiritual and gospel music firmly rooted in biblical texts. With the conversion of slaves from West Africa to Christianity, African Americans supplemented the officially sanctioned forms of preaching and worship provided by their masters with their own forms of worship, necessarily conducted in secret. This "invisible institution" of slave religion, as scholar Albert J. Raboteau calls it, included adaptation of spirituals, a form of religious folk music sung by blacks and whites but given special meaning in the slave communities. The biblical references are fundamental to the spirituals, providing symbols of hope and liberation, as well as sometimes encoding more concrete plans of escape to the North or communicating news of night worship. A former slave reported that when slaves went around singing "Steal away to Jesus," that meant there was a secret meeting for worship that evening (Raboteau 1978: 213). "Gospel music" is a more recent development, emerging as a style (as well as a new category of distinction) in the 1940s, but it developed out of these folk traditions of the nineteenth century (Moore 2002). Gospel music has made a mark on popular music, as Aretha Franklin ("The Queen of Soul"), Sam Cooke, and many others started out as gospel performers.

Some of our sources, such as "My Mother's Bible," further illustrate the degree to which those spiritual and gospel traditions gave rise to and continue to shape the broad genre of "country" music, the collection of uniquely American musical styles that has grown into another global, multibillion-dollar industry. The examples in the chapter demonstrate some of the original approaches for handling "The Book" in country music lyrics, in which bibles often are treated not simply as repositories of traditional wisdom and narrative but also as material objects replete with their own unique histories.

Not surprisingly, "The Book" also maintains a continued and imposing presence in almost every other American form of narrative production, showing the familiar patterns of diffusion, innovation, and inspiration. Biblical references abound in short stories, novels, plays, film features and shorts. Sometimes fleeting and subtle, sometimes extensive and explicit, the allusions serve different purposes and resonate with audiences in widely different ways.

The "antinomian strain" is especially pronounced in the American novel. Mark Twain once quipped about fellow novelist James Fenimore Cooper, that he saw "through a glass eye, darkly," suggesting that Cooper's novels never got the history or the writing quite right. In his deliberate mangling of Paul's statement in 1 Cor 13:12 ("Now we see in a mirror [glass] dimly, but then we will see face to face") Twain underscores what scholar Edwin Cady calls the "odd displacement of the Bible in major novels" of the nineteenth century (1983: 33). The pattern surfaces widely in North American novels well beyond that period. Narrative meets narrative – the biblical story serves as source and foundation in the American story – yet the reliance on the Bible is largely inverted. Scripture, invoked toward innovative ends, is constantly present in the texts yet appears in controlled, often veiled forms.

Despite the breadth and diversity of biblical references across American narrative traditions, we have opted to represent them through longer excerpts from two foundational novels emerging at critical moments in American cultural life. The first selection comes from *Moby Dick*, Herman Melville's 1851 epic sea adventure, while the second passage arises at the heart of James Baldwin's *Go Tell It on the Mountain*, written and released almost exactly a century later. Each work – undertaken at the middle of the nineteenth and twentieth centuries, respectively, amidst profound political, social, and economic change in the United States – reveals the similarly imaginative powers of two American literary giants intimately familiar with, deeply indebted to, but largely disaffected from the Bible of their religious upbringings.

Melville's and Baldwin's achievements stand as singular in many ways, yet their deep engagement with the Bible, at once both appreciative and unsympathetic, reverberates throughout the selections in this chapter and across the mixed, shifting terrain of the American cultural landscape. These days we can hear echoes across the United States of that ambivalence – that "antinomian strain" – every time players, young and old and engaged in a fierce game of *Rock Band*, hammer out their own inspired new version of "The Number of the Beast."

ART

EDWARD HICKS, *PEACABLE KINGDOM*

Edward Hicks (1780–1849) joined the Society of Friends as a young man. A coach, sign, and decorative painter, he became a minister in Pennsylvania. Realizing that painting provided a more secure means of supporting his family, he eventually left the ministry and spread his beliefs through his painting. This 1834 version of the painting is one of many he made over his lifetime, promoting a message of a peaceful and harmonious world. The background group is from Benjamin West's *Penn's Treaty with the Indians*, and the foreground depicts the vision of Isaiah 11:6–8. Some years before, Hicks' cousin, Elias Hicks, helped drive a schism in the Quakers between his own group, called Hicksites, and other Quakers.

Source: Reproduced by permission The National Gallery of Art.

Figure 5.1 Peacable Kingdom (1834)

HARRIET POWERS' BIBLE QUILT

Harriet Powers (1837–1910) was born into slavery. After Emancipation, she and her husband bought and worked a farm in Clarke County, Georgia. She displayed her quilt at the Athens Cotton Fair of 1886, and years later, hard times forced her to sell it for five dollars to a local artist, Jennie Smith. Unusual (for quilts) in its depiction of human figures, its eleven panels include biblical scenes such as Adam and Eve in the Garden, Jacob's dream, the crucifixion, and the Last Supper. Jennie Smith remarked on its boldness of style and "delicious" naivety, while contemporary historians have noted its resemblance to West African textiles.

Source: Reproduced by permission National Museum of American History, Smithsonian Institution.

Figure 5.2 Harriet Powers' quilt (1886)

EDMONIA LEWIS

Mary Edmonia Lewis (c.1843–c.1911), the child of a Chippewa mother and an Afro-Caribbean father, was orphaned young and raised by her mother's Chippewa family. She learned sculpture in the neo-classical style from Edward Augustus Brackett. Finding Europe more accepting of her as an artist of color, she settled permanently in Italy. She identified with the struggle of African Americans, producing a well-known sculpture, *Forever Free (Morning of Liberty)* in 1867–68. Scholar Lisa Farrington (2005: 53–60) explains that *Hagar* is semi-autobiographical. The biblical Hagar's expulsion parallels Lewis' own experiences of harassment in the United States, and self-generated exile to Europe, while the rounded limbs and face suggest she used herself as the model.

Source: Reproduced by permission, Smithsonian American Art Museum, Smithsonian Institution, gift of Delta Sigma Theta Sorority, Inc.

Figure 5.3
Hagar (1875)

BESSIE HARVEY

Bessie Harvey (1929–94) grew up among many siblings in Georgia in a life so difficult she said it would make *Roots* or *The Color Purple* look benign. Life did not improve when she married at fourteen and struggled to provide for her own children in Tennessee. She drew strength from nature and comfort from the natural world. From childhood she experienced intense images, or visions, which were the source of her art. Seeing God in art and nature, Harvey fashioned sculpture out of natural materials, especially wood, but also beads, hair, stone, and bits of metal. She made "little people," which, because she invested her works with spirit and power, others compared to "voodoo dolls." Harvey challenged the common misunderstandings (and misspelling) of Voudou upon which those assessments were based. Harvey insisted, the tradition "is a religion and it's not evil" (Farrington 2005: 248). In this work, Harvey combines familiar biblical images with the traditional notion in Voudou that the spirits possess, or "mount," capable individuals ("horses") as a regular means of communication and interaction with human communities.

Source: Reproduced by permission American Folk Art Museum, New York.

Figure 5.4
Black Horse of
Revelations (1991)

Tobi Kahn

Tobi Kahn is a painter and sculptor in New York. Drawing on themes of biblical reverence for the created world and attention to beauty, his work is predicated on the spiritual and healing potentialities of art. He has created ritual objects and sacred spaces, including a meditative space for the HealthCare Chaplaincy of New York. His 1999 Avoda project resulted in the participation of 9,000 college students in the creation of their own ceremonial objects for use in traditional and non-traditional ritual. The work *AHMA* (Shalom Bat chairs), created for the Shalom Bat ritual of a baby girl's welcome into the Jewish community, includes four chairs that call to mind the biblical matriarchs, Sarah, Rebecca, Rachel, and Leah.

Source: Reproduced by permission © 2009 Tobi Kahn.

Figure 5.5 AHMA (Shalom Bat chairs) (2009)

POETRY

Phillis Wheatley

Wheatley (c.1753–84) was bought as a slave at age seven or eight by John Wheatley of Boston and educated in the Bible, Latin, Greek, and literature. Her book of poems, published in 1772, includes an attestation of its authenticity, signed by a committee that included John Hancock and Thomas Hutchinson, the governor of Massachusetts. They had conducted an oral examination to satisfy any readers who doubted a young African slave could write verse in heroic couplets, sprinkled with references to the Bible and classical literature. With this volume of poems, Wheatley became the first African American published poet, and the second woman, after Anne Bradstreet, to be published in the colonies. This poem invites reflection on the Bible and slavery, and the spirit in which Wheatley writes.

Source: *Memoirs and Poems of Phillis Wheatley* (Boston: Geo. W. Light, 1834), 42; electronic edition, *Documenting the American South*, University Library, University of North Carolina at Chapel Hill, http://docsouth.unc.edu.

On being brought from AFRICA to AMERICA
'T WAS mercy brought me from my pagan land,
Taught my benighted soul to understand
That there's a God – that there's a Saviour too:
Once I redemption neither sought nor knew.
Some view our sable race with scornful eye –
"Their color is a diabolic dye."
Remember, Christians, Negroes black as Cain,
May be refined, and join the angelic train.

EMILY DICKINSON

Dickinson (1830–86), as a highly educated person of her time, would have known the King James Version of the Bible virtually by heart. She frequently invokes its language and imagery, but can be in creative opposition to it. In this poem, from around 1861, she draws on the story of the creation of Adam and Eve in Genesis, but also undermines Milton's interpretation of it in *Paradise Lost*. Against Milton's reading, which authorizes male dominance as divinely ordained, she indexes the vision of equality between two lovers as the nature of the true Eden (Wolff 1993: 129–31).

Source: *The Complete Poems of Emily Dickinson*, ed. Thomas H. Johnson (Boston: Little Brown, 1960) 112. Reproduced by permission of the publishers and the Trustees of Amherst College from THE POEMS OF EMILY DICKINSON, Thomas H. Johnson, ed., Cambridge, Mass. The Belknap Press and Harvard University Press, Copyright © 1951, 1955, 1979, 1983 by the President and Fellows of Harvard College.

246

Forever at His side to walk –
The smaller of the two!
Brain of His Brain –
Blood of His Blood –
Two lives – One Being – now –

Forever of His fate to taste –
If grief – the largest part –
If joy – to put my piece away
For that beloved Heart –

All life – to know each other –
Whom we can never learn –
And bye and bye – a Change –
Called Heaven –
Rapt Neighborhoods of Men –
Just finding out – what puzzled us –
Without the lexicon!

ROBERT LOWELL

Lowell (1917–77) came from a patrician New England background, as well as an extended family of distinguished poets that included James Russell Lowell and Amy Lowell. He was part of the New Criticism, a movement in mid-twentieth-century poetry that concentrated on the language and form of poetry, apart from the author's intention or reader's response. This poem is from the end of *Lord Weary's Castle* (1946), a volume which earned him a Pulitzer Prize in 1947. The poem, from the early stage of Lowell's career, coincides with a period after his conversion to Catholicism, and employs apocalyptic images culled from the Hebrew Bible and the New Testament to explore themes of constriction and liberation, hopelessness and possibility. It passes judgment on his native Boston, and by extension, American society, but also speaks to continuing divine presence.

Source: "Where the Rainbow Ends" from *Lord Weary's Castle*, copyright 1946 and renewed 1974 by Robert Lowell. Reprinted by permission of Houghton Mifflin Harcourt Publishing Company and Faber & Faber Ltd.

Where the Rainbow Ends

I saw the sky descending, black and white,
Not blue, on Boston where the winters wore
The skulls to jack-o'-lanterns on the slates,
And Hunger's skin-and-bone retrievers tore
The chickadee and shrike. The thorn tree waits
Its victim and tonight
The worms will eat the deadwood to the foot
Of Ararat: the scythers, Time and Death,
Helmed locusts, move upon the tree of breath;
The wild ingrafted olive and the root

Are withered, and a winter drifts to where
The Pepperpot, ironic rainbow, spans
Charles River and its scales of scorched-earth miles.
I saw my city in the Scales, the pans
Of judgment rising and descending. Piles
Of dead leaves char the air –
And I am a red arrow on this graph

Of Revelations. Every dove is sold.
The Chapel's sharp-shinned eagle shifts its hold
On serpent-Time, the rainbow's epitaph.

In Boston serpents whistle at the cold.
The victim climbs the altar steps and sings;
"Hosannah to the lion, lamb, and beast
Who fans the furnace-face of IS with wings:
I breathe the ether of my marriage feast."
At the high altar, gold
And a fair cloth. I kneel and the wings beat
My cheek. What can the dove of Jesus give
You now but wisdom, exile? Stand and live,
The dove has brought an olive branch to eat.

Samuel Menashe (1925–)

Samuel Menashe was born in New York city of Russian-Jewish parents, and fought in World War II in the Battle of the Bulge. His first poem was published in 1956 in the *Yale Review* and he attracted the attention of several British poets and critics. Recognition in the United States eluded him, however, until 2005, when he received the Poetry Foundation's first Neglected Masters Award. He has continued to write poetry for fifty years, while living in a Greenwich Village walk-up. His poetry is pithy, intense, and often joyful, and incorporates biblical images. Here two poems, the second untitled, evoke different episodes from the life of Moses.

Source: Samuel Menashe, *New and Selected Poems* (New York: The Library of America, 2005), 68, 71.

1
Reeds Rise from the Water

Rippling under my eyes
Bulrushes tuft the shore

At every instant I expect
What is hidden everywhere

2

Stone would be water
But it cannot undo
Its own hardness
Rocks might run
Wild as torrents
Plunged upon the sky
By cliffs none climb

Who makes fountains
Spring from flint
Who dares tell
One thirsting
There's a well

MUSICAL LYRIC

"THERE IS A BALM IN GILEAD"

African American spirituals stand as a critical and enduring sphere of
American cultural production and also as one of the most overtly biblical.
Central to the spiritual tradition is the continual reinvention of meaning
of the Bible's passages and allusions. The classic spiritual, "There is a
Balm in Gilead," exemplifies that interpretive tradition. The title draws
on the references in the Book of Jeremiah (8:22; 46:11 KJV) to the desire
for a magic elixir to heal the Hebrews' wounds. In the spiritual, that
Hebrew longing – inherited now by American slaves – finds redemption
in the New Testament's pronouncement of the Holy Spirit, embodied in
"your friend" Jesus, "to heal the sin-sick soul." The song probably dates
to the eighteenth century, even if the first documented version of the song
in its familiar form did not appear until the 1850s. Numerous American
cultural artifacts over the centuries invoke the passages from Jeremiah
(e.g. folk-rocker Rickie Lee Jones's 2009 album *Balm in Gilead*). Still, many
of the references – including Lanford Wilson's well-known 1965 play of
the same name – draw as much on "There is a Balm in Gilead" as on the
original biblical text, contributing to this particular spiritual's own lasting
legacy.

Source: traditional.

There is a balm in Gilead
To make the wounded whole
There is a balm in Gilead
To heal the sin-sick soul

Sometimes I feel discouraged
And think my work's in vain
But then the Holy Spirit
Revives my soul again

Don't ever feel discouraged
For Jesus is your friend
And if you lack of knowledge
He'll ne'er refuse to lend

If you cannot preach like Peter
If you cannot pray like Paul
You can tell the love of Jesus
And say, "He died for all".

"MY MOTHER'S BIBLE"

Charlie Tillman's classic tune, written in 1893 with lyrics by the preacher M. B. Williams, was not the first of the southern "gospel hymns" to invoke a mother's Bible and was far from the last. A popular song of the 1840s by the Hutchinson Family carried the same title, and mother's Bibles remained a common subject in country music throughout the first half of the twentieth century. Nevertheless, those later songs necessarily depended on Tillman's version. Not only did it turn up in various song-book collections and hymnals, but in 1924 the fiddler John Carson made Tillman's "My Mother's Bible" the first recorded Bible song in country music. Moreover, Williams' lyric – linking the memory of a "worn and faded" copy of the "Blessed Book" with the nostalgia for a dear mother's presence – codified the familiar country music theme.

Source: Broadman Press, *The American Hymnal* (Nashville, TN: Broadman Press, 1933), #485.

There's a dear and precious book,
Though it's worn and faded now,
Which recalls those happy days of long ago.
When I stood at mother's knee,
With her hand upon my brow,
And I heard her voice in gentle tones and low.

Refrain:
Blessed Book, precious book,
On thy dear old tear stained leaves I love to look;
Thou art sweeter day by day,
As I walk the narrow way
That leads at last to that bright home above.

Then she read the stories o'er
Of those mighty men of old,
Of Joseph and of Daniel and their trials,
Of little David bold,
Who became a king at last,
Of Satan and his many wicked wiles.
(Refrain)

Then she read of Jesus' love,
As He blessed the children dear,

How He suffered, bled and died upon the tree;
Of His heavy load of care,
Then she dried my flowing tears
With her kisses as she said it was for me.
(Refrain)

Well, those days are past and gone,
But their memory lingers still
And the dear old Book each day has been my guide;
And I seek to do His will,
As my mother taught me then,
And ever in my heart His Words abide.
(Refrain)

"THE GREATEST STORY EVER TOLD"

Many commentators, including many self-identifying "Deadheads," insist that the unique culture surrounding the renowned psychedelic band the Grateful Dead constitutes its own unique religion. In any case, at least one fact is certain: the band's music is filled with biblical references ranging from subtle to highly explicit. Among the most direct (and playful) examples is "The Greatest Story Ever Told," a tune first performed in 1971 and recorded in 1972. Robert Hunter, the band's longtime lyricist who set the words of the song to guitarist Bob Weir's music, has emphasized regularly his dependence on the Bible as "a great and enduring work of art" that provides "a rich source of symbol and reference, as [do] Shakespeare, Mother Goose, the famous poets everybody used to know, lyrics of popular songs, etc." (Miller 2006). In this case, Hunter and Weir mimic the title of the popular 1965 cinematic portrayal of Jesus' life (based on Fulton Ousler's well-known 1949 book of the same name), but they create a very different narrative by placing other familiar biblical characters in new – and somewhat more contemporary – situations.

Source: *The Complete Annotated Grateful Dead Lyrics*, eds. Alan Trist and David Dodd (New York: Free Press, 2007), 142–4. © Ice Nine Publishing.

Moses came riding up on a guitar
His spurs were a-jingling, the door was ajar
His buckle was silver, his manner was bold
I asked him to come on in out of the cold
His brain was boiling, his reason was spent
He said if nothing was borrowed then nothing was lent
I asked him for mercy, he gave me a gun
Said, 'Now n'again these things just got to be done'

Abraham and Isaac
sitting on a fence
'You'd get right to work

if you had any sense
Y'know the one thing we need
is a left-hand monkey wrench'

Gideon come in with his eyes on the floor
Says: 'Y'ain't got a hinge, you can't close the door'
Moses stood up a full six foot ten
Says: 'You can't close the door when the wall's caved in'
I asked him for water, he poured me some wine
We finished the bottle then broke into mine
You get what you come for, you're ready to go
It's one in ten thousand just come for the show

Abraham and Isaac
Digging on a well
Mama come quick
with the water witch spell
Cool clear water
where you can't never tell

"HALLELUJAH"

The appearances in popular culture of "Hallelujah" have been frequent and evolving since the Canadian-born singer-songwriter Leonard Cohen first wrote and recorded the song in 1984. In the original version, Cohen mined episodes in the Hebrew scriptures involving David and Saul and then David and Bathsheba (1, 2 Samuel) as well as Samson and Delilah (Judges) to create an image of a doubtful narrator brought, through awe, to utter "Hallelujah" ("Praise God!"). In 1988 Cohen introduced a different, less biblical set of lyrics, and since the mid-1980s the song has been widely covered in a range of styles by a multitude of artists (e.g. John Cale, Bob Dylan, Allison Crowe, k.d. lang, Willie Nelson) who often mix Cohen's versions or introduce their own changes. Nevertheless, the original lyrics remain the most familiar, owing to Jeff Buckley's well-known cover, Rufus Wainwright's version on the multi-platinum soundtrack to the 2001 film *Shrek*, and various performances over the years on the top-rated television show *American Idol*.

Now, I've heard there was a secret chord
That David played and it pleased the Lord
But you don't really care for music, do you?
It goes like this: the fourth, the fifth
The minor fall, the major lift
The baffled king composing Hallelujah

Hallelujah, Hallelujah
Hallelujah, Hallelujah

Your faith was strong but you needed proof
You saw her bathing on the roof
Her beauty and the moonlight overthrew you
She tied you to a kitchen chair
She broke your throne and she cut your hair
And from your lips she drew the Hallelujah

Hallelujah, Hallelujah
Hallelujah, Hallelujah

You say I took the name in vain
I don't even know the name
But if I did, well really, what's it to you?
There's a blaze of light in every word
It doesn't matter which you heard
The holy or the broken Hallelujah

Hallelujah, Hallelujah
Hallelujah, Hallelujah

I did my best, it wasn't much
I couldn't feel, so I tried to touch
I've told the truth, I didn't come to fool you
And even though it all went wrong
I'll stand before the Lord of Song
With nothing on my tongue but Hallelujah

Hallelujah, Hallelujah
Hallelujah, Hallelujah
Hallelujah, Hallelujah
Hallelujah, Hallelujah
Hallelujah, Hallelujah
Hallelujah, Hallelujah
Hallelujah, Hallelujah
Hallelujah, Hallelujah
Hallelujah

LAURYN HILL, "FORGIVE THEM FATHER"

On her Grammy-winning and best-selling 1998 album, *The Miseducation of Lauryn Hill*, the hip-hop artist perpetuates a practice established with her original band, The Fugees. Hill includes a plethora of biblical references (including frequent invocations of Zion, which is also the name of her son). In its title and from its first lines, the song "Forgive Them Father" most explicitly alludes to (and re-imagines) passages from the Bible. The published liner notes to the song identify it as an interpretation of Bob Marley's "Concrete Jungle." Hill's stated dependence on Marley's 1973 song – alongside invocations of figures like the ancient Ethiopian King Menelik – speaks to the deep and lasting influence through reggae of Rastafari's intricate biblical hermeneutics on the music and lyrics of Hill and of many other popular artists.

Source: "Forgive Them Father." Lyrics by Lauryn Hill. Copyright 1998 Sony/ATV Music Publishing LLC, Obverse Creation Music. All rights administered by Sony/ATV Music Publishing. All rights reserved. Used by permission.

Forgive us our trespasses as we forgive those that trespass against us
Although them again we will never, never, never trust

Dem noh know weh dem do, dig out yuh yei while dem sticking like glue,
Fling, skin, grin while dem plotting fah you,
True, Ah Who???

Forgive them father for they know not what they do
Forgive them father for they know not what they do

Beware the false motives of others
Be careful of those who pretend to be brothers
And you never suppose it's those who are closest to you, to you
They say all the right things to gain their position
Then use your kindness as their ammunition
To shoot you down in the name of ambition, they do

Forgive them father for they know not what they do
Forgive them father for they know not what they do

Why every Indian wanna be the chief?
Feed a man 'til he's full and he still want beef
Give me grief, try to tief off my piece
Why for you to increase, I must decrease?
If I treat you kindly does it mean that I'm weak?
You hear me speak and think I won't take it to the streets
I know enough cats that don't turn the other cheek
But I try to keep it civilized like Menelik
And other African czars observing stars with war scars
Get yours in this capitalistic system
So many caught or got bought you can't list them
How you gonna idolize the missing?
To survive is to stay alive in the face of opposition
Even when they comin' gunnin'

I stand position
L's known the mission since conception
Let's free the people from deception
If you looking for the answers
Then you gotta ask the questions
And when I let go, my voice echoes through the ghetto
Sick of men trying to pull strings like Geppetto
Why black people always be the ones to settle
March through these streets like Soweto

Like Cain and Abel, Caesar and Brutus, Jesus and Judas,
Backstabbers do this

Forgive them father for they know not what they do
Forgive them father for they know not what they do

It took me a little while to discover
Wolves in sheep coats who pretend to be lovers
Men who lack conscience will even lie to themselves, to themselves
A friend once said, and I found to be true
That everyday people, they lie to God too
So what makes you think, that they won't lie to you

Forgive them father for they know not what they do
Forgive them, forgive them
Forgive them father for they know not what they do
Forgive them, forgive them

Gwan like dem love while dem rip yuh to shreds,
Trample pon yuh heart and lef yuh fi dead,
Dem a yuh fren who yuh depen pon from way back when,
But if yuh gi dem yuh back den yuh mus meet yuh end,
Dem noh know wey dem do,
Dem no know, dem no know, dem no know,
Dem no know, dem no know wey dem do

THE NOVEL

HERMAN MELVILLE, SELECTION FROM *MOBY DICK*

The Bible is foundational to Melville's classic, *Moby Dick* (1851), an American original of sweeping grandeur. From a deeply religious, Dutch Reformed family, Melville (1819–91) grew up steeped in study of scripture. During the extensive seafaring travels of his early twenties, Melville began explicitly and radically to question the fundamental tenets of Christianity and the Bible. In the prefatory "excerpts" – even before the famous opening line ("Call me Ishmael") that introduces the story's narrator and the first of many biblically named characters – *Moby Dick* relentlessly invokes and reflects upon the Bible in content as well as theme, through sustained discussion as well as passing allusion. The following excerpt appears early in the narrative as the whaling ship *Pequod* sets out on its epic voyage. The section presents the text and context of the sermon delivered by an influential minister (prefaced with an adaptation of Psalm 18). In his discourse, Father Mapple discusses the biblical tale of the prophet Jonah, swallowed by a whale for disobeying God. Of course, Jonah's story foreshadows the subsequent narrative, but Father Mapple's exegesis also lays out the biblically based moral framework with which each of the characters – along with every one of Melville's readers – is forced to engage.

Source: Herman Melville, *Moby Dick; or, The Whale* [1851], 35–41. See www.gutenberg.org.

Chapter IX – The Sermon

Father Mapple rose, and in a mild voice of unassuming authority ordered the scattered people to condense. "Starboard gangway, there! side away to larboard – larboard gangway to starboard! Midships! midships!"

There was a low rumbling of heavy sea-boots among the benches, and a still slighter shuffling of women's shoes, and all was quiet again, and every eye on the preacher.

He paused a little; then kneeling in the pulpit's bows, folded his large brown hands across his chest, uplifted his closed eyes, and offered a prayer so deeply devout that he seemed kneeling and praying at the bottom of the sea.

This ended, in prolonged solemn tones, like the continual tolling of a bell in a ship that is foundering at sea in a fog – in such tones he commenced reading the following hymn; but changing his manner towards the concluding stanzas, burst forth with a pealing exultation and joy –

> "The ribs and terrors in the whale,
> Arched over me a dismal gloom,
> While all God's sun-lit waves rolled by,
> And lift me deepening down to doom.
>
> "I saw the opening maw of hell,
> With endless pains and sorrows there;
> Which none but they that feel can tell –
> Oh, I was plunging to despair.
>
> "In black distress, I called my God,
> When I could scarce believe him mine,
> He bowed his ear to my complaints –
> No more the whale did me confine.

"With speed he flew to my relief,
As on a radiant dolphin borne;
Awful, yet bright, as lightning shone
The face of my Deliverer God.

"My song for ever shall record
That terrible, that joyful hour;
I give the glory to my God,
His all the mercy and the power."

Nearly all joined in singing this hymn, which swelled high above the howling of the storm. A brief pause ensued; the preacher slowly turned over the leaves of the Bible, and at last, folding his hand down upon the proper page, said: "Beloved shipmates, clinch the last verse of the first chapter of Jonah – 'And God had prepared a great fish to swallow up Jonah.'

"Shipmates, this book, containing only four chapters – four yarns – is one of the smallest strands in the mighty cable of the Scriptures. Yet what depths of the soul does Jonah's deep sealine sound! what a pregnant lesson to us is this prophet! What a noble thing is that canticle in the fish's belly! How billow-like and boisterously grand! We feel the floods surging over us; we sound with him to the kelpy bottom of the waters; sea-weed and all the slime of the sea is about us! But what is this lesson that the book of Jonah teaches? Shipmates, it is a two-stranded lesson; a lesson to us all as sinful men, and a lesson to me as a pilot of the living God. As sinful men, it is a lesson to us all, because it is a story of the sin, hard-heartedness, suddenly awakened fears, the swift punishment, repentance, prayers, and finally the deliverance and joy of Jonah. As with all sinners among men, the sin of this son of Amittai was in his wilful disobedience of the command of God – never mind now what that command was, or how conveyed – which he found a hard command. But all the things that God would have us do are hard for us to do – remember that – and hence, he oftener commands us than endeavors to persuade. And if we obey God, we must disobey ourselves; and it is in this disobeying ourselves, wherein the hardness of obeying God consists.

"With this sin of disobedience in him, Jonah still further flouts at God, by seeking to flee from Him. He thinks that a ship made by men, will carry him into countries where God does not reign, but only the Captains of this earth. He skulks about the wharves of Joppa, and seeks a ship that's bound for Tarshish. There lurks, perhaps, a hitherto unheeded meaning here. By all accounts Tarshish could have been no other city than the modern Cadiz. That's the opinion of learned men. And where is Cadiz, shipmates? Cadiz is in Spain; as far by water, from Joppa, as Jonah could possibly have sailed in those ancient days, when the Atlantic was an almost unknown sea. Because Joppa, the modern Jaffa, shipmates, is on the most easterly coast of the Mediterranean, the Syrian; and Tarshish or Cadiz more than two thousand miles to the westward from that, just outside the Straits of Gibraltar. See ye not then, shipmates, that Jonah sought to flee world-wide from

God? Miserable man! Oh! most contemptible and worthy of all scorn; with slouched hat and guilty eye, skulking from his God; prowling among the shipping like a vile burglar hastening to cross the seas. So disordered, self-condemning is his look, that had there been policemen in those days, Jonah, on the mere suspicion of something wrong, had been arrested ere he touched a deck. How plainly he's a fugitive! no baggage, not a hat-box, valise, or carpet-bag, – no friends accompany him to the wharf with their adieux. At last, after much dodging search, he finds the Tarshish ship receiving the last items of her cargo; and as he steps on board to see its Captain in the cabin, all the sailors for the moment desist from hoisting in the goods, to mark the stranger's evil eye. Jonah sees this; but in vain he tries to look all ease and confidence; in vain essays his wretched smile. Strong intuitions of the man assure the mariners he can be no innocent. In their gamesome but still serious way, one whispers to the other – 'Jack, he's robbed a widow;' or, 'Joe, do you mark him; he's a bigamist;' or, 'Harry lad, I guess he's the adulterer that broke jail in old Gomorrah, or belike, one of the missing murderers from Sodom.' Another runs to read the bill that's stuck against the spile upon the wharf to which the ship is moored, offering five hundred gold coins for the apprehension of a parricide, and containing a description of his person. He reads, and looks from Jonah to the bill; while all his sympathetic shipmates now crowd round Jonah, prepared to lay their hands upon him. Frighted Jonah trembles, and summoning all his boldness to his face, only looks so much the more a coward. He will not confess himself suspected; but that itself is strong suspicion. So he makes the best of it; and when the sailors find him not to be the man that is advertised, they let him pass, and he descends into the cabin.

"'Who's there?' cries the Captain at his busy desk, hurriedly making out his papers for the Customs – 'Who's there?' Oh! how that harmless question mangles Jonah! For the instant he almost turns to flee again. But he rallies. 'I seek a passage in this ship to Tarshish; how soon sail ye, sir?' Thus far the busy captain had not looked up to Jonah, though the man now stands before him; but no sooner does he hear that hollow voice, than he darts a scrutinizing glance. 'We sail with the next coming tide,' at last he slowly answered, still intently eyeing him. 'No sooner, sir?' – 'Soon enough for any honest man that goes a passenger.' Ha! Jonah, that's another stab. But he swiftly calls away the Captain from that scent. 'I'll sail with ye,' – he says, – 'the passage money, how much is that, – I'll pay now.' For it is particularly written, shipmates, as if it were a thing not to be overlooked in this history, 'that he paid the fare thereof' ere the craft did sail. And taken with the context, this is full of meaning.

"Now Jonah's Captain, shipmates, was one whose discernment detects crime in any, but whose cupidity exposes it only in the penniless. In this world, shipmates, sin that pays its way can travel freely, and without a passport; whereas Virtue, if a pauper, is stopped at all frontiers. So Jonah's Captain prepares to test the length of Jonah's purse, ere he judge him openly. He charges him thrice the usual sum; and it's assented to. Then the Captain knows that Jonah is a fugitive; but at the same time resolves to help a flight that paves its rear with gold. Yet when Jonah fairly takes out his purse, prudent suspicions still molest the Captain. He rings every coin to find a counterfeit. Not a forger, any way, he mutters; and Jonah is put down for his passage. 'Point out my state-room, Sir,' says Jonah now. 'I'm travel-weary; I need sleep.' 'Thou look'st like it,' says the Captain, 'there's thy room.' Jonah enters, and would lock the door, but the lock contains no key. Hearing him foolishly fumbling there, the Captain laughs lowly to himself, and mutters something about the doors of convicts' cells being never allowed to be locked within. All dressed and dusty as he is, Jonah throws himself into his berth, and finds the little state-room ceiling almost resting on his forehead. The air is close, and Jonah gasps. then, in that contracted hole, sunk, too, beneath the ship's water-line, Jonah feels the heralding presentiment of that stifling hour, when the whale shall hold him in the smallest of his bowel's wards.

"Screwed at its axis against the side, a swinging lamp slightly oscillates in Jonah's room; and the ship, heeling over towards the wharf with the weight of the last bales received, the lamp, flame and all, though in slight motion, still maintains a permanent obliquity with reference to the room; though, in truth, infallibly straight itself, it but made obvious the false, lying levels among which it hung. The lamp alarms and frightens Jonah; as lying in his berth his tormented eyes roll round the place, and this thus far successful fugitive finds no refuge for his restless glance. But that contradiction in the lamp more and more appalls him. The floor, the ceiling, and the side, are all awry. 'Oh! so my conscience hangs in me!' he groans, 'straight upward, so it burns; but the chambers of my soul are all in crookedness!'

"Like one who after a night of drunken revelry hies to his bed, still reeling, but with conscience yet pricking him, as the plungings of the Roman race-horse but so much the more strike his steel tags into him; as one who in that miserable plight still turns and turns in giddy anguish, praying God for annihilation until the fit be passed; and at last amid the whirl of woe he feels, a deep stupor steals over him, as over the man who bleeds to death, for conscience is the wound, and there's naught to staunch it; so, after sore wrestlings in his berth, Jonah's prodigy of ponderous misery drags him drowning down to sleep.

"And now the time of tide has come; the ship casts off her cables; and from the deserted wharf the uncheered ship for Tarshish, all careening, glides to sea. That ship, my friends, was the first of recorded smugglers! the contraband was Jonah. But the sea rebels; he will not bear the wicked burden. A dreadful storm comes on, the ship is like to break. But now when the boatswain calls all hands to lighten her; when boxes, bales, and jars are clattering overboard; when the wind is shrieking, and the men are yelling, and every plank thunders with trampling feet right over Jonah's head; in all this raging tumult, Jonah sleeps his hideous sleep. He sees no black sky and raging sea, feels not the reeling timbers, and little hears he or heeds he the far rush of the mighty whale, which even now with open mouth is cleaving the seas after him. Aye, shipmates, Jonah was gone down into the sides of the ship – a berth in the cabin as I have taken it, and was fast asleep. But the frightened master comes to him, and shrieks in his dead ear, 'What meanest thou, O sleeper! arise!' Startled from his lethargy by that direful cry, Jonah staggers to his feet, and stumbling to the deck, grasps a shroud, to look out upon the sea. But at that moment he is sprung upon by a panther billow leaping over the bulwarks. Wave after wave thus leaps into the ship, and finding no speedy vent runs roaring fore and aft, till the mariners come nigh to drowning while yet afloat. And ever, as the white moon shows her affrighted face from the steep gullies in the blackness overhead, aghast Jonah sees the rearing bowsprit pointing high upward, but soon beat downward again towards the tormented deep.

"Terrors upon terrors run shouting through his soul. In all his cringing attitudes, the God-fugitive is now too plainly known. The sailors mark him; more and more certain grow their suspicions of him, and at last, fully to test the truth, by referring the whole matter to high Heaven, they fall to casting lots, to see for whose cause this great tempest was upon them. The lot is Jonah's; that discovered, then how furiously they mob him with their questions. 'What is thine occupation? whence comest thou? thy country? what people?' but mark now, my shipmates, the behavior of poor Jonah. The eager mariners but ask him who he is, and where from; whereas, they not only receive an answer to those questions, but likewise another answer to a question not put by them, but the unsolicited answer is forced from Jonah by the hard hand of God that is upon him.

"'I am a Hebrew,' he cries – and then – 'I fear the Lord the God of Heaven who hath made the sea and the dry land!' Fear him, O Jonah? Aye, well mightest thou fear the Lord God then! Straightway, he now goes on to make a full confession; whereupon the mariners became more and more appalled, but still are pitiful. For when Jonah, not yet supplicating God for mercy, since he but too well knew the darkness of his deserts, – when wretched Jonah cries out to them to take him and cast him forth into the sea, for he knew that for his sake this great tempest was upon them; they mercifully turn from him, and seek by other means to save the ship. But all in vain; the indignant gale howls louder; then, with one hand raised invokingly to God, with the other they not unreluctantly lay hold of Jonah.

"And now behold Jonah taken up as an anchor and dropped into the sea; when instantly an oily calmness floats out from the east, and the sea is still, as Jonah carries down the gale with him, leaving smooth water behind. He goes down in the whirling heart of such a masterless commotion that he scarce heeds the moment when he drops seething into the yawning jaws awaiting him; and the whale shoots-to all his ivory teeth, like so many white bolts, upon his prison. Then Jonah prayed unto the Lord out of the fish's belly. But observe this prayer and learn a weighty lesson. For sinful as he is, Jonah does not weep and wail for direct deliverance. He feels that his dreadful punishment is just. He leaves all his deliverance to God, contenting himself with this, that spite of all his pains and pangs, he will still look towards His holy temple. And here, shipmates, is true and faithful repentance; not clamorous for pardon, but grateful for punishment. And how pleasing to God was this conduct in Jonah, is shown in the eventual deliverance of him from the sea and the whale. Shipmates, I do not place Jonah before you to be copied for his sin but I do place him before you as a model for repentance. Sin not; but if you do, take heed to repent of it like Jonah."

While he was speaking these words, the howling of the shrieking, slanting storm without seemed to add new power to the preacher, who, when describing Jonah's sea-storm, seemed tossed by a storm himself. His deep chest heaved as with a ground-swell; his tossed arms seemed the warring elements at work; and the thunders that rolled away from off his swarthy brow, and the light leaping from his eye, made all his simple hearers look on him with a quick fear that was strange to them.

There now came a lull in his look, as he silently turned over the leaves of the Book once more; and, at last, standing motionless, with closed eyes, for the moment, seemed communing with God and himself.

But again he leaned over towards the people, and bowing his head lowly, with an aspect of the deepest yet manliest humility, he spake these words:

"Shipmates, God has laid but one hand upon you; both his hands press upon me. I have read ye by what murky light may be mine the lesson that Jonah teaches to all sinners; and therefore to ye, and still more to me, for I am a greater sinner than ye. And now how gladly would I come down from this mast-head and sit on the hatches there where you sit, and listen as you listen, while some one of you reads me that other and more awful lesson which Jonah teaches to me as a pilot of the living God. How being an anointed pilot-prophet, or speaker of true things, and bidden by the Lord to sound those unwelcome truths in the ears of a wicked Nineveh, Jonah, appalled at the hostility he should raise, fled from his mission, and sought to escape his duty and his God by taking ship at Joppa. But God is everywhere; Tarshish he never reached. As we have seen, God came upon him in the whale, and swallowed him down to living gulfs of doom, and with swift slantings tore him along 'into the midst of the seas,' where the eddying depths sucked him ten thousand fathoms down, and 'the weeds were wrapped about his head,' and all the watery world of woe bowled over him. Yet even then beyond the reach of any plummet – 'out of the belly of hell' – when the whale grounded upon the ocean's utmost bones, even then, God heard the engulphed, repenting prophet when he cried. Then God spake unto the fish; and from the shuddering cold and blackness of the sea, the whale came breeching up towards the warm and pleasant sun, and all the delights of air and earth; and 'vomited out Jonah upon the dry land;' when the word of the Lord came a second time; and Jonah, bruised and beaten – his ears, like two sea-shells, still multitudinously murmuring of the ocean – Jonah did the Almighty's bidding. And what was that, shipmates? To preach the Truth to the face of Falsehood! That was it!

"This, shipmates, this is that other lesson; and woe to that pilot of the living God who slights it. Woe to him whom this world charms from Gospel duty! Woe to him who seeks to pour oil upon the waters when God has brewed them into a gale! Woe to him who seeks to please rather than to appal! Woe to him whose good name is more to him than goodness! Woe to him who, in this world, courts not dishonor! Woe to him who would not be true, even though to be false were salvation! Yea, woe to him who, as the great Pilot Paul has it, while preaching to others is himself a castaway!"

He drooped and fell away from himself for a moment; then lifting his face to them again, showed a deep joy in his eyes, as he cried out with a heavenly enthusiasm, – "But oh! shipmates! on the starboard hand of every woe, there is a sure delight; and higher the top of that delight, than the bottom of the woe is deep. Is not the main-truck higher than the kelson is low? Delight is to him – a far, far upward, and inward delight – who against the proud gods and commodores of this earth, ever stands forth his own inexorable self. Delight is to him whose strong arms yet support him, when the ship of this base treacherous world has gone down beneath him. Delight is to him, who gives no quarter in the truth, and kills, burns, and destroys all sin though he pluck it out from under the robes of Senators and Judges. Delight, – top-gallant delight is to him, who acknowledges no law or lord, but the Lord his God, and is only a patriot to heaven. Delight is to him, whom all the waves of the billows of the seas of the boisterous mob can never shake from this sure Keel of the Ages. And eternal delight and deliciousness will be his, who coming to lay him down, can say with his final breath – O Father! – chiefly known to me by Thy rod – mortal or immortal, here I die. I have striven to be Thine, more than to be this world's, or mine own. Yet this is nothing; I leave eternity to Thee; for what is man that he should live out the lifetime of his God?"

He said no more, but slowly waving a benediction, covered his face with his hands, and so remained kneeling, till all the people had departed, and he was left alone in the place.

JAMES BALDWIN, SELECTION FROM *GO TELL IT ON THE MOUNTAIN*

Almost exactly a century after the publication of Melville's *Moby Dick*, James Baldwin (1924–87) produced another classic – and original American – novel by drawing heavily on the Bible in both content and theme. Like Melville, Baldwin drew extensively on scripture as part of his own – and, by extension, his readers' – process of critical engagement with religion in general and Christian traditions in particular. The novel's title, derived from the traditional African American spiritual that refers most directly to Moses' communion with God on Mount Sinai during the Israelite exodus, immediately reveals the central presence of the Bible in the novel. Again like Melville, Baldwin's upbringing was deeply religious. As an adolescent, he made a name for himself as fiery young preacher in the rapidly expanding African American "holiness" communities of late 1930s Harlem. That personal experience served as the basis for *Go Tell It on the Mountain* (1953), which recounts a 24-hour period – bridging "the Devil's Day" (Saturday) and "the Lord's Day" (Sunday) – in the life of a Pentecostal Harlem family at the height of racial segregation in the early 1930s. The narration of John – the family's adolescent second son

– frames the novel, but the story revolves around the "prayers" – the personal reflections and flashbacks – of the family's adults. At the very center of the story is each family member's relationship with Gabriel – the strict, religious father who works as the community's head deacon – as well as Gabriel's own conflicted history. In the excerpt below, taken from the section "Gabriel's Prayer," Gabriel remembers a momentous experience of his early adulthood as he struggled to transform himself from "sinner" to "saint." As in the excerpt above from *Moby Dick*, a sermon – full of biblical exegesis – sets the theological territory through which all the characters – and readers – must pass as they search for their own moral grounding.

Source: From *Go Tell It on the Mountain* by James Baldwin, copyright 1952, 1953 by James Baldwin. Used by permission of Doubleday, a division of Random House, Inc.

Now I been introduced
To the Father and the Son,
And I ain't
No stranger now.

When Florence cried, Gabriel was moving outward in fiery darkness, talking to the Lord. Her cry came to him from afar, as from unimaginable depths; and it was not his sister's cry he heard, but the cry of a sinner when he is taken in his sin. This was the cry he had heard so many days and nights, before so many altars, and he cried tonight, as he had cried before: "Have your way, Lord! Have your way!"

There was silence in the church … But now in this waiting, burdened silence it seemed that all flesh waited – paused, transfixed by something in the middle of the air – for the quickening power.

This silence, continuing like a corridor, carried Gabriel back to the silence that had preceded his birth in Christ. Like a birth indeed, all that had come before this moment was wrapped in darkness, lay at the bottom of the sea of forgetfulness, and was not now counted against him, but was related only to that blind, and doomed, and stinking corruption he had been before he was redeemed.

The silence was the silence of the early morning, and he was returning from the harlot's house. Yet all around him were the sounds of the morning: of birds, invisible, praising God; of crickets in the vines, frogs in the swamp, or dogs miles away and close at hand, roosters on the porch. The sun was not yet half awake; only the utmost tops of the trees had begun to tremble at his turning; and the mist moved sullenly, before Gabriel and all around him, falling back before the light that rules by day. Later, he said of that morning that his sin was on him; then he knew only that he carried a burden and that he longed to lay it down. This burden was heavier than the heaviest mountain and he carried it in his heart. With each step that he took, his burden grew heavier, and his breath became slow and harsh, and, of a sudden, cold sweat stood out on his brow and drenched his back.

... For he desired in his soul, with fear and trembling, all the glories that his mother prayed he should find. Yes, he wanted power – he wanted to know himself to be the Lord's anointed, His well-beloved, and worthy, nearly, of that snow-white dove which had been sent down from Heaven to testify that Jesus was the Son of God ...

Yes (walking homeward through the fleeting mist, with the cold sweat standing on his brow), yet, in vanity and the pride of conquest, he thought of her, of her smell, the heat of her body beneath his hands, of her voice, and her tongue, like the tongue of a cat, and her teeth, and her swelling breasts, and how she moved for him, and held him, and labored with him, and how they fell, trembling and groaning, and locked together, into the world again ... Then, in a moment, there was silence, only silence, everywhere – the very birds had ceased to sing, and no dogs barked, and no rooster crowed for day. And he felt that this silence was God's judgment; that all creation had been stilled before the just and awful wrath of God, and waited now to see the sinner – *he* was the sinner – cut down and banished from the presence of the Lord. And he touched the tree, hardly knowing that he touched it, out of an impulse to be hidden; and then he cried: "Oh, Lord, have mercy! Oh, Lord, have mercy on me!" ...

"Then," he testified, "I heard my mother singing. She was a-singing for me, ... like she knew if she just called Him, the Lord would come. ... Then I praised God, Who had brought me out of Egypt and set my feet on the solid rock." When at last he lifted up his eyes he saw a new Heaven and a new earth; and he heard a new sound of singing, for a sinner had come home.

And this was the beginning of his life as a man. He was just past twenty-one; the century was not yet one year old. He moved into town, in the room that awaited him at the top of the house in which he worked, and he began to preach ...

It was during this [time] that the town was subjected to a monster revival meeting. Evangelists from all the surrounding counties, from as far south as Florida and as far north as Chicago, came together in one place to break the bread of life. It was called the Twenty-Four Elders Revival Meeting, and it was the great occasion of that summer. For there were twenty-four of them, each one given his night to preach – to shine, as it were, before men, and to glorify his Heavenly Father. Of these twenty-four, all of them men of great experience and power, and some of them men of great fame, Gabriel, to his astonished pride, was asked to be one. This was a great, a heavy honor for one so young in the faith, and in years – who had but only yesterday been lying, vomit-covered, in the gutters of sin – and Gabriel felt his heart shake with fear as his invitation came to him. Yet he felt that it was the hand of God that had called him out so early to prove himself before such might men.

He was to preach on the twelfth night. ... When, at last, the Scripture lesson read, the testimonies in, the songs sung, the collection taken up, he was introduced – by the elder who had preached the night before – and found himself on his feet, moving toward the pulpit where the great Bible awaited him, and over that sheer drop the murmuring congregation, he felt a giddy terror that he stood so high, and with this, immediately, a pride and joy unspeakable that God had placed him there.

He did not begin with a "shout" song, or with fiery testimony, but in a dry, matter-of-fact voice, which trembled only a little, asked them to look with him at the sixth chapter of Isaiah, and the fifth verse; and he asked [his wife] Deborah to read it aloud for him.

And she read, in a voice unaccustomedly strong: "'Then said I, Woe is me! for I am undone; because I am a man of unclean lips, and I dwell in the midst of a people of unclean lips: for mine eyes have seen the King, the Lord of hosts.'"

Silence filled the lodge hall after she had read this sentence. For a moment Gabriel was terrified by the eyes on him, and by the elders at his back, and could not think how to go on. Then he looked at Deborah, and began.

These words had been uttered by the prophet Isaiah, who had been called the Eagle-eyed because he had looked down the dark centuries and foreseen the birth of Christ. It was Isaiah also who had prophesied that a man should be a hiding-place from the wind and tempest, Isaiah who had described the way of holiness, saying that the parched ground should become a pool, and the thirsty lands springs of water: the very desert should rejoice, and blossom as the rose. It was Isaiah who had prophesied, saying: "Unto us a child is born, unto us a son is given; and the government shall be upon His shoulder." This was a man whom God had raised in righteousness, whom God had chosen to do many might works, yet this man, beholding the vision of God's glory, had cried out: "Woe is me!"

"Yes!" cried a woman. *"Tell it!"*

"There is a lesson for all of us in this cry of Isaiah's, a meaning for us all, a hard saying. If we have never cried this cry then we have never known salvation; if we fail to live with this cry, hourly, daily, in the midnight hour, and in the light of the noonday sun, then salvation has left us and our feet have laid hold on Hell. Yes, bless our God forever! When we cease to tremble before Him we have turned out of the way."

"Amen!" cried a voice from far away. "Amen! You preach it, boy!"

He paused for only a moment and mopped his brow, the heart within him great with fear and trembling, and with power.

"For let us remember that the wages of sin is death; that it is written, and cannot fail, the soul that sinneth, it shall die. Let us remember that we are born in sin, in sin did our mothers conceive us – sin reigns in all our members, sin is the foul heart's natural liquid, sin looks out of the eye, amen, and leads to lust, sin is in the hearing of the ear, and leads to folly, sin sits on the tongue, and leads to murder. Yes! Sin is the only heritage of the natural man, sin bequeathed us by our nature father, the fallen Adam, whose apple sickens and will sicken all generations living, and generations yet unborn! It was sin that drove the son of the morning out of Heaven, sin that drove Adam out of Eden, sin that caused Cain to slay his brother, sin that built the tower of Babel, sin that caused the fire to fall on Sodom – sin, from the very foundations of the world, living and breathing in the heart of man, that causes women to bring forth children in agony and darkness, bows down the backs of men with terrible labor, keeps the empty belly empty, keeps the table bare, sends our children, dressed in rags, out into the whorehouses and dance halls of the world!"

"Amen! Amen!"

"Ah. Woe is me. Woe is *me*. Yes, beloved – there is no righteousness in man. All men's hearts are evil, all men are liars – only God is true. Hear David's cry: 'The Lord is my rock, and my fortress, and my deliverer; my God, my strength, in whom I will trust; my buckler, and the horn of my salvation, and my high tower.' Hear Job, sitting in dust and ashes, his children dead, his substance gone, surrounded by false comforters: 'Yea, though He slay me, yet will I trust Him.' And hear Paul, who had been Saul, a persecutor of the redeemed, struck down on the road to Damascus, and going forth to preach the gospel: 'And if ye be Christ's, then ye are Abraham's seed, and heirs according to the promise!'"

"Oh, yes," cried one of the elders, "bless our God forever!"

"For God had a plan. He would not suffer the soul of man to die, but had prepared a plan for his salvation. In the beginning, way back there at the laying of the foundations of the world, God had a plan, *amen!* to bring all flesh to a knowledge of the truth. In the beginning was the Word and the Word was with God and the Word was God – yes, and in Him was life, *hallelujah!* And this life was the light of men. Dearly beloved, when God saw how men's hearts waxed evil, how they turned aside, each to his own way, how they married and gave in marriage, how they feasted on ungodly meat and drink, and lusted, and blasphemed, and lifted up their hearts in sinful pride against the Lord – oh, then, the Son of God, the blessed lamb that taketh away the sins of the world, this Son of God was the Word made flesh, the fulfillment of the promise – oh, then, He turned to His father, crying: 'Father, prepare me a body and I'll go down and redeem sinful man.'"

"So *glad* this evening, praise the Lord!"

"Fathers, here tonight, have you ever had a son who went astray? Mothers, have you seen your daughters cut down in the pride and fullness of youth? Has any man here heard the command which came to Abraham, that he must make his son a living sacrifice on God's altar? Fathers, think of your sons, how you tremble for them, and try to lead them right, try to feed them so they'll grow up strong; think of your love for *your* son, and how any evil that befalls him cracks up the heart, and think of the pain that *God* has borne, sending down His only begotten Son, to dwell among men on the sinful earth, to be persecuted, to suffer, to bear the cross and *die* – not for His *own* sins, like our natural sons, but for the sins of *all* the world, to take away the sins of *all* the world – that we might have the joy bells ringing deep in our hearts tonight!"

"Praise Him!" cried Deborah, and he had never heard her voice so loud.

"Woe is me, for when God struck the sinner, the sinner's eyes were opened, and he saw himself in all his foulness naked before God's glory. Woe is me! For the moment of salvation is a blinding light, cracking down into the heart from Heaven – Heaven so high, and the sinner so low. *Woe is me!* For unless God raised the sinner, he would never rise again!"

"Yes, Lord! I was there!"

"How many here tonight had fallen where Isaiah fell? How many had cried – as Isaiah cried? How many could testify, as Isaiah testified, 'Mine eyes have seen the King, the Lord of hosts?' Ah, whosoever failed to have this testimony should never see His face, but should be told, on that great day: 'Depart from me, ye that work iniquity,' and be hurled forever into the lake of fire prepared for Satan and all his angels. Oh, would the sinner rise tonight, and walk the little mile to his salvation, here to the mercy seat?"

And he waited. Deborah watched him with a calm, strong smile. He looked out over their faces, their faces all upturned to him. He saw joy in those faces, and holy excitement, and belief – and they all looked up to him. Then, far in the back, a boy rose, a tall, dark boy, his white shirt open at the neck and torn, his trousers dusty and shabby and held up with an old necktie, and he looked across the immeasurable, dreadful, breathing distance up to Gabriel, and began to walk down the long, bright aisle. Someone cried: "Oh, bless the Lord!" and tears filled Gabriel's eyes. The boy knelt, sobbing, at the mercy seat, and the church began to sing.

Then Gabriel turned away, knowing that this night he had run well, and that God had used him. The elders all were smiling, and one of them took him by the hand, and said: "That was mighty fine, boy. Mighty fine."

References

Cady, Edwin. 1983. "'As Through a Glass Eye, Darkly': The Bible in the Nineteenth-Century American Novel." In G. B. Gunn, ed., *The Bible and American Arts and Letters.* Philadelphia, PA and Chico, CA: Fortress Press and Scholars Press.

Ellmann, Richard, and Robert O'Clair, eds. 1973. *The Norton Anthology of Modern Poetry.* 1st edn. New York: Norton.

Farrington, Lisa E. 2005. *Creating Their Own Image: The History of African-American Women Artists.* New York: Oxford University Press.

Gunn, Giles B., ed. 1983. "Introduction." In G. B. Gunn, ed., *The Bible and American Arts and Letters.* Philadelphia, PA and Chico, CA: Fortress Press and Scholars Press.

Iron Maiden. 1982. *The Number of the Beast.* Hollywood, CA: Harvest. Sound recording.

Johnson, Thomas H., ed. 1960. *The Complete Works of Emily Dickinson.* Cambridge, MA: Harvard University Press.

Kahn, Tobi. 2009. "The Meaning of Beauty." In E. G. Heller, ed., *Tobi Kahn: Sacred Space for the 21st Century.* London: MOBIA and D. Giles Limited.

Miller, Bryan. 2006. *Biblical Symbolics and the Grateful Dead.* Cited 14 June 2010. Available online at artsites.ucsc.edu/GDead/agdl/miller.html.

Moore, Allan F. 2002. *The Cambridge Companion to Blues and Gospel Music.* Cambridge: Cambridge University Press.

Raboteau, Albert J. 1978. *Slave Religion: The "Invisible Institution" in the Antebellum South.* New York: Oxford University Press.

Schneidau, Herbert. 1983. "The Antinomian Strain: The Bible and American Poetry." In G. B. Gunn, ed., *The Bible and American Arts and Letters.* Philadelphia, PA and Chico, CA: Fortress Press and Scholars Press.

Seldes, Lee. 1996. *The Legacy of Mark Rothko.* Revised edn. New York: Da Capo Press. Original edition, 1974.

Wolff, Cynthia Griffin. 1993. "Emily Dickinson." In J. Parini and B. C. Millier, eds, *The Columbia History of American Poetry* . New York: Columbia University Press.

Suggestions for further research

Boer, Roland. 1999. *Knockin' on Heaven's Door: The Bible and Popular Culture.* London and New York: Routledge.

Exum, J. Cheryl. 2006. *The Bible in Film – the Bible and Film.* Leiden: Brill.

NBC Studios. 2009. *Kings.* Television dramatic series.

Phy-Olsen, Allene. 1985. *The Bible and Popular Culture in America.* Philadelphia, PA and Chico, CA: Fortress Press and Scholars Press.

Reinhartz, Adele. 2003. *Scripture on the Silver Screen.* Louisville, KY: Westminster John Knox Press.

—— 2007. *Jesus of Hollywood.* New York: Oxford University Press.

Index

Biblical references

The Hebrew Bible, or Old Testament

The New Testament